# THE CHANGING LANDSCAPE OF SPANISH LANGUAGE CURRICULA

# THE CHANGING LANDSCAPE OF SPANISH LANGUAGE CURRICULA

## Designing Higher Education Programs for Diverse Students

*Alan V. Brown and Gregory L. Thompson*

*Foreword by Manel Lacorte*

Georgetown University Press / Washington, DC

The publisher is not responsible for third-party websites or their content. URL links were active at time of publication.

Library of Congress Cataloging-in-Publication Data

Names: Brown, Alan V., author. | Thompson, Gregory L., author.
Title: The Changing Landscape of Spanish Language Curricula : Designing Higher Education Programs for Diverse Students / Alan V. Brown and Gregory L. Thompson.
Description: Washington, DC : Georgetown University Press, 2018. | Includes bibliographical references and index.
Identifiers: LCCN 2017035595| ISBN 9781626165731 (hardcover : alk. paper) | ISBN 9781626165748 (pbk. : alk. paper) | ISBN 9781626165755 (ebook)
Subjects: LCSH: Spanish language—Study and teaching (Higher)—United States. | Universities and colleges—Curricula—United States.
Classification: LCC PC4068.U5 B76 2018 | DDC 468.0071/173—dc23
LC record available at https://lccn.loc.gov/2017035595

∞ This book is printed on acid-free paper meeting the requirements of the American National Standard for Permanence in Paper for Printed Library Materials.

19 18      9 8 7 6 5 4 3 2   First printing

Printed in the United States of America

Cover design by Martha Madrid.

# CONTENTS

*List of Illustrations*   *vii*
*Foreword by Manel Lacorte*   *ix*
*Acknowledgments*   *xiii*

1  The Changing Landscape of Spanish Language Education   1

2  The History and Evolution of Postsecondary Spanish Language Education in the United States   22

3  Helping Spanish Heritage Language Learners Find Their Place   47

4  Incorporating Meaningful Service Learning into Spanish Second-Language Curricula   72

5  Curricular and Programmatic Considerations in Spanish for Specific Purposes   98

6  Placement, Outcome, and Articulation Issues in Spanish Curricular Assessment   124

7  Connecting Spanish Language Education with Social, Economic, and Political Realities   151

8  Training Future Spanish Teachers   178

9  Technological Advances in Spanish Language Education   206

10  Charting a Course Forward   230

*Appendix: Description of Data Sets*   253
*Index*   259
*About the Authors*   277

# ILLUSTRATIONS

*Figures*

1.1   The Top Ten Foreign Language Enrollments in 2013   4
2.1   Enrollments in Spanish and Other Foreign Languages   30
2.2   World Language Advanced Placement Examination Totals   30
4.1   The Foreign Language NAEP Assessment Framework   77
7.1   A Sign Outside a Restaurant in Dimmitt, Texas, 1949   163
9.1   Community of Inquiry Model   213
10.1  Logo of the World-Readiness Standards for Learning Languages   244
10.2  Dubin and Olshtain's Model of Language Program Policy Design   246

*Tables*

1.1   The Top Twenty Languages Spoken at Home, Other Than English   3
2.1   Course Catalog Totals from Nine Universities   37
8.1   Key Competencies of Foreign Language and Second-Language
      Educators   199

# FOREWORD

Manel Lacorte
*University of Maryland*

The first two decades of the twenty-first century have been particularly positive for the teaching of Spanish as a foreign language (FL) or second language (L2) throughout the world, as should be expected in light of the ongoing consolidation of Spanish as an international language of culture, communication, business, and knowledge.

In the case of the United States, the teaching and learning of Spanish have enjoyed a quite extensive tradition since the early sixteenth century, as the authors of this volume skillfully describe as part of their effort to contextualize the present state of Spanish in US education. More than five hundred years after the first words of Spanish were spoken on the coast of what is now Florida, this language is now an academic subject for over 7.5 million students (out of a total of about 11 million) in the K–12 formal US education system, and about 800,000 learners in postsecondary centers—more than 50 percent of all L2 enrollments in this context. In addition, the United States is one of the most important research centers for the teaching, acquisition, and other applications of Spanish as an FL, L2, or heritage language (HL), with more than two hundred doctoral degree programs.

Strengthening the balance between a healthy demand for Spanish education at all levels—for K–16 and beyond—and a sizable body of high-quality research on Spanish as an FL/L2 will be an essential endeavor in the years ahead, considering possible trends that could affect L2 education, such as reductions in L2 requirements (especially in the natural and social sciences), more pressure on students to select options with more immediate financial promise, competition with other disciplines (e.g., computer sciences and information and communication technology), and a lack of institutional and/or financial support. Because the future of the humanities in US higher education—including L2 teaching and learning—does not look much more promising, it is crucial for the field of Spanish education to go beyond research focused on internal or external L2 learning processes and to devote more attention to larger and more complex institutional, social, cultural, and ideological issues in the teaching of Spanish as a FL/L2.

It is precisely for this reason that Alan Brown and Gregory Thompson's book will indeed become a reference for students, instructors, researchers, and administrators with interest in macroprogrammatic issues directly linked to Spanish university programs in the US. Drawing upon their own extensive experience and high-quality research, these authors have written a quite needed, exciting, and insightful analysis of programmatic and curricular trends, challenges, and opportunities in Spanish language education at the postsecondary level in this country, with the objective of providing realistic and valuable recommendations for the twenty-first century.

Brown and Thompson have keenly examined a significant amount of published and unpublished documents from a variety of sources, always aware of the place that Spanish has as a *second*, rather than as a *foreign*, language in many communities throughout the US. Precisely because of the distinctive history of Spanish in this country, and its current status as the language of the largest minority, the reevaluation of the structures and curricula of most Spanish programs involves challenges related to not only the traditional two-tiered configuration—languages versus literatures—and emphasis on achieving native-like competency in the language, but also the unique position of Spanish in the US, and the place that Spanish programs should have within institutions of higher education. Brown and Thompson address these challenges through an intelligent analysis of the historical, sociopolitical, and ideological circumstances that have shaped Spanish in the US, because they believe that these realities could bring about great opportunities "for Spanish language curriculum and course syllabus design, materials development, individual and programmatic assessment, and classroom pedagogy in the twenty-first century." As part of their analysis, the authors include topics as diverse as the country's evolving demographics, the historical and ideological construction of Spanish in the US, the cultural realities of many Spanish-speaking communities throughout the country, and the growing presence of HL learners in US universities due to (1) the overall growth of the Hispanic population and (2) the greater opportunities for Latino students to access higher education.

The need for rethinking and restructuring Spanish programs in the US is not only related to external causes. For decades, L2 departments have faced serious structural and curricular inconsistencies. First, the study of language and the study of literature have been for the most part based on different assumptions and goals. Second, this language-versus-content dichotomy has defined the division between lower- and upper-division courses in the curriculum. At the lower level, the main concern has traditionally been how to implement changing positions about L2 teaching and learning, often through textbooks and multimedia providing very limited and/or unrealistic views of US Spanish-speaking communities. At the upper level, the main stress has generally been on teaching canonical literature and/or culture, focusing on specific periods, geographical areas, and/or renowned authors. While taking into account differences in terms of program size and mission, academic emphasis, and human resources, a third distinction involves, on one hand, the teaching of lower-level courses by graduate teaching assistants, lecturers, or adjuncts following a relatively uniform structure, and on the other hand, the teaching of upper-level courses by tenure-track faculty in a more loosely coordinated structure with fewer hierarchy levels and a less strict chain of command.

With these inconsistencies in mind, Brown and Thompson have structured this book around a selection of areas of special interest for the future of Spanish as an FL/L2 in the US. More precisely, readers will find in one volume a solid historical overview of Spanish language education in the US, along with very informative and well-written discussions of L2 program articulation and development, HL programs, service learning, Spanish for specific purposes, placement and assessment, critical awareness and pedagogy, teacher education, and instructional technology. Each of these areas has been carefully developed with the support of high-quality scholarship, and each and every chapter should provide readers with a strong foundation for informed decision making in Spanish programs seeking to shake off traditional and/or outdated structures and focus instead on more productive challenges, such as developing coherent vertical and horizontal program articulation through the implementation of existing curriculum frameworks; creating a wider variety of courses for students to both increase discipline-specific knowledge and maintain intellectual rigor and cultural awareness; implementing a variety of in-class, hybrid, and online models of instruction in order to raise student learning and engagement; developing institutional and curricular infrastructure for HL students to become an essential part of Spanish programs and courses; furthering critical awareness of socioeconomic and sociopolitical realities of Spanish-speaking communities in the US; and preparing Spanish instructors and faculty truly equipped, in the authors' own words, "with adequate linguistic proficiency, cultural sensitivity, and pedagogical knowledge to effectively teach in any of the many twenty-first-century Spanish classrooms."

In these times of special emphasis on the implementation of strict guidelines and standards for teacher certification, another area of particular importance for the future of the field of Spanish education involves the need for preservice and in-service teacher development that takes into honest account the role of reflection and mediation in teaching, the diversity of learners' backgrounds, and the actual conditions of L2 learning and teaching in heterogeneous contexts. It is therefore important that L2 teachers gain knowledge not only about the subject that they teach (e.g., linguistic structures and categories, cultural products and artifacts, and other areas of the Spanish language and its cultures), and the pedagogical processes that may make L2 teachers' daily work in the classroom more effective (e.g., curriculum design, materials development, and classroom management). Preservice and in-service teachers also need to learn about and assess the institutional, social, and ideological conditions of L2/HL learning and teaching so they can, for instance, develop a better understanding of the connection (or lack thereof) between courses focused on different dimensions of Spanish as a subject matter—offered by Spanish programs—and courses on general curricular and pedagogical matters—offered as part of foreign language or world language education programs in schools of education. In this regard, this book will offer current and future professionals in the field many opportunities to reflect on and consider pedagogical and curricular applications suitable for a variety of settings, such as traditional secondary school L2 programs, elementary immersion programs, secondary immersion programs, and college/university environments.

A concluding point of interest about this book is how Alan Brown and Gregory Thompson have written it with the practitioner in mind, without losing sight of researchers seeking thoughtful information about the state of curricula for Spanish as an L2/HL in the US. Thus, the book provides an in-depth analysis of the state of Spanish postsecondary education in a quite accessible style, and in a way that allows readers to consider certain issues of special relevance from different perspectives, presented across multiple chapters.

Because there is no other text on the market that covers such a significant range of key programmatic and curricular issues, I am confident that this book will become an invaluable point of reference for instructors, program administrators, and teacher educators in the field of Spanish as an FL/L2, as well as for professionals in languages other than Spanish. Undeniably, this text will become an irreplaceable reference work for the development of individual critical thinking about all the above-mentioned areas of study in relation to local contexts in the United States for Spanish as an FL/L2 and beyond, if we keep in mind that a substantial part of the future of Spanish as a language of international communication is now developing in this country.

# ACKNOWLEDGMENTS

L ike any work of this magnitude, the time, talents, and overall goodwill of many were brought to bear in bringing this project to fruition, and we would be remiss not to mention their contributions. Cathy Brigham and Sherby Jean-Leger at the College Board were incredibly helpful in facilitating the preparation and licensing of the world languages Advanced Placement examination data, and Liz Stone at the Educational Testing Service was equally accommodating with the Praxis exam data. Nearly seven hundred Spanish language educators took the time to respond to our online survey, whose results figure prominently in the book, and we owe them heartfelt thanks. Earl K. Brown of Brigham Young University was masterful in his use of "R" to reconfigure the data sets for more efficient analysis. Our research assistants, Laura Shrake and Grace Webb, diligently endured the painstaking task of coding several universities' undergraduate Spanish courses from the late 1800s to the present. Finally, we thank God and our families for their fierce, undying support and loyalty.

# 1

# THE CHANGING LANDSCAPE OF SPANISH LANGUAGE EDUCATION

> Spanish. Bestow great attention on this, & endeavor to acquire an accurate knowledge of it. Our future connections with Spain & Spanish America will render that language a valuable acquisition. The ancient history of a great part of America, too, is written in that language. I send you a dictionary.
>
> —Thomas Jefferson, in a letter to Peter Carr, Paris, August 10, 1787

Many a Spanish language educator has invoked the prescient words of Thomas Jefferson from a letter he wrote to his nephew, Peter Carr, in 1787 as a means to impress upon contemporary students the need to learn Spanish and to learn it well. Little could Jefferson have imagined just how accurate his prediction would be, or that the need for Spanish language acquisition would one day apply to Anglo-American citizens who might never leave the borders of the United States, or ever interact with *foreign-born* speakers of Spanish. Given the historical context of Jefferson's letter and his use of "our" in contrast to "Spain & Spanish American," it seems that he was primarily thinking of the use of Spanish with nationals from other countries, not from his own. More than two centuries and many geopolitical events later, several contemporary scholars have reflected on the status of Spanish in present-day United States, and in the academy (Alonso 2007; Irwin and Szurmuk 2009; Leeman 2005; Macías 2014; Valdés et al. 2003), but within a completely transformed United States. In juxtaposition to Jefferson's eighteenth-century advice to his nephew, these scholars take the status of Spanish in the United States to another level entirely, particularly within the educational system, placing it nearly on par with English as the second national language. Although this assertion would have surely been labeled preposterous a few generations ago, the linguistic realities of twenty-first-century America make it now much more feasible. Macías (2014) identifies at least eight compelling arguments that explain why Spanish has achieved "unique status" in the United States, citing historical events such as imperialistic wars, ensuing territorial annexations, and the linguistic rights bestowed by corresponding peace treaties. Although no one would doubt that English remains the primary linguistic means of communication in the United States among the majority, very few would question the ubiquity of the Spanish language in the United States, regardless of location.

Census statistics are often cited as the most compelling evidence of the ethnic, cultural, and linguistic transformation of American society—and, indeed, they are convincing; see Lacorte and García (2014) and Carreira (2013) for additional discussions of census and other relevant statistics. As Field (2011, 12) notes, sometime between July 1, 2005, and July 1, 2006, Hispanics, or Latinos, surpassed blacks as the largest minority in the United States. The latest estimate published in 2013 by the US Census Bureau put the number of Hispanics or Latinos at nearly 54 million, while blacks or African Americans totaled just under 40 million. An overwhelming majority of participants in the 2013 American Community Survey indicated that—besides English—Spanish was by far the most commonly spoken language used in American households, as table 1.1 attests. In particular, southern states such as North Carolina, Kentucky, and Georgia have experienced sharp increases in Spanish use, as indicated by the US Census Bureau's data. Between 2005 and 2013, the number of people in North Carolina who reported using Spanish at home rose from 477,284 to 688,994—a 69 percent increase. Kentucky and Georgia saw slightly greater increases, of, respectively, 71 percent (74,780 to 105,204) and 75 percent (553,289 to 741,707).

The pervasiveness of Spanish in contemporary American society goes beyond statistical charts and surfaces in many facets of daily life, from the ever-present "Se habla español" in the storefront window to the Spanish language options at the automated teller machine or automated telephone menu to the bilingual (English/Spanish) customs form for American citizens returning to the United States. Loanwords from Spanish increasingly appear in contemporary American English and crop up in television programs and Hollywood films, such as the wildly popular phrase "Hasta la vista, baby," used by Arnold Schwarzenegger's cyborg in the well-known *Terminator* movies. Lacorte and García (2014) also note that during June and July 2013, the Spanish language television network Univisión was viewed by more eighteen- to forty-nine-year-olds than Fox, NBC, CBS, or ABC.

It comes as no surprise, then, that the Modern Language Association (MLA) has reported similar tendencies in response to its 2013 survey of foreign language (FL) enrollments in postsecondary institutions throughout the United States (Goldberg, Looney, and Lusin 2015). Among the 245 languages that enrolled one student or more at participating institutions from the undergraduate level, Spanish made up just over half (51.2 percent) of total

**Table 1.1    The Top Twenty Languages Spoken at Home, Other Than English**

| Language | Number | Percent of Total |
|---|---|---|
| Spanish or Spanish Creole | 38,417,235 | 62.2 |
| Chinese | 3,029,042 | 4.9 |
| Tagalog | 1,612,465 | 2.6 |
| Vietnamese | 1,428,352 | 2.3 |
| French (including Patois, Cajun) | 1,251,815 | 2.0 |
| Korean | 1,100,881 | 1.8 |
| Arabic | 1,052,938 | 1.7 |
| Other Asian languages | 1,016,905 | 1.6 |
| German | 984,669 | 1.6 |
| African languages | 967,886 | 1.6 |
| Russian | 895,902 | 1.5 |
| Other Indic languages | 886,013 | 1.4 |
| French Creole | 783,017 | 1.3 |
| Portuguese or Portuguese Creole | 677,329 | 1.1 |
| Hindi | 654,101 | 1.1 |
| Italian | 641,267 | 1.0 |
| Polish | 549,661 | 0.9 |
| Other Indo-European languages | 455,595 | 0.7 |
| Japanese | 454,997 | 0.7 |
| Urdu | 439,129 | 0.7 |

*Source:* US Census Bureau, 2013 American Community Survey.

FL enrollments, with French (12.7 percent) and American Sign Language (7.0 percent) coming a distant second and third. Spanish enrollments alone surpassed the enrollments of all other languages combined. Figure 1.1 displays the percentage distribution of the ten most commonly taught languages among institutions who participated in the 2013 survey.

According to the MLA's enrollment surveys, Spanish has maintained its position as the most commonly taught FL since 1969, and it appears that it will hold on to the top spot for the foreseeable future. In addition to the overwhelming majority of Spanish language enrollments, the 2013 survey also identified a trend that has not surfaced since 1968: a decrease in enrollments from the previous survey. In 2009, the MLA survey reported that postsecondary, undergraduate Spanish enrollments had hit an all-time high of 850,483 before decreasing to 781,634 in 2013—a reduction of nearly 70,000 students nationwide. This drop in enrollment numbers can be interpreted as reflecting college students' decreased interest in Spanish, and FLs more generally, or could simply be a by-product of increased competition for student enrollment due to overall curricular expansion (Ferdman 2015).

Figure 1.1    The Top Ten Foreign Language Enrollments in 2013 (percent)

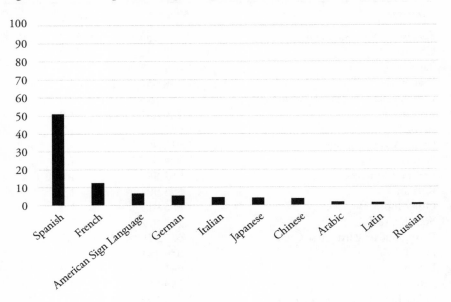

In spite of the decline in Spanish enrollments at the postsecondary level between 2009 and 2013, Spanish maintains a strong foothold in secondary school FL programs, as reflected in the number of high school students who take the Spanish language and Spanish literature Advanced Placement examinations administered by the College Board. Based on a data set assembled by the College Board that covers the period from 1994 to 2014, the number of high school students who took the two Spanish Advanced Placement exams increased 415 percent, from 36,822 in 1994 to 152,962 in 2014.[1] In 2014, the number of students who took the Spanish language and literature exams made up nearly 81 percent of all FL exams represented in the data set—namely, Chinese language, French language, French literature, German language, Italian language, and Japanese language. The above-mentioned statistics provide ample evidence of the large numbers of Spanish speakers in Anglo-American communities and Spanish language students in Anglo-American high school and college classrooms but do little to shed light on the sociolinguistic, socioeconomic, and sociocultural profiles of these individuals, and what these profiles mean for postsecondary Spanish language curricula and programs.

As Spanish language enrollments climbed, the renowned sociolinguist John Lipski (2002) addressed the status of Spanish in higher education by deconstructing the oft-heard phrase "the Spanish problem," used to refer to the unique situation that large Spanish enrollments—as compared with other FLs—present to university and FL program administrators. The fact that Spanish enrollments far outnumber those for other FLs implies certain logistical and staffing adjustments, but the differences between Spanish programs and other FL programs only begin there. Irwin and Szurmuk (2009) argue that though conventional wisdom seems to place Spanish on solid footing in the academy, highlighting precipitous drops in enrollments among other languages, Spanish is experiencing its own crisis. In their view, Spanish enrollments should be much higher than they are, even approaching enrollments of English departments. The *problems*—more appropriately labeled challenges, or even opportunities—that many Spanish language programs confront differ from those faced by other FL programs in several respects, not the least of which are the widely varying degrees of linguistic and cultural proficiency students bring with them due to previous experience with the language as heritage speakers, as one-way or two-way immersion students, or as participants in study abroad programs or other international travel, for example. Just as diverse are the types of motivations present among Spanish students, some of which Lipski (2002, 1248) calls "salutary" and others "disappointing," which result in levels of performance that "span an equally broad spectrum of dedication and achievement." Finally, the sociopolitical and sociocultural contexts in which Spanish is taught differ markedly from those for other modern languages and require a reconceptualization of its role in modern American society: "Until we radically rethink and restructure our programs . . . to reflect the reality of the contemporary role of Spanish in the United States and in the globalized Americas, and the role of nonliterary culture in the contemporary world, we are doing a great disservice to our students" (Irwin and Szurmuk 2009, 57).

The telling use of the acronym "LOTS"—for "languages other than Spanish"—to describe all other FLs besides Spanish evidences the unique status of Spanish and serves as a counterpoint to previously used acronyms that grouped FLs into two categories: CTL, for "commonly taught languages"; and LCTL, for "less commonly taught languages." Brown's (2009) comparative analysis of CTL (French, German, and Spanish) and LCTL (Arabic, Greek, Hebrew, Italian, and Japanese) students at the University of Arizona revealed stark academic and demographic differences between the two groups. Results from a self-reported questionnaire of over 1,400 students indicated that the CTL students were younger in age than the LCTL students, expected lower grades, reported lower grade point averages, and had studied a third language at a much lower rate. Because the Spanish students in Brown's study made up more than half the CTL group, it is safe to assume that, statistically speaking, they contributed strongly to the differences between the CTL and LCTL groups.

As a result of this status change, Spanish language programs at most institutions of higher education appear to be experiencing an identity crisis vis-à-vis traditional programmatic, curricular, and departmental structures. In an article written for the MLA publication *Profession*, Carlos Alonso (2007, 220) deconstructed this identity crisis and the challenges that accompany it, arguing convincingly that Spanish departments have become more like departments of "second national language and culture" and should behave as such within their respective institutions. Alonso affirmed Dasenbrock's (2004, 24) observation that "North America is now part of Latin America" and that the traditional cultural dichotomies that have reigned in scholarly discourse, such as North/South and American/Hispanic, are thus now obsolete and even counterproductive. According to Alonso, the new cultural and linguistic reality that has been unfolding in the United States' academy over the last twenty years necessitates a reconfiguration of strict intellectual and departmental boundaries. The tendency to place English, or American, studies on the other side of the administrative and intellectual fence from Spanish, or Hispanic, studies belies current sociocultural realities.

Increasing Spanish enrollments, in Alonso's (2007, 220) view, are driven by students' tacit understanding of this new cultural and linguistic reality, and by their concomitant perception "that Spanish is not just another foreign language, that they need to master it for reasons that transcend the foreign language label." In essence, for some students the study of Spanish may be more than just a course to be checked off on a graduation requirement sheet and subsequently erased from memory. Indeed, students are beginning to see Spanish more as a curricular and practical necessity than an intellectual and academic luxury, a trend that is both promising and troubling, according to Lacorte (2013), given the tendency to commodify language for strictly utilitarian means. One of Alonso's curricular recommendations, also included in the MLA report, encouraged the elimination of the strict division between the study of language and the study of literature and culture. Nevertheless, most of his proposals focus on administrative and structural alterations rather than exploring sociolinguistic and sociodemographic trends among contemporary Spanish language students and how these must find expression in twenty-first-century Spanish language programs and curricula. The latter objective—connecting social, linguistic, and pedagogical trends in contemporary Spanish language education to programmatic and curricular innovation at the postsecondary level—is the driving force behind this book.

## THE 2007 REPORT BY THE MODERN LANGUAGE ASSOCIATION'S AD HOC COMMITTEE

At nearly the same time that Alonso proposed the reconfiguration of language departments to more solidly embed Spanish as a *second*, rather than a foreign, language, an MLA ad hoc committee published (2007, 3) a call for sweeping curricular revisions of FL programs in the United States. This report, titled "Foreign Languages and Higher Education: New Structures for a Changed World," shook up the FL teaching world by proposing that curricular and programmatic changes in postsecondary programs were long overdue. According to the report, deep translingual and transcultural competence, however that might be defined, should be the overarching goal. The report bemoans the traditional "two-tiered configuration" that has defined FL departments for decades. Within this two-tiered structure, the elementary language sequence, with its focused language practice, is disconnected from upper-level courses in literature, culture, and linguistics that focus on *content* rather than language. The committee recommended that the teaching of language, culture, and literature in any given program be conceived as one continuous whole that permeates the entire curriculum and does not lead to hierarchical demarcations between *language*, or *service*, courses and *content* courses.

The committee also includes other noteworthy proposals in its report. First, FLs must expand beyond disciplinary and departmental lines, such that they permeate the curricula of other disciplines, not just FLs. The committee asserts that FLs should find their way into the requirements for nonlanguage majors in music, history, engineering, and law. Second, the committee recommends that department chairs and others involved in the curriculum design process consult with experts in applied linguistics who are formally trained in second-language (L2) acquisition, curriculum design, and language pedagogy. Finally, the committee encourages more inclusive and democratic departmental governance so that those teaching lower-level courses can play a greater role in decision making further along in the curriculum and so that tenure-line faculty can participate more actively in the design and teaching of the elementary language sequence.

The MLA report evoked strong reactions from some quarters of FL education (see Byrnes 2008), but what is truly compelling about the committee's analysis is the underlying assumption that (1) deep translingual and transcultural competence was *not* being fully achieved by students situated in traditional programmatic configurations, that is, those with clear delimitations between lower-level language studies and upper-level literature and culture studies; (2) alterations to pedagogical and curricular components could help remedy the situation; and (3) formally trained experts in disciplines such as applied linguistics and language pedagogy could make meaningful and necessary contributions to curriculum design. Undergirding these reformist tendencies is the pressing need many in the field of FL literature, culture, linguistics, and pedagogy (Corral and Patai 2008; Lipsett 2009; Norris and Mills 2014) feel to defend their raison d'être in the academy amid ubiquitous budget cuts and ever-shifting perspectives in society concerning the value of humanities and social science disciplines in higher education, a concern voiced by the MLA ad hoc committee.

A few years before the publication of the MLA report, one department in particular became quite well known as the standard bearer for curricular change and innovation. Georgetown University's German program underwent a curricular overhaul that resulted in several scholarly publications, most notably a 2010 monograph published by Byrnes, Maxim, and Norris (2010, 8) in the *Modern Language Journal* (also see Byrnes 2012). In their monograph, the authors offer a case study of their efforts to develop advanced FL writing ability while "pursuing a humanistic orientation for the field of FL studies that is at the same time language-based." The same undercurrents that led to the 2007 MLA report and the Georgetown University German program's reconfiguration have also led to other proposals for how best to update and transform the FL curriculum, such as Swaffar and Arens's (2005) multiple literacies approach. López Sánchez (2009, 32) argues that a multiple literacies approach that strives for symbolic competence is a viable candidate to replace communicative language teaching as the preferred approach to L2 pedagogy. She describes its focus as being "about gaining access to that 'axis of potential meanings' and restructuring (or redesigning) those meanings as we become members of a number of communities that use the language."

More recent calls for FL curricular and programmatic change surfaced in 2013 in a "Perspectives" discussion published in the *Modern Language Journal* (Tarone 2013) that focused on the training of preservice FL instructors and how curriculum design affects their preparedness as future language teaching professionals. Among the many issues broached in this "Perspectives" discussion was the need for curricular reform, such that undergraduate teaching majors could reach minimum levels of FL proficiency. For several of the contributors (Burke 2013; Fischer 2013; Moeller 2013) to the "Perspectives" discussion, minimum proficiency levels for teacher certification are a must and should not be compromised. Fischer also pointed to the frequent disconnect between preservice FL instructors' stellar academic achievement and their subpar performance on interactive assessments of oral and written proficiency, and he called for immediate attention to this issue.

These proposals surely have relevance for the teaching of Spanish as an FL in the United States, but fall short of concretely identifying the challenges unique to the teaching of Spanish in the United States as Spanish has become not just a foreign, but rather a *second*, language in many communities. As mentioned above, this rather recent transformation leads to unique opportunities and challenges for Spanish language curriculum and course syllabus design, materials development, individual and programmatic assessment, and classroom pedagogy in the twenty-first century.

## SECOND-LANGUAGE AND FOREIGN LANGUAGE CURRICULUM DESIGN

Brown (2011), Nation and Macalister (2010), and Richards (2001) are among scholars of L2 education who make a very strong case that a detailed needs analysis must precede any attempts at curriculum or syllabus design. This is to say that curriculum design, or redesign, of any sort is an iterative process and must be sensitive to the ebbs and flows of contemporary L2 acquisition and educational theory, sociocultural trends, and concrete logistical and institutional realities. Nation and Macalister discuss various models for conducting a needs analysis, but opt for a concise, tripartite approach focused on student learning that includes lacks, wants, and necessities. Relevant questions guiding this type of needs analysis are simply, 'What do learners need to learn given the hypothesized target language use situation or syllabus requirements?' (pertaining to necessities), 'What aspects of learners' language needs to improve?' (lacks), and 'What things do the students want to learn?' (wants). The key to an effective needs analysis is choosing instrumentation and data collection procedures that can provide appropriate data to answer these questions and inform subsequent decision making. In preparing to conduct the needs analysis, Brown (2011) recommends that curriculum designers define the purpose, delimit the student population, decide upon approaches and syllabuses, recognize constraints, and select data collection procedures. Once these steps have been completed, it is time to collect data, analyze them, and interpret the results. In Brown's view, the next step would be to use the results of the needs analysis to determine course and program objectives and, finally, to evaluate and report on the effectiveness of the needs analysis project.

Richards (2001, 54) problematizes facile explanations of the term *needs* by observing that "what is identified as a need is dependent on judgment and reflects the interests and values of those making such a judgment," and he notes that in some cases learners' needs transcend strictly language-related issues. Richards (2001) and Nation and Macalister (2010) recognize that a needs analysis alone is incapable of providing all the necessary information for effective curriculum design, and so they include another category, which they have respectively labeled *environment* and *situation* analysis.

Similar to their approach to needs analysis, Nation and Macalister's environment analysis focuses on three groups of factors that serve as constraints when writing a curriculum: learners, teachers, and situation. Richards points out that a situation analysis complements a needs analysis by providing information regarding contextual factors influencing language learning on different levels, including societal, project, institutional, teacher, learner, and adoption. Among many other possibilities that a situation, or environment, analysis might uncover are such things as the level of support from stakeholders within the institution and within the larger society; the level of teacher preparedness and experience; and other instructional realities, such as teaching load, and students' beliefs and perceptions regarding language learning and teaching. Similarly, Lacorte and García (2014, 131) highlight "the need to consider the teaching of Spanish from an emic perspective, which is to say, from within, in regard to pedagogical principles, curricular frameworks, local classroom and institutional realities, student characteristics, etc."[2] Indeed, curriculum design does not occur in a vacuum, and larger social, political, and cultural factors serve to constrain the nature and scope of curriculum design in significant ways. To ignore this fact is to doom any attempt at curricular innovation to failure.

The application of these foundational principles of L2 curriculum design to contemporary Spanish language teaching in the United States reveals a rapidly evolving and diverse set of *needs* and *environments*—to use Nation and Macalister's language—in which Spanish is taught in the United States. The question that Spanish programs from all environments must ask themselves is, simply, What programmatic and curricular structures will best address the needs of all Spanish language students? These structures must educate Spanish language students of all types, from the student with minimal proficiency, purely instrumental motivation, no interest in culture, and, potentially, deeply entrenched ethnic stereotypes of monolingual Spanish speakers in the United States to the heritage student whose ethnolinguistic and familial identity is closely aligned with one of the many Hispanic cultures and the Spanish language, to all the students in between.

Though the sheer size and diversity of the student population are key differences between the teaching of Spanish and other languages, what differentiates them even more is the incredibly charged sociocultural and political environment in which Spanish is taught, and the inextricable link to decisive events in the country's past. Lacorte (2013) and Macías (2014, 342–43) identify larger political and ideological forces at the societal, institutional, and departmental levels that influence the status of Spanish in the academy and in Anglo-American society, and that "will determine in great measure the global orientation toward the teaching of Spanish as a 'foreign' language or as a 'second' language in US universities." Macías (2014, 54) takes the discussion a step further, warning that even if Spanish achieves L2 status, without concomitant changes in language ideology, the classification "will be merely a descriptor of language diversity and nothing more." Educational institutions and their curricula can be powerful tools used for imbuing languages with social and cultural prestige and even political power, but only if they are responsive to contemporary realities, both within *and* beyond the classroom. It is with this understanding that we outline in the following section our vision for Spanish second curriculum design in the twenty-first century.

## CONTEMPORARY SPANISH LANGUAGE CURRICULUM DESIGN

The recent appearance of a scholarly journal solely dedicated to the teaching of Spanish language—the *Journal of Spanish Language Teaching*, published by Routledge—evidences the increased interest in and need for scholarship exclusively focused on the teaching of Spanish, particularly in the United States.[3] Although it is not possible to address every challenge facing Spanish language educators, administrators, and curriculum designers, some of the major issues that are dealt with in this book regarding Spanish language curricula in the twenty-first century are listed here. Throughout our discussion in the chapters that follow, we treat these issues holistically as interdependent, rather than independent, and discuss the challenges and opportunities they present:

- the creation of institutional infrastructure and mechanisms to establish heritage language courses, to increase enrollments in existing programs and courses, and to equip instructors with the necessary tools to properly teach them—see chapter 3;
- a broader and more sophisticated use of experiential learning (e.g., service learning and internships) in Spanish language, culture, literature, and linguistics classes, across all levels—see chapter 4;
- the creation of courses on Spanish for the professions that empower students with discipline-specific knowledge and linguistic skills while maintaining intellectual rigor and meaningful culture learning—see chapter 5;
- the creation and use of appropriate placement instruments that target a variety of language constructs to suit different proficiency profiles—see chapter 6;

- the establishment of coherent vertical program articulation, and sustained and deliberate oral proficiency development, throughout a language program—see chapter 6;
- developing students' critical awareness of the socioeconomic and sociopolitical realities of domestic Spanish-speaking communities by taking on politically charged issues, such as social injustice and marginalization—see chapter 7;
- preparing preservice Spanish instructors who are equipped with adequate linguistic proficiency, cultural sensitivity, and pedagogical knowledge to effectively teach in the wide variety of contexts in which Spanish will be taught in the twenty-first century (e.g., partial / full / dual immersion programs in elementary and secondary schools, heritage language courses, and service-learning courses)—see chapter 8; and
- effective design and implementation of online and blended models of delivery to maximize student learning and engagement—see chapter 9.

Although we are aware that Spanish is taught in diverse contexts at the tertiary level, our objective with this book is to conduct a needs and environment analysis, of sorts, of pressing issues that pertain to the postsecondary Spanish classroom context in the United States and that we consider crucial as we march further into the twenty-first century. Clearly, this analysis cannot and should not replace a detailed, locally driven analysis of the environment in which Spanish is taught and the needs of those who are engaged in teaching and learning it at each educational institution. Nevertheless, we feel that our target is sufficiently delimited to allow for meaningful and much-needed analysis to be undertaken. One strategy we employ throughout the book is to cite relevant data (see the appendix for a detailed description of the data sets) and statistics that strengthen our argument that the face of Spanish language education at the postsecondary level is changing and that these changes at once present challenges and opportunities. The data and statistics we cite are either ones we have computed ourselves from data we collected or ones that have been requested and provided to us by various organizations and institutions. Although this book does not primarily focus on L2 acquisition or classroom pedagogy, but rather on macro programmatic issues, some mention of how current understandings of L2 acquisition may influence curriculum design and pedagogy is included. We also propose concrete ways to address each challenge, and finally, we outline a productive research agenda for Spanish language curriculum design in the twenty-first century.

## THE ORGANIZATION OF THIS BOOK

This book seeks to unite in one volume both a cohesive and coherent discussion of the most pressing curricular and programmatic issues facing Spanish postsecondary education in the twenty-first century and also a consideration of how to convert them into opportunities. In this introductory chapter, we have presented a rationale for the book rooted in a macro needs analysis and have outlined the issues that have particular relevance for postsecondary Spanish language education. To frame our discussion, we have discussed the changing nature of Spanish in American society and its evolution from a foreign to a second language. In support of our underlying argument, we incorporated several relevant statistics to argue that changes are afoot among Spanish university programs. We have also briefly commented on the 2007 MLA report, which calls for increased translingual and transcultural competence, as well as noting the implications of this report for Spanish language curricula. Fundamental principles in curriculum design and needs analysis have been described to provide a larger framework within which our analyses will be embedded. Several curricular issues unique to Spanish language programs have been briefly outlined. We conclude this introductory chapter by providing a brief synopsis of each chapter that follows.

Chapter 2 traces the use of Spanish in the United States and the evolution of Spanish postsecondary education from colonial times to the present, and does so by framing it within contemporary sociocultural and political contexts of the time. Although this chapter does not provide an in-depth ethnographic analysis of Spanish use in the United States, the ebbs and flows of Spanish as an academic subject necessarily parallel historical events and social trends in American society. Hence, this chapter analyzes enrollment data gathered by the MLA census survey and also provides commentary on how Spanish enrollments might relate to social and political trends in society, as well as noteworthy historical events and legislation. The ambivalent attitudes of many Anglo-Americans toward bilingualism, the Spanish language, and native Spanish speakers are presented as a heuristic for understanding the place of Spanish in contemporary society. In addition, we cite statistics from the College Board related to the exponential increase in the number of Spanish language Advanced Placement exams given, and we offer our interpretations of what these increases might indicate for postsecondary Spanish education. We also make reference to the changing nature of course offerings, using our own descriptive analysis of several universities' course catalogs, before summarizing what we consider to be the current state of postsecondary Spanish language education in the United States.

Chapter 3 expands on the discussion of student diversity by focusing on the increasing numbers of Hispanic and non-Hispanic students with some degree of Spanish proficiency who are enrolling in postsecondary institutions. The exponential growth of Spanish heritage learners has paralleled the overall growth of the Hispanic population in the United States, and has many institutions working hard to meet these students' linguistic and cultural needs. Hispanic students, many of whom have some degree of proficiency in Spanish, are enrolling in increasing numbers in postsecondary institutions. In spite of the increasing numbers of heritage learners in the classroom, there are still numerous programs that do not offer courses designed specifically for these students, and among the programs that have such courses, there are still many questions regarding how to best meet these learners' needs. Given the lack of Spanish heritage language programs, many postsecondary institutions combine heritage learners with nonheritage students in language courses. In this chapter, we explore the many challenges and opportunities these classroom configurations present for teachers, not to mention both sets of students. Also, there is a growing need for more research and for materials developed specifically to meet the linguistic and cultural needs of heritage learners of Spanish. This chapter addresses the development of curricula for heritage learner classes and examines programmatic difficulties that may arise. As part of the chapter, we provide suggestions based on current research on the curricular changes needed for heritage learners who are in mixed classes. We also discuss how the abilities and skills of Spanish heritage language learners can be utilized to benefit other heritage language learners, L2 learners, and the community.

Chapter 4 highlights the increased opportunities for experiential learning that are made available by the presence of Spanish-speaking communities in the United States. Experiential learning can meet many of the prerequisites for meaningful L2 learning to take place by employing elements that are key to language acquisition, namely, interpersonal interaction, negotiation of meaning, comprehensible input and output, and high levels of motivation. As part of this discussion, we consider the ways in which service learning represents an ideal pedagogical approach through which the American Council on the Teaching of Foreign Languages' World-Readiness Standards may find expression. Beyond the potential for linguistic gains, experiential learning may serve as a vehicle for attitude change, promoting positive perspectives among students toward the target culture. With the increase in experiential learning programs, language departments are discovering a useful outlet for their students to implement skills acquired in the classroom out in the community. Because Spanish represents the most commonly spoken second language in the United States, opportunities exist in many more communities across the nation than for other second languages. In this chapter, we review research on how experiential learning is currently being used in postsecondary Spanish language programs and the concomitant set of challenges it brings. Information is also provided on how to effectively integrate experiential learning into programs, both at home and during study abroad. Finally, we offer suggestions regarding how to integrate experiential learning into the curricula of a wide range of courses and with Spanish students representing a variety of proficiency levels.

In chapter 5 we begin by outlining the history of languages for specific purposes, particularly English, and trace its origins to well-known theories of language—for example, Halliday's systemic functional linguistics and Hymes's conceptualization of communicative competence—and to larger trends in European and North American society for large numbers of individuals to pursue language acquisition for vocational advancement. Given that Spanish use has grown in all sectors of American society (e.g., health, business, and education), specialized courses for developing the necessary skills to work in these areas are being designed and taught in increasing numbers. Although we do not delve into the daily pedagogy of Spanish for specific purposes, our analysis focuses on what these courses should accomplish and what they imply for students' perceived needs and wants from a curricular perspective. We also look at what employers and businesses have identified as the necessary skills and abilities that they require in their employees, which many of these courses offer. This chapter also comments on the conflicting tensions these courses represent for language departments and for instructional staff. Some language departments may not have qualified instructors to offer such courses, or they may consider them the domain of other departments. Others might argue that courses on Spanish for specific purposes have been a boon to Spanish programs because they bolster enrollments, particularly by nonmajors from outside the humanities.

Chapter 6 addresses the unique challenges that surface with regard to accurate placement testing, articulation of student learning outcomes, vertical program articulation, and proficiency development, given the rapidly evolving nature of Spanish curricula and students' sociolinguistic profiles. L2 programs of all types conduct myriad assessments of their students' language abilities, at both the classroom and programmatic levels, upon entry and even upon exit. Recent calls for greater programmatic transparency and accountability have heightened language educators' and administrators' awareness of the importance of valid and reliable assessment procedures, particularly with regard to program assessment, and have shed light on well-crafted and well-publicized student learning outcomes. Though all languages must deal with assessment, unique challenges surface for the Spanish language context, given the sheer size of many programs. The logistical challenges associated with size are exacerbated by the widely varying levels of Spanish ability that students bring with them from their secondary education or from naturalistic acquisition at home or abroad. In this chapter, we identify the nature of these struggles for programs that must necessarily accommodate an ever-increasing array of student proficiency and sociolinguistic profiles while targeting the same programmatic learning outcomes.

Chapter 7 squarely places the teaching and learning of Spanish into the greater socioeconomic and political contexts in the United States and discusses the importance of helping Spanish L2 students of all sociocultural backgrounds develop critical awareness of the socioeconomic and sociopolitical realities of Spanish-speaking populations within their own communities. Unlike many other languages taught at the postsecondary level, the teaching of Spanish as an L2 in the United States benefits from the presence of millions throughout the country who speak Spanish as their first language, many of whom are Spanish-dominant bilinguals or even monolinguals. As we discuss in chapter 4, the pedagogical implications of this reality are numerous because students are able to engage in meaningful, face-to-face exchanges using the language outside the classroom. However, Spanish language education in the United States does not take place in a social, economic, or political vacuum. This chapter relates constructs and social processes from linguistic anthropology and sociolinguistics—such as so-called standard language ideology, language subordination, and language variation—to the teaching and learning of Spanish. The argument is made that these phenomena are relevant in the daily lives of not only Spanish-speaking Hispanics but also those Anglo-American Spanish students who form part of a society in which Spanish and those whose identity is inseparable from it are often encountered on a daily basis. Within this chapter, we analyze the disconnect between the cultural content of the postsecondary Spanish curriculum and the cultural realities of many Spanish-speaking communities throughout the United States. This chapter proposes ways to help Spanish L2 students develop critical awareness of the socioeconomic and sociopolitical realities of Spanish-speaking populations within their own communities. Additionally, in order to bridge the gap between the somewhat idealistic portrayals of international Spanish-speaking communities in textbooks and multimedia and the serious challenges many domestic Spanish-speaking communities face, we recommend that Spanish curricula do more to take on politically charged issues, such as social injustice and marginalization, even at the beginning levels.

Chapter 8 analyzes the training of future Spanish teachers by focusing on two primary challenges: (1) the wide variety of backgrounds that prospective teachers will represent (native speakers, heritage speakers, immersion students, FL students, etc.); and (2) the settings where they will teach, such as traditional secondary school FL programs, elementary immersion programs, secondary immersion programs, and the college/university level. Education is one of the most frequently cited professional outlets presented to FL majors. For many students, this seems like a natural fit because they desire to parlay their enthusiasm for language learning and previous successes in the classroom into their own livelihoods. Moreover, the large numbers of high school Spanish positions that become available each year seem to augur well for preservice students. Unfortunately, many of these preservice Spanish instructors are not fully prepared to enter the Spanish classroom on four main fronts: (1) L2 speakers' subpar levels of oral Spanish when compared with state education requirements; (2) heritage speakers' command of standard, academic Spanish; (3) large numbers of high school students motivated solely by the precollege language requirements; and (4) the growth of immersion programs that require not only Spanish language competence but also command of discipline-specific language and content knowledge in areas such as biology, physics, and mathematics. Finally, we offer suggestions to assist preservice Spanish language education programs as they strive to ensure high-quality instruction at the elementary and secondary levels.

Chapter 9 takes on the issue of technology in the Spanish language curriculum, specifically the increasing demand for Spanish courses delivered completely online or in a blended format. The current generation of Spanish language students seeks these courses out, especially to fulfill general education requirements, and in some cases they have begun to expect their availability. Online and blended courses now permeate many programs' course catalogs, and the demand for these courses only increases each year. In spite of their commonplace appearance in most institutions' catalogs, the designs of these courses vary. Additionally, there is a plethora of studies and research currently being published on the *best* way to develop these courses and how to adapt the content to guide students toward the same or superior fluency, as compared with traditional face-to-face courses. Some argue that online language courses can never help students achieve the levels of oral/aural ability needed in real-time, face-to-face encounters, and could potentially be detrimental to course articulation further along in the curriculum. Others disagree completely. Online and blended courses are not unique to Spanish, but the ubiquitous nature of Spanish in the US context presents an ideal opportunity to maximize the effectiveness of these alternative delivery models. In this chapter, we discuss the feasibility of incorporating online and blended courses into the Spanish language curriculum, noting valid concerns and potential solutions.

In chapter 10 we provide analysis of the results from two sections of our national survey not addressed in previous chapters: *other* and *national standards*.

The application of the National Standards to postsecondary Spanish language education is explored. In this chapter, we also provide a synthesis and summary of the book's content, using the curricular frameworks proposed by Nation and Maclister (2010) and Dubin and Olshtain (1986). Finally, we conclude this chapter by highlighting several topics that merit further attention, such as the quandary of widespread access to affordable study abroad and the appearance of postsecondary Spanish content immersion programs.

At the end of each chapter, we include two types of expansion activities. First are reflection questions, whose purpose is to allow readers to extend the discussion of the chapter's content beyond the text and to apply it to their local context and personal experiences. In a classroom setting, these reflection questions may be asked at the whole-class level directed by the instructor or be left to small-group and even pair work. At the personal level, readers might benefit from raising these questions with departmental colleagues, either informally as part of workplace conversations or formally during faculty meetings. Though complete neutrality on many issues broached in this book is impossible, our goal has been to formulate these questions in such a way so as to trigger deep reflection that could lead to a variety of interpretations and responses.

Second, with the exception of chapter 1, each chapter also includes a set of exercises that we have labeled "Pedagogical Activities," which include a variety of tasks, ranging from classroom-based action research to stakeholder interviews to lesson planning. All these activities relate directly to the content of the chapter, and they differ from the reflection questions in that they require practical application of the content to the reader's own context and they are designed to be completed after a classroom or departmental discussion.

Together, these expansion activities enrich the text by allowing readers to experience firsthand the complexities of postsecondary Spanish language curriculum description, design, and evaluation at the local level. A variety of activity types are included to allow for instructors at different stages in their careers, but readers are encouraged to adapt them further as needed.

## REFLECTION QUESTIONS

1. How has the status of Spanish changed from Jefferson's time to the present day with regard to its use in the United States? How have attitudes toward Spanish among Anglophones evolved from the time of Jefferson's letter to today? Finally, what geopolitical events in American history might have exerted influence over the use of Spanish since Jefferson's time?

2. Besides the data from census statistics, what other evidence is there to corroborate the argument that Spanish has become the country's second national language,

as Alonso claims? How would you describe the nature of the Spanish you see or hear with respect to dialect, register, or function?

3. Although university students take courses for a variety of reasons, what different types of motivation are present among Spanish students at your institution? How do their motivational types resemble or differ from those of students taking less commonly taught languages, such as Japanese, Chinese, and Arabic? How can these different types of motivation affect the teaching and learning that take place in the classroom?

4. What does it mean to be a *second* language rather than a *foreign* language, and what are the implications for university Spanish departments in the US? How would you describe "the Spanish problem," and what challenges might likely arise in Spanish language programs that would be less of an issue for other languages? What is the best way to deal with them?

5. Why does the 2007 MLA report recommend the elimination of a two-tiered programmatic structure, whereby language courses are considered "service" rather than content courses? What are the repercussions of two-tiered programs, and what might have been the rationale for this structure?

8. Outline two Spanish language learning contexts for which a needs analysis would return very different results. How does each context differ with regard to the profile of the students, the teachers, the institution, and the community?

9. What other curricular challenges and opportunities unique to Spanish language education in the twenty-first century would you add to this list? How pressing are these issues, and for which contexts?

## NOTES

1. This data set includes de-identified, aggregated results from each state and basic demographic information such as gender and ethnicity. The College Board licensed the data set to the authors for research purposes.

2. Original Spanish: "La necesidad de considerar la enseñanza del español desde una perspectiva émica, es decir, 'desde dentro,' con respecto a principios pedagógicos, marcos curriculares, condiciones locales del aula y el contexto institucional, características de los estudiantes, etc." All translations of quoted material throughout the book are ours.

3. Although the American Association of Teachers of Spanish and Portuguese has published *Hispania* for nearly a hundred years, *Hispania* is not exclusively dedicated to scholarship on language teaching in the strict sense because it also includes articles on literature and linguistics.

## REFERENCES

Alonso, Carlos J. 2007. "Spanish: The Foreign National Language." *Profession 2007* (Modern Language Association): 218–28.

Brown, Alan V. 2009. "LCTL and CTL Students: A Demographic and Academic Comparison." *Foreign Language Annals* 42, no. 3: 405–23.

Brown, James D. 2011. "Foreign and Second Language Needs Analysis." In *The Handbook of Language Teaching*, edited by Michael H. Long and Catherine J. Doughty. Malden, MA: Wiley-Blackwell.

Burke, Brigid. 2013. "Looking into a Crystal Ball: Is Requiring High-Stakes Language Proficiency Tests Really Going to Improve World Language Education?" *Modern Language Journal* 97, no. 2: 531–34.

Byrnes, Heidi, ed. 2008. "Perspectives." *Modern Language Journal* 92, no. 2: 284–312.

———. 2012. "Of Frameworks and the Goals of Collegiate Foreign Language Education: Critical Reflections." *Applied Linguistics Review* 3, no. 1: 1–24.

Byrnes, Heidi, Hiram H. Maxim, and John M. Norris. 2010. "Realizing Advanced FL Writing Development in Collegiate Education: Curricular Design, Pedagogy, Assessment." *Modern Language Journal* 94: 1–221.

Carreira, María. 2013. "The Vitality of Spanish in the United States." *Heritage Language Journal* 10 no. 3: 103–19.

College Board. 2015. Unpublished Data Set of Foreign Language Advanced Placement Scores 1994–2014, derived from data provided by the College Board. Copyright © 1994–2014 The College Board, www.collegeboard.org.

Corral, Will H., and Daphne Patai. 2008, June 6. "An End to Foreign Languages, An End to the Liberal Arts." *Chronicle of Higher Education* 54, no. 39: 30.

Dasenbrock, Reed W. 2004. "Toward a Common Market: Arenas of Cooperation in Literary Study." *ADFL Bulletin* 36, no. 1: 20–26.

Dubin, Fraida, and Elite Olshtain. 1986. *Course Design: Developing Programs and Materials for Language Learning*. Cambridge: Cambridge University Press.

Ferdman, Roberto A. 2015. "Americans are Beginning to Lose their Love for Foreign Languages." *Wonkblog*, February 19. www.washingtonpost.com/news/wonk/wp/2015/02/19/americans-are-beginning-to-lose-their-love-for-foreign-languages/?utm_term=.bbba7cba70ef.

Field, Frederic. 2011. *Bilingualism in the USA: The Case of the Chicano-Latino Community*. Philadelphia: John Benjamins.

Fischer, Gerhard. 2013. "Professional Expectations and Shattered Dreams: A Proficiency Dilemma." *Modern Language Journal* 97, no. 2: 545–48.

Goldberg, David, Dennis Looney, and Natalia Lusin. 2013. "Enrollments in Languages Other Than English in United States Institutions of Higher Education, Fall 2013." Modern Language Association. www.mla.org/content/download/31180/1452509/EMB_en rllmnts_nonEngl_2013.pdf.

Irwin, Robert, and Mónica Szurmuk. 2009. "Cultural Studies and the Field of 'Spanish' in the US Academy." *A Contracorriente: A Journal of Social History and Literature in Latin America* 6, no. 3: 26–60.

Jefferson, Thomas J. 1787. "The Letters of Thomas Jefferson: To Peter Carr Paris, Aug. 10, 1787." www.let.rug.nl/usa/presidents/thomas-jefferson/letters-of-thomas-jefferson.

Lacorte, Manel. 2013. "Sociopolitical and Institutional Conditions for Teaching Spanish as an L2 in US Universities." *Spanish in Context* 10, no. 3: 331–49.

Lacorte, Manel, and Jesús Suárez García. 2014. "La Enseñanza del Español en los Estados Unidos: Panorama Actual y Perspectivas de Futuro." *Journal of Spanish Language Teaching* 1, no. 2: 129–36.

Leeman, Jennifer. 2005. "Engaging Critical Pedagogy: Spanish for Native Speakers." *Foreign Language Annals* 38, no. 1: 35–45.

Lipsett, Anthea. 2009. "Threat of Closure for University Language Departments." *The Guardian*, June 11. www.theguardian.com/education/2009/jun/11/universities-language-departments-close.

Lipski, John. 2002. "Rethinking the Place of Spanish." *PMLA* 117, no. 5: 1247–51.

López Sánchez, Ana. 2009. "Re-writing the Goals of Foreign Language Teaching: The Achievement of Multiple Literacies and Symbolic Competence." *International Journal of Learning* 16, no. 10: 29–38.

Macías, Reynaldo F. 2014. "Spanish as the Second National Language of the United States: Fact, Future, Fiction, or Hope?" *Review of Research in Education* 38: 33–57.

MLA (Modern Language Association). 2007. "Foreign Languages and Higher Education: New Structures for a Changed World." https://www.mla.org/Resources/Research/Surveys-Re ports-and-Other-Documents/Teaching-Enrollments-and-Programs/Foreign-Languages -and-Higher-Education-New-Structures-for-a-Changed-World.

Moeller, Aleidine J. 2013. "Advanced Low Language Proficiency: An Achievable Goal?" *Modern Language Journal* 97, no. 2: 549–53.

Nation, I. S. P., and John Macalister. 2010. *Language Curriculum Design*. New York: Routledge.

Norris, John, and Nicole Mills. 2014. "Innovation and Accountability in Foreign Language Program Evaluation." In *Innovation and Accountability in Language Program Evaluation*, edited by John Norris and Nicole Mills. Boston: Cengage Learning.

Richards, Jack C. 2001. *Curriculum Development in Language Teaching*. New York: Cambridge University Press.

Swaffar, Janet, and Katherine Arens. 2005. *Remapping the FL Curriculum: An Approach through Multiple Literacies*. New York: Modern Language Association of America.

Tarone, Elaine, ed. 2013. "Perspectives." *Modern Language Journal* 91, no. 2: 528–60.

US Census Bureau. 2013. "American Community Survey." www.census.gov/programs-sur veys/acs/.

Valdés, Guadalupe, Sonia González, Dania García, and Patricio Márquez. 2003. "Language Ideology: The Case of Spanish Departments of Foreign Languages." *Anthropology and Education Quarterly* 34, no. 1: 3–26.

# 2

# THE HISTORY AND EVOLUTION OF POSTSECONDARY SPANISH LANGUAGE EDUCATION IN THE UNITED STATES

The key issue that departments of Spanish are currently facing is their change in status from a department of foreign language to something resembling a department of second national language and culture in this country.

— Carlos Alonso, "Spanish: The Foreign National Language," 2007

The declaration that postsecondary Spanish language educators in the United States should consider Spanish a sort of national language, second only to English, comes approximately five hundred years after the first words of Spanish were spoken in what is now Florida, presumably by Juan Ponce de Leon and his crew in 1513. Less than forty years later, Spanish could also be heard by Juan Rodríguez Cabrillo and his men on the coast of present-day California when they arrived in San Diego Bay in September 1542. Use of the Spanish language within the borders of the modern-day United States has a long and complicated history. This chapter seeks to not only trace the historical evolution of Spanish language education and the sociopolitical events and educational trends that influenced its trajectory, but also analyze the current state of Spanish in collegiate institutions. These data will shed light on recent trends in Spanish language curricula and programs, and on what the future augurs for subsequent generations of Spanish language educators, their students, their programs, and their institutions.

We begin this chapter with a brief summary of the history of Spanish language education from the arrival of the Spanish explorers in the New World to the integration of Spanish into postsecondary curricula throughout the United States in the nineteenth and twentieth centuries to its current status in academia. Given the scope of this book, the present discussion focuses on the evolution of macroprogrammatic issues over time—such as enrollment trends, curricular foci, and societal perceptions—with only limited space dedicated to specific teaching methodologies.[1] Nevertheless, certain pedagogical innovations and other relevant scholarship in related fields such as linguistics, psychology, and second-language acquisition are woven into the narrative when deemed pertinent.

## SPANISH LANGUAGE EDUCATION FROM CONTACT TO THE NINETEENTH CENTURY

Though little detailed historical documentation is available, the teaching of Spanish most surely was undertaken for the first time in the Western Hemisphere by the Spanish clergy after having come into contact with the indigenous peoples of the Americas and having set up permanent settlements in the New World. As early as 1516, the Spanish monarchs and the Catholic Church expressed their desire to teach the indigenous people Spanish when Francisco Cardinal Jiménez (Ximenes) de Cisneros identified the teaching of Spanish as a crucial component of Spain's colonization and Christianization of the New World.[2] However, Sánchez Pérez observed that a formal, systematic, and enduring approach to Spanish instruction was not instigated for many years after initial contact between the Europeans and the indigenous peoples of the Americas, and "was spread and learned most often by way of 'natural' means."[3] Indeed, the current linguistic landscape of most of Central and South America is a testament to how indiscriminate and thorough this natural learning of Spanish was in supplanting indigenous languages, when not in competition with the languages of other colonial powers.

Within territory that would eventually fall under the rule of the United States, the teaching and learning of Spanish would develop differentially along two separate geographic axes in the late eighteenth and early nineteenth centuries: (1) the Eastern Seaboard and adjacent territories dominated by Anglophones from the original thirteen colonies, and (2) the southern and southwestern lands liberated from Spanish rule before annexation by the United States by purchase or by treaty. Unlike the lands of the American colonies, much of the southern and southwestern territory was already populated by Spanish-speaking mestizos and criollos when English-speaking Americans arrived.

Several individuals throughout the American colonial period identified the potential market for Spanish instruction, targeting clients seeking fruitful commercial relationships with Spain and its extensive colonies in the Western Hemisphere, such as Augustus Vaughn, John Clarke, and Garret Noel. Leavitt (1961, 123) identifies the Public Academy of the City of Philadelphia—that is, the University of Pennsylvania—as the first institution of higher education to identify the need for Spanish instructors in its 1749 Constitution. By 1766 Paul Fooks was installed as professor of Spanish and French at the Public Academy, while an Italian, Carlo Bellini, was charged with teaching French,

Spanish, and Italian at William and Mary College in 1779. Nevertheless, the well-traveled and rather cosmopolitan Francisco de Miranda from Venezuela noted in his diary after visiting Harvard College in the 1780s that "it is extraordinary that there is no chair whatever of living languages," a rather prescient observation that would be addressed in time.

## SPANISH IN THE ACADEMY IN THE NINETEENTH AND EARLY TWENTIETH CENTURIES

In spite of these early initiatives at establishing Spanish systematically in university curricula, the teaching of Spanish at the postsecondary level in "a really serious way" (Leavitt 1961, 593) would not commence until 1815, when Abiel Smith bequeathed $20,000 to Harvard University for a professorship in French and Spanish. George Tickner and the poet Henry Longfellow were the first to fill the Smith Professorship, and they, along with subsequent Smith professors, had a profound impact on the direction and focus of Spanish teaching at the collegiate level that can still be felt today—namely, a concentration on literary texts written by authors from the Iberian Peninsula. In referring to the Smith professors, Spell (1927, 151) concludes that it would be difficult to accurately gauge "the influence these men . . . exerted on the development of Spanish teaching in the United States."

The Harvard professors' methodological focus, which placed a premium on the use of literary texts and literary analysis for language instruction, was so strong that institutions with even "the most utilitarian motives used texts whose purpose was to introduce students to the treasures of Spanish literature" (Spell 1927, 151). This bias in favor of Peninsular Spanish and Spanish literature and culture continued on into the 1900s and only started to recede toward the close of the third decade of the twentieth century, when the Harvard Council on Hispano-American was organized in 1929. By 1961, Leavitt (1961, 616) proclaimed that Latin American studies "are now firmly entrenched in the colleges and universities of the United States." However, the dominance of literature in university curricula and faculty scholarship continues rather strongly to the present day (VanPatten 2015). Serious scholarly research and teaching within the fields of Hispanic linguistics and applied linguistics would not appear until many decades after Spell's 1927 article.

Throughout the 1800s, Spanish instruction at institutions of higher education continued to spread, both in terms of the number of institutions teaching Spanish and in terms of the prestige given the language vis-à-vis instructors' academic appointments and the acceptance of Spanish courses toward degree requirements. By 1832, at least fourteen institutions offered Spanish, and though many still employed instructors, several universities established similar professorships to the Smith Professorship at Harvard. Throughout the nineteenth century, many other universities, both public and private, introduced Spanish, and others began accepting Spanish courses to fulfill graduation requirements. The establishment of the Modern Language Association (MLA) in 1883 and the publication of the *Modern Language Journal* in 1916 provided additional evidence of the growing interest in the study of world languages in higher education, but more specifically the study of a language's literary canon and high culture. The American Association of Teachers of Spanish was formed in 1917, and the first issue of its journal *Hispania* came out in 1918.

Notwithstanding the integration of Spanish at the most prestigious and best-known universities, Leavitt (1961) notes that the growth of Spanish teaching was not continuous and that interest was sporadic. He argues that if all American universities are considered, Spanish only rarely was part of the curriculum and in some cases was relegated to an extracurricular subject to be studied outside class, with no official credit being awarded. Leeman (2006) notes that in 1910 not one of the 33 percent of US colleges that required two to four years of modern language study accepted Spanish. Cook's (1922, 276–77) indictment of Spanish as bereft of any cultural value within the educational context is indicative of prevalent biases against Spanish during this time: "German and French are the languages of great literatures as well as of science; Spanish, relatively speaking, is the language of neither." Writing in 1927, Spell laments the fact that Spain seemed to monopolize the Spanish postsecondary curriculum as instructors directed students' attention solely to the life, culture, and literature of the Spanish Peninsula, and those who traveled abroad "have sought Spain as their Mecca, not Spanish America"(Spell 1927, 158). He also hints at the irony that most of the graduate programs in Spanish at the time his article was published were offered by institutions in the East, far removed from lands formerly part of the Spanish Empire, where native Spanish could still be heard as a means of communication. Leeman connects racial prejudice to the sociocultural marginalization of Spanish speakers in the nineteenth and early twentieth centuries, arguing that some feared that a further expansion in Mexico and the Caribbean would threaten the maintenance of the United States as a "white English-speaking nation" (Leeman 2006, 35).

## TERRITORIAL EXPANSION IN THE NINETEENTH CENTURY: FROM MAJORITY TO MINORITY

By the early and middle nineteenth century, Spanish had been firmly established as the primary means of communication among longtime residents throughout the extensive Spanish territories along the southern and southwestern axis. The outbreak of revolutionary movements among many Spanish-American colonists in the early 1800s engendered sympathy for Spain's subjects and broad interest in Spanish America among Anglo-Americans from the East (Spell 1927). Several events within a fifty-year period transformed sympathy and interest to massive migration as English-speaking Americans poured into lands formerly ruled by Spain but still populated by Spanish-speaking majorities, starting with the purchase of Louisiana in 1803 and Florida in 1819. The annexation of Texas in 1846, the signing of the Treaty of Guadalupe Hidalgo in 1848, the discovery of gold in California in 1848, and the annexation of lands included in the Gadsden Purchase in 1853 served to further increase the contact of English and Spanish speakers and sparked Anglo-American interest in the prospect of economic benefit in these newly acquired lands and, consequently, in the Spanish language. Unlike the Anglophones striving to learn Spanish from the mid-eighteenth to the early nineteenth centuries along the Eastern Seaboard, who constituted the linguistic majority in their communities, those who flooded into lands recently liberated from Spanish rule were initially a linguistic minority, but they came from an ascending regional and international political superpower. In many cities and towns throughout the Southwest and West, Spanish-speaking majorities were completely replaced by English-speaking settlers within two or three generations, such that English became the majority language in much of the southwestern and western United States by the dawn of the twentieth century.

Field (2011, 6) points out that contact between speakers of diverse languages may be the result of conflict and the "apparently human urge to conquer, dominate, and expand ethnic or national frontiers." To some degree, this seems to have been the case for Anglo-Americans in the nineteenth century as they moved across the continent with their culture and language in tow. Ironically, it was Americans' perceptions of the Germans' desire to conquer and dominate that led to reduced interest in the study of German following World War I. Though German had been the default foreign language—with its connection to science, psychology, and philosophy—Spanish enrollments at all levels increased as a result of the resentment many Americans felt toward the German language during and after World War I.

In spite of the drop in German enrollments and the increase in Spanish enrollments following World War I, and even World War II, Sánchez Pérez (1992) cites survey research conducted in the 1930s and 1940s (Leavitt 1936; Walsh 1947) indicating that Spanish might have been doing well quantitatively but not qualitatively: "In many places Spanish is relegated to second-class status and is not considered worthy as a requirement for other courses of study."[4] For most of the nineteenth and early twentieth centuries, foreign languages were thought of as tools for achieving greater depth in and enriched study of a particular field—such as literature, culture, psychology, and philosophy—and not as objects of study themselves akin to the modern study of linguistics or the acquisition of practical communicative ability. As such, one index of a language's prestige within an institution was the number of academic programs that required students to achieve reading mastery as a prerequisite for advanced disciplinary study. For most of the eighteenth and nineteenth centuries, and even portions of the twentieth century, French and German were considered more academically prestigious languages because they provided access to works of the great German and French authors, philosophers, and scientists. As is demonstrated elsewhere, other sociocultural, ethnic, racial, and linguistic ideologies also exerted great influence on the assignment of prestige to different languages.

## IMMIGRATION AND THE PERSISTENCE OF UTILITY IN THE TWENTIETH CENTURY

The story of the Spanish language and its instruction within the borders of the United States took a distinct turn in the twentieth century. By the mid-1900s, few could argue that English was not the language of power, commerce, and governance across nearly all communities in the United States. The territorial borders of the continental United States had been solidified, and contact between Spanish and English in the United States no longer was due to territorial expansion and imperialism, strictly speaking, but rather national security, free trade, and, most important, foreign immigration. After the close of World War II, the onset of the Cold War, and Russia's launch of Sputnik in 1957, the American government felt the need to improve education at all levels and in all subjects, including foreign languages, as a way to remain competitive internationally and as a way to effectively defend itself against communism (Heining-Boynton 2014). The National Defense Education Act of 1958 was the legislative manifestation of this angst and injected unprecedented amounts of tax money into schools at all levels.

However, as America's standing as the preeminent economic, cultural, and political superpower became undeniable, it also became clear that America's international status had severely undermined foreign language learning. English became a lingua franca worldwide, and the United States' cultural and economic power reached into even the most remote villages of Asia, Africa, and Latin America. As such, Americans found less and less reason to learn other languages and monolingualism continued as the norm. A different sort of national security surfaced in the United States that might better be referred to as apathy. Many felt secure with their identity as citizens of the most powerful and influential country and as speakers of one of the most widely used languages in the world. Although some surely felt that the world's desire to learn the language of the United States was a feather in its cap, Paul Simon (1980) famously bemoaned America's entrenched monolingualism in his oft-cited *The Tongue-Tied American: Confronting the Foreign Language Crisis*. The relative calm that accompanied America's apparent triumph over its perennial Cold Ward rival—Russia—was short-lived. The September 11, 2001, terrorist attacks on America, at the dawn of the twenty-first century, and the ensuing war on terror led the US government to, once again, address America's linguistic deficiencies and to identify *critical* needed languages. Government agencies formed partnerships with universities to offer scholarships for students willing to engage in advanced study of critically needed languages such as Arabic, Chinese, and Farsi. As Field (2011) so accurately observed, conflict is one of the strongest motivators for language learning at the national level; nevertheless, national security may be the most ephemeral of motivations because armed conflicts on foreign lands in the modern era tend to dissipate in the public's consciousness much faster than it takes most postpubertal adults to achieve functional proficiency in the second language.

An additional utilitarian motive for the teaching and learning of foreign languages, and Spanish specifically, is identified by Field (2011) as economic cooperation, or exploitation—depending on the power differential between nations. From the earliest evidences of Spanish instruction in the thirteen colonies, Spanish language learning has been connected to economic gain for the learner because it allows access to previously inaccessible markets. The rapid globalization of world markets in the late twentieth and early twenty-first centuries led to several free trade agreements, including the North American Free Trade Agreement of 1994. Though hotly debated and quite controversial, this pact, along with other free trade agreements, made it more profitable for American companies to do business in other countries. As transnational American companies poured into Spanish-speaking countries—such as Mexico, Panama, Costa Rica, Guatemala, and Colombia—the need for Spanish proficiency among domestic employees and employees stationed abroad became more acute. The rise of business Spanish courses in the United States is but one tangible example of how free trade agreements have affected the teaching and learning of Spanish. Sánchez Pérez provides a somewhat scathing conclusion from an outsider's perspective regarding Americans' interest in learning Spanish: "In the United States, what has most driven the learning of our language [Spanish] has been the reality and need for trade with Latin American countries. While aesthetic, literary, and even romantic motives cannot be discounted, they are not substantial enough, quantitatively or qualitatively, to attract the attention of Americans."[5]

As the twentieth century came to a close, Spanish-speaking markets were not only made available abroad but also became increasingly viable domestically, with large numbers of Spanish-dominant consumers residing within the borders of the United States. The following observation made by Leeman (2006, 37) rings true, especially for Spanish in the United States during the twentieth and early twenty-first centuries: "Second-language ability is increasingly commodified as a job skill, rather than a symbol of education and cultural capital."

From the *bracero* program of the 1940s and 1950s that provided American farmers with laborers from Mexico to the political refugees fleeing Cuba in the late 1950s and early 1960s and the economic refugees in the early 1980s, to the thousands of Puerto Ricans established along the Eastern Seaboard to the undocumented Mexicans and Central Americans who cross the southwestern border seeking greater economic opportunity, the twentieth century has been marked by large numbers of foreign-born, Spanish-speaking immigrants to the United States. As we noted in chapter 1, Hispanics make up the largest ethnic or racial minority in the US, and Spanish is the most commonly spoken language in American homes besides English, by a large margin. Several states have seen increases of more than 60 percent in the number of Spanish speakers in less than ten years (2005–13). These waves of Spanish-speaking immigrants have had a profound impact on several sectors of American society, not the least of which is education, particularly Spanish language education.

As the numbers of Spanish speakers in the last several decades of the twentieth century grew, Spanish quickly became the default foreign language course at all levels, from elementary to secondary to postsecondary. The MLA's periodic survey of collegiate foreign language enrollments indicates that Spanish enrollments surpassed those of all other languages in approximately 1970. From 1985 to 2009, the gap widened between Spanish and the other languages so quickly that since 1995 Spanish enrollments have totaled more than all the other languages combined (figure 2.1), notwithstanding a slight dip in Spanish enrollments from 2009 to 2013. In like manner, the number of Advanced Placement examinations given by the College Board to high school students in Spanish language and Spanish literature between 1979 and 2014 increased from 4,378 to 152,962. In 1979 the two Spanish exams represented 46 percent of modern foreign language Advanced Placement exams given, while in 2014 this proportion had risen to 81 percent (figure 2.2). The logic for why many high school and university students opt for Spanish over other languages is sound: the likelihood of using oral Spanish in their day-to-day lives with native and Spanish-dominant speakers either at work or in the community regardless of location is much higher than it is with other

**Figure 2.1    Enrollments in Spanish and Other Foreign Languages, 1958–2013**

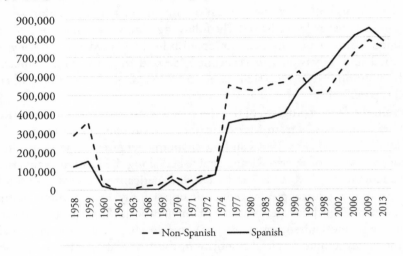

**Figure 2.2    World Language Advanced Placement Examination Totals, 1979–2014**

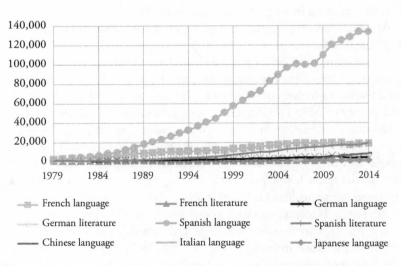

*Source:* Data from Alan V. Brown and Gregory L. Thompson, "The Evolution of Foreign Language AP Exam Candidates: A 36-Year Descriptive Study," *Foreign Language Annals*, June 17, 2016. © 2016 American Council of Teachers of Foreign Languages; reprinted by permission.

languages. This practical, performance-based approach to language learning received scholarly support from movements in applied linguistics and foreign language education that enthroned communicative competence and proficiency as the hallmarks of second-language learning.

## CHANGING DEMOGRAPHICS AND DIVERSE NEEDS IN THE TWENTY-FIRST CENTURY

As the country's demographics have changed, with large numbers of immigrants arriving from Spanish-speaking countries, so too has the makeup of many of America's schools. Many of the children of immigrant families that enrolled in elementary schools and high schools had limited, or no, English skills, and as a result they struggled to progress academically and even failed miserably, leading to disillusioned, disenfranchised, and disgruntled parents. These students' language learning and cultural needs were addressed by a series of legislative acts—no doubt facilitated by the civil rights movement—passed by the US Congress throughout the 1960s and 1970s.[6] Foremost among these, insofar as Spanish language education is concerned, were the Elementary and Secondary Education Act of 1965 and the Bilingual Education Act (Title VII of the Elementary and Secondary Education Act) of 1967.

These progressive pieces of legislation were designed to allow students with limited English skills to make use of, and even improve, their first language (Spanish) as a means of improving their second-language skills in English. From a cognitive, linguistic, and acquisition perspective, this approach seemed reasonable, grounded in sound second-language acquisition theory, and offered a practical solution to academic underachievement and failure among the thousands of schoolchildren from Spanish-speaking homes with limited proficiency in English. As a result, bilingual programs began sprouting up across the country in areas with large Spanish-speaking populations. One school in Miami—Coral Way Elementary School—was looked to as an example of how to run a successful bilingual program, where English-speaking students learned Spanish, but, more important for the Anglophone majority, where Spanish-speaking students learned English.

However, as Field (2011) notes, it became apparent rather early on that there were as many definitions of bilingual education as there were bilingual schools and that socioeconomic and sociocultural variables exerted great influence on learning outcomes, as did teacher expertise and commitment. Bilingual programs were initially portrayed as somewhat of a panacea for teaching migrant children English, but many stakeholders felt that these programs did not live up to their billing. Unfortunately, in many cases bilingual programs were only bilingual in name, given that the curricula, pedagogy, and culture at many schools were subtractive in nature and undermined maintenance of the first language. It was clear that what many in society wanted was for Hispanic, Spanish-dominant bilingual children to become English-dominant monolinguals as quickly as possible. The apparent failure of bilingual programs—coupled with strong political, economic, and social forces decrying illegal immigration—led to many English-only campaigns across the country. These movements seemed to devalue bilingualism specifically among Latinos, which in turn created a rather hostile environment in those US states that aggressively pursued English-only laws. Several states that had large conservative voting blocs and also had large Spanish-speaking populations—such as California, Arizona, and Texas—voted to dismantle traditional bilingual programs, leaving only remnants of the original models and severely limiting the use of students' native language in the school setting.

The traditional approach to school-based foreign language learning, which delayed formal coursework until the secondary level and was oriented toward English-dominant monolinguals, became the norm for all but students with the most limited English proficiency. Rather than strengthening both of a bilingual child's languages from the beginning of his or her school career to facilitate greater outcomes by high school graduation, traditional curricular models made Spanish-English bilinguals wait until their native language proficiency fell below the level of their second language, English, before allowing them to renew study in the first language, Spanish, at the high school level. Students' bilingualism was essentially viewed as a liability to be dealt with and delayed rather than an asset to be capitalized on from the outset. A 1972 white paper published by the American Association of Teachers of Spanish and Portuguese (1972, 19) stated, rather poignantly, that as an organization, it was compelled to reject "the embarrassing anomaly of a language policy for American education which on the one hand seeks to encourage and develop competence in Spanish among those for who it is a second language, and on the other hand, by open discouragement, neglect, condescension, destroys it for those who speak it as a mother tongue."

Ruiz (1990), who found that ethnic languages for minority-language populations are construed as problematic, identified the underlying ideology and clear paradox exposed by this approach to Spanish, observing that foreign languages for majority-language populations are seen as resources. Correa (2011, 315) states this quite succinctly: "Spanish enjoys different status depending on who the learner is (FL [foreign language] or HL [host language])."

Not surprisingly, this subtractive—or at the least *delayed*—approach failed to produce satisfactory results because many bilingual students, in spite of perfect mastery of conversational English, struggled to acquire academic registers of English and Spanish and continued to underachieve academically.

Many Spanish-speaking Latino students came from socioeconomically underprivileged families with little social capital. These students also struggled emotionally and socially at school, as many felt that their bilingual and bicultural identity were to be apologized for and dismissed rather than highlighted and celebrated. In some cases, linguistic biases harbored against Spanish-dominant Latinos in the United States represented only the surface of deeper racial and ethnic prejudices in the country.

The civil rights movement and the tireless efforts of prominent activists like César Chávez made great strides in imbuing the Mexican-American identity, language, and culture with pride. But it was not until much later that the presence of Hispanic, Latino, and Chicano students in traditional courses on Spanish as a foreign language resulted in widespread curricular change. In the 1990s and early 2000s, more and more Spanish language educators at the secondary and postsecondary levels were confronted with nearly fully bilingual students in their beginning classes. These students had developed solid receptive and fairly strong productive abilities in Spanish in their homes and communities as children. As their numbers increased, it became apparent rather quickly that these students (1) represented a very diverse group linguistically and culturally, (2) possessed linguistic and cultural competence that was quantitatively and qualitatively different from their monolingual Anglo-American classmates, and (3) required an alternative pedagogical approach catered to their needs. The term *heritage* or *native* was used to refer to these students, given their familial and childhood connections to the language, culture, or both, and courses were developed to address their needs. Textbooks were written especially for this population (Marqués 2000; Roca 1999), entire curricula and academic programs were designed (Beaudrie 2011), and a flourishing research program within applied linguistics was born (Beaudrie and Fairlough 2012).

Today, throughout the United States, collegiate Spanish language curriculum designers are confronted with incoming students at all levels but, quite ironically, relatively few that would be considered true beginners. In fact, it is safe to say without fear of misrepresentation that the large majority of students who enroll for the first time in any level of Spanish at a given tertiary institution, either as incoming freshmen or as transfer students, have previously studied the language formally, either in high school or at other postsecondary institutions. In many cases this holds true for introductory, first-year, first-semester courses, such as the proverbial Spanish 101. At the University of Kentucky (UK) from 2008 to 2016, the average share of Spanish 101 students with *no* high school Spanish was 24 percent, while the average proportion with two or more years of high school Spanish was 74 percent. These realities have led many programs, including UK's, to create courses designed for "false beginners" that allow them to take only one course that equates to two semesters of the elementary language sequence. Indeed, the nature of Spanish 101 insofar as classroom pedagogy and language use are concerned would not strike an outside observer with no Spanish ability as a true beginning-level class. Although heritage students' exposure to Spanish outside class may exceed their in-class exposure, traditional students may have very little contact with the language. The consequences of this disparity and the wide diversity of student abilities in Spanish at the postsecondary level have ramifications for the establishment of appropriate curricular-level structures; the design of *accelerated, high beginner / intermediate, intensive,* and *heritage* classes; the assessment of students' abilities; the specification of programmatic student learning outcomes; and the deployment of classroom instruction.

## PEDAGOGICAL PROGRESS AND THE PROGRESSIVE EXPANSION OF SPANISH CURRICULA

Since Spanish was first taught formally in Philadelphia in the mid-1700s, postsecondary Spanish curricula have undergone notable changes, despite a strong undercurrent of tradition. Many of these changes reflect trends in teaching methodologies, scholarly research in linguistics and second-language acquisition, and reconceptualizations of higher education and its goals. In this section, we briefly review these major trends, citing the results of our own analysis of several university course catalogs during the mid–twentieth and early twenty-first centuries as a means of systematically charting the growth of undergraduate course offerings and program configurations.

During much of the nineteenth century, Spanish language teaching was considered an intellectual exercise consisting of grammatical analysis and cross-linguistic translation, both of which facilitated analysis of literary masterpieces by prominent Spanish authors. Reading and writing were the preferred modalities, and grammatical and lexical accuracy were emphasized. In a typical college-level Spanish course in the 1800s in the United States, the medium of instruction was English, not the foreign language, and the development of students' extemporaneous oral ability was not the focus. Many nonnative Spanish professors, potentially including some holders of the Smith Professorship at Harvard, would have struggled to conduct literary and grammatical analyses exclusively in spoken Spanish.

By the end of the nineteenth century, a reform movement in language teaching arose that looked to the first language and naturalistic acquisition as the model to follow in teaching second languages (Richards and Rodgers 2001). The Direct Method, as it was called, focused on oral communication reflective of daily communicative tasks, placed a premium on mastery of the sound system, and prescribed exclusive use of the target language during class. This approach to classroom language learning garnered many supporters and caught on well in private language schools with highly motivated learners in small classes, but failed to achieve the same success in public school classrooms with large groups of adolescents or even university students. With generally unsatisfactory learning outcomes in foreign language classes, the 1929 Coleman Report represented the culmination of a nationwide study that sought to identify reasonable goals for foreign language education in the public school system. The report recommended that a more realistic approach to language learning would be to focus on developing students' reading ability, rather than trying to incorporate the time-consuming and exhausting techniques of the Direct Method.

The methodological pendulum would swing back again in the direction of naturalistic approaches after World War II, as government agencies realized that functional oral-aural interpersonal skills in critical foreign languages were a rarity among nonnative military personnel and civil servants alike. The Army Specialized Training Program was born out of this need, and was boosted by theoretical support from B. F. Skinner's well-known approach to the analysis of human behavior—including language and language learning—called, simply, *behaviorism*. The theoretical foundation of behaviorism hinged on the organizing principle of stimulus–response psychology and led to an academic adaptation called the Audio-Lingual Method, which prioritized oral language, memorization and mimicry, and pronunciation, while demanding impeccable grammatical accuracy. In time, it too began to fall from grace after Noam Chomsky's (1959) sharp critique of Skinner's (1957) *Verbal Behavior*. Chomsky's (1965) insights gave rise to modern linguistics and provided theoretical models for the structure, representation, and acquisition of language, all of which represented a significant departure from the structuralist tradition of the early to middle twentieth century. Although Chomsky criticized Skinner's work, Dell Hymes (1966) did the same to Chomsky's, finding several tenets of Chomsky's theory of language competence deficient. Hymes argued that a speaker's ability to use language in real time with the constraints imposed by situational factors demanded a broader conceptualization of language ability that transcended strict grammatical competence and captured what he called *communicative competence*. From the theoretical foundations laid by Chomsky and Hymes, scholars interested in language learning, such as Corder (1967), began to systematically study the acquisition of second languages, considering it a qualitatively different enterprise than the process by which infants learn their first language. The study of second-language acquisition was established as a scholarly field in its own right, and began to inform classroom pedagogy.

At the same time that researchers, teachers, and students' perspectives on language teaching and learning were undergoing a transformation, so too was American higher education. Starting in the 1950s and 1960s, the numbers of young people in the United States who attended college began growing rapidly. A university education was not just for the social and economic elite who came from privileged backgrounds but was also made accessible to the working and middle classes of society (Bok 2006). As such, a college education was not solely to stimulate reflection and broaden students' intellectual horizons or to develop an informed and civically active citizen, but rather to equip him or her with knowledge and skills that would lead to gainful employment. Heining-Boynton (2014, 143) notes that, by the mid-1970s, "students demanded real-world relevance in all of their college courses" and "enrolled in courses that they believed would help them in their jobs and careers." This growing sentiment among college students that valued practical and even vocationally oriented curricula, coupled with developments in second-language acquisition, triggered an explosion of new courses in Spanish programs.

A strictly textual and quantitative analysis of selected American universities' undergraduate Spanish course titles and course descriptions substantiates this trend. The course catalogs of nine prominent universities were studied longitudinally at regular intervals to determine how postsecondary Spanish course offerings have evolved over time. Academic years 1970–71 and 2015–16 were chosen as points of comparison because 1970–71 was the first year in which all nine schools' catalogs were available for analysis and, given the use of modern conventions, for the reporting and publication of course titles and descriptions. Table 2.1 includes the total number of courses for each category, along with the average per school and the percentage change from 1970–71 to 2015–16. Overall, the total number of undergraduate courses offered across all schools nearly doubled, from 397 to 781. The subjects that saw the greatest increase were, in descending order, courses in translation and interpretation, heritage/native Spanish language, service-learning, and Spanish for the professions, from twenty-eight-fold (translation and interpretation) to six-and-a-half-fold (Spanish for the professions). Culture increased nearly fourfold, and it added the most courses in raw numbers (219), while linguistics and independent and directed study also saw their numbers more than double. The only area with fewer courses in the 2015–16 catalog than appeared in the 1970–71 catalog was literature, which fell 12 percent, from 167 to 147 courses. Nevertheless, when culture and literature are combined, they total 421, more than all the other nine categories combined (360). As such, courses categorized as literature and culture continue to dominate the undergraduate curriculum, with the percentage of culture courses rising dramatically from 1970–71 to 2015–16. In spite of Irwin and Szurmuk's (2009) conclusion that Spanish

Table 2.1    Course Catalog Totals from Nine Universities, 1970–71 and 2015–16

| Subject | 1970–71 | Average per School | 2015–16 | Average per School | % Total Change |
|---|---|---|---|---|---|
| Elementary language | 71 | 7.9 | 89 | 9.9 | +25 |
| Advanced language | 52 | 5.8 | 68 | 7.6 | +31 |
| Linguistics | 22 | 2.4 | 64 | 7.1 | +191 |
| Literature | 167 | 18.6 | 147 | 16.3 | −12 |
| Culture | 55 | 6.1 | 274 | 30.4 | +398 |
| Spanish for the professions | 4 | 0.4 | 30 | 3.3 | +650 |
| Translation and interpretation | 1 | 0.1 | 29 | 3.2 | +2,800 |
| Heritage/native Spanish language | 2 | 0.2 | 23 | 2.6 | +1,050 |
| Teaching | 6 | 0.7 | 8 | .9 | +33 |
| Service learning | 0 | 0 | 9 | 1 | +900 |
| Independent/directed study | 17 | 1.9 | 40 | 4.4 | +135 |
| Total | 397 | 44.1 | 781 | 86.8 | +97 |

programs have been less willing, or able, than German and French programs to adopt a cultural studies approach to postsecondary language education, our course catalog analysis seems to indicate that changes are indeed afoot, at least among these nine Spanish programs.

## THE NEED FOR CHANGE AND THE INTRANSIGENCE OF TRADITION

Although our analysis of university Spanish curricula appears to paint a picture of progressive evolution and positive transformation, the actual situation is much more complex and nuanced. The wide variety of courses that have surfaced in the course catalogs during the second half of the twentieth century indicate the need for change insofar as course offerings were concerned, most likely due to student demand, administrative mandate, and advocacy from selected members of the faculty. Yet the fact that a course appears in a catalog gives no indication of whether it is taught each term or how many sections are available, or what the academic profile and rank of those who teach them might be, or whether the courses are coherently and cohesively integrated into an academic program of study with clear learning outcomes, or how well they match the research, training, and pedagogical inclinations of the majority of the professoriate. Many collegiate Spanish programs maintain a two-tiered approach to formal language learning, in which lower-level elementary language instruction has been programmatically and culturally separated from upper-level courses in literary, cultural, and linguistic studies. Although the

lower-level language courses are often taught by part-time, adjunct, or graduate student instructors, in many universities the upper-level courses appear
to be the domain of tenured or tenure-line faculty. This comes in spite of
repeated calls by scholars in applied linguistics, foreign language education,
and instructed second-language acquisition for the eradication of this long-
standing configuration and for a more equitable distribution of undergraduate courses among instructors of all ranks. All this must be placed within the
broader sociocultural and socioeconomic context in American higher education, in which the humanities, and foreign languages more specifically, are under pressure to "express a renewed sense of value" (Norris and Mills 2014, 1).

The long-standing programmatic bifurcation of language departments, in
which lower-level courses focus on the development of day-to-day conversational language and upper-level courses focus on the reading and analysis of
literary texts, reflects a deeper intellectual division in language departments
throughout the academy. At the close of the twentieth century, Bernhardt
(1998, 51) concluded that postsecondary language teaching has experienced,
and continues to experience, a sort of schizophrenia: "The tension between
the traditional, humanities-based, reading-oriented study of belles lettres and
views advocating functionality and oral proficiency; the paradoxical image
of language as part of the humanities but simultaneously in the service of
government and the military; the social problematic of maintaining and valuing a cultural identity while encouraging people to assume another; and the
economics of promising in a short term what can be delivered only in the
long term."

The tension many departments feel between developing a functionally oriented curriculum that would facilitate students' acquisition of interpersonal,
primarily oral, proficiency—as compared with more academic, primarily
written, competencies—is felt nowhere stronger than in Spanish programs.
Added to this tension are the "fissure between peninsularists and Latin Americanists" (Irwin and Szurmuk 2009, 44), the contested displacement of traditional literary approaches in favor of a cultural studies focus (Irwin and
Szurmuk), and the apparent hesitance among both parties to accept that "they
are responsible for teaching and producing scholarship about an increasingly
national cultural reality rather than a foreign one" (Alonso 2007, 225). Irwin
and Szumurk make a strong argument for the elevation of US Latino studies,
Mexican studies, and Latin American studies within curricular hierarchies, at
the expense of Spain and Peninsular studies, anecdotally noting that they are
not familiar with any department with more Mexicanists than Peninsularists. Given the ubiquity of Spanish and Spanish-dominant speakers in US
society, many of whom are of Mexican and Mexican-American heritage, students are attracted to Spanish because of the perceived utility for their future

professional and personal lives, as opposed to their intellectual and academic lives.

Though many university students see the practical benefits of language study, they appear to be uneasy limiting their choice of major solely to language, and thus they often combine their language major with another major. A recent MLA report, "Data on Second Majors in Language and Literature, 2001–2013," revealed that—not surprisingly—the number of foreign languages, literatures, and linguistics *second* majors surpassed the number in any other discipline within the sciences or humanities. Additionally, among all disciplines included in the US Department of Education Integrated Postsecondary Education Data System, foreign languages, literatures, and linguistics had the highest rate of second majors as a percentage of total majors, at 38.6 percent in 2013. In the case of Spanish language and literature, second majors made up 48.3 percent of all Spanish majors, while many other languages had even higher proportions—Romance (82.4 percent), Italian (60.6 percent), French (54.7 percent), and German (50.1 percent). Probably the most telling statistic included in the MLA report came from the Humanities Departmental Survey of 2012–13, which found that 61 percent more minors (49,200) had been completed in languages other than English than had majors (30,240). In sum, students are increasingly pairing their language studies with studies in other disciplines, an implicit sign of academic pragmatism.

The curricular and programmatic manifestations of this intellectual struggle between pragmatism and intellectualism go beyond the well-known, two-tiered structure of many programs and may influence the identification of coherent student learning objectives overall. Byrnes, Maxim, and Norris (2010) identify two overarching learning goals that many foreign language programs espouse: (1) to acquire intellectually meaningful cultural knowledge about the pertinent areas and the peoples who speak the foreign language, and (2) to acquire the ability to use the foreign language (FL) effectively across a variety of contexts. However, many contemporary FL programs struggle to operationalize concrete and coherent learning objectives that would guide syllabus design. Byrnes, Maxim, and Norris (2010, 4) offer the following detailed and rather compelling explanation as to why this might be:

> Among the results of this unresolved dilemma are bifurcated programs that relate largely content-indifferent and content-underspecified and textbook-driven language instruction to roughly the first four semesters of study and that shift to largely language-indifferent or language-underspecified and faculty interest-driven content instruction in the remaining course offerings that pursue their cultural studies mission. With both programmatic halves existing in a nonarticulated relationship toward each other, the one

undisputed characteristic of any successful FL acquisition to advanced ca-
pacities—namely, its long-term cumulative nature—remains unaddressed.
As a consequence, collegiate FL studies departments are unable to create
statements of valued and realistic learning outcomes for each of the major
stages of their undergraduate programs in the humanities.

Foreign language curricula often reflect tradition as well as faculty interests
and training. In practice, and even in theory, many academic programs do not
map out a clear pathway to meaningful linguistic and cultural competence in
the second language over the span of their college career.

As we observed in chapter 1, the 2007 MLA white paper called for fundamental changes to curricular and programmatic structures that seemed to
perpetuate the two-tiered model. In order to achieve deep translingual and
transcultural competence among students, the committee recommended the
inclusion of more faculty trained in applied linguistics, greater collaboration
between faculty of all disciplines and ranks, and the involvement of senior
faculty in the teaching of lower-level courses. Soon after the publication of the
Ad Hoc Committee's report, the Teagle Foundation published a report concerning the state of the undergraduate major in language and literature. The
Teagle Report (MLA 2009) reaffirmed the importance of language, literacy,
and literature, while echoing much of what appeared only two years earlier,
namely, greater collaboration among colleagues of all disciplines, greater efforts at achieving seamless articulation across levels, and greater accountability
vis-à-vis the use of learning outcome measures.

VanPatten (2015) voiced unequivocal criticism of many foreign language
departments for the lack of applied linguists, or what he called language scientists. The casual use of "language departments," he argues, to describe departments that house non-English disciplines presupposes that they are made
up of language experts—an assertion he refutes. VanPatten (2015, 4) claims
that specialists in literary and cultural studies are not trained during graduate
school, or even during their entire careers, to understand the intricacies of language and language acquisition: "The point is simply that the vast majority of
scholars populating academic 'language' departments are not experts in language or language acquisition." He presents findings from his analysis of the
specialty areas of faculty from several Spanish and French departments at well-
known research-intensive universities—six from the West Coast, six from the
East Coast, and an additional fifteen primarily from the Midwest. VanPatten
found that an overwhelming majority of faculty members specialized in literary and cultural studies, as compared with linguistics, language acquisition,
or other disciplines. In Spanish the rate of professors with expertise in literary and cultural studies was 76 percent among the Midwestern institutions

and 90 percent among the six prominent West Coast schools. Even in 2015, faculty members who specialized in literary and cultural studies continued to represent a large majority of collegiate faculty, a reality that VanPatten claims may have had detrimental consequences.

A fairly recent article by Hertel and Dings (2014) aimed at assessing the extent to which the 2007 MLA report had affected the state of the under-graduate Spanish major. The authors designed a survey based on the rec-ommendations from the MLA ad hoc committee and distributed it to 400 faculty members, with 104 completing the survey. The responses to ques-tions regarding the types of courses offered and the number and nature of required courses indicated that literature courses represented the core of the curriculum. Over two-thirds of institutions (69 percent) required three or more literature courses, while only a quarter (25 percent) did so for advanced language courses. Moreover, nearly all institutions (98 percent) represented by the survey respondents offered a course giving an introduction to litera-ture, and 68 percent required it. In the case of linguistics, the introductory course was offered at 68 percent of institutions but was only required by 30 percent. Courses on Spanish for specific purposes, such as business Spanish and translation, were the least-offered and least-required courses. Only 28 percent of institutions offered specific concentrations within the major, while the other 72 percent had a general track allowing students to take a variety of courses in different disciplines. Most institutions (70 percent) required 30–36 credit-hours of coursework to complete the major, and only 18 percent indicated that the completion of an experience of study abroad was required. Participants' responses varied with regard to the extent to which the MLA report influenced program requirements and offerings. Some respondents felt that the reports had exerted influence on their programs, while others were quite resistant to the report, and still others voiced frustration with their col-leagues' resistance. Finally, faculty members rated study abroad as the most important experience for students, at 4.58 out of 5, with advanced grammar a close second, at 4.39—ostensibly indicating a desire for improved language skills, among other abilities. Introduction to literature was rated at 4.36, and introduction to linguistics was rated at 3.62.

## CONCLUSION

By the time the formal teaching of Spanish made its way into the higher edu-cation system of the Anglo-American colonies, it had already been firmly es-tablished as a commonly used medium of communication in lands claimed by the Spanish crown in the southern and southwestern portions of the present-day United States. Many scholars consider the establishment of the Smith

Professorship in French and Spanish at Harvard as a watershed moment in the teaching of Spanish in higher education, because it elevated Spanish and Spanish language literatures and cultures to subjects worthy of serious study. Yet the status of Spanish in university curricula did not follow an unbroken, linear ascent in the society dominated by Anglo-American culture. Geopolitical events such as armed conflict, commercial trade, and foreign immigration have all influenced the teaching of Spanish, as have paradigm shifts in linguistics and applied linguistics. Spanish has become the second-most-commonly spoken language in the country and the most commonly taught second language in America's colleges and universities, with learners coming from a wide variety of proficiency profiles and sociolinguistic backgrounds. In order for Spanish instruction in the twenty-first century to flourish in the academy, deeply entrenched curricular and programmatic structures must be updated, ethnic and racial stereotyping of native-speaking populations must be addressed, effective pedagogies and realistic learning outcomes for all learners must be identified and implemented, and utilitarian and humanistic approaches to curriculum design must be seamlessly interwoven to achieve enduring translingual and transcultural competence. From our own analysis of course offerings and from research conducted by Hertel and Dings (2014) and VanPatten (2015), it is apparent that though change may be afoot in Spanish language departments, it moves at a slow pace and "without significantly upsetting the status quo" (Irwin and Szurmuk 2009, 52).

## REFLECTION QUESTIONS

1. In your view, what criteria must be met for a language to officially be declared a *second* language at the local, regional, or national level? Does Spanish meet these criteria in your local community? What about regionally and nationally?

2. What social, economic, and cultural circumstances made the replacement of indigenous languages by Spanish so complete across such a large expanse of territory, from northern Mexico to southern Argentina, with very few exceptions? Why has English become such a globalized language and the lingua franca in so many areas of transnational intercourse?

3. What other major geopolitical events during the twentieth century influenced the teaching and learning of Spanish or other languages, in the United States?

4. Identify the pros and cons of learning a second language solely for instrumental, utilitarian reasons, such as to get a job or a raise, as well as the implications for classroom teaching and learning.

5. What might have caused the slight downturn in Spanish enrollments at the university level from 2009 to 2013? To what extent should Spanish language educators be concerned?

6. Regardless of your personal stance, articulate arguments that can be made for and against English-only legislation in the United States. What documents and services would most likely only be made available in English? How might English-only legislation and the discourse surrounding it affect bilingual education programs for minority children and foreign language programs for language majority students at the secondary level? What implications are there for university foreign language programs?

7. In some Spanish departments, there are deep divisions, and even resentment, between faculty members trained in literary and cultural studies and those trained in linguistics, applied linguistics, and foreign language education. How are these manifest in terms of the curriculum and programmatic configurations, and how might such territorialism be minimized?

8. In the appendix, we describe several data sets that have informed our analysis of Spanish language curricula at the postsecondary level in the twenty-first century, but we realize even these only paint a partial picture. Assume that you could access any relevant data regarding Spanish language teaching and learning at the university level, and then name three data sets that would shed further light on university Spanish language education. How would you analyze these data, and what would you expect to find? Would there be any clear curricular or programmatic implications?

## PEDAGOGICAL ACTIVITIES

1. With a partner, begin to roughly outline an *ideal* undergraduate Spanish curriculum for either a small, selective liberal arts college with 1,500 to 5,000 students or a large, research-intensive public school with 15,000 to 30,000, or any other type of institution, by completing one or all of the following tasks:

   a. Draft a short, one-paragraph mission statement with three to five broad goals from which more specific student learning outcomes could be derived.

   b. How many credit-hours will be required, and at what level(s)? Will there be any core courses, and will non-Spanish courses be allowed? Will there be a capstone project, experience, or education abroad trip required, or even an exit exam with a minimum level of proficiency?

   c. Without specifying the title of each course, identify the types of courses offered and how many of each category will be required.

   d. What programs of study will be available to students—for example, major with various tracks, minor with various tracks, teaching certification/licensure, translation/interpretation certificate?

   e. What will the professional and demographic makeup of instructional staff be?

2. Conduct an analysis of your department's curriculum and program by completing one or all of the following tasks:

   a. Review the résumés of all full-time faculty and categorize them according to the discipline in which they received their highest academic degree and their appointment status (e.g., tenured/tenure-line, lecturer, visiting professor, full-time instructor, part-time adjunct). What categories did you use? Which category had the greatest number of instructors? Calculate percentages for each category.

b. If possible, determine how many students in a given semester are taught by instructors of different academic rank and contractual status (e.g., full professor, associate, assistant, lecturer, part-time adjunct, graduate student instructor, etc.) and the level of the courses taught (first-year beginning language, fifth-semester advanced grammar/composition, third/fourth-year introduction to literature/linguistics, etc.). Describe any trends that you discover.

c. Using the same disciplinary categories from 2a above, categorize all course offerings in the Spanish Department and calculate a percentage. Compare the percentage from 2a to 2c, and explain the match or mismatch.

d. Identify at least three additional courses that are not currently taught that you feel merit inclusion in the departmental offerings, and explain why.

e. Where feasible, contact either departmental or college-level administrators to request the total number of Spanish majors and majors from two other disciplines not in the humanities, such as biology, psychology, and business. In the case of the Spanish majors, request that they be broken down by primary/single majors, primary/double majors, secondary/double majors, single minor, double minor. What trends are detectable in the data across disciplines and within the Spanish major, and what might they indicate?

## NOTES

1. Among the many historical overviews of second language teaching methodologies available for interested readers, we recommend Richards and Rodgers (2001), Grittner (1990), and Mitchell and Vidal (2001).

2. Readers are encouraged to consult Spell (1927), Leavitt (1961), and Sánchez Pérez (1992, chap. 5) for in-depth accounts of the history of Spanish teaching in the United States, from the arrival of the Spanish to the early and middle twentieth century. Heining-Boynton's (2014) review provides much less detail of the early years of Spanish instruction in the US and throughout the nineteenth century, but it does include a more holistic perspective on issues of current relevance that are not accessible in other comprehensive reviews such as Doyle (1925) and Nichols (1945). Leeman (2006) also provides a history of the teaching of Spanish in the US with an eye to language ideology and the status of Spanish in the academy. Our review relied heavily on Heining-Boynton, Leavitt, Sánchez Pérez, and Spell.

3. Original Spanish: "Se expandía y aprendía sobre todo por medios 'naturales'" (Sánchez Pérez 1992, 250).

4. Original Spanish: "En muchos centros el español se deja en segunda fila o no se contempla como 'requirement' para otros estudios" (Sánchez Pérez 1992, 302).

5. Original Spanish: "En los Estados Unidos es la realidad y la necesidad del intercambio comercial con las naciones Hispano-Americanas la que ha promovido y empujado el aprendizaje de nuestro idioma. No se excluyen razones estéticas, literarias y hasta románticas, pero éstas no son lo suficientemente sustantivas ni cuantitativas para que el español atrajese la atención de los norteamericanos" (Sánchez Pérez 1992, 305).

6. See Field (2011, chap. 6) for further discussion of legislative acts that influenced bilingual education.

# REFERENCES

Alonso, Carlos J. 2007. "Spanish: The Foreign National Language." *Profession 2007*, 218–28.

American Association of Teachers of Spanish and Portuguese. 1972. "Teaching Spanish in School and College to Native Speakers of Spanish." *Hispania* 55: 619–31.

Beaudrie, Sara. 2011. "Spanish Heritage Language Programs: A Snapshot of Current programs in the Southwestern United States." *Foreign Language Annals* 44, no. 2: 321–37.

Beaudrie, Sara, and Marta Fairclough, eds. 2012. *Spanish as a Heritage Language in the United States: State of the Field.* Washington, DC: Georgetown University Press.

Bernhardt, Elizabeth B. 1998. "Sociohistorical Perspectives on Language Teaching in the Modern United States." In *Learning Foreign and Second Languages: Perspectives in Research and Scholarship*, edited by Heidi Byrnes. New York: MLA.

Bok, Derek. 2006. *Our Underachieving Colleges: A Candid Look at How Much Students Learn and Why They Should Be Learning More.* Princeton, NJ: Princeton University Press.

Brown, Alan V., and Gregory L. Thompson. 2016. "The Evolution of World Language AP Exam Candidates: A 36-year Descriptive Study." *Foreign Language Annals* 49, no. 2: 235–51.

Byrnes, Heidi, Hiram H. Maxim, and John M. Norris. 2010. "Realizing Advanced FL Writing Development in Collegiate Education: Curricular Design, Pedagogy, Assessment." *Modern Language Journal* 94: 1–221.

Chomsky, Noam. 1957. *Syntactic Structures*. New York: Mouton de Gruyter.

———. 1959. "Reviews: Verbal Behavior by B. F. Skinner." *Language* 35, no. 1: 26–58.

———. 1965. *Aspects of the Theory of Syntax*. Cambridge, MA: MIT Press.

Cook, William. 1922. "Secondary Instruction in Romance Languages." *School Review* 30, no. 4: 274–80.

Corder, Stephen P. 1967. "The Significance of Learners' Errors." *International Review of Applied Lingustics* 5: 161–70.

Correa, Maite. 2011. "Advocating for Critical Pedagogical Approaches to Teaching Spanish as a Heritage Language: Some Considerations." *Foreign Language Annals* 44, no. 2: 308–20.

Doyle, Henry G. 1925. "Spanish Studies in the United States." *Bulletin of Spanish Studies II*, 163–73.

Field, Frederic. 2011. *Bilingualism in the USA: The Case of the Chicano-Latino Community.* Philadelphia: John Benjamins.

Grittner, Frank. 1990. "Bandwagons Revisited: A Perspective on Movements in Foreign Language Education." In *New Perspectives and New Directions in Foreign Language Education*, edited by Diane W. Birckbichler. Lincolnwood, IL: National Textbook Company.

Heining-Boynton, Audrey L. 2014. "Teaching Spanish Pre K–16 in the US: Then, Now, and in the Future." *Journal of Spanish Teaching* 1, no. 2: 137–53.

Hertel, Tammy J., and Abby Dings. 2014. "The Undergraduate Spanish Major Curriculum: Realities and Faculty Perceptions." *Foreign Language Annals* 47, no. 3: 546–68.

Hymes, Dell H. 1966. "Two Types of Linguistic Relativity." In *Sociolinguistics*, edited by William Bright. The Hague: Mouton.

Irwin, Robert, and Mónica Szurmuk. 2009. "Cultural Studies and the Field of 'Spanish' in the US Academy." *A Contracorriente: A Journal of Social History and Literature in Latin America* 6, no. 3: 26–60.

Leavitt, Sturgis E. 1936. "The Status of Spanish in the South Atlantic States." *Hispania* 19, no. 1: 37–40.

————. 1961. "The Teaching of Spanish in the United States." *Hispania* 44, no. 4: 591–625.

Leeman, Jennifer. 2006. "The Value of Spanish: Shifting Ideologies in United States Language Teaching." *ADFL Bulletin* 38, nos. 1–2: 32–39.

Marqués, Sarah. 2000. *La Lengua que Heredamos: Curso de Español para Bilingües*. Hoboken, NJ: John Wiley & Sons.

Mitchell, Cheryl B., and Kari E. Vidal. 2001. "Weighing the Ways of the Flow: Twentieth-Century Language Instruction." *Modern Language Journal* 85, no. 1: 26–38.

MLA (Modern Language Association). 2007. "Foreign Languages and Higher Education: New Structures for a Changed World." www.mla.org/Resources/Research/Surveys-Reports-and-Other-Documents/Teaching-Enrollments-and-Programs/Foreign-Languages-and-Higher-Education-New-Structures-for-a-Changed-World.

————. 2009. "Report to the Teagle Foundation on the Undergraduate Major in Language and Literature: Executive Summary." www.mla.org/pdf/2008_mla_whitepaper.pdf.

————. 2015. "Data on Second Majors in Language and Literature, 2001–2013." www.mla.org/Resources/Research/Surveys-Reports-and-Other-Documents/Teaching-Enrollments-and-Programs/Data-on-Second-Majors-in-Language-and-Literature-2001-13.

Nichols, Madaline W. 1945. "The History of Spanish and Portuguese Teaching in the United States." In *A Handbook of the Teaching of Spanish and Portuguese, with Special Reference to the Latin America*, edited by Henry G. Doyle. Boston: D. C. Heath.

Norris, John M., and Nicole Mills. 2014. "Innovation and Accountability in Foreign Language Program Evaluation." *Innovation and Accountability in Language Program Evaluation*, edited by John M. Norris and Nicole Mills. Boston: Cengage.

Richards, Jack C., and Theodore S. Rodgers. 2001. *Approaches and Methods in Language Teaching*, 2nd ed. New York: Cambridge.

Roca, A. 1999. *Nuevos Mundos: Lectura, Cultura y Comunicación, Curso de Español para Bilingües*. Hoboken, NJ: John Wiley & Sons.

Ruiz, Richard. 1990. "Official Languages and Language Planning." In *Perspectives on Official English: The Campaign for English as the Official Language of the USA*, edited by Karen Adams and Daniel Brink. Berlin: Mouton de Gruyter.

Sánchez Pérez, Aquilino. 1992. *Historia de la Enseñanza del Español como Lengua Extranjera*. Madrid: Sociedad General Española de Librería.

Simon, Paul. 1980. *The Tongue-Tied American: Confronting the Foreign Language Crisis*. New York: Continuum International.

Skinner, Burrhus F. 1957. *Verbal Behavior.* Acton, MA: Copley.

Spell, Jefferson R. 1927. "Spanish Teaching in the United States." *Hispania* 10, no. 3: 141–59.

VanPatten, Bill. 2015. "Hispania White Paper: Where Are the Experts?" *Hispania* 98, no. 1: 2–13.

Walsh, Donald D. 1947. "A Survey of the Teaching of Spanish in the Independent Schools of New England." *Hispania* 30, no. 1: 270–71.

# 3

# HELPING SPANISH HERITAGE LANGUAGE LEARNERS FIND THEIR PLACE

> Learning your ethnic language at school makes you feel like a whole person. You don't have to feel ashamed of your culture; on the contrary, you can feel that you are as good as anyone else. And it hasn't hurt my English or any other subject.
>
> —Grace Feuerverger, "University Students' Perceptions of Heritage Language Learning," 1991

Arguably, one of the biggest differences between Spanish and other commonly taught non-English languages, such as French and German, is the number and proportion of heritage language learners (HLLs) who have intimate sociocultural and familial connections with the language and who make up an ever-growing proportion of Spanish classes at all levels. The exponential growth of Spanish HLLs has paralleled the overall growth of the Hispanic population in the United States, and increasing numbers of them are enrolling in postsecondary institutions. In spite of the increasing numbers of heritage learners in the classroom, there are still numerous programs that struggle to address these students' unique linguistic and cultural needs. Given the lack of Spanish heritage language programs, many postsecondary institutions combine heritage learners with nonheritage students in language classes, which can lead to unfavorable results.

In this chapter, we explore the many challenges and opportunities that the increasing number of heritage speakers present for teachers, for heritage and traditional students, and for the programs of which they form a part. In addition, there is a growing need for more research and for materials developed specifically to meet the linguistic and cultural needs of Spanish HLLs. This chapter addresses the development of curricula for HLL courses and also provides suggestions based on current research for curricular changes that are needed to maximize success for both traditional and heritage Spanish language students in mixed classes. We also discuss how the abilities and skills of Spanish HLLs can be utilized to benefit other HLLs, second-language (L2) learners, and the community.

To address the curricular needs of HLLs, it is important to define who these learners are and what makes their needs uniquely different from those of traditional L2 learners. The difficulty with defining HLLs is the wide variety of proficiency levels and sociolinguistic profiles they represent. One definition frequently used in studies on HLLs is that offered by Valdés (2000, 1), who describes a heritage learner as a person who is raised in a home where a non-English language is spoken, who speaks or merely understands the heritage language, and who is to some degree bilingual in English and the heritage language. The definition by Valdés highlights the variety of skill levels that HLLs may possess with regard to their receptive and productive oral proficiency. Montrul (2016, 249) also recognizes their diversity and describes them as native speakers who have variable levels of "ultimate attainment." Fishman (2001) provides an even broader view of HLLs, stating that being able to communicate in the heritage language is not a requirement to be considered an HLL. If a language has familial or cultural relevance for the learner, it constitutes a heritage language, regardless of whether it is spoken or understood.

Spanish heritage speakers represent the largest heritage language population in the United States by far (Hancock 2002). Hispanics have officially been the largest minority in the United States since the 2010 US Census, and they make up over 19 percent of all college students from age eighteen to twenty-four years (Fry and Lopez 2012). Roberts (2008) projects that minorities, largely composed of Hispanics, will constitute the majority of school-age students by 2020. These demographic trends qualitatively change the horizon for Spanish and English education from the elementary to postsecondary levels and have far-reaching ramifications.

In spite of the relatively large numbers of HLLs and the recent creation of courses for these learners, the study of heritage learners in the language classroom is relatively young in comparison with other areas of language research. Early studies can be traced to the 1970s but really began in earnest in the early 1980s, with the publication of Guadalupe Valdés's edited volume titled *Teaching Spanish to the Hispanic Bilingual: Issues, Aims and Methods* (Valdés, García-Moya, and Lozano 1981). Early heritage language curricula in the United States were predominantly subtractive because the goal was to eradicate the use of colloquial varieties of the language and any type of code-switching in order to produce more "polished" speakers of the language. This approach often undermined the language ego and identity of speakers and led to attrition and complete language loss. Marrone (1981) analyzed how early heritage language textbooks responded to code-switching in the classroom, citing examples from the text *Español para el bilingüe* (which was published in

1972). In a chapter dedicated to the study of "*barbarismos*" (barbarisms), the textbook declared: "Barbarism is the vice or defect of language that consists in pronouncing or misspelling words, or using inappropriate words. Here we will deal with 'barbarisms' that characterize the Hispanic speech in the southwestern region of our country."[1]

This text and many other texts of the 1960s and 1970s pointed out to students that their Spanish was full of barbarisms, archaisms, Anglicisms, and "other bad forms to be extirpated like cancer before progress could be made in the reading and writing of Spanish" (Foster 1982, 72). Foster argues that the eradication of the student's "familial" style "battered away at a very sensitive area—self-esteem. Successful application of the normative approach was thus analogous to the clinical situation wherein the 'disease' is contained but the patient turns comatose." Other language instructors stated that these HLLs had no native language, and thus they had no language at all (Sánchez 1981, 92). The curricular design for these early courses thus focused on the elimination of any informal and contact varieties of Spanish and attempted to instill in HLLs that only the formal, academic variety was worthy of use. This initial tack, aimed at eliminating the "informal" style of Spanish among bilinguals, was shown to be detrimental in the classroom and to the language abilities of the learners. As a result, many researchers and practitioners consider it much more effective to build on the abilities that the students already possess. The instructor's role, then, is to help HLLs complement their linguistic repertoire by adding a more formal dialect to be used in situations where their informal dialect would not be appropriate, thus converting them into bidialectal speakers.

## HERITAGE LANGUAGE PROGRAMS

The stark contrast between heritage and traditional learners led to research into these learners' unique curricular needs, which depended on their level of proficiency and exposure to the Spanish language. Beaudrie (2011, 2012) conducted a large-scale survey to determine the current state of heritage language course offerings across the United States. She surveyed more than 422 universities with at least 5 percent Hispanic enrollment to determine if these institutions had a Spanish heritage language program and also what kinds of courses they offered for HLLs. She found that 40 percent of participating universities offered at least one course for heritage students. This was a dramatic increase from previous research by Brecht and Ingold (2002), which found that only 17.8 percent of programs offered at least one course for HLLs. Beaudrie additionally noted a positive relationship between the number of Hispanic students enrolled at a given university and the availability of a course for heritage speakers. In spite of this positive correlation, she also discovered that some schools in areas with large concentrations of Hispanics (i.e., more than 1,000 students)—in California, Texas, Arizona, Colorado, and Utah—did not offer a single course. Overall, she found that heritage language courses are currently being offered in twenty-six states as well as the District of Columbia (Beaudrie 2012). Yet these figures only reflect the number of courses, not the total number of sections offered, average class size per section, or total student enrollments, which would provide a more accurate estimate of the reach of heritage language programs in contemporary postsecondary education.

Although the dramatic increase in programs is very positive for HLLs, Beaudrie (2012, 210) observed that most programs only offered one or two courses (81 percent), with the majority offering one course. She also concluded that programs with "four or more courses are practically nonexistent." The two areas of the country with the highest number of programs are the Southwest and Northeast. And though close to 65 percent of the programs in the Northeast only offer one course for HLLs, almost 50 percent of the programs in the Southwest offer two courses for these learners. Beaudrie attributes this to the longevity of many of the programs in the Southwest, which have been around for several decades serving a larger Hispanic population. Many universities that did not have programs simply included the HLLs in courses with L2 learners. It remains to be seen how institutions in the Southeast will adjust their curricula, given the large influx of Spanish speakers in states like North Carolina, South Carolina, Georgia, Alabama, and Kentucky.

At the University of Kentucky, for example, some progress has been made toward addressing the needs of Spanish HLLs. After years when native speakers were enrolling in Spanish courses at all levels, the university's Hispanic Studies Department began training instructors of lower-level courses to immediately send native speakers to the director of undergraduate studies for proper placement within the first few days of the semester. As the numbers of HLLs rose, the department created two courses for bilingual students: one at the intermediate level—Science Practical Assessment (SPA) 205—and one at the high intermediate level (SPA 215). The course textbooks were carefully chosen from the many on the market designed specifically for Spanish HLLs. With textbooks selected, syllabi designed, and the blessing of the faculty senate, a curricular space had been carved out for Spanish heritage learners at the University of Kentucky. To further incentivize enrollment, SPA 205 was approved as the curricular equivalent of both second-year courses (SPA 201 and 202), and SPA 215 fulfilled both fifth-semester courses for traditional students (SPA 210 and 211). Unfortunately, because the courses first appeared in the 2009–10 course catalog, they have still not been taught due to insufficient enrollment. A simple explanation would point to the limited availability a single section offers students with busy schedules, which surely is a crucial factor; but a closer look at larger institutional forces and economic exigencies may shed much-needed light on why some programs struggle to establish HLL programs.

In many respects, the situation of most language programs at Brigham Young University (BYU) is rather unique because over two-thirds of the students enrolled at BYU speak an L2, and many are at the advanced level following eighteen- to twenty-four-month missionary service abroad without having completed equivalent coursework. This reality has concrete implications for the creation of Spanish heritage language courses at BYU, or the lack thereof. Highly proficient Spanish HLLs are either placed into courses with advanced L2 students, most of whom learned their foreign language during missionary service, or into one of the three levels preceding the advanced level. Given the broad range of students and language experiences at BYU, the Spanish and Portuguese Department created three years of course work preceding the advanced-level courses. It offers a first-year set of courses (SPAN 101–102) designed for true beginners. The second-year courses (SPAN 105–106) are at the low intermediate level, designed for students who have taken one to two years of high school Spanish and also for speakers of other Romance languages. The third-year courses (SPAN 205–206) are designed to move students into the intermediate high or advanced low range to prepare them to take courses alongside students who have been immersed in the language for eighteen to twenty-four months during their missionary service. Hence, the curriculum offers no courses geared specifically to HLLs. Part of the rationale for not offering specific courses for Spanish HLLs is the assumption that one of these levels will be able to address the needs of these learners with lower levels of proficiency and that the needs of those with advanced-level proficiency are not distinct enough from traditional L2 learners to merit separate courses. Because the advanced courses are largely populated by students with advanced listening and speaking skills but limited experience with reading and writing, the Spanish HLLs are placed into these mixed courses with the notion that they will be similar linguistically to their L2 peers. However, these assumptions may be reductive because they minimize the unique path of acquisition of each group (prepubescent/familial vs. adult/naturalistic in foreign country/culture) and their disparate cultural connection to the language.

## SECOND-LANGUAGE LEARNERS AND HERITAGE LANGUAGE LEARNERS

Although the HLL population has continued to grow, Leeman and Martinez (2007) mention that, at least in the United States, there has been a much greater focus on L2 students than HLLs. Additionally, due to the fact that early heritage language courses were initially labeled as Spanish for native speakers, many of the less proficient HLLs either self-selected out of these courses or they were placed into courses for L2 learners. Also, because many programs even today only offer courses for intermediate or advanced HLLs, many receptive, bilingual HLLs are forced to take L2 courses.

Studies of HLLs have determined that the biggest problem with the inclusion of HLLs in the standard L2 classroom is that the skills that are needed by L2 learners are not the same ones that HLLs need to improve. Carreira (2003) and Fairclough (2005) describe how many HLLs possess highly developed receptive language skills, such as listening and reading, and are often placed into courses with L2 learners because of their weak oral skills. Unlike traditional L2 learners, HLLs comprehend most of what is being said in Spanish in the classroom but struggle to express themselves in Spanish. Because one of the foci of the beginning language courses is on the acquisition of aural skills, many teachers modify their speech to assist students who have never heard Spanish before and develop a curriculum with an extensive focus on aural activities. HLLs have often been exposed to Spanish since birth, and they generally understand the majority of conversations typically included in most beginning textbooks, such as family, school, daily activities, and leisure. Fairclough (2011) studied a group of HLLs with only receptive language skills and gave them a lexical recognition task to determine their knowledge of common Spanish vocabulary words. She found that these HLLs had a passive knowledge of half the 5,000 most common words in Spanish, and yet many first-year courses spend enormous amounts of time teaching these words to the L2 and the HLLs taking them. The result of this is a set of students who not only do not learn from the instruction given them but often become bored and disinterested in learning Spanish because of the emphasis on material they already know or skills they have already acquired.

Potowski (2002) administered a questionnaire to a group of HLLs to assess their opinions regarding their inclusion in traditional L2 classrooms. She determined that the students were generally dissatisfied with the experience, for a variety of reasons. First, the HLLs reported that the teachers had higher expectations of them than the L2 students and, subsequently, they were graded more harshly. This resulted in lower scores among HLLs than L2 students. Second, the HLLs felt their grammatical knowledge was inferior to that of their L2 classmates. Finally, the HLLs felt that they were judged more critically because of their nonstandard use of Spanish. Felix (2004) found similar results in her research on HLLs in L2 courses. She observed that the HLLs in her study did not feel that their needs were being met through the mixed classroom. They wanted more assistance with the development of their reading and writing skills, in addition to the other language skills. They also felt judged by their peers for having taken the course for an "easy" A that required little effort on their part. Felix concludes that separate courses designed for HLLs are needed in order to better focus on heritage students' unique needs and more effectively facilitate their linguistic and cultural development.

Beaudrie (2006) carried out a unique study that focused on low-level, passive, bilingual HLLs who were enrolled in first-year courses for heritage learners and compared them with heritage learners with the same receptive skills who were enrolled in first-year courses for traditional L2 students. She found that the students in the heritage courses were much more satisfied with their courses with regard to content as well as design, which included a focus on developing oral skills. Additionally, these students reported a greater degree of satisfaction overall and appreciated the ability to interact with other heritage learners who had similar language skills and whose cultural identity aligned more closely with theirs. The HLLs enrolled in the traditional courses did not have the same positive experience. They reported being dissatisfied with many aspects of the course, from the cultural content to the disconnect between the linguistic content and the way they used Spanish in their daily lives. Given that the majority of courses for heritage learners are not at the beginning levels, Beaudrie suggests the creation of heritage language courses for all levels of learners, and recommends that these courses will be valuable because they enhance HLLs' language learning experiences. Lynch (2008, 274) found that even though there are many similarities between lower-level L2 learners and HLLs at the same level, specific courses need to be developed for these learners that include sound principles from both L2 acquisition and from heritage language research. Lynch declares:

> Unless we begin to implement particular courses more in line with problems of L2 acquisition than with formal L1 [first-language] development for heritage language learners at intermediate and lower points along the bilingual continuum, the rapidly growing pool of third- and fourth-generation Spanish speakers in the United States who have a more limited —but nonetheless vital—prior social experience with Spanish will continue to be placed in traditional L2 classrooms. There they will spend extensive amounts of time formally studying some basic elements of the language that they already control and not giving adequate attention to other basic elements that they do not.

In spite of the attention given to the need to develop heritage courses that are specific for HLLs, Montrul and Bowles (2017, 3) declare that "the *outcomes* of classroom [heritage language] instruction have been largely understudied." They go on to state that the entire field of instructed heritage language acquisition is in need of more empirical studies and of additional research to determine how HLLs differ from L2 learners and in what areas they benefit most from formal instruction. The lack of empirical evidence regarding the differences between HLLs and L2 learners is an area of concern, especially given that the field of instructed L2 acquisition has received extensive attention (Loewen 2015).

### Language Standards: Standards-Based Approaches to the Teaching of HLLs

The American Council on the Teaching of Foreign Languages (ACTFL) is one of the leading organizations in the United States that is looking at improving language learning through providing learner standards. These standards are designed to help language educators as they develop curricula and programs to meet the needs of their students by focusing on those areas that assist learners in developing the necessary skills to communicate with the maximum number of speakers in the widest variety of settings. ACTFL defines its mission thus: "Language and communication are at the heart of the human experience. The United States must educate students who are linguistically and culturally equipped to communicate successfully in a pluralistic American society and abroad. This imperative envisions a future in which ALL students will develop and maintain proficiency in English and at least one other language, modern or classical" (National Standards Collaborative Board 2015, 1).

ACTFL has established the World-Readiness Standards as one way to address the needs of learners and help them to become competent multilinguals, and it has continually revised them to meet the needs of an ever-changing population and the demands on today's language learners. ACTFL states, "The World-Readiness Standards for Learning Languages create a roadmap to guide learners to develop competence to communicate effectively and interact with cultural understanding" (para. 5). The World-Readiness Standards for Learning Languages include what are known as the 5 Cs: communication, cultures, communities, connections, and comparisons. These five areas delineate the areas that are essential for learners to become proficient in a language. These standards are not limited to L2 learners only, but were developed to include the full spectrum of language learners at all levels. According to ACTFL, the World-Readiness Standards are equally applicable to all learners, including pre-kindergarten through postsecondary students, native speakers and heritage speakers, students of English as a second language, speakers of American Sign Language, and learners of Latin and Greek.

Although most people consider the World-Readiness Standards to be focused on the L2 learner, they not only can be applied to HLLs but were actually developed with the heritage student in mind. Martinez (2012, 68) affirms that the earliest version of the Standards for Foreign Language Teaching, published in 1996, "reserved a clear and unambiguous place for heritage learners in language education," and, according to Valdés (2000), were written to simultaneously address the needs of traditional learners and the strengths of heritage learners. Valdés (2001, 66) further argues that standards help HLLs increase "their competence to carry out face-to-face interactions, comprehend live and recorded and extended oral texts, comprehend written texts, and use language in written and oral form to present information to groups of listeners or readers."

The use of the World-Readiness Standards for Learning Languages in the heritage language classroom and also in mixed classrooms can provide a useful tool to help construct a curriculum that will aid these learners in developing their linguistic and cultural knowledge in a broad spectrum of areas. Heritage students have a unique advantage in meeting many of the language standards but often need additional guidance in order to maximize their full potential. The World-Readiness Standards that are often difficult for L2 learners to meet are those of connections and especially communities. Not only does the L2 learner often have trouble making the connection between the content of the course being studied and other curricular areas, but these learners frequently do not have easy access to the Hispanic community. Nevertheless, HLLs form part of the Hispanic community, and they have access to the social and cultural elements that are important in developing proficiency in learners. Additionally, they can make connections between their studies, their culture, and the acquisition of Spanish. The advantage of having mixed classes with both HLLs and L2 students, especially at higher proficiency levels, is that they can help each other meet many of these language standards. HLLs do not have to be cultural and linguistic experts when working with L2 students, but they can access their own personal experiences, and those of friends and family members, and can share this knowledge with the classroom. Language educators can then view HLLs as a resource in the classroom who can access different members of the Hispanic community and share this information with the classroom.

At the University of Central Florida, for instance, many students enrolled in Spanish courses are fluent bilinguals whose ancestors hailed from many different parts of the Spanish-speaking world and who bring with them a variety of native accents. On one occasion, a phonetics class taught by one of the authors had students who were either native speakers or heritage speakers from fourteen different Spanish speaking countries in addition to many English-dominant L2 learners of Spanish with experience living abroad. As different speech varieties and phonological variations were discussed in the class, the HLLs and native speakers were able to naturally demonstrate many of the unique features of their respective dialect, showing everyone the great variety that exists in the Spanish language. This served as a concrete demonstration of how there is *not* one way of speaking that is correct and that it is precisely due to the contributions of these different accents that Spanish has become the intricate and exquisite tapestry that it is. It brought to life the words and concepts printed in the textbook, as students' speech was held up as embodied manifestations. This was a powerful lesson for both the HLLs and the L2 learners and served as one of the benefits of having a mixed classroom.

**AP Exam Data: HLL Results and Implications**

One area where the changes in the number of heritage learners and the number of Hispanics can be noted is in the Advanced Placement (AP) examinations offered by the College Board. We conducted original research based on an exclusively licensed AP exam data set from 1979 to 2014. The results of this data set coincide with early research into HLLs as well as the current state of heritage students in the schools. In 1979, Hispanic students represented less than 25 percent of those taking the Spanish language and Spanish literature AP exams. However, in 2014, nearly 84 percent of those taking the Spanish literature exam and almost 65 percent of those taking the Spanish language exam were identified as Hispanic, reflecting the growing Hispanic population in secondary and postsecondary schools and also the overall population of the United States. These statistics also reflect the increasing numbers of Spanish-speaking Hispanics who are not only going on to college more than previous generations but are also deliberately pursuing university credit, even before they start their first college classes. Even as their numbers increase, Hispanic AP candidates are performing rather well on the AP Spanish language and AP Spanish literature exams. In order to receive credit at the majority of the universities, students need to get a score of 3 or better on the AP Spanish language and culture and Spanish literature and culture exams, which are scaled from 1 to 5. In 2014, of those who identified as Hispanic, over 90 percent scored 3 or better on the language exam, and 75 percent scored 3 or better on the literature exam. Unlike the language exam, the literature exam requires much more extensive exposure to authentic literary texts and literary analysis, areas to which many heritage learners have little exposure in their daily lives.

In 2004, the College Board began asking candidates about their use of the language outside the classroom. Until that point, they had simply been categorized as Hispanic according to the demographic information that was collected. In the data set prepared for the authors, the College Board classified as "heritage" speakers those who had lived or studied for one month or more in a country where the language is spoken *and* those who spoke the language regularly at home. Although the requirement that students respond positively to both questions to qualify as a "heritage" speaker is problematic, given that many HLLs have not had the chance to visit the country where their parents or grandparents are from, this gives a conservative estimate as to the number of heritage learners who are taking the AP exam. The numbers of those identified as heritage learners is understandably close to the number of students who identified as Hispanic. In 2004, only 28 percent of those who took the AP Spanish literature exam and 47 percent of those who took the AP Spanish language exam were classified as heritage speakers of Spanish. However, in 2014, about 80 percent of those who took the AP Spanish literature exam and 62 percent of those who took the AP Spanish language exam were identified as heritage learners. The question then arises as to what universities are doing from a curricular and programmatic standpoint to receive these students and effectively educate the increasing numbers of Spanish HLLs at the collegiate level. Whether they are prepared for them or not, these heritage students are arriving on campus in hopes that they can further their Spanish language education in programs that are sensitive to their needs.

## SPANISH POSTSECONDARY PROGRAM AND CURRICULUM SURVEY RESULTS

As described in chapter 2, we distributed our Spanish postsecondary program and curriculum survey electronically to postsecondary educators across the United States, who ranged from full professors at research-intensive institutions to adjunct faculty at two-year community colleges to inexperienced first-year graduate students teaching beginning courses. The purpose of the study was to gain a better understanding of their perceptions of the issues presented to them in the survey and to what level they were concerned about these issues in their own institutions. The survey included seven specific questions of potential concerns that participants had regarding heritage language teaching. The participants were allowed to write in an additional item that they perceived as a concern.

Postsecondary educators were asked to rank each item according to the level of concern that they had for each of the following issues related to heritage language students and teaching. All the instructors ranked each item on a scale of 1 (very much a concern) to 5 (not a concern at all). At the end of each item listed below, we include the item's mean and overall rank across all fifty-five survey items with regard to the level of perceived concern. These means and ranks were calculated from responses given by approximately seven hundred instructors of all academic backgrounds, ranks, ages, and from all institution types. Any items with mean scores under 3 indicate a concern, while means over 3 indicate that the item is not a concern. The results of the survey show the areas within heritage language teaching where the instructors surveyed are most concerned and how these questions ranked in the overall survey. The percentage listed last under each question below represents the number of participants who felt that the item did not apply to their program:

- Effective mechanism for proper placement of heritage/native speakers: 2.56 / 16th / 5 percent;
- Adaptation of instruction to address diverse proficiency levels among heritage/native language learners: 2.67 / 26th / 6 percent;
- Adaptation of instruction for mixed classes with traditional L2 and heritage/native speakers: 2.73 / 29th / 6 percent;
- Creation of Spanish for heritage/native speaker courses: 2.81 / 31st / 6 percent;
- Availability of materials designed for heritage/native language learners: 2.86 / 36th / 7 percent;
- Adequate training for instructors in heritage/native language teaching: 2.99 / 42nd / 8 percent; and
- Achieving sufficient enrollment in existing heritage/native speaker courses: 3.20 / 48th / 19 percent.

The results show that the greatest concern among the instructors in this survey is regarding the proper placement of HLLs. This is valuable information, because it reflects ongoing research in the field of heritage language studies demonstrating the vast range of abilities of HLLs and the struggles that many programs have in properly placing them. What is not clear from this survey is whether the individuals surveyed have specialized courses for heritage students. The areas of least concern relate to the training of instructors of heritage speakers and achieving sufficient enrollment in heritage courses, and this was also the question that 18 percent stated did not apply to their program, which could mean several different things. It could be that the individuals surveyed have courses for HLLs that have sufficient enrollment and well-trained teachers so they are not concerned about this. It may also be the case that many of the instructors at these postsecondary schools do not offer specific courses for heritage learners, and so these above-mentioned areas are not a concern. If the individuals surveyed do not have courses for HLLs, then this would imply that the proper placement of the HLLs refers to placing them into mixed classes with heritage learners and L2 learners. This notion is further supported by the subsequent areas of greatest concern in heritage language teaching, which refer to the adaptation to teach not only HLLs at different levels of proficiency but also to teach these learners who are in mixed classrooms. Given the scope of the survey, we can only speculate as to why instructors expressed concern about placement; but the data seem to indicate that this is due either to deficient placement instruments or inappropriate programmatic structures.

Of the nine categories in the survey, concern about heritage language issues was ranked sixth overall but was still of concern for many of the participants in this survey. Notable differences surfaced when the results of the survey were analyzed according to the area of specialty of the respondents. The participants were asked to describe the general area of their highest degree according to four broad descriptions, including literature and culture, general linguistics, applied linguistics, and other. When analyzing the data based on these divisions, we found that those instructors whose highest degree was in the area of literature and culture were least concerned about heritage language programs and curriculum, while those whose highest degree was in linguistics or applied linguistics were most concerned. One of the greatest differences between these two groups' responses to the survey is related to the creation of Spanish for heritage/native speaker courses. Those whose highest degree was in the area of literature and culture ranked this item fortieth out of fifty-five items, whereas those whose highest degree was in linguistics or applied linguistics ranked it seventeenth out of fifty-five items. This difference is very likely due to the administrative responsibilities given to instructors based on their area of specialization. Many times, those involved in linguistics and applied linguistics are assigned as coordinators of entire elementary language programs or specific multisection courses and are asked to create language courses for an ever-growing heritage population. Consequently, these learners and their curricular needs are on the forefront of their minds. Literature and culture faculty, conversely, find many of these students in their advanced content courses and may struggle with their contact variety of Spanish, feeling that they have been misplaced. Absent from this survey is information regarding the demographics of the individual schools, making it impossible to link responses to percentages of heritage students in a particular school. The relative lack of concern about heritage issues among survey participants as compared to other issues in the postsecondary setting is quite telling. Normally, those involved with creating and teaching the heritage language curriculum are a relatively small segment of the instructional staff of a department or institution. Therefore, unless many of those involved with heritage courses completed the survey, it is understandable that many of these issues appeared to be of little concern for an instructor who only has minimal contact with this group in his or her classes.

## PLACEMENT TESTING FOR HLLS

As mentioned in the survey that we conducted, the greatest concern regarding heritage students, regardless of the instructor's training and educational background, was the proper placement of these students. The best-designed curriculum will likely be negatively affected by incorrect placement of students into that curriculum. Fairclough (2015, 143) argues that "all postsecondary institutions need to identify SHL [Spanish for heritage learners] learners using objective methods such as well-designed and reliable questionnaires and measure their linguistic proficiency in the HL [heritage learning] by means of solid assessment tools to successfully place them at the right level." Indeed, a great deal of research in recent years has examined the assessment and placement of HLLs (Beaudrie and Ducar 2012; Beaudrie 2012; Potowski, Prada, and Morgan-Short 2012; Wilson 2012).

To place HLLs into the proper class, some researchers have chosen to look at their linguistic competencies, such as syntactical competence, grammar use, and vocabulary knowledge (Achugar 2003; Fairclough 2011; Fairclough and Mrak 2003; Fairclough and Ramírez 2009; Keating, VanPatten, and Jegerski 2011; Lam, Perez-Leroux, and Ramírez 2003; Montrul 2010; Valdés 1998). Fairclough (2011, 274) found that the majority of programs use standardized computerized exams relying on "questionnaires, self-placement, interviews, and locally designed exams to place their students." The main problem with many of these instruments is that they are not practical to administer to large numbers of students because of the tremendous amount of resources and time required to administer them and arrive at an accurate placement decision. She declares that in order for a placement instrument to be of practical value to most programs, it needs to be a computerized exam that provides results immediately upon completion. But the larger issue is whether a placement exam can meaningfully discriminate between the various levels of HLL proficiency, and particularly between receptive HLLs and traditional foreign language students at the same level.

Fairclough (2006) analyzed the placement exam results of HLLs at the University of Houston, using a placement exam that focused on verb morphology and overall writing in response to short essay prompts. She analyzed the results of students who placed into one of four distinct university classes and gathered her data over two academic years. She found that students were most successful on the use of the impersonal form of the verb *haber* (to have) as well as with the copula verbs. The students struggled most with the subjunctive, and especially with compound tenses. Although the students placed into four distinct classes, the data were analyzed in the aggregate, which did not allow for students' proficiency level to be connected to their scores on each section of the placement exam.

Lynch (2008) conducted a study of oral interviews comparing the differences between HLLs and foreign language learners enrolled in intermediate to advanced language courses. He observed that though some distinctions could be made about the participants, the similarities between the groups were what was most salient to him. He found that all participants were quite successful in their noun–adjective agreement and the use of copula verbs. However, the HLLs were more accurate overall in their use of aspectual distinction in Spanish. Both groups struggled with their use of the subjunctive, with the highest degree of accuracy coming from a foreign language learner who used it correctly 69 percent of the time. Fairclough and Ramírez (2009) studied the use of the lexical decision task (LDT) with HLLs to determine if there was a correlation between the LDT and overall vocabulary knowledge and proficiency. These authors found that there was a strong correlation between LDT and proficiency and claimed that "there is a close relationship between passive knowledge of vocabulary and general knowledge of the language."[2] They assert that the use of LDT for the placement of HLLs appears to have great potential and would be easy to administer and inexpensive. Fairclough (2011) had similar results in her research, finding that the occurrence of high-frequency words was useful in separating lower- from higher-level learners but was less effective in distinguishing among higher-level HLLs, a result she attributes to a ceiling effect.

Although placement exams vary in their design and content, many focus on writing ability and specific grammatical and lexical abilities that are perceived to be vital to success in academic programs. Lynch (2008, 253) describes the speech of HLLs based on their contact with English, stating that "the restricted social use of minority languages in a situation of language contact leads to a grammatically simplified system and introduces innovative, that is, nonnormative, elements at the lexical and discourse levels." Silva-Corvalán (1994) concurs, noting that for many HLLs with limited language proficiency, the use of the language becomes a series of memorized phrases and formulaic responses to specific prompts. Low-proficiency HLLs do have certain abilities, but they are compartmentalized in specific chunks of knowledge and preformulated answers. It is possible that many lower-level HLLs have simply memorized chunks of language and that their placement scores thus are not an accurate reflection of their productive morphosyntactic knowledge or overall proficiency. Being able to distinguish between actual proficiency and memorized chunks would contribute to greater accuracy in the placement of HLLs. If researchers and educators are able to understand the language competencies of HLLs as they enter programs, they will be better equipped to place them into the proper class and develop a curriculum that maximizes their skills while helping them increase their proficiency.

Aside from considering the linguistic ability of HLLs, current research into the placement of these learners is considering the role of other social and cultural factors in proper placement. Alarcón (2010) encourages the development of a complete profile of these learners by obtaining more information about their linguistic and cultural backgrounds, and their attitudes, behaviors, and motivations. Alarcón (2010, 270–71) states, "The HL [heritage language] learner profile becomes even more intricate when accounting for additional issues these students bring into the classroom, such as the amount of previous language(s) exposure, the quality and frequency of social interactions in the HL, identity and cultural questions, attitudes toward the HL, and unique linguistic strengths and weaknesses."

Thompson (2015, 85) declares, "The difficulty lies in finding a way to incorporate such aspects of a HLL's life into a proper placement exam as well as determining how these aspects influence language proficiency and placement." And if those aspects of an HLL's life are reflected in the placement exam, they should also be reflected in the curriculum.

Although the researchers mentioned above have found interesting patterns regarding language use among HLLs as they relate to linguistic competence and overall proficiency, much more research is needed to see if predictable patterns can be established between speakers at different levels and what can be done to properly place HLLs based on those patterns. Valdés (2006, 242) states that the field of heritage language research and teaching needs a clear research agenda. She recommends several areas of focus; the first one is the need to "develop language evaluation/assessment procedures that can identify key differences among heritage learners." Previous studies have begun this process, but further studies are needed to assist in parsing out the differences between HLLs.

## CURRICULAR CONSIDERATIONS

The curricular needs of heritage learners and programs are vast and urgent, yet Beaudrie (2012, 215) states that "research on SHL programmatic and curricular issues is still in its infancy." The goal of many veins of SHL research is to be able to develop curricular goals and materials that are applicable to the widest possible audience. Heritage programs need to focus on several different aspects of their students in order to meet their needs. First, programs need to look at developing a sequence of courses to address the needs of HLLs at all levels, from the receptive learner to more proficient speakers. One of the challenges of the heritage language classroom is the fact that many programs only offer one or two courses for all HLLs from different backgrounds and with varying language abilities. Too many of these programs only offer one intermediate-level course, which is supposed to bring HLLs in line with L2 learners who have been studying the language for many years. Not only does this not work, but it may also alienate HLLs from taking further courses beyond the one designed for them because they cannot relate to the content and do not find it beneficial to their language development. They may perceive that the heritage language classroom is simply a class of Spanish for native speakers, a class in which they feel inadequate. Where a critical mass of HLLs exists, programs need to offer a series of well-articulated courses (4–6) specifically designed for these learners that address their needs and abilities. Where a critical mass does not exist, instructors who teach classes with mixed students should review their program and determine if their approach is undermining the heritage learners' progress or promoting undeserved stereotypes. The lack of vertical articulation evident at the postsecondary level has its roots in elementary schools. Postsecondary programs should work with both elementary and secondary programs to develop a sequence of courses with which higher education curricula would articulate to advance the HLL's development (Valdés 2011). All these initiatives presuppose substantive and ongoing training in the fundamentals of heritage language pedagogy for instructors.

Second, the heritage learner curriculum needs to focus on those aspects of language and culture that would be of greatest use to these students. Montrul (2016, 289) states that curricular development needs to be based upon sound research: "Identifying how L2 learners and heritage speakers differ in their linguistic competence and processing is a critical step toward developing efficient pedagogical solutions for language teaching." The teaching of culture within the curriculum of the heritage language classroom warrants further study as well. Beaudrie, Ducar, and Relaño-Pastor (2009) found that heritage learners were much more interested in learning about culture and assert that its role should be prominent in the heritage language classroom. The students in their study expressed the desire to learn more about the perspectives and practices of the culture with less interest in the products of any given culture. The study of culture in the classroom also will lead these students to greater self-awareness and help them develop an understanding of the Hispanic community around them as well as their own role in it. Thompson (2015) surveyed HLLs regarding what they learned most from their interactions through service learning in the Hispanic community where they lived. Though the students themselves were Hispanic, and they served within local

Hispanic communities, they indicated that they learned the most about people from social or cultural backgrounds *different* from theirs. Not only did the students gain valuable life skills and cultural insights, but the experience also made them feel more a part of their own community and more eager to give service to others. A curriculum that includes a significant community service-learning component geared toward HLLs and that addresses not just cultural products but also cultural practices and perspectives would greatly enhance the heritage language curriculum.

Third, Beaudrie (2012, 216) argues that three important questions remain to be answered and need to shape the discussion of heritage language program design. First, what is the minimum proficiency level required for entrance into each course on Spanish for heritage learners? Placing students into courses below or beyond their level may negatively affect their level of motivation and their language ego, problems that can surface in the L2 classroom as well. Second, how many language courses do learners at different programmatic levels need to reach desired proficiency levels? This question assumes that programs for heritage learners have established specific proficiency goals for their students and have designed a curriculum to meet these goals. Third, where should these courses be placed in the undergraduate curriculum? Do certain courses need to be dropped or not required of HLLs? Could these courses count toward other requirements currently in the undergraduate curriculum? Moreover, in cases where heritage language courses are available, curriculum designers must decide at what point in the curriculum to allow traditional L2 learners and heritage speakers' programs of study to intersect and merge. These questions not only need to be addressed at the programmatic level but also are concerns for broader academic entities, such as the college or university and its requirements.

Fourth, one of the main concerns in the US heritage language context is the troubling prevalence of "standard" language ideology and other ideologies that undermine language learning among certain populations in the United States. Although people find it interesting to know that a majority language speaker has mastered another language, this country has historically tended to promote assimilationist approaches to language learning and bilingualism among minority groups that are subtractive and lead to monolingualism. This is often the case for children who go to schools where their heritage language is not understood, or valued, or both. The best-designed curriculum will not be effective until HLLs, their parents, and society at large begin to value bilingualism and language maintenance. Even in the field of heritage language research, there has been an overriding concern with the development of a standard variety of the language, and this has had an impact on classroom practices in many ways (Fairclough 2015; Villa 2002). Fairclough (2015, 138) concurs with other scholars of Spanish for heritage learners that the "language-as-resource orientation . . . will contribute to maintenance of the HL."

Fifth, even the best-designed heritage language curriculum will be rendered ineffective if HLLs are not properly placed. Heritage language students need to be placed into a class that not only challenges them but also aligns well with their current level of competence, which will lead to greater levels of student satisfaction and retention. Gloria and others (2005) identified the lack of social support as one of the characteristics that most negatively affected retention rates of Hispanic students. Given that many HLLs are members of the first generation in their families to attend a postsecondary institution, proper placement into language classes may have an impact on their decision to stay in school. Choy (2001) found that first-generation college students are twice as likely to drop out when compared with their peers. Aside from the academic benefits, placing HLLs with other learners from similar backgrounds will help them to feel less isolated socially at their postsecondary institution, which can also lead to greater retention (Hahs-Vaughn 2004).

Sixth, one of the major factors in all language learning is motivation. Montrul and Bowles (2017) state that the field of heritage learner research needs to study how to motivate HLLs so they have a desire to improve their language skills and enrich their linguistic repertoire at the same time. Within applied linguistics, there is a significant focus on how to motivate L2 learners, but there also needs to be a concerted effort to specifically integrate motivation into the heritage language curriculum. Spanish language educators need to determine best practices for encouraging students to take these courses, continue their education, and maintain their language outside the classroom. It is not yet known if the same types of instructional strategies and curriculum that motivate L2 learners have the same effect on HLLs.

Finally, Fairclough (2015, 142) emphasizes the role of professional training for those instructors who will be working with HLLs. She states that "one of the most important keys to successful HLE [heritage language education] is to have sociolinguistically informed instructors who are sensitive to SHL learners' linguistic needs." These instructors need to be trained not only in recognizing the needs of HLLs but also in how to use materials designed for these learners and how to effectively differentiate instruction. Lacorte (2016, 108) emphasizes the need of programs to look at everything from the treatment of language varieties in textbooks to the sequencing and articulation of courses specifically designed for HLLs and L2 students with mixed courses. He notes that the diverse "cultural and linguistic backgrounds of HL learners require teacher preparation activities that allow instructors to become more familiar with current approaches to curricular development." Moreover, he encourages programs to involve HLLs in service learning as a way to not only help them use their language outside the classroom but also connect with the Spanish-speaking community around them.

## CONCLUSION

Unfortunately, the deficit model in Spanish for heritage learners, which views heritage learners' dialects as inferior, still persists in many programs today and undermines the ability of administrators and educators to recognize HLLs' curricular needs. More needs to be done to develop materials and textbooks that address HLLs' cultural and linguistic needs, so they can develop their skills and awareness in the most efficient and productive manner. Additionally, Beaudrie (2012) expressed concern that much of the research to date has been carried out using survey data and that a broad range of methodologies and techniques should be developed to give researchers and practitioners the most current and up-to-date information on the needs of these learners. To try to meet the needs of practitioners, in their recent book, Beaudrie, Ducar, and Potowski (2014) offer a variety of practical suggestions, based on current research and their personal experience, that can be used in the classroom to teach HLLs.

Additionally, many programs in the US still suffer from a lack of funding, trained instructors, and support from administration (Valdés and Geoffrion-Vinci 2011). Many schools struggle to fill positions for traditional L2 courses and would be hard pressed to find qualified instructors for courses for heritage learners. Additional funding needs to be secured to increase the growth and effectiveness of these programs, with an understanding that not only are students learning a language but they are also maintaining their identity and culture, which can then be passed on to future generations to avoid language loss (Cazzoli-Goeta and Young-Scholten 2007).

Montrul and Bowles (2017) highlight the comparative lack of research regarding instructed language teaching with heritage learners, citing such basic questions as to the learning gains made by instructed, classroom-based HLLs and uninstructed, naturalistic HLLs who solely receive input in their communities. Bowles (2016, 2) articulates these questions in the following way: "(1) Is instruction in a classroom setting beneficial for heritage language acquisition, and if so, (2) What features make such instruction most effective?" The answer(s) to these classroom-based questions are necessarily implicated in addressing larger programmatic issues critical to the development of robust heritage language curricula in the twenty-first century.

## REFLECTION QUESTIONS

1. What are the respective benefits and challenges of having a native, nonnative, and heritage speaker of Spanish in class?

2. Many educational institutions as well as private companies have exams that they claim will accurately place HLLs. However, some scholars state that heritage placement exams should be developed for the region and population specific to a particular area and institution. Do you believe this is necessary? Why? Could a general placement exam for HLLs work for a general population across the country?

3. Many HLLs use features reflective of US Spanish—such as code-switching, calques, loan words, and neologisms—when they speak because this is often the speech used in their communities. Such uses are often marginalized and considered unacceptable for academic work by instructors and other authority figures. Should these nonstandard features be accepted in formal presentations and writing in higher education? Why? How can programs value the variety of language that each heritage student brings to the classroom?

4. Many institutions do not have specific courses for HLLs, and thus they end up in mixed classes with L2 students. Based on this chapter and your own experience, what are some of the strategies that can be used to ensure that mixed classes are beneficial for both groups of students?

5. One area where more research is needed in pedagogy for Spanish for heritage learners relates to the development of assessments adapted specifically to HLLs. How should assessments of HLLs differ from those for L2 learners? What are some of the skills that might not be reflected in traditional assessments for L2 learners?

6. The placement of students into the appropriate class is difficult for L2 learners and even more problematic for HLLs. Why do you think that is? What can be done to make sure these students are placed at the level that is appropriate for them?

7. Some individuals argue that the World-Readiness Standards are designed for L2 learners and not for HLLs. How would you respond to this statement?

8. The AP Spanish language exam candidates consist of greater numbers of HLLs each year, but still reflect a very small portion of the HLLs in the public schools. What can be done to encourage more HLLs to take the AP Spanish language and literature exam? How might this be beneficial to college and university programs?

## PEDAGOGICAL ACTIVITIES

1. One of the challenges facing Spanish HLLs is the lack of specific assignments designed to meet their needs. Develop an activity of any type—for example, form-focused and communicative—that can be used for Spanish HLLs in a mixed classroom. This activity can target any of the language modalities and should be designed for a course that you are currently teaching or will teach in the future. Keep in mind the specific skills that many HLLs possess as well as the level for which the activity will be used.

2. As discussed in this chapter, placement exams for Spanish HLLs are being developed by individual institutions. These exams are designed to meet the specific needs

of the HLLs in the region where the institution is located. Write an outline (i.e., test specifications) of a placement instrument that could be used for the Spanish HLLs in your institution. What are some of the general characteristics of the students at your institution, and how do those influence the sections and type of items you include in the placement test?

3. Interview a student currently enrolled in a course on Spanish for HLLs regarding his or her experience with such a course. Use the following questions as well as others that you find to be pertinent to your institution. Take notes as you interview the HLL and write up a summary of the interview.

a. To what extent have your Spanish classes addressed your linguistic and cultural needs?

b. How would you change courses on Spanish for HLLs that you have taken at your institution?

c. Would you like to see additional courses on Spanish for HLLs offered at your school? If so, why and which courses?

d. What could be done to better help you in learning Spanish at this institution?

## NOTES

1. Original Spanish: "Barbarismo es el vicio o defecto del lenguaje que consiste en pronunciar o escribir mal las palabras, o en emplear vocablos impropios. Aquí vamos a tratar de los 'barbarismos'que caracterizan el habla del hispano en la región suroeste de nuestro país" (Marrone 1981, 72).

2. Original Spanish: "La alta correlación entre los resultados de la prueba léxica y el cloze-test indica que hay una estrecha relación entre el conocimiento pasivo del vocabulario y un conocimiento general de la lengua" (Fairclough and Ramírez 2009, 96).

## REFERENCES

Achugar, Mariana. 2003. "Academic Registers in Spanish in the US: A Study of Oral Texts Produced by Bilingual Speakers in a University Graduate Program." In *Mi Lengua: Spanish as a Heritage Language in the United States,* edited by Ana Roca and M. Cecilia Colombi. Washington, DC: Georgetown University Press.

Alarcón, Irma. 2010. "Advanced Heritage Learners of Spanish: A Sociolinguistic Profile for Pedagogical Purposes." *Foreign Language Annals* 43, no. 2: 269–88.

Barker, Marie Esman. 1972. *Español para el Bilingüe.* Skokie, IL: National Textbook Company.

Beaudrie, Sara M. 2006. "Spanish Heritage Language Development: A Causal-Comparative Study Exploring the Differential Effects of Heritage versus Foreign Language Curriculum." PhD diss., University of Arizona.

———. 2011. "Spanish Heritage Language Programs: A Snapshot of Current Programs in the Southwestern United States." *Foreign Language Annals* 44, no. 2: 321–37.

———. 2012. "Research on University-Based Spanish Heritage Language Programs in the United States: The Current State of Affairs." In *Spanish as a Heritage Language in the United States: The State of the Field,* edited by Sara M. Beaudrie and Marta Fairclough. Washington, DC: Georgetown University Press.

Beaudrie, Sara M., and Cynthia Ducar. 2012. "Language Placement and Beyond: Guidelines for the Design and Implementation of a Computerized Spanish Heritage Language Exam." *Heritage Language Journal* 9, no. 1: 77–99.

Beaudrie, Sara M., Cynthia Ducar, and Ana María Relaño-Pastor. 2009. "Curricular Perspectives in the Heritage Language Context: Assessing Culture and Identity." *Language, Culture and Curriculum* 22, no. 2: 157–74.

Beaudrie, Sara M., Cynthia Ducar, and Kim Potowski. 2014. *Heritage Language Teaching: Research and Practice.* New York: McGraw-Hill Education.

Brecht, Richard D., and Catherine W. Ingold. 2002. *Tapping a National Resource: Heritage Languages in the United States.* Washington, DC: ERIC Clearinghouse on Languages and Linguistics.

Carreira, María. 2003. "Profiles of SNS Students in the Twenty-First Century: Pedagogical Implications of the Changing Demographics and Social Status of US Hispanics." In *Mi Lengua: Spanish as a Heritage Language in the United States,* edited by Ana Roca and M. Cecilia Colombi. Washington, DC: Georgetown University Press.

Cazzoli-Goeta, Marcela A., and Martha Young-Scholten. 2007. "Attrition at the Interface vs. Competing Grammars." Paper presented at European Second Language Association Conference, Newcastle, UK.

Choy, Susan P. 2001. *Students Whose Parents Did Not Go to College: Postsecondary Access, Persistence, and Attainment.* NCES Report 2001-126. Washington, DC: US Department of Education, National Center for Education Statistics. http://nces.ed.gov/pubs 2001/2001126.pdf.

Fairclough, Marta. 2005. *Spanish and Heritage Language Education in the United States: Struggling with Hypotheticals.* Madrid: Vervuert.

———. 2006. "La Enseñanza del Español como Lengua de Herencia: Un Curso de Preparación para Docentes." *Revista Iberoamericana de Lingüística* 1: 31–50.

———. 2011. "Testing the Lexical Recognition Task with Spanish/English Bilinguals in the United States." *Language Testing* 28, no. 2: 273–97.

———. 2015. "Spanish as a Heritage Language." In *Routledge Handbook of Hispanic Applied Linguistics,* edited by Manel Lacorte. New York: Routledge.

Fairclough, Marta, and N. Ariana Mrak. 2003. "La Enseñanza del Español a los Hispanohablantes Bilingües y Su Efecto en la Producción Oral." In *Mi Lengua: Spanish as a Heritage Language in the United States,* edited by Ana Roca and M. Cecilia Colombi. Washington, DC: Georgetown University Press.

Fairclough, Marta, and Carlos Ramírez. 2009. "La Prueba de Decisión Léxica como Herramienta para Ubicar al Estudiante de Español en los Programas Universitarios." *Íkala, Revista de Lenguaje y Cultura* 14, no. 21: 85–99.

Felix, Angela. 2004. "The Adult Heritage Spanish Speaker in the Foreign Language Classroom." PhD diss., Capella University.

Feuerverger, Grace. 1991. "University Students' Perceptions of Heritage Language Learning and Ethnic Identity Maintenance." *Canadian Modern Language Review* 47, no. 4: 660–77.

Fishman, Joshua. 2001. "Three Hundred-Plus Years of Heritage Language Education in the United States." In *Heritage Languages in America: Preserving a National Resource,* edited by Joy Kreeft Peyton, Donald A. Ranard, and Scott McGinnis. McHenry, IL: Delta Systems Co. and Center for Applied Linguistics.

Foster, William. 1982. "A Comparison of Three Current First-Year College-Level Spanish-For-Native-Speakers Textbooks." *Bilingual Review* 22, no. 5: 72–81.

Fry, Richard, and Mark Hugo Lopez. 2012. "Hispanic Student Enrollments Reach New Highs in 2011." Pew Hispanic Center, Washington. www.pewhispanic.org/files/2012/08 /Hispanic-Student-Enrollments-Reach-New-Highs-in-2011_FINAL.pdf.

Gloria, Alberta M., Jeanett Castellanos, Ambrocia G. Lopez, and Rocio Rosales. 2005. "An Examination of Academic Nonpersistence Decisions of Latino Undergraduates." *Hispanic Journal of Behavioral Sciences* 27, no. 2: 202–23.

Hahs-Vaughn, Debbie. 2004. "The Impact of Parents' Education Level on College Students: An Analysis Using the Postsecondary Students Longitudinal Study 1990–92/94." *Journal of College Student Development* 45, no. 5: 483–500.

Hancock, Zennia. 2002. *Heritage Spanish Speakers' Language Learning Strategies.* Report ERIC, EDO-FL-02-06. Washington, DC: Center for Applied Linguistics.

Keating, Gregory D., Bill VanPatten, and Jill Jegerski. 2011. "Who Was Walking on the Beach?" *Studies in Second Language Acquisition* 33, no. 2: 193–221.

Lacorte, Manel. 2016. "Teacher Development in Heritage Language Education." In *Innovative Strategies for Heritage Language Teaching: A Practical Guide for the Classroom,* edited by Marta Fairclough and Sara M. Beaudrie. Washington, DC: Georgetown University Press.

Lam, Y., Ana T. Pérez-Leroux, and Carlos Ramírez. 2003. "Using Lexical Decision for Spanish Language Placement Testing." Paper presented at annual meeting of American Association for Applied Linguistics, Arlington, VA, March 22–25.

Leeman, Jennifer, and Glenn Martinez. 2007. "From Identity to Commodity: Ideologies of Spanish in Heritage Language Textbooks." *Critical Inquiry in Language Studies* 4, no. 1: 35–65.

Loewen, Shawn. 2015. *Introduction to Instructed Second Language Acquisition.* New York: Routledge.

Lynch, Andrew. 2008. "The Linguistic Similarities of Spanish Heritage and Second Language Learners." *Foreign Language Annals* 41, no. 2: 252–381.

Marrone, Nila. 1981. "Español para el Hispano: Un Enfoque Sociolingüístico." In *Teaching Spanish to the Hispanic Bilingual: Issues, Aims and Methods,* edited by Guadalupe Valdés, Anthony G. Lozano, and Rodolfo García-Moya. New York: Teachers College Press.

Martinez, Glenn. 2012. "Policy and Planning Research for Spanish as a Heritage Language." In *Spanish as a Heritage Language in the United States,* edited by Sara M. Beaudrie and Marta Fairclough. Washington, DC: Georgetown University Press.

Montrul, Silvina. 2010. "How Similar Are Adult Second Language Learners and Spanish Heritage Speakers? Spanish Clitics and Word Order." *Applied Psycholinguistics* 31, no. 1: 167–207.

———. 2016. *The Acquisition of Heritage Languages.* Cambridge: Cambridge University Press.

Montrul, Silvina, and Melissa Bowles. 2017. "Instructed Heritage Language Acquisition." In *The Routledge Handbook of Instructed Second Language Acquisition,* edited by Shawn Loewen and Masatoshi Sato. New York: Routledge.

National Standards Collaborative Board. 2015. *World-Readiness Standards for Learning Languages,* 4th ed. Alexandria, VA: National Standards Collaborative Board. www.actfl.org /publications/all/world-readiness-standards-learning-languages.

Potowski, Kim. 2002. "Experiences of Spanish Heritage Speakers in University Foreign Language Courses and Implications for Teacher Training." *ADFL Bulletin* 33, no. 3: 35–42.

Potowski, Kim, Mary Ann Parada, and Kara Morgan-Short. 2012. "Developing an Online Placement Exam for Spanish Heritage Speakers and L2 Students." *Heritage Language Journal* 9, no. 1: 51–76.

Roberts, Sam. 2008. "In a Generation, Minorities May Be US Majority." *New York Times*, August 13. www.nytimes.com/2008/08/14/washington/14census.html.

Sánchez, Rosaura. 1981. "Spanish for Native Speakers at the University: Suggestions." In *Teaching Spanish to the Hispanic Bilingual: Issues, Aims and Methods*, edited by Guadalupe Valdés, Anthony G. Lozano, and Rodolfo García-Moya. New York: Teachers College Press.

Silva-Corvalán, Carmen. 1994. *Language Contact and Change: Spanish in Los Angeles*. New York: Oxford University Press.

Thompson, Gregory L. 2015. "Understanding the Heritage Language Student: Proficiency and Placement." *Journal of Hispanic Higher Education* 14, no. 1: 82–96.

Valdés, Guadalupe. 1998. "The World Outside and Inside Schools: Language and Immigrant Children." *Educational Researcher* 27, no. 6: 4–18.

———. 2000. "The ACTFL–Hunter College FIPSE Project and Its Contributions to the Profession." In *Teaching Heritage Learners: Voices from the Classroom*, edited by John Webb and Barbara Miller. ACTFL Foreign Language Education Series. New York: American Council on the Teaching of Foreign Languages.

———. 2001. "Heritage Language Students: Profiles and Possibilities." In *Heritage Languages in America: Preserving a National Resource. Language in Education: Theory and Practice*, edited by Joy K. Peyton, Donald A. Ranard, and Scott McGinnis. Crystal Lake, IL: Delta Systems Company.

———. 2011. "Ethnolinguistic Identity: The Challenge of Maintaining Spanish-English." In *Bilingual Youth: Spanish in English-Speaking Societies*, edited by Kim Potowski and Jason Rothman. Amsterdam: John Benjamins.

Valdés, Guadalupe, Joshua A. Fishman, Rebecca Chávez, and William Perez. 2006. *Developing Minority Language Resources: The Case of Spanish in California*. Bristol, UK: Multilingual Matters.

Valdés, Guadalupe, Rodolfo García-Moya, and Anthony G. Lozano, eds. 1981. *Teaching Spanish to the Hispanic Bilingual: Issues, Aims, and Methods*. New York: Teachers College Press.

Valdés, Guadalupe, and Michelle Geoffrion-Vinci. 2011. "Heritage Language Students: The Case of Spanish." In *The Handbook of Hispanic Sociolinguistics*, edited by Manuel Díaz-Campos. Hoboken, NJ: John Wiley & Sons.

Villa, Daniel J. 2002. "The Sanitizing of US Spanish in Academia." *Foreign Language Annals* 35, no. 2: 222–30.

Wilson, Damian Vergara. 2012. "Developing a Placement Exam for Spanish Heritage Language Learners: Item Analysis and Learner Characteristics." *Heritage Language Journal* 9, no. 1: 27–50.

# 4

## INCORPORATING MEANINGFUL SERVICE LEARNING INTO SPANISH SECOND-LANGUAGE CURRICULA

> On one issue, . . . there is no contradiction: In most areas of the United States, it is no longer necessary to teach Spanish only as a foreign language. . . . Growing Latino communities throughout the United States allow more and more Spanish instructors to connect to those communities and to learn from them.
>
> —Annie Abbott, *Comunidades*, 2010

Service learning is not a new instructional strategy in education and has existed under various names since the 1860s in the United States (Liu 2000). However, the writings of the educational philosopher John Dewey in the early twentieth century helped to solidify what we now refer to as *service learning*. Despite its nineteenth-century origins and many contemporary educators' interest in service learning, research examining the utility of service learning in the second-language (L2) classroom has been lacking, and even less available are inquiries into the curricular implications of incorporating service learning into postsecondary language programs. In 1999, Wehling declared that "research regarding service learning with a foreign language class is virtually non-existent" (Wehling 1999, 44). Fortunately, since Wehling's observation, there has been an increase in research not only into the use of service learning in a wide variety of settings and disciplines but also, specifically, in the acquisition of a second language. In the last twenty years, this growing body of research appears to have indicated that service learning may contribute to greater second-language competency. Researchers are also examining how to effectively employ service learning in the language classroom to maximize the benefits to students and to the community. The increased presence of Spanish-speaking communities in the United States and the need for students with real-world knowledge and effective communication skills have led to experiential-based learning being used more frequently in the Spanish language classroom (Lafford, Abbott, and Lear 2014). Service learning fulfills many of the known prerequisites for meaningful second-language learning to take place by employing elements that are key to language acquisition, namely, interpersonal interaction, negotiation of meaning, comprehensible input and output, and high levels of motivation. Beyond the potential for linguistic gains, experiential learning may serve as a powerful vehicle for attitude change, promoting positive perspectives among students toward the target culture. With the increase in service-learning projects, language departments are discovering a useful outlet for their students to implement skills in the community that they have acquired in the classroom. Because Spanish represents the most commonly spoken second language in the United States, opportunities for it exist in many more communities across the nation than for other second languages. In this chapter, we begin by providing necessary background on service learning in the second-language context before outlining how service learning presents an ideal mechanism to address national standards for second-language learning. We then review research on how service learning is currently being used in postsecondary Spanish language programs and the concomitant set of opportunities and challenges it brings from a curricular and programmatic perspective. Finally, information is also provided on how to effectively integrate service learning into a range of language programs and at various curricular levels.

## SERVICE LEARNING IN L2 EDUCATION

The skill sets that university students need to acquire have evolved, and the same holds true for second-language students because the professional world they enter will require practical communicative skills and cultural sensitivity. As noted above, the demand for courses in the humanities overall has decreased in recent years both in the United States and abroad, and those in the humanities disciplines continuously strive to reverse this trend (Abbott 2011; Paton 2013; Levitz and Belkin 2013). For the first time in the history of the Modern Language Association's survey of enrollments in languages other than English, the number of students studying Spanish declined from 2009 to 2013. Many foreign languages in the US suffered even greater losses over that period (Goldberg, Looney, and Lusin 2015), despite the fact that the 2009 survey found that most languages experienced continued growth in the face of economic downturns (Furman, Goldberg, and Lusin 2010). Notwithstanding the slight downturn in the number of students studying Spanish, more students continue to study Spanish than all other foreign languages combined (Goldberg, Looney, and Lusin 2015). Postsecondary second-language students in the United States live in a linguistically and culturally diverse country, wherein access to native speakers of *foreign* languages outside the walls of the classroom but within the community is becoming increasingly available, particularly in the case of Spanish. A responsive twenty-first-century Spanish language curriculum should reflect these changes and assist L2 students in successfully navigating this reality. As we have argued, along with others, one compelling way to help Spanish L2 students be successful in the foreign language is through service learning.

As a pedagogical approach, service learning uses community involvement to apply theories or skills being taught in a course while giving meaningful service to the community. Service learning is also referred to as "community" service learning, to highlight the context in which students' service is embedded. "Experiential learning" is a superordinate term that refers more broadly to learning that is hands on and completed through actual lived experiences rather than intellectual reflection or discussion, and may take place in the classroom or outside it, as in credit-bearing internships. As a branch of experiential learning, service learning is more targeted because it strives to further the learning objectives of the academic course while addressing community needs. Adler-Kassner, Crooks, and Watters (1997, 4) summarize the potential of service learning for integrating the university and the community: "The most immediate effect of service learning is to rearticulate the college or university as part of rather than opposed to the local community. This is a crucial and difficult rearticulation. Sometimes a large portion of the college population—especially the student portion—have no past relation to the surrounding community, and often come from different class, ethnic, or national backgrounds, as well."

Thus, the implementation of service learning in a community can break down barriers within the community and especially with members and groups that do not actively associate with the college or university. The authors further describe how service learning can integrate university-age students from other regions into a community that is not their own and with which they are likely unfamiliar. It is often the case that university students go about their daily lives attending class and social events, going to work, and participating in clubs with minimal interactions with outside community members. Universities and colleges are actually structured so that students have everything they need on campus—including food courts, entertainment venues, financial institutions, and the like—and do not need to enter the community unless they choose to do so. Students at commuter-oriented institutions often come to the university in their personal vehicles only to attend class and then return to their place of residence with minimal contact with the surrounding neighborhoods and communities.

As students become involved in service learning, they practice civic engagement while taking academics out of the classroom and into the community. Moreover, service learning may help faculty members to reinvigorate their teaching, ground it in societal realities, and add variety to their pedagogical quiver. Service learning assists students in connecting theory to practice, as well as providing community members with an infusion of human capital and access to university resources. To maximize the impact of service learning, it should

1. be reciprocal in nature, so that students and community members benefit;
2. require students to consider how the service and learning relate, how they are able to apply this knowledge, and how they might make the most out of their experience;
3. trigger personal growth and leadership throughout the process so that students who start are not the same ones who finish the service-learning experience;
4. provide a meaningful service to the community and its members, as opposed to a superficial project meant only to complete a course assignment;
5. increase civic responsibility in students, creating not just individuals who complete a project to fulfill a requirement but also actively involved community members; and
6. expose students to the diverse nature of the community where they live and extract them from their own social "bubble."

Service learning differs from volunteerism in that both groups need to learn and benefit from the experience. For example, participating in a service project where university students plant trees as part of an urban revitalization project is beneficial to the community, and the students would gain intrinsic satisfaction from completing the project—but this is simply service, not service learning. Service learning in L2 curricula forces students to interface with an added layer of linguistic and cultural diversity that English-language projects may not.

Each year, a national coalition of college and university presidents titled Campus Compact conducts a survey of its members to determine the impact of the service provided by participating institutions and their students. In its 2012 survey, a total of 557 member campuses responded to the survey, which indicated that "an average of 44% of students participated in some form of community engagement during the 2011–12 academic year, contributing an estimated $9.7 billion in service to their communities" (Campus Compact 2012, 5). Given that only about half the institutions participated in the survey and that many other institutions participate in service-learning programs, the actual benefits and value of these programs are likely to be much greater.

## SERVICE LEARNING AND NATIONAL STANDARDS

One of the challenges in the language classroom is engaging students in meaningful, relevant, and motivating encounters with the language that challenge them and, at the same time, provide enough context to allow their language skills to develop. With this in mind, and with an eye to curricular reform, the American Council on the Teaching of Foreign Languages (ACTFL) developed the World-Readiness Standards for Learning Languages. As part of these language standards, ACTFL categorized language learning into five main areas that are essential in the acquisition of a foreign language and labeled them the 5 Cs: communication, cultures, connections, comparisons, and communities. According to ACTFL's executive summary on its Web page, *communication* is defined as the ability to "communicate effectively in more than one language in order to function in a variety of situations and for multiple purposes"; *cultures* refers to the ability to "interact with cultural competence and understanding"; *connections* refers to the how the language learner is able to "connect with other disciplines and acquire information and diverse perspectives in order to use the language to function in academic and career-related situations"; *comparisons* address how the language needs to "develop insight into the nature of language and culture in order to interact with cultural competence"; and finally, *communities* refers to the skills developed by the language learner and how they employ these skills to "communicate and interact with cultural competence in order to participate in multilingual communities at home and around the world" (National Standards Collaborative Board 2015, 1).

All these 5 Cs form a vital part of language learning in the classroom as well as out of the classroom (Lear and Abbott 2008). Service learning enables students to develop these skills and not only use them in the nearby community and around the world but also subsequently bring them back into the classroom to share with their classmates. One can envision a classroom where the teacher provides topics and assignments that require the students to leave the walls of the institution in which they are studying. The students then enter the community where they live and provide meaningful service to community members while learning and practicing the target language in face-to-face encounters. After completing their service learning, students bring what they have learned back into the classroom to share with the instructor and fellow students, who are then able to make connections between the content, community, and cultures being studied. Abbott and Lear (2010, 242) found in their research that students were able to make connections to course content through service learning. They state that programs "need to

**Figure 4.1   The Foreign Language NAEP Assessment Framework**

*Note:* This figure originally appeared in "Framework for the 2004 Foreign Language National Assessment of Educational Progress Pre-Publication Edition," a report published by the American Councils of Teachers of Foreign Languages, and is reprinted by permission.

infuse civic engagement in an explicit manner" in Spanish service-learning courses and throughout the curricula.

Service learning can connect all the language modalities to the 5 Cs in an integrated and seamless way that allows students to develop their language skills, as displayed in the National Assessment of Educational Progress (NAEP) framework shown in figure 4.1. Interpersonal, interpretive, and presentational skills can all be addressed as language students complete appropriately designed tasks rooted in the service-learning experience. Face-to-face encounters with native speakers of Spanish may elicit oral/aural skills when transmitting information but also could include reading and writing in a tutoring session. Finally, Spanish language students are able to present their findings and experiences with the class through oral and written presentations.

## RESEARCH ON SERVICE LEARNING IN THE L2 CURRICULUM

As mentioned above, much research has been emerging on service learning in the second-language classroom, especially in the last twenty years (Bataller

2010; Cohen et al. 2005; Martinsen et al. 2011; Sanders 2005). Although the increase in the number of studies has helped to develop a better picture of the impact of service learning on language teaching and student learning, more research is needed to fully explore the impact of service learning on the concrete acquisition of Spanish as well as how curricular and programmatic considerations factor in—for example, vertical articulation, incorporation of service learning at all levels and for all subject areas, valid assessment practices, and instructor training and buy-in.

**Increasing Oral Proficiency**

One of the challenges that many language educators face is being able to move students from one proficiency level to the next. Students will at times plateau, creating challenges for instructors to move them forward. Lee (2000, 134) conducted a study investigating the characteristics of the oral proficiency level of second year Spanish students. She looked at the time they had spent learning Spanish as well as their contact with Spanish outside of the classroom. She found that those rated as Intermediate High on the Oral Proficiency Interview were the students who had engaged with native speakers outside the classroom, leading her to conclude that interaction with native speakers "may be an important factor in reaching higher levels of oral proficiency." She adds that "opportunities to use the language outside the classroom should be created to help students attain higher levels of language proficiency." Indeed, students who did not have contact with native speakers outside the classroom achieved a maximum of Intermediate Mid on the Oral Proficiency Interview.

Although the need for interactions with native speakers may seem apparent with regard to language acquisition, the question arises as to why so few programs make these opportunities available to their students. Given the ubiquity of Spanish and Spanish speakers in the United States and the limited resources of many agencies that serve underprivileged and diverse populations, why have so few institutions established extensive service-learning programs for their second-language programs?

One challenge in developing oral proficiency in the classroom is the lack of communicative need (Gass and Mackey 2006). Students are aware that they may at any point revert to a common first language with their classmates if the need arises. Thompson (2015, 124) investigated the use of service learning with advanced conversation courses to increase oral proficiency and interaction with native speakers while giving meaningful service. He found that students reported a much higher level of comfort in using the language, especially when they worked with children. One participant described her experience in the following way:

In a foreign environment, it is sometimes a little uncomfortable, but in this it was very comfortable and it was fine if we made a mistake. I believe that this is the best way to learn and practice a language. Sometimes I did not know a word or something but a boy would help me and he was happy to speak with me even when I made a mistake. I believe that speaking with children is the best way to learn a language. You can practice without being judged.

In addition to these comments by nonnative speakers of Spanish, Thompson also surveyed native and heritage speakers of Spanish to determine the perceived benefits of their oral language skills that they experienced through service learning. These learners, who spoke Spanish and often used it in their homes, reported that service learning helped them to become aware of lexical gaps in their Spanish due to extensive contact with English. They realized that they discussed certain topics only in English, and that when forced to engage in dialogue with other speakers in Spanish, they struggled to complete the tasks. Other heritage and native speakers of Spanish also stated that working with a wider range of speakers helped learners to become "more well-rounded in his/her speech and understanding" (Thompson 2015, 125). Much more research must be done to determine how best to incorporate meaningful service-learning projects into heritage and native speaker courses. The value of service learning over the range of a semester is that it can help students, even highly proficient heritage speakers, to develop linguistically and to strengthen their confidence in their ability to communicate with native speakers of Spanish in a variety of contexts.

Barreneche (2011) found that one of the advantages of providing service learning in elementary schools was that his students were teaching a live audience and thus had to not only prepare the material for the class but also had to make online adjustments and modifications to their speech. Additionally, elementary school children ask a wide variety of questions, some related to the material being covered and others rather unrelated, both of which stretched the university students. The ability to adapt one's speech during a dynamic conversational encounter in which topics, semantic domains, and interlocutor identity may change unexpectedly in the course of a language class, and during a real-world conversation, is a useful skill for all language learners. Several of the students' comments from the study by Barreneche (2011, 110–11) reflect how beneficial it was for them to have a real need to be spontaneous and be prepared for all questions and comments: "The experience I had with JA gave me the advantage of being able to practice my Spanish speaking skills, translating the things I need to say in the moment I think them, rather than planning everything I say beforehand. This is important because in important conversations I will not be able to plan out how to say things, or whip out my trusty dictionary."

This student recognized how her service-learning experience could prepare her to be successful for more high-stakes settings. Another student felt increased motivation to improve her proficiency after being required to speak in front of an audience.

> In a paper or written assignment, we have time to think about exactly what we want to say. . . . In a conversation, this is [not] possible, so the experience of teaching gives great practice because you do have a lesson plan as a guide of what you will say but students have questions and other things need to be addressed, so you are forced to step out of the preplanned comfort zone and think spontaneously—which is how real conversations are carried on in everyday life when you would actually use your Spanish skills. (Barreneche 2011, 111)

Bloom (2008) noted that much service-learning research that had been carried out to date focused on the intermediate- to advanced-level speakers. She states that effective programs can be designed at all levels of learning, including first-year language students. In her course, students worked in elementary schools helping Hispanic students improve their reading in Spanish. The author chose books related to the content of the course and to the lives of elementary students. To mitigate the fact that first semester Spanish students have limited language ability, she waited until midsemester to begin the service-learning assignment. She discovered that service learning had a positive impact on the cultural sensitivity of some students. Although Bloom (2008, 114, 116) considers the program to have been successful, she offers many valuable suggestions for instructors considering the incorporation of service learning with beginning-level students. Primarily, she felt that students would have found the service-learning project "less daunting" if a more structured approach to the service-learning assignment had been adopted with linguistic support and a concrete beginning, middle, and end. Many of the gains for these students will be made through careful observations and through their direct interactions with native speakers. Bloom also found that a careful orientation to the service-learning project and to the community where the project was to be completed led to greater success. Because students are not always familiar with the community outside their own social networks, this orientation is a valuable tool to prepare them and allay any concerns they may have. Finally, the author emphasizes the need to have the syllabus and curriculum "mesh seamlessly" with the service-learning component. She found that even when this was the case, student reflections still tended to be superficial, highlighting some of the difficulties that come with incorporating service learning with a lower-level speaker. Bloom recommends that with any service-learning experience instructors must train students on how to engage in critical thinking and reflection as a means to maximize the service-learning experience.

## Service Learning and Culture

One of the areas that has received attention pertains to the acquisition of cultural knowledge and cultural sensitivity through service learning. Barreneche (2011) studied students at a small, private liberal arts college in Winter Park, Florida, who were working with Junior Achievement on a service-learning project over a four-year period. In this project, Spanish language students worked with elementary schools, teaching lessons about economics and career planning designed for young learners. He found that the students in his study were not aware of many of the issues facing local immigrants in the community where they lived. He also found that the college students became aware of differences in perceptions and behaviors between themselves and the Hispanic students with whom they interacted. Although Barreneche's conclusions ostensibly point to a tremendous opportunity afforded by service learning, it could also present a difficult challenge by deepening some students' long-standing stereotypes of racial, linguistic, or ethnic groups.

One of the areas of particular interest has resulted from studies that have looked not solely into how the university students benefited from service learning but also how the community members were affected. Research in this area is relatively new, and studies have had some difficulty in ascertaining the true feelings that community members held toward the college students and the benefit of the encounter. D'Arlach, Sánchez, and Feuer (2009, 6) identify the difficulty of ascertaining community partners' honest opinions, noting that they are "unlikely to repudiate or jeopardize a partnership with a well-funded university by making negative comments in a university-sponsored survey. The best they can do is ask for more voice in the collaboration." Community organizations are often run by a few dedicated individuals who are trying to address more needs than their resources can meet, so their receiving any assistance at no cost to them through service learning has a positive impact. Several qualitative studies have been carried out to capture the true nature of these interactions and receive feedback on the performance of students performing service learning. D'Arlach, Sánchez, and Feuer (2009) employed field notes and interviews with community members to allow them to reflect upon their experience with the university students. These authors found that the community members felt comfortable interacting with the university students after a short time, which reduced stereotypes: "Community students stopped seeing the university students in terms of class or race, and began to see them as human beings with stories, aspirations, and struggles similar to their own" (d'Arlach, Sánchez, and Feuer 2009, 9).

Unfortunately, not all the university students behaved in the same manner, and surely some of the students' behavior perpetuated negative stereotypes among their community counterparts. Several students formed exclusive "cliques" and refused to interact with their community partners and made it obvious that they did not want to be there. The community partners were aware of this group, and often referred to them as the "young ones," "the negative ones," or "snobs" (d'Arlach, Sánchez, and Feuer 2009, 9). Notwithstanding the difficulties from this group of students, community members were most surprised to find that the university students were similar to them. Because the community participants in this service-learning project were mainly "undocumented immigrants with limited English language skills," they were surprised to find that the students struggled and missed their families just as they did. The community members also felt a degree of empathy toward the students, and both groups struggled to communicate in a nonnative language. Schmidt and Robby (2002) also interviewed the community partners in their research after their university students tutored over 250 elementary school children. These authors found that the children responded more positively to the university students who were interested in issues related to diversity and social justice. In addition, they found a positive correlation between university students and children who were similar in race, ethnicity, and socioeconomic status and who were interested in the overall success of the child in the service-learning experience.

University students need to become more familiar with other cultures and customs as they leave their familiar settings at home and enroll in ever-more-diverse universities and colleges. Instructors must help students develop an understanding of and appreciation for other cultures and peoples while facilitating the development of the necessary skills to interact with diverse populations. Petrov (2013, 310–11) found that the primary benefits of service learning had less to do with linguistic gains and more to do with "achieving attitudinal learning goals, encouraging development of positive Latino identities, and effecting increased engagement with the Latino communities." Nevertheless, personal prejudices and worldviews are not easily altered and may hijack efforts to increase appreciation of diversity.

Holsapple (2012, 10) conducted a meta-analysis of research, looking at the impact of service learning on students' diversity-related outcomes. He compared more than fifty-five studies and found that through service learning, students could interact with individuals with whom they had little or no previous contact and were also able to confront stereotypes about the target culture. He identified six common characteristics related to stereotypes that surfaced from his meta-analysis of the research. First, he found that students confronted stereotypes that they previously held about the community members and that service learning led to a reduction in the quality and quantity of students' stereotypes. Second, he found that students gained knowledge about the target population. Students acquired factual knowledge of the people and their countries, of cultural practices, and, finally, of the diversity that exists within the same community. Students had previously thought of the community "as a homogenous group, with the same experiences, backgrounds, and perspectives; this changed during the program." Third, students learned to value diversity within their own and the target populations. They also began to appreciate the richness that diversity brings to the culture and to their own community. Fourth, students developed a tolerance for differences, an essential characteristic in developing cultural proficiency. Eyler and Giles (1999) researched the development of tolerance for difference and found that students involved in service learning were more tolerant than students who did not participate. Other research found that students developed greater respect for the views of others, lessened their ethnocentrism, and increased their global understanding through service learning (Marullo 1998; Spiezio, Baker, and Boland 2006; Borden 2007; Astin et al. 2000). Fifth, students who participated in service learning were more likely to interact with people who they found to be different from them as well as their fellow students. Finally, service learning helps learners to realize that despite many differences in language and culture between groups, there are many similarities as well.

These studies demonstrate that great care must be taken when incorporating service learning into the curriculum because individual students' levels of cultural sensitivity will vary. Increasing cultural knowledge and sensitivity should be a goal of all programs, and service learning can assist in fulfilling this goal—but only if the instructor helps students overcome their stereotypes and prejudices.

## Service Learning and Student Retention

One of the factors that is often not considered in service-learning research relates to student retention. Many programs and universities are concerned with retaining new students as well as continuing students. The National Center for Educational Statistics (2014, para. 1) found that "59% of first-time, full-time students who began seeking a bachelor's degree at a 4-year institution in fall 2006 completed the degree at that institution within 6 years." This does not necessarily mean that the other 40 percent dropped out of school or are no longer enrolled, but rather that they did not graduate within six years. Regarding service learning, several studies have found a relationship between involvement in service learning and student retention. Keup (2005, 82) reports that service learning increases students' intention to return by enhancing the "quality and quantity of faculty interaction" and by promoting "positive academic experiences for students in their adjustment to college in the first year." Axsom and Pilland (1999) compared students in two different English composition courses. One course had a service-learning component, but the other did not, respectively leading to 78 percent retention for males and 83.6 percent for females in the service-learning classes and 65.3 percent and 63.5 percent retention in the traditional classes—a statistically significant difference for females. Of the participating students, 79 percent came from ethnic minority groups, with 25 percent of the population being first-generation Hispanic college students. This research points to the effectiveness of service learning as a tool to increase student retention, particularly among minority students who are at most risk of discontinuing their study after the first year.

Bringle, Hatcher, and Muthiah (2010) surveyed over seven hundred first-year university students at a variety of institutions and in different programs regarding their intentions to reenroll and remain at the institution the next year. The researchers found that the students who were enrolled in courses that included service learning had an impact on a student's reenrollment in a significant way, although this was mitigated somewhat when the quality of instruction and the results from a presurvey were considered. Nevertheless, 85 percent of the students reenrolled the following fall, with a higher rate of students who had participated in service-learning courses returning than those who had not. The students who participated in a course with service learning not only reenrolled but also reported greater satisfaction with their courses and found them to be of higher quality. The students in service-learning courses also reported increased peer and faculty interaction, greater course satisfaction, and more active learning. For instructors incorporating service learning into their classrooms, serious consideration needs to be given regarding the promotion of Spanish language classes, not only as a place for majors in the humanities but also as a place where double majors and minors can gain valuable skills for their chosen careers. Lafford, Abbott, and Lear (2014) consider courses on Spanish for the professions to be ideal places to integrate service learning into postsecondary Spanish language education. They propose that, when done properly, the integration of service learning into courses on Spanish for specific purposes allows students to appreciate how Spanish can prepare them to work in business, medicine, and education with the large and growing Hispanic population in the United States and abroad.

## SPANISH POSTSECONDARY PROGRAM AND CURRICULUM SURVEY RESULTS

Our national survey (see the appendix for a description) included seven specific questions regarding how much of a concern service learning was for the participants in this study. The postsecondary educators were asked to rank each item according to the level of concern that they had for each of the following issues related to the use and integration of service learning into classes and curriculum. All the instructors ranked each item on a scale of 1 (very much a concern) to 5 (not a concern at all). We also include the overall rank of the item's mean across all fifty-five survey items with regard to the level of perceived concern. The results of the survey show the areas where the instructors surveyed are most concerned and how these questions ranked in the overall survey. The percentage listed last under each question represents the number of participants who felt the item did not apply to their program:

- Establishment of productive partnerships with the Spanish-speaking community: 2.62 / 22nd / 4 percent;
- Integration of service-learning projects into existing courses: 3.06 / 44th / 6 percent;
- Creation of new service-learning courses in the curriculum: 3.07 / 45th / 6 percent; and
- Adequate training for instructors on the use of service learning: 3.11 / 47th / 6 percent.

The results show that the greatest concern for the instructors surveyed related to the establishment of productive partnerships with the Spanish-speaking community. The establishment of productive partnerships is one of the keys in establishing successful service-learning programs and courses and was ranked twenty-second out of the fifty-five items on the survey. This item was the only one whose mean was less than 3, or neutral. The next-highest-ranking item of concern regarding service learning was quite a bit lower, at forty-fourth. Apparently, service learning as expressed in these items was a matter of excessive concern for participants. The lowest-ranked item, and the one of least concern, related to adequate training for instructors on the use of service learning. For the population that took this survey, training was not a concern for the vast majority. It is also important to note that the majority of instructors in our survey found these items to be relevant, with only between 4 and 6 percent marking the questions as not applicable. Of the nine areas presented in this survey, the service-learning category overall ranked between sixth and eighth across disciplines.

One noteworthy aspect of this category is that it received the most qualitative comments and the largest number who used the "other" category. A total of eighty-nine participants marked the "other" category, twenty-six of whom included an additional item or left comments explaining their concern. The additional concerns were very telling and included such issues as "staffing a service-learning course," "level of proficiency among staff," establishing "international service-learning programs," and "developing effective service-learning courses for study abroad."

Other concerns related to attracting students to service-learning courses and getting the support of colleagues and administrators. One participant noted the need to increase "participation in our service learning, which is well established," which mirrored another respondent, who observed that "we created a service-learning class but it didn't fill." Faculty indifference seemed to describe one instructor's perspective, as she wanted to get "colleagues to see the need for service learning." Some comments transmitted frustration, noting that"bureaucratic obstacles" and the perception that the participant's "institution doesn't care about service learning."

It was also found that several participants were concerned about how the development of service-learning programs might affect them professionally and whether they would be recognized for their attempts at pedagogical innovation: "Adequate recognition for service-learning faculty in issues of promotion and tenure," "Appreciation of the work in SL," and "pedagogical value vs. effort required vs. payoff in tenure/promotion for SL." In addition, several participants saw the need to better articulate service learning into the overall Spanish curriculum, stating, "Development of a cohesive SL program—not isolated classes" and "creation of a continuum of community engaged learning across several courses; also, we tend to use 'community-engaged learning' rather than 'service learning' to better describe what we do." Finally, though some participants expressed the desire of "getting colleagues to understand what service learning is!" others were still a little confused, asking "what is service learning?" The wide variety of comments illustrates the ongoing struggles of implementing service learning in the Spanish curriculum. From articulation to enrollment to institutional support and recognition, the survey participants voiced many areas of concern that need to be addressed in the future.

## CURRICULAR CONSIDERATIONS FOR THE IMPLEMENTATION OF SERVICE LEARNING

Throughout this chapter, we have outlined many of the opportunities available for Spanish language educators and curriculum designers who wish to engage their students more meaningfully with Spanish and with those who use it as their native language. Indeed, the educational benefits afforded by service learning in the Spanish language classroom are plentiful and promising, but effective implementation of service learning in postsecondary Spanish language curricula in the United States is not without its challenges. In this final section of the chapter, we take stock of these opportunities and challenges, summarizing some we have already alluded to while introducing others we have not.

In many cases, effective service learning carries an additional burden for instructors, language program directors, and departmental administrators, especially when initially introduced into a program's curriculum, or even just into one particular course. Community contacts must be made and nurtured, and student placements must be organized and tracked, taking into account the needs of the student, the community partner, and the instructor—not to mention the learning objectives. Instructors are often concerned with how to oversee and supervise students who are off campus, and many believe that service learning requires the expenditure of additional energy and resources that are beyond their ability or willingness to provide, or is simply beyond their job description. Some instructors may consider on-site observations and meeting with community partners outside class an unreasonable burden on their time. As such, program administrators who desire to incorporate service learning in all courses and at all levels may encounter resistance. What instructors must remember is that service learning requires an initial investment of time and energy, but much of the training and observations can be done by the community partner and relayed thereafter to the instructor. Instructors may want to make initial visits to the service-learning sites before using them; but formal evaluations are carried out through structured reflections, community partners' feedback, and other reports based on the instructors' goals. Additionally, instructors need to consider the time investment required to develop any high-quality project that promotes student engagement.

One of the additional challenges facing language teachers is locating interested community partners whose needs match the curricular goals set forth by the instructor. Finding a balance between what the community partner wants and needs and what the instructor-authored student learning outcomes prescribe may be difficult or may need to be adjusted. Instructors also must carefully negotiate the extent to which they or a member of the community partner's administrative body will supervise students and assess their achievement of agreed-upon objectives or goals. For example, many nonprofit organizations need materials translated into Spanish or initial drafts of documents prepared for further review. However, if the focus of the course is on conversation and improving oral and aural abilities, this type of service-learning experience, though perfect for a translation course, would be inappropriate. Instructors need to interview the community organizations to determine how the needs of both the students and the community can best be served. Community organizations are likely to have needs based on the population they serve, so instructors should find out what levels of proficiency students require to carry out the project, whether students would benefit from cultural awareness training, and how the community partner sees its role in assisting with the project. These initial inquiries will help avoid future problems and help to properly place students.

In spite of the difficulties in establishing service-learning programs and developing community partnerships, language educators must realize that success does not solely rely on them. Many resources exist to assist in the development of programs and in establishing links with community partners. Thompson (2012) describes how he created a partnership with the United Way of Central Florida, which in turn was able to send out information about his students' project and what they were required to do as part of the course. He found that this assistance greatly facilitated the instructor's work. In this case, not only did the students benefit from working with the United Way but the United Way was also able to use its resources to serve the community as a nonprofit organization. In addition to community organizations, an increasing number of colleges and universities have established a centralized office on campus to assist professors and connect them to community agencies with diverse needs. These offices go by many names, such as the Office of Experiential Learning, the Center for Service and Learning, and the Office of Service Learning and Civic Engagement. One potential problem with these campus offices is that they may have never worked with bilingual service-learning encounters. They may require a certain amount of education on how to best integrate service learning into language courses at a wide range of levels. Regardless of the level of experience, these campus offices have staff and resources dedicated to the establishment of community outreach programs, with instructors at all levels and in all disciplines, and they can find organizations that fit the curricular needs of different language courses. Furthermore, they can assist in instructing language teachers regarding the inclusion of service learning in their courses. One benefit of service learning is that an instructor does not need to be an expert in the area where the students are giving service because the community partner will work with the students and train them according to their needs.

At Brigham Young University (BYU), the office in charge of helping students find service opportunities as well as helping instructors set up service-learning opportunities for their courses is called Y-Serve. The center's goal is to support one of the key aims of BYU, which is to help students develop a pattern of lifelong learning and service in collaboration with one of its seventy community service programs, many of which work with the local Spanish-speaking community. During 2016, 10,653 BYU students provided over 100,983 hours of service estimated to be valued at over $2 million. The academic programs that work with the local Spanish-speaking community provide a range of services, some of which have been incorporated into classes provided by BYU's Department of Spanish and Portuguese. For example, the Spanish translation and interpretation courses require students to provide translation and interpretation services for various nonprofit community organizations. The goal is to prepare students to work in jobs within the area of translation and interpretation, and the professors involved in this program find that service learning provides not only practical hands-on training but also valuable service to the local community.

There are also many other resources that can assist the instructor interested in integrating service learning into his or her curriculum, such as the aforementioned Campus Compact, whose central purpose is campus-based civic engagement through service learning. Its website, www.compact.org, offers a plethora of resources that can assist in establishing a program or modifying a program to better meet students' needs. In addition, many publications focus on service-learning research, such as the *Michigan Journal of Community Service-Learning*. This peer-reviewed, academic publication addresses many of the concerns that teachers face when implementing service learning in the classroom.

## Assessing Service Learning

One of the concerns that arises with the incorporation of service learning into the Spanish language curriculum relates to assessment. How do instructors fairly assess student performance, and how will participation in service-learning projects affect students' final course grades? Thompson (2012, 118) found that initial attempts to include service learning resulted in slight grade inflation, given that grades were based almost entirely on simple completion of the tasks, rather than a careful examination of the quality of that completion. Students generally received full points for completion of the components of a service-learning project, in some cases resulting in increases of an entire letter grade. He suggests that attempts be made to measure "the quality of their service and reflection during the course of the class" and not simply the completion of the assignment.

The question then arises as to how an instructor can validly measure and evaluate the quality of the service learning performed and the achievement of student learning outcomes without having been present on site. Most assessments seem to rely on students' reflections on their experience rather than on direct, quantifiable, and, ostensibly, objective measures of language or culture learning. Nevertheless, several strategies can make the assessment of service learning more valid and defensible. Instructors might divide the service-learning project into several components, depending on the content of the course. For a conversation course, an instructor could have students present on what they have learned during the service-learning project several times during the semester, whereas in a literature course, students might write up an analysis comparing their experiences to situations in the works of literature they are covering in class. Literature students could also read excerpts of Spanish language works to Spanish-speaking elementary or high school students in heritage language classes and then engage them in a meaningful discussion. Where appropriate and approved by the community partner, students could audio-record a common verbal exchange completed early during their service-learning assignment and then toward the end of the semester, regardless of the context. These audio recordings could be transcribed and analyzed for grammar, fluency, vocabulary, and pragmatics. Instructors who want to focus on the development of grammar in writing could assign unique topics for each service-learning encounter that would require students to employ the language skills they are developing in the classroom. If a class is being taught on the use of the past tense, an instructor could assign his or her students to write about what they learned concerning the target community during their experience or how the experiences of the young Hispanics they served compare with their own childhood.

Another source of feedback that can be used for the evaluation of students comes from community partners. Although such evaluations can be problematic, given the tendency of community partners to appreciate any help that is given, these partners can be provided with targeted, confidential online surveys where they can evaluate or even rank the students who worked with them. This feedback could be included with other considerations relating to the students' performance in the completion of their service-learning assignment, such as self and peer evaluations. Self-evaluations can be a useful part of assessing a student's performance in his or her project. They can be asked questions related to the completion of tasks, on-time arrival at service-learning assignments, completion of total hours, the quality of interpersonal interaction, and social skills. In addition, many service-learning projects send students in cohorts to carry out service learning. In these situations, students could evaluate each other on their individual contributions to the project. These evaluations, along with the other assessments, help to paint a more complete picture of student performance and the overall quality of the service-learning site and student experience.

### Service Learning and Teacher Training

Teacher training programs also need to consider whether to require students to complete service learning as part of their language program. Many language teacher education programs require students to achieve a prescribed level of proficiency to be certified to teach. A required service-learning project in the Spanish-speaking community, and particularly in schools with large numbers of Spanish-speaking students, would help preservice language teachers who may not be able to travel abroad increase their proficiency in preparation for certification. Moreover, many states are developing dual language immersion programs that require not only a high level of proficiency but also the ability to teach a broad range of types of subject matter. A carefully constructed service-learning component as part of teacher training would serve as a valuable experience in developing language skills as well as teaching skills. Many of the service-learning programs mentioned in this chapter have dealt with some form of teaching adults and children. Thus, students involved in service learning would be able to work on their language skills as well as apply their pedagogical knowledge to their teaching, all in preparation for their practicum and future employment.

### Service Learning in All Language Classrooms

Although it may seem that only certain types of courses and levels lend themselves to effective service learning, many different types of Spanish language classrooms can benefit from well-planned service learning, from the high-beginner language class to the senior-level literature class to the introductory linguistics class. The only limitation to meaningfully applying service learning to the classroom lies in the language course instructor's creativity and vision. One of the most obvious best fits for the use of service learning is in courses where the focus is on oral production. Many programs offer Spanish conversation courses at intermediate levels and beyond. The purpose of these courses is to engage learners, assist them in expanding their vocabulary, and help them interact in a wide range of settings with native speakers. Often, these courses are designed around readings on stimulating topics, where the members of the class defend their point of view related to the topic. Students are also often called upon to give presentations on topics and to discuss how these relate to their own lives and the lives of their classmates. In these situations, the teacher functions as a facilitator who provides the means for a lively discussion or debate.

Nevertheless, intermediate conversation courses are not the only place in the curriculum that allows for the incorporation of meaningful service-learning projects. Spanish literature and linguistics courses may also find meaningful service-learning projects at local libraries, community centers, and schools that serve Spanish-speaking populations. Whether students are required to read from the literary canon to heritage language classes and to conduct a discussion on a particular movement, genre, or author, or to teach first-language literacy and grammar to Hispanic migrants, service learning is a viable option. In the case of the literature course, many students find a disconnect between the material covered in class and their daily lives. However, instructors can assign a contemporary Hispanic American short story, in which the aspects of culture and history presented in the text resemble to some extent the circumstances of their service-learning placement. Students are also able to talk with native speakers and obtain perspectives on the readings that they may not have previously considered. Students can learn about social issues and develop a greater understanding of the motivations behind certain behaviors through careful observation and analysis. Finally, one of the skills needed in literature courses is the ability to express oneself through writing. Service learning requires careful and purposeful reflection to help students integrate what they have learned and how it relates to them, both as individuals and as members of a particular cultural group.

Beginning, or high beginning, students may also take advantage of service-learning projects when paired with upper-level students, or even alone, if their responsibilities are designed to match their level. For example, beginning students might be required to attend a Latino health fair attended by predominantly bilingual speakers rather than monolingual speakers and given the assignment to provide basic directions to various events or booths. As with the use of nearly all authentic texts—spoken or written—it is the nature of the task, not the text, that makes the difference.

With service learning, students are given more independence and autonomy as they choose service-learning assignments that are of most interest to them. From their interactions with community members who are native speakers of the language, they are able to discover topics of interest to them and to consult with native speaking informants regarding their views and then bring this information into the classroom to share. Here, the teacher's role is to assist in guiding students in discussion and to present different points of view that the students will be able to explore within their own community.

Many universities have conversation courses with the goal of allowing students at a variety of levels to practice their language skills. Depending on the level of the class, the curriculum of these courses is based on a variety of different foci. For example, advanced-level students can look at authentic texts or audio clips and then respond and debate their content. Students at the intermediate or novice level can make inferences regarding text type and function based on key words. These courses serve a valuable function, but what is lacking in many of them is the legitimate need to communicate in an authentic environment. Through service learning, students can practice these same skills while observing their impact on the community and making positive connections between the college or university and the surrounding community. Students can then return to the conversation classroom, where they will be able to present the information that they have collected through their interactions with their service-learning partners.

## CONCLUSION

Of all the second languages currently being taught in the United States, none is more properly situated to maximize the impact of service learning on second-language curricula than Spanish. With few communities in the United States that do not have a sizable number of native Spanish speakers, Spanish language educators and program administrators would do well to fully incorporate meaningful and useful service-learning projects into their courses of all disciplines and levels. In this chapter we have argued that the opportunities afforded by service learning far outweigh whatever difficulties may arise insofar as students' acquisition of Spanish goes and their appreciation of diverse cultures.

As is indicated by the title of Barreneche's (2011) article, "Language Learners as Teachers," service learning allows instructors to transfer the onus of learning squarely back to the learners. Even in today's era of the flipped classroom, too often the Spanish language classroom centers on the teacher. Service learning allows the teacher to place the onus of learning back on the students. One of the benefits of sending students into the community is that they not only make gains in the development of their language skills and cultural knowledge but they are also able to bring this back into the classroom to share with their instructors and peers. The knowledge and skills gained go far beyond simple language acquisition because students become more civically minded and apply the experience from service learning to other areas of study. Service learning in the Spanish language classroom has the potential to change the whole framework of classroom language teaching and learning. Barreneche (2011, 111) concurs, noting that "as a result, much in the same way study abroad and immersion experiences heighten language acquisition and translingual skills by removing the student from a less natural classroom environment that is directed by the instructor, the student of an integrated community engagement project takes ownership of his or her language learning."

Carney (2004, 270) sums up how university students can benefit from their involvement in service learning:

1. Awareness of social problems and the need for community involvement to solve them.
2. A change in student perception of the "immigrant problem" as something complex and irreducible to quick fixes.
3. Self-discovery, which includes self-doubt, self-reflection, self-assurance, and self-worth.
4. Application of disciplinary knowledge in meaningful contexts: students testing academic ideas/terms/knowledge in the "messy" real world.
5. Development of problem-solving initiative (agency).
6. Respect for others, not as different or needy, but as fellow human beings negotiating a path within a particular set of circumstances.

As we advance farther and farther into the twenty-first century, and as the Spanish language continues to establish its place as the second national language of the United States, it is high time that postsecondary Spanish language education make much greater use of one of the most potent tools available to achieve the lofty goals it has set for itself, namely, service learning.

## REFLECTION QUESTIONS

1. This chapter contends that service learning is a valuable tool in all Spanish language classes. Are there classes where this does not seem to be the case, or where service learning would not be beneficial? Explain your response.

2. Thinking specifically about the community where you live, where might service-learning opportunities be established? How would the students, community, and instructor benefit from implementing service learning in your community?

3. Studies on study abroad have sometimes found that students who go abroad return with more stereotypes than they had before going abroad. Would this be a concern for service learning? How could these issues be mitigated by the instructor?

4. One of the goals of service learning is to increase civic awareness and engagement. How does service learning in the Spanish language classroom achieve this? Are there other ways to create more civically minded students other than service learning? Should this be an important goal of the language classroom?

5. Scholarship on service learning has focused on the affective benefits but less on proficiency gains. This may be due to the fact that more than a semester is often needed to produce measurable gains, and to the difficulty of isolating service learning as the key component in these gains. How could research be carried out to specifically look at gains based on a service-learning component in a classroom?

6. One of the main concerns regarding the implementation of service learning in the Spanish language curriculum is the increased workload added to an already-overburdened schedule. How would you respond to this based on the information given in this chapter?

7. Heritage language learners already speak the language to differing degrees, and often use the language in authentic settings. What would be the advantage of using service learning in classes for heritage speakers of Spanish? What considerations should be taken into account when creating projects for heritage learners of Spanish?

8. What role could service learning play in hybrid or online courses? How could it be integrated into this type of classroom to help students improve their language skills and cultural sensitivity? How would students share their experiences with service learning in an online setting?

## PEDAGOGICAL ACTIVITIES

1. Often, it is easier to incorporate meaningful service-learning projects into advanced-level courses. Develop a plan describing how to integrate service learning into the curriculum of first- and second-year Spanish language courses. What types of projects would be a good fit for these lower-level students? What about the advanced students? What projects in your community would best be suited for students of various levels?

2. Visit the office at your institution that assists instructors in developing connections with the community or in establishing service-learning courses. Find out what organizations it works with that address the needs of Spanish-speaking members of the local community. Determine if any current language courses have a service-learning component as part of their syllabus. How is it being implemented? Ask for advice on how you could incorporate service learning into the courses that you are currently teaching or that you will teach in the future.

3. Develop a lesson plan that includes a mini-service-learning component for a course that you have taught or have taken. Plan the lesson with the service-learning component that helps students to further their knowledge of the content you are teaching. This plan can be completed with the data gathered from the previous activity regarding the agencies with which your institution is currently working.

4. Interview an instructor at your institution who uses service learning as part of the curriculum. Find out their perspective on the benefits and challenges of service learning based on their experience. Ask for any advice that this person may have for someone who is planning on using service learning in the future.

## REFERENCES

Abbott, Annie R. 2010. *Comunidades: Más Allá del Aula*. Upper Saddle River, NJ: Prentice Hall.

Abbott, Annie R. 2011. "Putting Students to Work: Spanish Community Service Learning as a Countervailing Force." In *Creating Infrastructures for Latino Mental Health*, edited by Lydia P. Buki and Lissette M. Piedra. New York: Springer.

Abbott, Annie R., and Darcy Lear. 2010. "The Connections Goal Area in Spanish Community Service Learning: Possibilities and Limitations." *Foreign Language Annals* 43, no. 2: 231–45.

Adler-Kassner, Linda, Robert Crooks, and Ann Watters. 1997. *Writing the Community: Concepts and Models for Service-Learning in Composition.* Washington, DC: Stylus.

Astin, Alexander W., Lori J. Vogelgesang, Elaine K. Ikeda, and Jennifer A. Yee. 2000. *How Service Learning Affects Students.* Los Angeles: University of California, Los Angeles, Higher Education Research Institute.

Axsom, Trish, and William Piland. 1999. "Effects of Service Learning on Student Retention and Success." *NSEE Quarterly* 24: 15–19.

Barreneche, Gabriel Ignacio. 2011. "Language Learners as Teachers: Integrating Service-Learning and the Advanced Language Course." *Hispania* 94, no. 1: 103–20.

Bataller, Rebeca. 2010. "Making a Request for a Service in Spanish: Pragmatic Development in the Study Abroad Setting." *Foreign Language Annals* 43, no. 1: 160–75.

Bloom, Melanie. 2008. "From the Classroom to the Community: Building Cultural Awareness in First Semester Spanish." *Language, Culture and Curriculum* 21, no. 2: 103–19.

Borden, Amanda Welch. 2007. "The Impact of Service-Learning on Ethnocentrism in an Intercultural Communication Course." *Journal of Experiential Education* 30, no. 2: 171–83.

Bringle, Robert G., Julie A. Hatcher, and Richard N. Muthiah. 2010. "The Role of Service-Learning on the Retention of First-year Students to Second Year." *Michigan Journal of Community Service Learning* 16, no. 2: 38–49.

Campus Compact. 2012. "Annual Member Survey." www.compact.org/wp-content/up loads/2013/04/Campus-Compact-2012-Statistics.pdf.

Carney, Terri M. 2004. "Reaching Beyond Borders through Service Learning." *Journal of Latinos and Education* 3, no. 4: 267–71.

Cohen, Andrew D., R. Michael Paige, Rachel L. Shively, Holly Emert, and Joseph Hoff. 2005. "Maximizing Study Abroad through Language and Culture Strategies: Research on Students, Study Abroad Program Professionals, and Language Instructors." *Final Report to the International Research and Studies Program, Office of International Education, DOE.* Minneapolis: Center for Advanced Research on Language Acquisition, University of Minnesota.

d'Arlach, Lucia, Bernadette Sánchez, and Rachel Feuer. 2009. "Voices from the Community: A Case for Reciprocity in Service-Learning." *Michigan Journal of Community Service Learning* 16, no. 1: 5–16.

Eyler, Janet, and Dwight E. Giles Jr. 1999. *Where's the Learning in Service-Learning? Jossey-Bass Higher and Adult Education Series.* San Francisco: Jossey-Bass.

Furman, Nelly, David Goldberg, and Natalia Lusin. 2010. "Enrollments in Languages Other Than English in United States Institutions of Higher Education, Fall 2009." Modern Language Association, New York. www.mla.org/pdf/2009_enrollment_survey.pdf.

Gass, Susan M., and Alison Mackey. 2006. "Input, Interaction and Output: An Overview." *AILA Review* 19, no. 1: 3–17.

Goldberg, David, Dennis Looney, and Natalia Lusin. 2015. "Enrollments in Languages Other Than English in United States Institutions of Higher Education, Fall 2013." Modern Language Association, New York. www.mla.org/content/download/31180/1452509 /EMB_enrllmnts_nonEngl_2013.pdf.

Holsapple, Matthew. 2012. "Service-Learning to Encourage Openness to Diversity: A Meta-Analysis of Current Support." *Michigan Journal of Community and Service-Learning* 18, no. 2: 5–18.

Kena, Grace, Susan Aud, Frank Johnson, Xiaolei Wang, Jijun Zhang, Amy Rathbun, Sidney Wilkinson-Flicker, and Paul Kristapovich. 2014. *The Condition of Education 2014.*

Report NCES 2014-083. Washington, DC: National Center for Education Statistics, Institute of Education Sciences, US Department of Education.

Keup, Jennifer R. 2005. "The Impact of Curricular Interventions on Intended Second Year Re-enrollment." *Journal of College Student Retention: Research, Theory & Practice* 7, no. 1: 61–89.

Lafford, Barbara A., Ann Abbott, and Darcy Lear. 2014. "Spanish in the Professions and in the Community in the US." *Journal of Spanish Language Teaching* 1, no. 2: 171–86.

Lear, Darcy W., and Annie R. Abbott. 2008. "Foreign Language Professional Standards and CSL: Achieving the 5 C's." *Michigan Journal of Community Service Learning* 14, no. 2: 76–86.

Lee, Lina. 2000. "Evaluating Intermediate Spanish Students' Speaking Skills through a Taped Test: A Pilot Study." *Hispania* 83, no. 1: 127–38.

Levitz, Jennifer, and Douglas Belkin. 2013. "Humanities Fall from Favor." *Wall Street Journal*, June 6. www.wsj.com/news/articles/SB10001424127887324069104578527642373232184?mod=WSJ_hps_LEFTTopStories.

Liu, Goodwin. 2000. "Knowledge, Foundations, and Discourse: Philosophical Support for Service-Learning." In *Beyond the Tower: Concepts and Models for Service-Learning in Philosophy*, edited by C. David Lisman and Irene Harvey. Sterling, VA: Stylus.

Martinsen, Rob A., Wendy Baker, Jennifer Bown, and Cary Johnson. 2011. "The Benefits of Living in Foreign Language Housing: The Effect of Language Use and Second-language Type on Oral Proficiency Gains." *Modern Language Journal* 95, no. 2: 274–90.

Marullo, Sam. 1998. "Bringing Home Diversity: A Service-Learning Approach to Teaching Race and Ethnic Relations." *Teaching Sociology* 26, no. 4: 259–75.

National Standards Collaborative Board. 2015. *World-Readiness Standards for Learning Languages*, 4th ed. Alexandria, VA: National Standards Collaborative Board. www.actfl.org/publications/all/world-readiness-standards-learning-languages.

Paton, Graeme. 2013. "University Fee Rise Sparks Surge in Demand for 'Jobs-Based' Degrees." *The Telegraph*, August 13. www.telegraph.co.uk/education/universityeducation/clearing/10238399/University-fee-rise-sparks-surge-in-demand-for-jobs-based-degrees.html.

Petrov, Lisa Amor. 2013. "A Pilot Study of Service-Learning in a Spanish Heritage Speaker Course: Community Engagement, Identity, and Language in the Chicago Area." *Hispania* 96, no. 2: 310–27.

Sanders, Robert F. 2005. "Community-Based Learning in Rural Guatemala." *Hispania* 88, no. 1: 182–89.

Schmidt, Adeny, and Matthew A. Robby. 2002. "What's the Value of Service-Learning to the Community?" *Michigan Journal of Community Service Learning* 9, no. 1: 27–33.

Spiezio, Kim E., Kerrie Q. Baker, and Kathleen Boland. 2005. "General Education and Civic Engagement: An Empirical Analysis of Pedagogical Possibilities." *Journal of General Education* 54, no. 4: 273–92.

Thompson, Gregory L. 2012. *Intersection of Service and Learning: Research and Practice in the Second Language Classroom*. Charlotte: Information Age.

———. 2015. "Engaging Second Language Learners: Developing Cultural Knowledge and Language Proficiency through Service-Learning." In *Productive Foreign Language Skills for an Intercultural World: A Guide (Not Only) for Teachers*, edited by Michal Paradowski. New York: Peter Lang.

Wehling, Susan. 1999. "Service-Learning and Foreign Language Acquisition: Working with the Migrant Community." *Dimension* 99: 41–55.

# 5

## CURRICULAR AND PROGRAMMATIC CONSIDERATIONS IN SPANISH FOR SPECIFIC PURPOSES

> LSP [language for specific purposes] is a square peg that we are trying to fit into the round hole of traditional university language curricula (literature and linguistics).
>
> —Barbara Lafford, Ann Abbott, and Darcy Lear,
> "Spanish in the Professions," 2014

The movement advocating language for specific purposes (LSP)—or, more specifically, Spanish for specific purposes (Spanish LSP[1])—represents a crucial component of twenty-first-century Spanish curricula because it aims to bridge the gap between what students learn in the classroom and their use of it outside the classroom. The World-Readiness Standards for Learning Languages—from the American Council on the Teaching of Foreign Languages, with its 5 Cs—have particular relevance for Spanish LSP, especially connections, comparisons, and communities. Although postsecondary foreign language (FL) curricula have included LSP courses for several decades, current trends in higher education have placed LSP courses squarely in the spotlight as the embodiment of the conflicted nature of contemporary collegiate FL curricula more specifically. Despite pedagogic and curricular innovations, LSP represents the tension that exists between traditional, humanistic curricula on one hand and practical, vocationally focused curricula on the other hand. As Lafford, Abbott, and Lear (2014) point out in the epigraph above, LSP—and in our case, Spanish for specific purposes (Spanish LSP)—often seems to occupy the liminal and somewhat marginalized space between purely literary, cultural, or linguistic approaches to language study, and vocationally targeted approaches to practical language learning and contextualized use.

Scholars such as Beltrán (2004) cite the confluence of economic, social, intellectual, and political factors soon after the close of World War II that propelled English to the status of international lingua franca and precipitated the subsequent appearance of the LSP movement. Factors that led to heightened demand for second-language (L2) pedagogy tailored to specific academic and professional domains include the rapid rate of scientific discovery and innovation, the increase of transnational trade, the speed and facility of information dissemination, the rise of the United States as an economic superpower, and the evolution of various subfields within linguistics (applied linguistics, sociolinguistics, psycholinguistics) (Beltrán 2004). The field congealed more firmly in the United Kingdom after Halliday, Strevens, and McIntosh (1964) advocated for research that could empirically validate the professional language presented in pedagogical materials aimed at equipping learners of English with domain-specific linguistic skills. José María de Tomás Puch (2004, 1149) argues that technological innovations and the appearance of electronic communication have led to increased contact between professionals from different countries and have generated foreign language students with a profile "very different from years past."[2]

Additional momentum for LSP was provided by several scholars in the fields of linguistics, philosophy, and L2 acquisition. Hymes's (1972) conceptualization of communicative competence directly countered Noam Chomsky's assertions regarding language competence by arguing that true competence in any interpersonal communicative interaction requires more than a mastery of highly abstract syntactic rules and universal principles and parameters. Of a somewhat similar intellectual persuasion was Halliday (1961), whose systemic-functional linguistics claimed that the language system and the functions for which it is used maintain a bidirectional relationship rather than a unidirectional one in which the linguistic system dictates how certain communicative functions can be fulfilled. Hyland (2011) argues for specificity in L2 pedagogy, as in the case of LSP, from even the most elementary levels, given the nonlinear nature of L2 acquisition and the fact that learners acquire features of the language as they need them rather than in a specific order. He cites social constructivism as additional theoretical support for the LSP enterprise, given its claim that each profession and discipline constructs its own worldview via unique discourses. These scholars' contributions have provided additional theoretical and intellectual backing for the LSP movement among L2 educators, who began to appreciate the value in instructing learners explicitly in domain-specific discourses and genres embedded within their corresponding social and cultural milieus.

The changing nature of modern higher education in the United States and its principal objectives also have contributed to the rise of LSP in collegiate curricula on many US campuses. Most notably, Derek Bok (2006) has examined the tension that has arisen for many universities between the need to simultaneously provide students with a liberal, humanistic education—historically focused on intellectual discovery, character development, and mental discipline—while also preparing them for gainful employment and a successful career by equipping them with practical knowledge and skill sets. José (2014, 15) discusses this debate and recounts the difficult conversations that one of his students frequently had with her parents while deciding on a major. On one occasion, while he was meeting with the student in his office, her parents texted the following message: "[Humanities majors] are unemployed, unemployable and bound to menial jobs." Instead of simply preparing university students to become informed, engaged members of an educated citizenry committed to the betterment of society, university studies are seen as a financial investment whose corresponding curricula must respond to the larger socioeconomic forces at play. This is directly reflected in the large numbers of university students who choose business as a major and the diminishing number who pursue studies in the arts and sciences.

In their seminal article on LSP in American higher education, Grosse and Voght (1991, 29) attributed the inclusion of LSP in the FL curriculum to the general need to promote greater foreign language study, to expand the curriculum, and to incorporate humanistic approaches into professional education, and also as a way to address calls for the internationalization of university curricula. Nevertheless, they do acknowledge "diverse and powerful forces" that have led to the inclusion of LSP courses in FL curricula, citing Kramsch's (1989) rather candid assessment of the state of foreign language teaching and learning in the late 1980s: "Kramsch attributes the national trend toward broadening the nature of language study to economic and political pressures, rather than to a renewed interest in humanistic education per se" (Grosse and Voght (1991, 31).

In the ensuing years since 1989, and even since the 2007 MLA report, it has become quite clear that foreign language departments—like all disciplines in the humanities—have had to become much more responsive to the socioeconomic and sociopolitical realities students face upon exit from their programs in the design and deployment of their curricula. The creation of LSP courses and programs represents one concrete instantiation of this reality.

## CONTEMPORARY DEFINITIONS OF LSP

Several useful definitions of LSP have surfaced over the ensuing years, as the field has striven to demarcate its own intellectual borders. Ken Hyland (2011, 201), a preeminent scholar in the field of English for specific purposes, offers the following definition: "Specific purposes teaching refers to a distinctive approach to language education based on identification of the specific language features, discourse practices, and communicative skills of target groups, and on teaching practices that recognize the particular subject matter needs and expertise of learners."

Arnó-Macià (2012, 90) states that LSP centers on "the learner's need to participate effectively in the target academic or professional community. LSP courses are thus cost-effective and rooted in the texts and practices of the target disciplines." Lafford (2012, 2) provided a rather succinct, yet precise, definition, asserting that the primary goal of LSP is "to prepare language students for the practical application of their L2 in professional environments."

Dan Douglas (2000, 19), an assessment specialist, offers an implicit definition of LSP, while differentiating LSP tests from general second-language tests: "Test content and methods are derived from an analysis of a specific purpose target language use situation, so that test tasks and content are authentically representative of tasks in the target situation, allowing for . . . inferences about a test taker's capacity to use language in the specific purpose domain."

These definitions have several things in common: (1) they all differentiate LSP pedagogy and assessment from traditional second-language pedagogy, using such terms as *distinctive*—essentially carving out a unique intellectual space for LSP within applied linguistics; and (2) they highlight the importance of accurately identifying the specific discursive, linguistic, cultural, and communicative characteristics of each specific-use context before any attempts at instruction or assessment are made. Though other scholars have problematized these characterizations of LSP (Lafford, Abbott, and Lear 2014; Sullivan 2012) for various reasons, it is clear that effective LSP pedagogy and assessment is context dependent and heavily reliant upon an accurate needs analysis, characteristics of LSP that Basturkmen (2012, 62) calls "key course design processes."

In more concrete terms, scholars have found that LSP courses cover a wide variety of subject areas in addition to business and medicine. In their 2011 survey, which replicated Grosse and Voght's (1990) research, Long and Uscinski (2012) added four more disciplines—education, nursing, translation, and engineering—to the previous six that Grosse and Voght included—business, medicine, law, public programs, technology, and other—for a total of ten. In the 2011 version, the second-most-used category of the ten was "other," making up 21 percent of courses, as compared with 12 percent in Grosse and Voght's research in the late 1980s. Not surprisingly, the subject areas that Long and Ucsinski reference as examples of the increasingly diverse nature of LSP offerings come from Spanish curricula: "Spanish for hotel, tourism and restaurant management" and "Spanish for criminal justice," though the majority of Spanish LSP courses relate to business and medical Spanish.

## SPANISH LSP

As a now-well-established field within applied linguistics, LSP has its own research agenda and preferred teaching methodology. Empirical studies in

LSP draw upon research methods in related areas within applied linguistics, such as critical genre analysis, conversation analysis, register analysis, and corpus-based lexical analysis (Bowles 2012). Likewise, LSP pedagogy presents a hybridized approach, with many methods being adopted and adapted from communicative language teaching, task-based language teaching, and content-based instruction. José (2014) highlights the potential of LSP pedagogy to bridge the gap between the educational and professional spheres, as it transitions students from producing low-stakes work for private consumption—that is, the course instructor—to higher-stakes projects open to public scrutiny by much larger audiences—for example, potential employers and customers. In terms of both research and teaching, English has been the primary focus of LSP around the globe for several decades, given its status as a lingua franca in many domains, for example, information technology, business, and medicine. Nevertheless, other superlanguages, such as Chinese and Spanish, are gaining ground in the field of LSP (Hyland 2011).

Fryer (2012) cites Eastern Michigan University as one of the first institutions to undertake non-English LSP curriculum development in 1979, arguing that the number of undergraduate programs subsequently skyrocketed in the 1990s. Beltrán (2004, 1113–14) traces the increased demand for and consolidation of Spanish LSP, primarily business Spanish, back to the 1980s, and he notes "interest on the part of academic and professional institutions to harness this demand (universities, cabinets of commerce and industry, language academies, etc.) and the resulting start of publishing activity in the field."[3] Surveys of collegiate course offerings conducted over the past thirty years (Grosse 1985; Grosse and Voght 1990; Schulz 1979) have corroborated the solid footing that LSP has achieved in postsecondary curricula.

More recent survey research conducted by Long and Uzcinski (2012) has indicated that among non-English LSP programs, Spanish LSP programs were by far the most common. Long and Uscinski also found that 43 percent of all non-English business courses were ones in Spanish business. Our own analysis of nine prominent American universities' course catalogs indicated that the average number of Spanish for the professions courses increased from four to thirty between academic years 1970–71 and 2015–16, and courses in translation and interpretation increased from one to nine during the same period. Moreover, Peris and Cubillos (2015) noted that among the three most prominent North American publishing houses, there are approximately twenty-seven titles in Spanish for special purposes, with Cengage responsible for seventeen of the twenty-seven. Along with the numbers of Spanish LSP textbooks being published by large publishing houses, the American Association of Teachers of Spanish and Portuguese has published several volumes related to Spanish LSP (Doyle 1945; Fryer and Guntermann 1998; Walsh

1969), foremost among them being an edited, textbook-length volume titled *Spanish and Portuguese for Business and the Professions* (Fryer and Guntermann 1998). Finally, the inception of academic programs of study (majors, minors, tracks, etc.), federally funded research centers (Centers for International Business Education and Research), scholarly journals (*Revista Ibérica*), and international conferences (International Symposium on Languages for Specific Purposes) that focus on LSP all attest to the significant presence of LSP among postsecondary Spanish FL curricula.

José (2014, 18) argues that the field shows signs of "both maturity and infancy" in his discussion of current issues and conversations, in what he calls "language studies." In spite of the increased attention paid to LSP courses and curricula in contemporary postsecondary Spanish programs, there are indications that the outlook for LSP is not quite as bright as it may superficially appear and that significant obstacles still need to be overcome on many levels before Spanish LSP courses are coherently and effectively integrated into current curricular structures in American higher education. For example, Long and Uscinski (2012) found that the percentage of institutions offering LSP courses had not significantly changed over the nearly thirty-year period between Grosse's 1985 survey and their own published in a special issue of the *Modern Language Journal* in 2012. Furthermore, Abbott (personal communication) points out that what appears to be a surge in LSP textbook publishing due to increased Spanish LSP enrollments in universities may more accurately reflect aggressive marketing campaigns aimed at recouping costs.

The next section systematically addresses issues that apply directly, and at times uniquely, to collegiate Spanish programs as they seek to successfully integrate LSP courses into their curricula. The analyses of the difficulties outlined in the literature are complemented by our own experiences with Spanish for specific purposes at our respective institutions and from the results of survey research targeting the issues that contemporary Spanish programs face with regard to Spanish for specific purposes. To conclude the chapter, we take stock of the implications of our analyses regarding future opportunities and challenges that courses and programs on Spanish for specific purposes present for Spanish language programs in the twenty-first century.

## CHALLENGES FOR SPANISH FOR SPECIFIC PURPOSES

Scholars raise similar challenges for LSP in slightly different ways throughout the literature, some of which seem to apply to all second-language and foreign language contexts, some solely to English as a second language, and others to Spanish as a nonmajority language—the focus of this book. In this section, we examine potential difficulties for LSP at the postsecondary level in general, while highlighting key differences between Spanish LSP courses in the United States and other languages and contexts. The challenges that postsecondary Spanish language educators may face have been organized into three general categories, which are discussed in turn: (1) Spanish LSP students, their profile, and their needs; (2) Spanish LSP curricula; and (3) instructional staff and institutional culture. As we have done throughout the book thus far, we have interwoven our own experiences with the issues raised here in order to provide background for and concrete examples of the challenges we cite.

### The Spanish LSP Student Profile

The bedrock of curricular innovation in any foreign language program or department is, or should be, a thorough and accurate needs analysis. This is especially true of Spanish LSP at the undergraduate level in the Anglo-American academy, for several reasons. First, although surely many Spanish LSP students in Anglo-American institutions are sufficiently motivated—particularly those embedded in highly specialized and structured programs, such as the School of Foreign Service Program at Georgetown University described by Martinez and Sanz (2008)—some may lack motivation or struggle to relate their learning to future employment opportunities. It would come as no surprise if the average English for specific purposes (ESP) student enrolled in an English-medium intensive language institute, or even matriculated students in credit-bearing courses, felt much more urgency to master the course material than the average Spanish LSP student enrolled in a three-year business Spanish course as an elective toward his or her general Spanish major. For the ESP student embedded in an English dominant society, mastery of the course content is fundamental for employment, while some Spanish LSP students may view the course(s) as an additional line on the transcript or résumé aimed at impressing future employers or graduate school admissions officers.

As Lafford, Abbott, and Lear (2014) point out, undergraduate students are often unsure of the specific profession they will pursue after finishing their college degrees, or are unable to anticipate professional opportunities that may arise midcareer, or may simply be forced by circumstances out of their control to change careers multiple times over their lifetime. As such, students who are not sure of their needs or of how Spanish LSP might fit into their larger academic and professional goals may struggle to muster the motivation necessary to learn about liabilities, risk management, or supply chains in Spanish. If a Spanish LSP course simultaneously fulfills an elective for the general Spanish major and at the same time a core requirement for an interdisciplinary double major in international studies and economics, student motivations, proficiency, and background knowledge can vary tremendously.

The more specific the content focus of the Spanish LSP course, the more homogeneous one would expect students' motivations and professional aspirations to be. Nevertheless, greater specificity comes at a cost, for the pool of students will inevitably shrink, leading to reduced enrollments—a cardinal sin in an era of revenue-generating budget models. Conversely, as the needs and abilities of students in the same course or of those who pursue the same program of study become more diverse, it becomes more difficult to appropriately cater instruction.

What compounds the situation even further is the textbook-driven nature of many Spanish programs and how a textbook-driven curriculum may appear to obviate the need for detailed needs analyses. Although Hyland (2011, 204) calls needs assessment in LSP "foundational" and a "continuous process," in many cases it appears to have been relegated to textbook companies. The applied linguist Bill VanPatten (2015, 10) bemoans the overuse of textbooks in Spanish language teaching more generally and argues that, despite competition, "language textbooks look amazingly alike, with only superficial differences." To maximize their profitability, textbooks must assume a certain degree of homogeneity to be marketable to the widest audience possible. The perennial issue of finding the appropriate degree of authenticity and specificity in LSP (Arnó-Macià 2012) that matches local students' needs is particularly pronounced in Spanish LSP courses, which may attract a wide variety of students enrolled in the course to fulfill a multiplicity of requirements.

In theory, an effective needs analysis for Spanish LSP would achieve the maximum degree of alignment between course content (i.e., linguistic, cultural, and disciplinary) and students' future use of it in work-related contexts, or what Lafford (2012, 3) has called "potential applicability." An example of misalignment occurs in undergraduate programs that use business Spanish textbooks that focus on terminology and concepts geared toward graduate students seeking managerial degrees (e.g., MBA, MPA), who will most likely be responsible for weighty administrative matters such as supply chains, risk management, and insurance liability in international contexts. In contrast, the majority of students in undergraduate courses will most likely be called upon to use their Spanish domestically to interface with lower-middle-class to working-class Spanish speakers in customer service or sales encounters. The Hispanic and Spanish-speaking market is growing tremendously in the United States, according to Nataly Kelly, in her 2014 *Harvard Business Review* article "Will Spanish Help You Reach the US Hispanic Market? It Depends." Kelly notes that by 2050, Hispanics could make up 30 percent of the US population, and she outlines concrete strategies for marketing online to Hispanics. She cites Humphries (2012), who projected that Hispanics' purchasing power would reach $1.5 trillion by 2015.

The number of Hispanics in the United States is not only increasing precipitously among the general population but also within elementary, secondary, and postsecondary classrooms. As the number of heritage language learners has risen, so too has the number of educational programs designed to address these students' unique sociolinguistic profile in the Spanish classroom. Heritage learners bring to the Spanish classroom a set of characteristics that differ markedly from traditional students of Spanish as a foreign language, for linguistic, cognitive, cultural, and social reasons. Even within the heritage language learner population, there is a wide variety of proficiency levels in Spanish, and the strength of learners' connections to Hispanic cultures also varies.

Nevertheless, the Spanish LSP classroom has the potential to maximize heritage language learners' linguistic, cultural, and social capital. Lear's (2012, 164) argument that community service learning (CSL) "provides unique opportunities for heritage learners" and allows them to "bring their strengths to bear in CSL language courses" can easily be applied to Spanish LSP. Spanish LSP courses—such as business, medical, and legal Spanish, along with translation—quite naturally lead to interaction with native speakers of students' heritage language and culture outside the classroom. However, the incorporation of heritage language learners into Spanish LSP classrooms—and particularly community, site-based projects—must be done carefully, taking into account heritage learners' cultural, social, and linguistic profiles, so as to maximize each student's learning potential and his or her contribution to the community.

Although the number and purchasing power of Hispanic and Spanish-speaking consumers is growing in the United States, what is much less clear is the extent to which Spanish is needed among upper-level management and to what degree business professionals interface with Spanish-dominant or monolingual Spanish speakers in the domestic, Anglo-American context. What business Spanish students need from a linguistic standpoint seems to be more closely tied to retail sales and customer service than human resources, insurance, supply chains, or banking. In fact, it may be that for many students, even those who plan on using their Spanish abroad but especially those who plan on using Spanish domestically, the higher they aim as far as their professional and managerial aspirations are concerned, the less imperative it becomes that they master complex business concepts in Spanish. Orlando Kelm (2014, 45) discusses this issue at length by presenting several personal anecdotes that corroborate his conclusion "that English as a lingua franca has a stronghold among international professionals." As a result, he recommends that "the need, role, and scope of teaching other foreign languages for professional purposes" be reassessed.

One poignant example comes from the experience of an upper-level manager who was invited to speak to business Spanish students at the University of Kentucky. The students were impressed that the guest speaker had obtained some proficiency in Spanish after a religious mission, but when pressed about his experiences using Spanish extensively as a professional with international clients abroad, he admitted that most interactions abroad were conducted in English, after simple pleasantries had been exchanged in Spanish. He bemoaned the fact that in spite of his extensive travel in Spanish-speaking countries, his Spanish was not what it used to be because most business meetings and negotiations were conducted in English to accommodate the US-based transnational corporation. Unlike ESP contexts, in which a lack of proficiency in professional and academic discourses in English serves to limit access to powerful communities of practice (Hyland 2011), the situation is much less dire for English-dominant learners of Spanish LSP, especially in the domestic university context. As fluent speakers of the world's lingua franca, aspiring business students in Anglo-American institutions who do not take business Spanish are not affected nearly as much as limited proficient users of English who are unable to enroll in business English. Moreover, Kedia and Daniel (2003) found that employers ranked cross-cultural sensitivity as the most desirable international skill among their employees, while foreign language skills received the lowest rating on the survey. Although the smaller businesses in José's (2014) study did not seem as concerned about cultural awareness among employees, the larger companies expressed a clear preference for employees who demonstrate cultural sensitivity.

Similarly, students enrolled in a course on Hispanic bilingualism in the US at the same university who expressed interest in using their Spanish while helping Hispanic children with their homework at a local public library were disappointed to learn that almost all the children spoke English perfectly and preferred English over Spanish. During her visit as a guest speaker to the class, the branch librarian clarified that in most cases Spanish proficiency was not needed for the children's learning issues, but rather to help their parents successfully complete required forms and to navigate a completely unfamiliar educational system. In the educational and commercial contexts cited above, it was not that Spanish proficiency was not needed, but that it did not seem to reflect what was offered via a formal course.

Indeed, some students may ultimately find themselves in situations that require the highly technical and discipline-specific language covered in Spanish LSP courses, but these contexts also require high levels of overall proficiency and oral fluency, usually beyond what is generally attainable after a four-year degree program. For example, a Spanish major who has taken a course in medical Spanish may aspire to work as a hospital interpreter, only to quickly realize that her command of domain-specific vocabulary does not compensate for underdeveloped language proficiency, particularly aural comprehension deployed during emotionally charged encounters. She may find herself relegated to tasks that mostly require general Spanish terminology as she helps direct Spanish-speaking patients to the right office or wing of the hospital, or she may potentially use a limited amount of her medical Spanish during very basic and brief triage encounters. Somewhat ironically, Kelm (2014, 50) defends the development of LSP proficiency as a way "to be part of the nonbusiness side of business," citing greater understanding of current events, politics, religion, local culture, and other areas accessible via general L2 proficiency.

The Office of Postsecondary Education (2010) noted that employers wanting to expand their business abroad struggle to find multilingual applicants who have achieved advanced or superior levels of proficiency. Long and Uscinski (2012) found that though more lower-level courses are being offered than in the past, higher-level courses still make up a large majority of LSP course offerings. Unfortunately, research has demonstrated that a typical four-year sequence at the university level is insufficient for students to achieve high levels of proficiency (Magnan 1986; Norris and Pfeiffer 2003; Swender 2003). Lafford (2012) attributes the relatively low levels of proficiency among students entering LSP classes to weak or nearly nonexistent FL programs in the elementary schools. Similarly, Kelm (2014) laments the limited time made available to Anglo-American primary and secondary students to learn additional languages.

For Spanish LSP courses to be more relevant for university students and more successful in the twenty-first century, more meaningful and valid needs analyses must be done that extend beyond textbook selection and that do not assume, necessarily, that students will use their newly acquired skills abroad, or that they will form part of upper-level management, or that they will engage in emotionally charged, highly technical health care encounters as interpreters. In spite of some domain-specific needs analyses, such as that done by Lear (2005), Spanish language educators must do more to focus on the needs of *their* LSP students and to determine how their program's students are actually using Spanish on the job after graduating and how these uses correspond to the content and learning objectives of Spanish LSP courses. Ideally, as advocated by José (2014), students' needs would align well with their employees' perceived needs with regard to Spanish language use in the workplace. When asked why they incorporated LSP into their curricula, Long and Uscinski (2012) found that educational institutions ranked employers' needs the lowest. Although the institutional needs of universities and their efforts at self-preservation are always present, and at times are incredibly powerful, students' well-assessed needs should remain paramount so as to avoid the "tendency to accept institutional imperatives in defining needs too readily" (Hyland 2011, 215), especially when done under the auspices of addressing student demand, attracting new students, or grooming future donors (Lear 2012; Long and Ucsinski 2012).

### The Spanish LSP Curriculum

Regardless of language, LSP courses must find a balance between what Doyle (2012, 108) calls a "tripartite integrated curricular structure," in which topical knowledge interfaces with domain-specific linguistic skills, and cultural knowledge. Whether the task is to design a single Spanish LSP course or a series of courses, the question remains the same: To what extent should the course, or courses, focus on content and concepts unique to the specific subject matter, on lexicogrammatical and discursive features most common to the domain, or on the sociocultural mores that characterize each respective speech community? These features of an LSP course are only complicated by varying levels of language proficiency, background knowledge, and cultural awareness among students, which makes vertical articulation and the use of prerequisites so crucial to the success of any Spanish LSP course or program (Brown 2014).

The issue of balancing topical knowledge versus language ability in LSP is particularly salient when designing valid assessments because a defining characteristic of LSP is the ability to communicate about topics within a specific domain, and not just about general interest topics. Bachman and Palmer (1996) outline three possibilities for addressing the interaction between language ability and content knowledge on second-language assessments, asserting that inferences from test results may focus (1) solely on language ability among students whose background knowledge varies widely, (2) on language ability *and* background knowledge among a rather homogeneous group of students, and (3) on two separate constructs if test developers are unsure of students' background knowledge. Douglas (2000, 22) opines that the first scenario laid out by Bachman and Palmer is "not relevant to the LSP testing enterprise," and it may not be for a fine-tuned ESP program with clear, curricular-level structures, placement procedures, and enrollment guidelines in place. But for a Spanish undergraduate LSP course or program, it may very much represent reality. Hyland (2011, 212) proposes an "adjunct model," in which an LSP course is linked with a content course, a somewhat common approach used for international students associated with an intensive English institute, but a much more difficult proposition for Spanish language departments and programs, given the limited personnel and resources most programs can allocate to perceived overlaps in course coverage and staffing.

As mentioned above, one of the greatest challenges for Spanish LSP courses and LSP courses in any language is drastic diversity in language proficiency, background knowledge, or both. Course prerequisites may serve to reduce differences among students, but whether to impose language-based or content-based prerequisites can be difficult to determine. Clapham's (1996) study of the relationship between topical knowledge and general language proficiency indicated that until students reached a certain threshold of language ability—specifically, structural understanding—their topical knowledge could not be fully activated. Nevertheless, if minimum proficiency levels had been reached, topical knowledge had a stronger effect on student performance when presented with reading texts that were highly specific. For many years, the University of Kentucky had one business Spanish course, whose only prerequisite was the successful completion of the fifth-semester grammar and conversation courses. This course enrolled students from both extremes of the topical and language proficiency continuum. At one end of the continuum were the students pursuing a double major in business or economics and Spanish, who possessed strong Spanish skills and had extensive exposure to fundamental business concepts. At the other end of the spectrum sat the Spanish minors, who had just completed their 200-level, fifth-semester courses, who possessed somewhat weak Spanish skills, and who had no exposure to any business concepts at all. Due to this tremendous diversity, along with other factors discussed in the following section, Spanish LSP courses may present quite a challenge to instructors striving to find a balance between developing topical knowledge and language proficiency. As a result, the ability to maintain ecological validity for each respective LSP student and his or her needs in LSP testing is formidable (Lafford 2012).

The third element that should form part of LSP curricula and that has recently received greater attention in the LSP literature pertains to the cultural and discursive contextualization of specific LSP domains. Although the debate over how much language to teach and how much topical content to include will surely persist, Bowles (2012, 53) notes that current issues relate to the "greater contextualization of discourse, moving away from a concentration on lexicogrammatical features of text to include analysis of spoken and written discourses of specific domains as they occur in real time"—and, one might add, in real social and cultural groups. Professional communities of all types not only have their own technical jargon and unique discourse but also their own sociocultural values, mores, and power structures that make that discourse interpretable. Second-language learners must understand the cultural subtleties associated with each domain's discourse to become legitimate peripheral participants in a specific community of practice—using Lave and Wenger (1991) and Wenger's (1998) terminology. In Doyle's (2012) discussion of the cultural implications of business language studies, he cites a poignant observation made by Galloway (1987, 69) that to develop students' linguistic skills without sensitizing them to the surrounding cultural context is "to provide students with the illusion that they are communicating." Cross-cultural sensitivity weighs heavily on the minds of international companies looking to hire employees (Kedia and Daniel 2003), and more recent research (Language Flagship 2008) has indicated that companies desire employees with much greater language proficiency. However, many surveys of international companies' needs are quite general and do not specify the exact nature of the cross-cultural sensitivity needed or the linguistic competence required of employees at different levels who fulfill diverse functions. What sort of cultural and linguistic proficiency, for example, would an appliance salesperson or customer service representative need to interact with Spanish-speaking colleagues?

Another cultural component of LSP curricula that is particularly relevant for Spanish courses and programs relates to the larger sociopolitical realities, hierarchies, and power structures into which Anglo-American students will most likely deploy the knowledge and skills they acquire in LSP courses. Previously, we highlighted Hyland's (2011) observation that to *not* offer ESP courses to students of English as a second language would be to disempower and potentially disenfranchise them from the surrounding society, especially those working in English-majority societies. In the case of the Anglo-American student, the potential exists that added Spanish LSP knowledge and skills will unwittingly lead to the perpetuation of sociopolitical and socioeconomic inequities, both domestically and abroad. As native speakers of English from the wealthiest and largest capitalist economy in the world, Anglo-American students who add Spanish LSP knowledge to the social, cultural, and linguistic capital they already possess are perfectly situated to assume a position of power in future professional endeavors. Not all Spanish LSP students will ultimately possess this capital and wield this power, but they will surely be exposed to social injustice as they interact with repressed and marginalized Spanish-speaking populations on American soil and abroad.

This fact was made clear to one of the authors on two occasions: (1) during a study abroad trip to Ecuador with a service-learning focus, and (2) during the presentation of a local business executive to business Spanish students. As part of the study abroad program, the Anglo-American students were briefly trained in dental terminology so they could engage in free dental fairs for

underprivileged populations in Ecuador. After efforts to serve the Afro-Ec-
uadorean population in northern Ecuador were rebuffed by the province's
minister of health, presumably to avoid the appearance of needing help from
Americans, one student reacted strongly to the perceived injustice in her class
journal: "It just seems to be that people of color, especially of African descent,
seem to be so suppressed everywhere around the world. . . . It just made me
think what the real reason . . . behind not allowing free aid to those who
needed it?! It's ridiculous!"

The second experience illustrating the reality of socioeconomic inequities
that relate to Spanish LSP occurred when an executive from a transnational
business who had spent time in Guatemala was invited to speak to business
Spanish students at the University of Kentucky. His business specialized in
outsourcing the processing of credit card applications and insurance claims
to offshore, international locations. The executive explained to students how
he struggled to transform the workplace culture to align more closely with a
merit-oriented system and how this transformation required that some un-
derperforming workers be laid off. As a result of these personnel decisions
and other policy changes, he and his family were threatened with physical
violence through anonymous letters and workplace graffiti. He recounted to
the business Spanish students that in response to these threats, he convened a
meeting with all the workers and told them quite candidly that if the threats
persisted, the company would simply close the center and exit the country,
leaving all the workers unemployed. The tactic apparently worked because the
threats ceased and operations at the center improved. Although it is hard to
determine what would have been the best course of action for this American
executive in these circumstances, it is easy to note the tremendous power differential between the executive, the American company he represented, and
the Guatemalan workers.

In summary, it is inevitable that the students who choose to parlay the
skills and knowledge they acquire in a Spanish LSP course into a career will
confront, at some point, issues of social injustice and inequity. Students
may encounter these inequities in a remote village in northern Ecuador, at
an American-run factory in Guatemala, in a free health clinic for Spanish-
speakers in the US, or even within the walls of their local elementary school.
The forward-thinking Spanish educator must determine to what extent the
Spanish LSP curriculum should empower Anglo-American students with the
linguistic and content skills needed to interface with Spanish-speaking populations without informing them of larger social issues that professionals in
these fields often confront. In essence, should the socially responsible Spanish
LSP curriculum include greater emphasis on macro sociopolitical issues and
not just micro linguistic and content issues?

In a recent review article on the current state of Spanish in the professions, Lafford, Abbott, and Lear (2014, 176) note the ever-increasing number of diverse LSP courses cropping up in foreign language programs and make a somewhat provocative proposal: "a single foundational course on translingual and transcultural issues in professional contexts." In their view, the increase in more, and more specific, LSP courses presupposes a more static professional environment than most contemporary college graduates will face. They envision a course that broaches skills that nearly all college graduates should develop, from task-specific skills used while engaging in a telephone conversation or giving/taking instructions to broader skills such as teamwork, creativity, and respect for diversity. Not surprisingly, the skills that Lafford, Abbott, and Lear propose for a redesigned LSP course mirror those chosen by employers surveyed by José (2014). They further argue that key professional skills should be not be limited to a single LSP course and should be distributed throughout the curriculum, permeating all levels and topical areas. In line with the sort of curricular overhaul envisioned in the 2007 MLA report, Lafford and her colleagues champion a "paradigmatic restructuring" of the curriculum that would integrate "professionalism and interdisciplinarity throughout the language course sequences" (Lafford, Abbott, and Lear 2014, 183). Indeed, such efforts would constitute a true curricular overhaul and a rather radical departure from business as usual in many postsecondary Spanish programs.

Finally, LSP curricula for all languages must respond to a much larger, and somewhat threatening, question that can be stated simply: *Does it work?* In the case of ESP, Master (2005, 111) notes that "despite 30 years of calls for empirical research demonstrating the efficacy of ESP, not a single published study has appeared to this end." Lear (2012) also comments on the need for program evaluation in LSP. In concrete terms, do university students who enroll in Spanish LSP courses perform better in subsequent, real-life encounters that require mastery of domain-specific content, culture, and language; or would it be better to continue developing general proficiency without the added topical focus—a possibility tentatively supported by Clapham's (1996) research? Are students' needs with regard to their use of Spanish in the work environment sufficiently delimited to warrant the time and effort spent in Spanish LSP courses? In programs with only one or two Spanish LSP courses of a particular domain—for example, business or medical—that are loosely connected to an academic major or minor, these questions demand close scrutiny.

### The Instructional Staff and Institutional Culture

Within the field of foreign language teaching at the collegiate level, there is little debate that curricular change is necessary to maintain relevance in the academy, as the case of Spanish LSP clearly illustrates. Closely connected to curricular revision and essential to its success are the instructors who are tasked with implementing the changes in the classroom. The instructional staff members who constitute the foundation of any language program have a deep impact on and are affected by curricular changes, regardless of their academic and professional profile, and this is especially the case in Spanish LSP. Moreover, they influence and are influenced by institutional culture and the degree to which this culture values and prioritizes the goals and pedagogy that lie at the heart of Spanish LSP. In this section of the chapter, we look more closely at Spanish LSP postsecondary instructional staff members and their profile, along with worrisome trends with regard to institutional culture that plague many disciplines in the academy.

One of the foremost challenges Spanish language programs of all sizes have faced with regard to LSP has been the ability to hire qualified instructors from within their own ranks to teach courses with a nonhumanistic focus, such as Spanish for business professionals, or medical Spanish, or Spanish for social workers. In their survey research, Long and Uscinski (2012) report that most LSP courses are taught in language departments rather than discipline-specific departments. Nevertheless, 81 percent of language departments noted that they had non-LSP faculty teaching LSP courses. Many Spanish departments, their faculty, and their curricula have been slow to evolve from a traditional, humanities-centered program with literature, culture, and linguistics at the core to a dynamic, interdisciplinary program that is much more expansive and eclectic in its offerings and pedagogies. It is the latter configuration that society seems to be demanding of language programs, and the former that needs updating. In their review of LSP over twenty years ago, Grosse and Vaught (1991) highlighted the widely varying levels of training among LSP instructors in the field of the LSP course. Ene (2012) observed that in many cases, current LSP practitioners and researchers who received their degrees in traditional language and literature departments got their start as LSP instructors with no experience in the domain area—for example, business, health care, and engineering.

The expertise and training in the content domain or in LSP pedagogy that many Spanish LSP instructors bring with them to their first day of class, in most cases, is minimal or nonexistent. The lingering question in LSP pedagogy and language programs is whether it is more effective to have a content specialist or a language specialist at the front of the classroom, assuming that both are available. Master (2005) discusses this issue in some detail, and cites opposing arguments made by Taylor (1994) and Troike (1994), both of whom appear to be language specialists. Although Taylor feels comfortable claiming that English language teaching specialists with the right attitude and enough interest are better equipped to help students develop LSP proficiency than content experts, Troike does not. He argues that it is far easier to train a content specialist in the basics of language pedagogy than the reverse—that is, to train language educators in the technical content of the LSP domain. Even when a course is team taught, Basturkmen (2012, 66) points out that the language instructor is often considered the "junior partner."

The preceding discussion of instructor expertise and training seems to make several subtle assumptions: (1) that Spanish instructors asked to teach LSP courses are interested in teaching them, (2) that Spanish instructors are willing to remediate any deficiencies in technical content knowledge, and (3) that subject specialists might be available and willing to co-teach or consult a Spanish LSP course—a contingency more likely in the ESP than the Spanish LSP context, given greater access to subject specialists proficient in English. Experience has proven time and again that when a disconnect occurs between an instructor's training and the courses he or she is asked to teach, the results are less than favorable. VanPatten (2015) has argued this point quite convincingly with regard to the impact that the overall lack of language specialists in language departments has on program effectiveness. His review of departmental websites from French and Spanish programs at research, doctoral-granting institutions in the Midwest, in the East, and on the West Coast revealed that among full-time, tenured, and tenure-line faculty members, scholars trained in literary and cultural studies were grossly overrepresented. The lowest proportion of literary and cultural studies scholars was slightly more than three-fourths (76 percent), in the case of Spanish departments in the Midwest, though the highest proportion was found for French scholars in the East, who made up 96 percent of language professors. The highest rate for scholars of literature and culture in Spanish programs was found among the West Coast schools, with 90 percent. When all the programs and geographic areas were averaged together, nearly 80 percent of all tenured/tenure-line scholars in French and Spanish specialized in literary and cultural studies. Experience has shown that the teaching pool within a language department from which to select even semiqualified instructors for Spanish LSP courses has been quite small, and that some within this pool demonstrate great resistance to teaching Spanish LSP courses, such as business Spanish.

The hesitancy that many non-LSP instructors display when asked to teach an LSP course or to be trained to teach such courses may reflect a much larger issue in contemporary higher education, that is, the creation of disciplinary "silo walls" (Lafford, Abbott, and Lear 2014, 174). In fact, Lafford and her colleagues call it the "biggest challenge for . . . LSP" (p. 180), while Fryer (2012, 134) points out the "willfully obstructionist" stance that some faculty have taken toward the integration of LSP into the curriculum and toward overall curricular reform. The resistance by many faculty to welcome Spanish LSP into the standard curriculum may also manifest itself negatively in promotion and tenure cases for candidates who specialize in LSP research and teaching. The perception among some scholars of Spanish literature, culture, and linguistics that their colleagues in Spanish LSP are vocationally oriented and intellectually soft with a limited research agenda may introduce professional bias and undermine prestige. The clearest indicator of this trend is the overwhelming number of LSP practitioners who are contract faculty members without permanent status within the department—for example, part-time instructors, adjunct faculty, and graduate student instructors (Lafford, Abbott, and Lear 2014). Although it is difficult to pinpoint whether such resistance by core tenured faculty to LSP is simply a tactic of self-preservation and professional survival or truly a manifestation of deep disciplinary hubris and intellectual elitism, it presents a formidable stumbling block to the progress of Spanish LSP programs, their instructors, and their instructors' careers. Curriculum designers thus must confront this uncomfortable question: Are faculty members' professional aspirations and intellectual inclinations driving postsecondary Spanish curricula or learners' educational and professional needs?

In an explicit recognition of this uphill battle to garner intellectual and institutional respect for business LSP, Doyle (2012, 105) has argued quite compellingly for the need for "a more rigorous toponymic identity by which to identify itself as a theory-based field of scholarship." As is the case in many fields, proper nomenclature and theoretical discourse represent the first steps toward disciplinary respect from outsiders. As such, he proposes that the official name of business LSP be "Business Language Studies." As Doyle (2010, 2013, 2014) delineates the linguistic and cultural complexities of the field of business language studies and Spanish LSP more broadly, it becomes apparent that the quest for prestige and validation for the LSP profession and LSP professionals transcends simple semantics or a turn of phrase, and must be rooted in substantive and rigorous inquiry into the interface between language, culture, and content.

## SPANISH POSTSECONDARY PROGRAM AND CURRICULUM SURVEY RESULTS

The "Spanish for Specific Purposes" section of our survey had six questions, with the option to manually write in a seventh. These items included the following issues, which are presented below in order from the one of most concern to the least, with mean scores at the end of each item, on a scale of 1 (very much a concern) to 5 (not a concern at all). We also include the overall rank of the item's mean across all fifty-five survey items with regard to the level of perceived concern. The percentage of respondents who chose the sixth response option, "not applicable to my program," appears last among the information at the end of each item:

- Finding appropriate balance between language, topical, and cultural content: 2.43 / 10th / 4 percent;
- Ensuring coherent integration of courses into academic program of study (e.g., major, minor): 2.57 / 17th / 6.2 percent;
- Availability of appropriate classroom materials (e.g., textbook, selected readings): 2.59 / 19th / 3.8 percent;
- Adapting instruction to address the future needs of individual Spanish for specific purposes students (e.g., business Spanish, medical Spanish, translation): 2.63 / 24th / 5.6 percent;
- Finding qualified instructors for each topical area (e.g., business Spanish, medical Spanish, legal Spanish): 2.88 / 37th / 7.1 percent; and
- Integrating external instructors into the academic life of the department: 3.23 / 50th / 10.3 percent.

Although the differences between the mean values for items related to Spanish for specific purposes are not large, all but one of the items scored below a 3, or *neutral*. That is to say that, on average, for approximately seven hundred instructors, the level of concern for five of the six issues lay somewhere between *somewhat of a concern* and *neutral*. The issue of most concern points to the difficulty of knowing how much to focus on language, disciplinary content, or cultural content, while the two items that generated the least amount of concern in this category have to do with personnel issues. Though the survey is clearly quite general and does not allow for detailed analyses of why the survey participants responded as they did, it does help to compare the tendencies in how subgroups ranked different categories' items. For example, when participants' responses to the six Spanish LSP questions were analyzed by academic rank (tenured / tenure track and nontenure track) the overall mean from Spanish LSP varied little, with a difference of 0.02 on a 5-point scale (2.74 = tenured; nontenured = 2.72). However, those trained in literary and cultural studies (2.55) appeared a bit more concerned about issues related to Spanish LSP as compared with their counterparts in linguistics and applied linguistics (2.93), where the lower the value indicates more concern.

Somewhat ironically, the most telling result of this national survey that reflects directly on the field of Spanish LSP came from an item not included in the Spanish LSP category. Under the *other* category, we asked that respondents indicate how much of a concern it was for their program to help "students value learning Spanish for reasons other than employment." Of the fifty-five items for which mean values were calculated and for which the lower the score the greater the concern, this item had the lowest mean response and was the item of most concern. Once again, the survey was not designed to delve into the rationale behind each concern or what served as the basis for the concern for each individual; it simply asked participants for their perceptions "of the most pressing programmatic and curricular issues in Spanish education at your institution overall." Evidently, this sample of approximately seven hundred postsecondary Spanish educators consider it somewhat worrisome that students might only want to learn Spanish to further their employment prospects and not for other reasons. Further research is needed to more clearly elucidate what lies at the root of this concern, and what has brought it to the fore for these instructors.

## CONCLUSION

Targeted, discipline-specific learning of Spanish in the United States postsecondary context seems to make intuitive sense: maximize students' time by focusing on the linguistic structures and lexical items that provide access to the topical content. However, as this chapter has shown, intuition and logic may not be enough to seamlessly incorporate Spanish LSP into collegiate Spanish programs and curricula. The initial surge of Spanish LSP courses and programs into traditional curricular structures and strictures may have subsided due to incoherent integration into existing curricula and programs of study, unclear connections between course content and subsequent student use of Spanish LSP, and significant pushback from the professoriate, or all three. Several scholars have noted that Spanish LSP lends itself particularly well to service learning (Lafford, Abbott, and Lear 2014; Lear 2012; Sánchez-López 2014, 163), with Sánchez López calling it "worrisome" that service learning might not be included in programs on Spanish for specific purposes. Spanish LSP course instructors should take advantage of the widespread use of Spanish and the presence of Spanish-dominant speakers outside the language classroom by integrating greater service-learning opportunities into their course syllabus. Nevertheless, the instructors who responded to our survey appear to be anxious that students not only engage with Spanish for strictly utilitarian or professional motives but also for something more intellectually oriented. This apparent ambivalence toward the place of Spanish LSP among core faculty members may reflect the narrow and uninformed perspective that many Spanish instructors of all backgrounds have on the field of Spanish LSP. To the extent possible, it may be time to make the necessary adjustments in Spanish departments and programs to round off the edges of the Spanish LSP square peg (Lafford, Abbott, and Lear 2014) to fit the round hole of traditional Spanish curricula or to cut out edges in the round hole of these curricula to fit the square peg of Spanish LSP.

## REFLECTION QUESTIONS

1. What characteristics of community service learning make it such a good fit for LSP courses? Are there other pedagogic techniques that might lend themselves better to an LSP course than a traditional language course? Why, and how so?

2. In your opinion, how important are the economic and professional benefits of foreign language study as compared with cognitive and interpersonal benefits? What about Spanish language majors and minors at your institution? How does this compare with other foreign language majors, such as French, German, and Chinese?

3. Early in the chapter, we stated that LSP courses represented "the embodiment of the conflicted nature of contemporary collegiate FL curricula." Explain the nature of this conflict and to what extent it has manifested itself in your program.

4. Which LSP courses are offered at your institution, and which ones do you feel should be added, if any? Does your institution offer a specific certificate or emphasis in any area of Spanish LSP, and if not, should it?

5. How would you characterize the linguistic and cultural needs of Spanish LSP students at your institution who enroll in business Spanish, medical Spanish, translation, and the like? How do the majority of students use the knowledge acquired in those classes outside class or after graduation?

6. Taylor (1994) and Troike (1994) offer somewhat opposing perspectives on the effectiveness of a content specialist as an LSP instructor as compared with a language specialist. Which type of instructor would be more effective in your mind, a content specialist with superficial language training or a language specialist with only basic knowledge of the content area?

7. In the chapter, we cited instances in which an imbalance of power seemed to be implied in LSP teaching and learning, but differentially for students of English for specific purposes and of Spanish LSP. Explain how the status of English as a lingua franca and the pervasiveness of US culture internationally can serve to empower Spanish LSP students.

8. What can be done to imbue LSP courses, instructors, and research with greater intellectual and disciplinary prestige among professors of literature, culture, and linguistics, or even applied linguistics? How will this affect Spanish programs, their curricula, and their programs overall?

9. Our survey research does not identify why the respondents chose the responses they did. For example, the individual respondent may not have any problem with LSP courses but may perceive that his or her colleagues do, or the administration. As you look over the results from our survey, discuss potential reasons why participants might have responded the way they did.

## PEDAGOGICAL ACTIVITIES

1. For an undergraduate business Spanish course, assign students to design and administer a short survey to businesses, nonprofits, or organizations from different sectors of the local economy to discover (1) how often Spanish is used by their employees or volunteers to conduct business, and (2) the nature of the Spanish that is used (e.g., conversational Spanish, formal written Spanish). Compare the responses from at least three different organizations, and then analyze how these compare with at least one business Spanish textbook. In what ways do the survey results correspond to the language and language skills covered in the textbook?

2. For a medical Spanish or translation course, have students contact a local hospital or health clinic and inquire about the hiring process for paid and volunteer medical interpreters and the minimum qualifications required (e.g., required certifications, proficiency minimums). Also inquire about the nature of the tasks they are asked to complete (e.g., assisting with intake forms, interpreting for receptionists, nurses, and physicians). Finally, find out the particulars of the position, such as hours per week, benefits, whether it is part time or full time, and so on.

3. For a translation course, ask students to collect three or four sample tests from large organizations like the American Translator's Association or the Federal Court Interpreter's Program or from smaller regional organizations and translation houses. After students have collected the tests, ask them to analyze the nature of the language tested as well as the characteristics of the test tasks. Have them reflect on what level of overall proficiency would be needed to complete the various tasks for each assessment instrument.

## NOTES

1. We use "Spanish LSP" deliberately, rather than "Spanish SP" or "SPP," given the familiarity with and widespread use of the acronym "LSP" in the literature, and to clearly differentiate it from the commonly used acronym "ESP," for English for specific purposes.

2. Original Spanish: "muy diferente al existente en épocas anteriores" (Puch 2004, 1149).

3. Original Spanish: "un interés por parte de las instituciones académicas y profesionales por canalizar esta demanda (universidades, Cámaras de Comercio e Industria, academias de idiomas, etc.) y el consiguiente inicio de la actividad editorial en este campo" (Beltrán 2004, 1113–14).

## REFERENCES

Arnó-Macià, Elisabet. 2012. "The Role of Technology in Teaching Languages for Specific Purposes Courses." *Modern Language Journal* 96 (Focus Issue): 89–104.

Bachman, Lyle F., and Adrian S. Palmer. 1996. *Language Testing in Practice*. Oxford: Oxford University Press.

Basturkmen, Helen. 2012. "Languages for Specific Purposes Curriculum Creation and Implementation in Australia and Europe." *Modern Language Journal* 96 (Focus Issue): 59–70.

Beltrán, Blanca A. 2004. "La Enseñanza del Español con Fines Profesionales." In *Vademécum para la Formación de Profesores: Enseñar Español como Segunda Lengua (L2) / Lengua Extranjera (LE)*, edited by Jesús S. Lobato and Isabel S. Gargallo. Madrid: Sociedad General Española de Librería.

Bok, Derek. 2006. *Our Underachieving Colleges: A Candid Look at How Much Students Learn and Why They Should Be Learning More*. Princeton, NJ: Princeton University Press.

Bowles, Hugo. 2012. "Analyzing Languages for Specific Purposes Discourse." *Modern Language Journal* 96 (Focus Issue): 43–58.

Brown, Alan V. 2014. "Foreign Language Course Grades as Prerequisites and Programmatic Gatekeepers." In *AAUSC 2014 Volume: Innovation and Accountability in Language Program Evaluation*, edited by John Norris and Nicole Mills. Boston: Cengage.Clapham, Caroline. 1996. *The Development of IELTS: A Study of the Effect of Background Knowledge on Reading Comprehension*. Cambridge: Cambridge University Press.

Douglas, Dan. 2000. *Assessing Languages for Specific Purposes*. Cambridge: Cambridge University Press.

Doyle, Henry G., ed. 1945. *Handbook on the Teaching of Spanish and Portuguese, with Special Reference to Latin America*. Boston: D. C. Heath.

Doyle, Michael S. 2010. "A Responsive, Integrative Spanish Curriculum at UNC Charlotte." *Hispania* 93, no. 1: 80–84.

———. 2012. "Business Language Studies in the United States: On Nomenclature, Context, Theory, and Method." *Modern Language Journal* 96: 105–21.

———. 2013. "Continuing Theoretical Cartography in the LSP Era." In *Scholarship and Teaching on Languages for Specific Purposes*, edited by Lourdes Sánchez-López. Birmingham, AL: UAB Digital Collections.

———. 2014. "Guest Editor Remarks: Adding Thickness and Granularity to SSP." *Cuaderns de ALDEEU* 28 (número especial): 8–14.

Ene, Estela. 2012. "Language for Specific Purposes in Eastern Europe." In *The Encyclopedia of Applied Linguistics*, vol. 5, edited by Carol Chapelle. Malden, MA: John Wiley & Sons.

Fryer, T. Bruce. 2012. "Languages for Specific Purposes Business Curriculum Creation and Implementation in the United States." *Modern Language Journal* 96 (Focus Issue): 122–39.

Fryer, T. Bruce, and C. Gail Guntermann. 1998. *Spanish and Portuguese for Business and the Professions*. Lincolnwood, IL: National Textbook Company.

Galloway, Vicki. 1987. "From Defining to Developing Proficiency: A Look at the Decisions." In *Defining and Developing Proficiency: Guidelines, Implementation, and Concepts*, edited by H. Byrnes and M. Canale. Lincolnwood, IL: National Textbook Company.

Grosse, Christine U. 1985. "A Survey of Foreign Languages for Business and the Professions at US Colleges and Universities." *Modern Language Journal* 69: 221–26.

Grosse, Christine U., and Geoffrey M. Voght. 1990. "Foreign Language for Business and the Professions at US Colleges and Universities." *Modern Language Journal* 74: 36–47.

———. 1991. "The Evolution of Languages for Specific Purposes in the United States." *Modern Language Journal* 75: 181–95.

Halliday, Michael A. K. 1961. "Categories of the Theory of Grammar." *Word* 17, no. 3: 241–92.

Halliday, Michael A. K., Peter Strevens, and Angus McIntosh. 1964. *The Linguistic Sciences and Language Teaching*. London: Longman.

Humphries, Jeffrey. 2012. *The Multi-Cultural Economy: 2012*. Athens: Selig Center for Economic Growth, Terry College of Business, University of Georgia.

Hyland, Ken. 2011. "Specific Purpose Programs." In *The Handbook of Language Teaching*, edited by Michael H. Long and Catherine J. Doughty. New York: Wiley-Blackwell.

Hymes, Dell H. 1972. "On Communicative Competence." In *Sociolinguistics: Selected Readings*, edited by J. B. Pride and J. Holmes. Harmondsworth, UK: Penguin.

José, Alán. 2014. "Language Studies: Implicit Associations and Cognitive Dissonances in How the Field Is Described, Perceived, and Expected to Perform." *Cuadernos de ALDEEU* 28: 15–38. http://aldeeu.org/cuadernos/index.php/CALDEEEU/issue/view Issue/50/62.

Kedia, Ben L., and Shirley J. Daniel. 2003. *US Business Needs for Employees with International Expertise*. Paper presented at the Needs for Global Challenges Conference, Duke University, Durham, NC.

Kelly, Nataly. 2014. "Will Spanish Help You Reach the US Hispanic Market? It Depends." *Harvard Business Review*, February. https://hbr.org/2014/02/will-spanish-help-you-reach -the-u-s-hispanic-market-it-depends/.

Kelm, Orlando R. 2014. "The Use of English as a Lingua Franca: Where Does Foreign Language Education Fit?" *Cuadernos de ALDEEU* 28: 39–55. http://aldeeu.org/cuadernos /index.php/CALDEEEU/issue/viewIssue/50/62.

Kramsch, Claire. 1989. "New Directions in the Study of Foreign Languages." *ADFL Bulletin* 21, no. 1: 4–11.

Lafford, Barbara A. 2012. "Languages for Specific Purposes in the United States in a Global Context: Commentary on Grosse and Voght (1991) Revisited." *Modern Language Journal* 96 (Focus Issue): 1–27.

Lafford, Barbara A., Ann Abbott, and Darcy Lear. 2014. "Spanish in the Professions and in the Community in the US." *Journal of Spanish Language Teaching* 1, no. 2: 171–86.

Language Flagship. 2008. "What Business Wants: Language Needs in the 21st Century." www.thelanguageflagship.org/media/docs/reports/what_business_wants_report_final _7_09.pdf.

Lave, Jean, and Etienne Wenger. 1991. *Situated Learning: Legitimate Peripheral Participation*. Cambridge: Cambridge University Press.

Lear, Darcy. 2005. "Spanish for Working Medical Professional: Linguistic Needs." *Foreign Language Annals* 38, no. 2: 223–35.

———. 2012. "Languages for Specific Purposes Curriculum Creation and Implementation in Service to the Community in the United States." *Modern Language Journal* 96 (Focus Issue): 158–72.

Long, Mary K., and Izabela Uscinski. 2012. "Evolution of Languages for Specific Purposes Programs in the United States: 1990–2011." *Modern Language Journal* 96 (Focus Issue): 173–89.

Magnan, Sally S. 1986. "Assessing Speaking Proficiency in the Undergraduate Curriculum: Data from French." *Foreign Language Annals* 19, no. 5: 429–38.

Martinez, Ana M., and Cristina Sanz. 2008. "Instructors' and Administrators' Beliefs within a Spanish LSP Program." In *AAUSC 2007, From Thought to Action: Exploring Beliefs and Outcomes in the Foreign Language Program*, edited by H. Jay Siskin. Boston: Thomson Heinle.

Master, Peter. 2005. "Research in English for Specific Purposes." In *Handbook of Research in Second Language Teaching and Learning*, edited by Eli Hinkel. Mahwah, NJ: Lawrence Erlbaum Associates.

Norris, John M., and Peter C. Pfeiffer. 2003. "Exploring the Use and Usefulness of ACTFL Oral Proficiency Ratings and Standards in College Foreign Language Departments." *Foreign Language Annals* 36: 572–81.

Office of Postsecondary Education. 2010. "International Education Programs Service: Alternative Modes of Instruction." www2.ed.gov/about/offices/list/ope/iegps/language-instruction.html.

Peris, Ernesto M., and Jorge H. Cubillos. 2015. "Publishing." In *The Routledge Handbook of Hispanic Applied Linguistics*, edited by Manel Lacorte. New York: Routledge.

Puch, José M. 2004. "La Enseñanza del Español Comercio." In *Vademécum para la Formación de Profesores: Enseñar Español como Segunda Lengua (L2) / Lengua Extranjera (LE)*, edited by Jesús S. Lobato and Isabel S. Gargallo. Madrid: Sociedad General Española de Librería.

Sánchez-López, Lourdes. 2014. "An Analysis of the Integration of Service Learning in Undergraduate Spanish for Specific Purposes Programs in Higher Education in the United States." *Cuadernos de ALDEEU* 28, no. 1: 155–70.

Schulz, Renate. 1979. *Options for Undergraduate Foreign Language Programs. Four-Year and Two-Year Colleges*. New York: MLA.

Sullivan, Barry. 2012. "Assessment Issues in Languages for Specific Purposes." *Modern Language Journal* 96 (Focus Issue): 71–88.

Swender, Elvira. 2003. "Oral Proficiency Testing in the Real World: Answers to Frequently Asked Questions." *Foreign Language Annals* 36: 520–26.

Taylor, M. 1994. "How Much Content Does the ESP Instructor Need to Know?" *TESOL Matters* 4 (February–March): 14.

Troike, Rudolph. 1994. "The Case for Subject-Matter Training in ESP." *TESOL Matters* 3, no. 6: 7.

VanPatten, Bill. 2015. "Where Are the Experts?" *Hispania* 98, no. 1: 2–13.

Walsh, Donald D., ed. 1969. *A Handbook for Teachers of Spanish and Portuguese*. Lexington, MA: D. C. Heath.

Wenger, Etienne. 1998. *Communities of Practice*. Cambridge: Cambridge University Press.

# 6

# PLACEMENT, OUTCOME, AND ARTICULATION ISSUES IN SPANISH CURRICULAR ASSESSMENT

> Absent a systematic approach to assessment that reflects curricular artic-
> ulation, FL [foreign language] studies programs tend to be hard-pressed
> to understand or interpret student learning in relation to fully conceived
> programs of study or to utilize assessment information for improving
> curriculum and instruction.
>
> —Heidi Byrnes, Hiram Maxim, and John Norris,
> "Realizing Advanced FL Writing Development," 2010

More than ten years ago, Norris (2006) and other researchers (Bernhardt 2006; Chase 2006; Kiely 2006; Morris 2006; Sullivan 2006; Wright 2006) sounded the clarion call for greater attention to the assessment of collegiate foreign language programs across the United States, encouraging foreign language educators to improve their assessment literacy and practices. The importance of accountability was highlighted, as was the prediction that without sound assessment practices at the individual course and program levels, foreign language education would continue to lose ground in the academy. *Accountability* has generally been understood to mean the extent to which university foreign language programs can empirically demonstrate improvements in targeted learning outcomes as a result of instruction.

Though classroom-level assessment is addressed to some extent in this chapter, our focus is on the programmatic concerns faced by many Spanish language programs. We trace the journey of university Spanish students from placement through their coursework and, finally, on to completion and graduation. As we chart this journey from beginning to end, we point out potential pitfalls and how they may be turned into opportunities. Increasingly, in the Spanish language context, this journey is begun by linguistically and culturally diverse students with equally diverse communicative abilities, motivations, and professional trajectories. Logistical constraints due to many Spanish programs' sheer size must also be addressed. As we have done elsewhere, we cite real and relevant examples from our own experiences as Spanish postsecondary educators.

## PLACEMENT PROCEDURES AND TESTING

American students enter a collegiate Spanish program from a variety of contexts and represent a host of proficiency levels with diverse linguistic, social, and cultural backgrounds. Some come with no or negligible communicative skills and cultural awareness after exposure to one year of subpar teaching at the high school level, while others arrive less than five months removed from high-achieving K–12 immersion programs with college-level credits already granted. Still others come with native-like conversational ability, having spoken nothing but Spanish at home since birth; yet their mastery of formal academic writing leaves much to be desired.

Upon arrival in a Spanish program, these diverse students, regardless of background, may ask the simple question "Where do I start?"—sometimes followed by "Why there?" Though apparently simple questions, myriad considerations lurk beneath that often boil down to a placement test. In most cases, placement tests discriminate among beginning to low-intermediate levels of ability rather well but are less effective at higher levels, given the difficulty of testing productive skills accurately, validly, and efficiently. More labor-intensive and time-consuming procedures are generally reserved for high intermediate, advanced, and heritage students—an ever-increasing percentage of incoming Spanish students—but these assessment procedures may also be a bit reductive. Few placement procedures transcend the language-focused approach aimed at separating those who need more grammar or writing at the fifth-semester level (high intermediate) and those who are ready for upper-level literature, linguistics, and culture courses. For reasons of expediency and efficiency, placement procedures are often limited to testing language ability at a very general level, thus falling short of achieving any diagnostic value for students with regard to the particulars of the curriculum or its courses and masking significant differences between upper-level students.[1]

For many years, one of the most commonly used placement instruments in the United States for Spanish, and other frequently taught languages, was an examination created at Brigham Young University and ultimately placed on the internet—the WebCAPE, or Web-Based Computer Adaptive Placement Exam, which includes multiple-choice items calibrated for difficulty and is incredibly efficient. In spite of its weaknesses, the widespread use of this exam is testament to the great need among language programs for accurate, efficient, and cost-effective placement tests.

As Green (2012, 168) observed, for some language learning contexts, placement testing is low-stakes and incorrect placements are easily rectified, but such is not the case for large university Spanish programs that place hundreds, and sometimes thousands, of students a year into several different programmatic levels. Inaccurate placement into a large Spanish program may lead to additional coursework and corresponding tuition costs, delayed graduation, "considerable inconvenience and disaffection," and abandonment of language study altogether—particularly among those who study Spanish as a minor or secondary major. Many full-time students' schedules are as full as the courses they wish to take, making the adjustment of incorrect placements a logistical nightmare for the student, the adviser, and the department. Indeed, to devalue the importance of placement testing and accurate placement procedures is to undermine the entire enterprise of collegiate foreign language education.

This was made evident at the University of Kentucky when the WebCAPE exam—a placement exam—was replaced by the American Council on the Teaching of Foreign Languages' (ACTFL's) Assessment of Performance toward Proficiency in Languages (AAPPL) interpretive reading and listening exams, in order to incorporate an instrument more closely aligned with the ACTFL proficiency guidelines and to transform, simultaneously, the university foreign language requirement from seat time to proficiency. The change seemed ideal on paper, and though the AAPPL implied additional cost, the convenience of using a performance-based exam of receptive abilities as a placement exam *and* as a rough measure of general proficiency seemed to outweigh the additional expense. The performance levels were converted into numeric values and added together to produce a composite score that served as the student's placement exam score. Cut scores were set for each level after pilot data were collected, with current students in the program at the target levels. Following the pilot, hundreds of incoming freshmen completed the exam and enrolled in their first university Spanish course. Unfortunately, the experiment did not go as planned for several reasons: (1) The exam's construct definition and relatively low level of difficulty resulted in inflated scores that did not align student ability well with the program's curriculum; (2) college-level administrators received complaints from students who felt that they were incorrectly placed into higher-level courses, for example, fifth-semester grammar course, and that their low course grades were the result of the misplacement; and (3) the recurring cost of the exam, coupled with student complaints, led to increased pressure from college deans to begin looking for more accurate and cost-effective means for placing students. Another layer of difficulty that compounded the situation was the fact that in many cases, general academic advisers with limited knowledge of language acquisition, the variable influence of prior high school coursework, and the subtleties of the Spanish curriculum were called upon to counsel students on registration decisions that often had to be made during a one-hour advising session the day after the exam. These difficulties make no mention of the crude placement procedures used for the growing number of heritage speakers enrolling in courses of all levels at the university and the all-too-common lack of appropriate coursework to receive them.

Placement exams and general placement procedures are most effective when they maintain a dialogic, ongoing, and bidirectional relationship with the curriculum, its communicative goals, and programmatic level structures. Research that would provide guidance on how to establish this relationship exists but is scant (Green and Weir 2004; Wall, Clapham, and Alderson 1994; Wesche, Paribakht, and Ready 1996) due to limited scholarly scrutiny of placement testing and, as a result, minimal funding (Green 2012). However, in a reading course on English for academic purposes, Clark and Ishida (2005) found that promoted students' vocabulary knowledge was inferior to students who placed directly into the course. Although this course's context is very different from a Spanish postsecondary context, Clark and Ishida's design could be replicated longitudinally in Spanish programs to determine students' levels of grammatical ability or lexical knowledge among those who were promoted sequentially from the 101 course and those who placed directly into the more advanced course. Research of this type could help track down the weak link in the curricular chain: the placement exam, the lack of vertical articulation between courses, vague course-level student learning outcomes, or simply poor teaching and unmotivated learning. Incorrect placements are inevitable in large Spanish programs with such a wide variety of linguistic and cultural needs among the students and given the limited resources allocated to placement testing due to tight budgets and the temporal constraints imposed on the retrieval of results. Notwithstanding this inevitability, some Spanish departments may be too quick to adopt external instruments of questionable fit with limited piloting at the local level to determine cut scores, and they pay the price, literally and figuratively.

Norris (2004) recounts the design, validation, and implementation of a placement test used in Georgetown University's German Department. This cloze test, which was created and validated by Norris and local stakeholders, was accompanied by a complete curricular overhaul to focus on genre and writing as the unifying thread across all curricular levels. Clearly, placement exams should not be expected to test all, or even most, of the abilities and dispositions targeted by an entire university Spanish curriculum (Green and Weir 2004), but they should capture enough of those needed at each target course level to start students off on the right foot. As Green (2012) points out, and as Norris's dissertation (2004) confirms, indirect tests of language competence—in the form of dictations, cloze tests, vocabulary and grammar tests, and even elicited imitation tests (Cox and Davies 2012)—may work well as placement instruments, but only after they have been aligned with corresponding courses, which should, in turn, align with larger curricular and programmatic goals. Even with this alignment intact, empirical evidence must be brought to bear on the accurate setting of cut scores.

## CURRICULAR CONTENT AND ACHIEVEMENT IN SPANISH LANGUAGE PROGRAMS

So now that our students have been told where to start their language learning journey in the program, the next series of questions they could reasonably ask are "What will I learn?" and "Where will I end up?"—followed by "How do I get there?" and even "How will I know I'm there?" The question of what can, or should, reasonably be taught, much less learned, in a two- or four-year collegiate Spanish language program is a complicated one that goes beyond the scope of this chapter. Our intent here is not to provide an exhaustive treatment of the issue, but rather to discuss and problematize crucial considerations in achieving a coherent and cohesive Spanish language program, from entry to exit. Ideally, a statement of the overall mission of a university Spanish program would guide the creation of program-wide student learning objectives, which would lead to the identification of appropriate courses aimed at meeting these objectives. The goal would be to identify course-level objectives informed by those of adjacent levels and distinct content areas, with all building toward the achievement of overarching curricular objectives. Classroom assessments would be designed to reflect classroom teaching, which would support course learning objectives, with each course making a unique and meaningful contribution to the ultimate attainment of well-articulated, achievable curricular goals. Such an approach should produce some semblance of parity with respect to communicative abilities and cultural dispositions—or, in the words of the MLA (2007), report deep translingual and transcultural competence. This mechanistic approach to language teaching and learning based on differential inputs that are somehow mysteriously transformed into uniform outputs rarely, if ever, pans out. Within curriculum studies, a crucial distinction is made between intended, enacted, assessed, and learned curricula. What designers set out to teach (the intended curriculum)—as specified on official documents, such as a syllabus—may be different from what is actually taught (the enacted curriculum), and what is taught may not align perfectly with what is tested (the assessed curriculum). Finally, what is assessed may not reflect all that individual students have acquired (the learned curriculum), or, quite commonly, it may highlight the discrepancy between what they have concretely learned and what they should have learned based on the original intended curriculum.

During the last several decades, various researchers from a variety of contexts have directly addressed the question of what level of proficiency students can expect to achieve during and upon completion of college language study (Carroll 1967; Rifkin 2005; Magnan 1986; Swender 2003; Tschirner 2016). Though Carroll found that the average graduating senior was at an Interagency Language Roundtable 2+ level, roughly equivalent to ACTFL's Advanced Mid or High, Tschirner (2016) notes that Carroll's findings must be interpreted with caution because they do not align with other studies that used the ACTFL scale and the Oral Proficiency Interview (OPI). Nevertheless, even with students achieving, on average, the Advanced level on the ACTFL scale, Carroll (1967, 134) commented on "the generally low median levels of attainment in audio-lingual skills." Magnan (1986) found that four of the ten fourth-year French students in her study were rated at the Intermediate Mid or High level, while six were rated Advanced or Advanced plus. Of the 501 students from seven different languages in Swender's study, 53 percent scored at the Intermediate High level or lower. The Spanish cohort performed similarly, with 57.4 percent at that level or lower. According to ACTFL (2012, 7), Intermediate High speakers can deal with "routine tasks and social situations" and can handle "uncomplicated tasks and social situations requiring an exchange of basic information"—hardly what one would consider deep translingual competence. Though the fourth-year Spanish students in Tschirner's study were rated, on average, Advanced Low in reading proficiency, their listening proficiency remained at Intermediate High. At the time this book went to press, scholars were analyzing thousands of proficiency tests given to college students at various large state institutions as part of the Flagship Proficiency Initiative (Fernando Rubio, personal communication). Apparently, and not surprisingly, questions regarding the level of proficiency attained by students from college-level study remains relevant. As investigations using primarily cross-sectional samples, what these studies do not include is information related to students' individual progress over time, their mastery of skill sets related to a liberal arts education such as critical and analytical thinking, or their cultural competence.

Byrnes, Maxim, and Norris (2010, 15) problematize the commonly accepted approach to collegiate language education that would prioritize "transactional, interactional, oral language learning." The authors trace the bias for oral proficiency back to Canale and Swain's (1980) conceptualization of communicative competence, widespread use of Omaggio Hadley's (1986) well-known textbook *Teaching Language in Context*, the creation of the ACTFL (1986) oral proficiency guidelines, and the language learning interests expressed by many US students. One of the most powerful forces mentioned by Byrnes, Maxim, and Norris (2010) driving contemporary lower-level Spanish curricula are the World-Readiness Standards for Learning Languages (formerly the National Standards for Foreign Language Learning; see National Standards in Foreign Language Education Project 1996). The widely known five goal areas, or 5 Cs, include communication, cultures, connections, comparisons, and communities and provide targets for language learners and programs. The communication goal specifies three modes of communication: interpersonal, interpretive, and presentational. As a large and influential professional organization, ACTFL's 5 Cs have exerted tremendous influence on foreign language curricula, particularly at the secondary level. Many introductory college textbooks explicitly note connections between unit and activity objectives and the National Standards. Indeed, the National Standards helped propel the swing of the methodological pendulum toward communicative language teaching and a focus on performance indicators, embodied by "can-do" statements and integrated performance assessments. However, the influence of the standards in many university programs quickly wanes as students advance to higher-level literature, culture, and linguistics courses, where instructors are less likely to make explicit connections between course content and the standards.

In spite of the momentum created by the proficiency movement to develop curricula grounded in oral-based communicative competence, some claimed that it was unrealistic (Byrnes 2006; Schulz 2006)—reminiscent of the report by Coleman (1929)—and neglected deeper issues such as cross-cultural awareness, social justice, and mastery of symbolic competence (Kramsch 2006). As part of their rationale for a genre-focused approached to advanced foreign language writing development, Byrnes, Maxim, and Norris (2010) bemoan the disconnect between language and culture learning in foreign language programs, particularly at the lower levels, and the apparent disregard for textual interpretive abilities—the hallmark of a humanities-focused education.

Though Byrnes, Maxim, and Norris's (2010) well-known and carefully conceived German curriculum at Georgetown University seems a lofty goal for many university programs, it has shed light on the need within the academy for deliberate foreign language curricular reform grounded in a solid conceptual and theoretical frame. Other scholars have offered up similar proposals for collegiate foreign language curriculum design that would more seamlessly interweave language, content, and culture across all levels of a program, but particularly at the lower levels. Swaffar and Arens (2005) provide a comprehensive proposal for the reconfiguration of foreign language curricula based on *literacy* as the appropriate merging of form and meaning in all its various manifestations—for example, literary, cultural, linguistic, and historical.

Arens (2009) problematizes the culture curriculum as currently instantiated in the academy and reimagines the Standards for Foreign Language Learning in the 21st Century to more closely approximate an interdisciplinary approach, similar to the field of cultural studies. Others (Kramsch 2000; Swaffar 2006; Rossomondo 2012) have offered up innovative and forward-thinking curricular proposals that would redefine the enterprise of collegiate language learning as an indispensable component of humanities-based learning of culture. In contrast to these proposals for integrating culture through multiple literacies and a reconceptualization of foreign language curricula and pedagogy, Lee and VanPatten's (2003, 5) perspective on teaching students culturally appropriate linguistic behavior in the classroom is a bit more measured: "In terms of culturally appropriate linguistic behavior, classrooms isolated from the second-language community will always do poorly in preparing students to conform to certain norms."

However, for Spanish programs the issue of determining which communicative skills to teach and how to balance these with topical content—literary, linguistic, and cultural—across the span of a degree program has been particularly difficult, for many reasons. First, the wide range of communicative abilities and cultural awareness students possess when they first enter a program may result in quite varied outcomes upon completion of each course and entry into the next, and upon completion of the entire degree program. For true beginners enrolled in Spanish 101 with no previous experience, functional mastery of several elements of oral communicative competence and meaningful cultural awareness by graduation may be far-fetched. However, for the increasingly common high-intermediate to advanced traditional and heritage-language student who places directly into upper-level Spanish courses, achieving a semblance of oral communicative competence and cross-cultural competence by the completion of his or her degree is much more realistic. Second, students' perceived communicative needs in Spanish after graduation are primarily oral, transactional, and interactional rather than written and academic. The situation grows even more complicated when students' perceived needs are mixed with their professional aspirations. The proficiency needs of an aspiring preservice Spanish teacher who must reach a certain level on ACTFL's oral proficiency scale will differ from those of a double major in business, social work, or premed, all of which will differ from a Spanish minor wanting to simply "keep up" his or her Spanish for personal reasons. Third, culture is not monolithic for any language, but particularly for the varieties of Spanish used internationally and domestically, which in turn represent a wide variety of cultures. Irwin and Szurmuk (2009, 46) argue that in the United States, a major producer of transnational Spanish language mass media, Spanish "cannot merely be thought of in national or geographic terms." As such, identifying cultural targets for any approach—for example, textual, generic, traditional (both big C and little c culture), or otherwise—in the Spanish curriculum is inherently problematic. Finally, the preferred learning goals and focus of instructional staff members, particularly veteran tenured and tenure-track faculty members who teach upper-level courses, may not coincide with students' perceived needs and with recent trends in foreign language education and second-language acquisition. Curricular innovations undertaken by departments to approximate the ideals of the report by the MLA (2007) may further distance the modern curriculum from a subset of faculty members whose training more closely parallels the traditional two-tiered curriculum.

## STUDENT LEARNING OBJECTIVES: DESIGN, DELIVERY, AND ASSESSMENT

Nearly every Spanish program has a statement that encapsulates its overall mission, whether it be on the departmental website or in the university bulletin, and that can be accessed by current and prospective students. Often these statements express lofty ideals at an abstract level that speak of students becoming global citizens who are culturally sensitive and who are equipped with myriad skills, such as analytical and critical thinking, interpersonal communication, and bilingual competence, among others. The mission statement for the Department of Hispanic Studies at the University of Kentucky, for example, speaks of improving students' linguistic and critical thinking skills, deepening their cultural understanding, and heightening "their awareness of their role as local and global citizens in a pluralistic society" (University of Kentucky 2015, 156). Such mission statements are easy to write but hard to operationalize and enact, and are often not well known to students or faculty.

At some point, the mission statement of a program must find expression in programmatic student learning objectives that are stated with sufficiently concrete verbiage to render them assessable. But these student learning outcomes (SLOs) must be grounded in a larger conceptual framework that provides coherence and structure to the curriculum. For example, does the program desire to adopt a standards-based model for the curriculum using the World-Readiness Standards to determine what is to be learned, ACTFL's Integrated Performance Assessment model to monitor progress, and the ACTFL (2012) proficiency assessments and scale to gauge language ability at set intervals and at graduation? Conversely, is a seat-time, credit-hour-based curriculum (Schmitt 2014) with clear objectives deployed by skilled instructors for motivated students enough to ensure achievement of prescribed SLOs? Indeed, answers to these questions depend on myriad factors unique to the local context, but must be rooted in a sound understanding of instructed second-language acquisition.

Once the overall mission and targets for learning are set for a program, and an appropriate curricular framework is adopted, more granular SLOs must be written for the entire program and for individual courses. Davis (2012, 2015, 2016) reviews the outcomes assessment movement in the United States as it applies to foreign language education, noting the "unprecedented scrutiny" (2016, 377) to which foreign language instructors' practices are subjected in the current educational climate. He argues that contemporary approaches to outcomes assessment are rooted in a seventy-year-old framework proposed by Tyler (1949) for the evaluation of curriculum and instruction that centered on the development and assessment of SLOs, which then facilitated the diagnosis of curricular and pedagogical weaknesses. According to Davis (2016, 378), "SLO assessment may prove to be one of the most pervasive changes to US postsecondary educational practice in recent history," and it is tied to reforms aimed at improving US language education and to changes in higher education accreditation. Far from being an evaluative panacea, outcomes-based methodologies suffer from several weaknesses: (1) a limited ability to directly improve programs; (2) a tendency to focus on a narrow set of outcomes that are not reflective of the program's global aims; (3) a propensity to choose outcomes that are most easily measured, as compared with those that are most important; and (4), in a high-stakes context, issues of measurement and reporting are emphasized to the detriment of probing inquiry and innovation (Davis 2016). However, Davis is quick to note that under the right conditions, SLO-focused assessment can effect positive change by identifying gaps in the curriculum, inducing deeper program understanding, aligning coursework and other program components with a shared set of values, establishing a foundation for continuing inquiry, and triggering changes that result in concrete improvements of teaching and learning.

Klee, Melin, and Soneson (2014) describe the complex and lengthy process undertaken at the University of Minnesota to move from the selection of an overarching framework for general education to the alignment of this framework with models of language learning to the identification of SLOs and the integration of ongoing evaluation. As a testament to the comprehensive nature of their programmatic revisions, the authors include in the appendix fifty-three total student language learning outcomes spread across two-year and four-year sequences of language learning; Tier 1 and Tier 2 languages; and interpretive, interpersonal, and presentational modes of communication. These SLOs could then be aligned with the curriculum in such a way as to identify how each course contributes to the introduction, emphasis, or mastery of each SLO in the form of a curriculum map.

The experience of the University of Minnesota illustrates well how the determination of coherent SLOs for an entire program is a monumental undertaking requiring the expertise of many and input from all. It is somewhat doubtful, however, that many Spanish programs have the institutional will, monetary resources, and professional expertise to engage in such a thorough approach to the identification of programmatic SLOs, much less the creation of corresponding assessment instruments. Moreover, the articulation of SLOs at the programmatic level must be informed by local students' necessities, lacks, and wants (Nation and Macalister 2010), and thus not solely be the product of a faculty committee's deliberations or a national organization's standards. The art, and science, of writing fruitful SLOs for any program resides in the unique ways that they are customized to fit the students who will strive to achieve them. Locally driven and thorough needs assessment has a rich history in English language learning (Brown 2011), but much less so in foreign language programs in the US academy, where general education and graduation requirements are based on seat-time and credit-hour completion. In many cases, costly textbooks from large publishing houses are used as proxies for a true needs assessment and are leaned upon to identify what students should learn, how they should learn it, and in what order (VanPatten 2015).

Once learning objectives at the program level have been identified and we know the types of knowledge and abilities students should acquire, they must then be tied to course-level outcomes that facilitate vertical articulation from lower- to upper-level courses, as well as horizontal articulation across multiple sections of the same level. Paesani and Barrette (2005) identify the following four guidelines for effective program articulation: (1) consideration of the program overall, as well as the individuals and individual perspectives included therein; (2) development of a cohesive relationship between instruction, content, goals, and assessment; (3) appreciation of language learning as constituted by process and product; and (4) development of content knowledge and proficiency at all levels of the program. The mapping of targeted SLOs must start from the first entry-level course through the last upper-level course students may complete.

Often, however, curriculum mapping of desired learning outcomes becomes increasingly fragmented and disconnected as students move through a program. One of the unfortunate by-products of a bifurcated programmatic structure—that is, lower-level language versus upper-level content—is the tacit acceptance that once students have graduated from the closely coordinated elementary and intermediate levels of primarily language study, they have acquired the necessary skills and knowledge to succeed in literature, culture, and linguistics courses, and that there is much less need for carefully articulated objectives and dialogue between courses because their focus is topical, not linguistic. Lord and Isabelli-García (2015, 153) point to the loose coordination of upper-level courses and resulting consequences: "The so-called 'content' courses—courses in culture, literature, linguistics, and so on—are often on their own with little or no supervision. The lack of supervision or oversight also implies that the relationship of these courses to the others in the department is sporadic, at best."

The *relationship* between courses that Lord and Isabelli-García mention alludes to several crucial components of a well-articulated curriculum, such as mutually informed SLOs that introduce new material, both cultural and linguistic, while also recycling previously learned concepts and skills. Another crucial relationship is the one that the instructors for each course, particularly those at different levels, maintain with each other, as well as with the SLOs of their colleagues' courses and the overall program.

Lafford, Abbott, and Lear (2014, 175) used the metaphor of "silo walls" in speaking of potential stumbling blocks for the meaningful integration of a Spanish language service provider (LSP) into Spanish postsecondary curricula. Yet the silos that have been built up within many Spanish departments are not only injurious to curricular innovations like Spanish LSP and community service learning, but also to the coherence of mainstream programs with fairly standard course offerings in language, literature, culture, and linguistics. Although the silo metaphor can represent personal, disciplinary, and intellectual tendencies among colleagues, it is most deleterious when it accurately reflects curricular, programmatic, and pedagogical isolation. The faculty member who solely teaches upper-level courses in literature or linguistics may also be the one who routinely complains that his or her students are introducing themselves with "*Me llamo es . . .*" on the first day of class. The complaints may also center on the heritage speaker with a Hispanic surname who speaks perfectly in class but who turns in written work riddled with orality, leading to low grades and disappointed instructors and students. In many cases, especially at large universities with graduate student instructors, seasoned faculty members become disconnected from the elementary levels, having had limited, if any, experience or even familiarity with beginning- and intermediate-level courses, the SLOs attached to them, and the linguistic production of the students enrolled in them.

Effective vertical programmatic articulation may be further complicated by course prerequisites and by idiosyncratic grading practices. Brown's (2014) analysis of the course catalogues issued by public, research-intensive universities found that just over half of the seventy-three institutions reviewed had at least one undergraduate course with a grade-based course prerequisite, the most common of which was a finite course grade—as opposed to grade point average or major average. The empirical validation of grade-based prerequisites at one of the programs demonstrated that grades were not strongly correlated with students' scores on a third-party, measure-of-proficiency exam and that students with A grades, for example, received a wide range of scores on the three sections of the test. Brown (2014, 201) concludes: "As we reconcile our educational values with our programmatic goals and the realities of instructed SLA, we may find current policies and practices that restrict the ability of course grades to serve as effective prerequisites and accurate indicators of achievement and proficiency." Absolute uniformity in grading and student achievement, as reflected by a course grade, are not necessary to facilitate vertical articulation but do contribute to the predictive ability of a curriculum to achieve desired SLOs.

One of the key components of ensuring seamless horizontal and vertical articulation within a Spanish program and achievement of SLOs is the appropriate design and use of language tests. Students who progress through a postsecondary Spanish curriculum will inevitably be confronted by myriad language tests, from those used for placement to those used for assessing students' learning of course material and assigning course grades to those employed for the verification of proficiency level, and, finally, to those used for evaluating program effectiveness (Bordón and Liskin-Gasparro 2015). The preparation of useful language tests that target course-level SLOs is no small or simple task, as Bachman and Palmer (1996) have demonstrated. Despite the many practical guides to language testing in print (Bachman and Palmer 1996; Brown and Abeywickrama 2010; Hughes 2003; McNamara 2000), Spanish language educators must always confirm that their assessments are tied to course-level SLOs, which in turn contribute to the achievement of programmatic objectives.

Bordón and Liskin-Gasparro (2015) identified three issues of particular relevance to contemporary postsecondary Spanish language educators, their programs, and their students: (1) the debate surrounding performance-oriented and ability-oriented approaches to language testing, (2) the use of technology in language testing, and—arguably the most important of the three—(3) the adequate training of Spanish instructors in the basics of classroom assessment. Although the theoretical debate regarding the merits of a performance- or construct-focused approach surely deserves attention, it resides beyond the scope of this chapter. The use of technology and instructors' assessment literacy have particular relevance for Spanish language programs, which tend to be the largest non-English-language programs at most institutions.

As mentioned above, the computer-based WebCAPE has allowed many programs to quickly and rather accurately place hundreds of students into their programs using test items that have been calibrated for difficulty with Item Response Theory. For many years, the WebCAPE was the gold standard for placement exams because it took relatively little time (e.g., 30 minutes), was cost-effective, and produced a score immediately upon completion that could be used to make enrollment decisions on the spot. Other computer-based alternatives exist for placement, performance, and proficiency testing—such as third-party, measure-of-proficiency exams, ACTFL's AAPPL, and Lancaster University's Dialang diagnostic exam. At the completion of a language major, particularly language teaching majors, many programs require students to demonstrate proficiency by participating in a costly and cumbersome ACTFL OPI. The Oral Proficiency Interview by computer (OPIc) was created as a cost-effective alternative to the OPI and allowed students to record their responses to questions asked by a computer avatar. The OPIc results in ratings that are similar to those for the OPI (Thompson, Cox, and Knapp 2016), with some differences in lexical diversity and density as well as temporal and discursive fluency (Brown, Cox, and Thompson 2017). Indeed, advances in language testing technology may prove to be a boon for Spanish postsecondary education, particularly at the beginning and end of a student's program of study, given shrinking budgets, increasing numbers of students, compressed timelines for enrollment decisions, and increased calls for accountability and objectivity. What remains to be seen is how technology might be used effectively by instructors to facilitate testing in their courses, assuming that instructors possess basic assessment literacy.

In many Spanish programs, the instructional corps come from a wide variety of academic backgrounds with limited formal training in assessment, which has implications for curricular coherence and vertical articulation. The graduate student instructor, who only three and a half months earlier finished his or her undergraduate degree, may be teaching Spanish 101 in a classroom adjacent to the veteran colleague teaching senior seminars in literary or cultural studies. Malone (2011, 1) defines assessment literacy as an "understanding of the measurement basics related directly to classroom learning"—such as validity, reliability, practicality, and impact. Unfortunately, many Spanish language educators with little or no training in assessment, such as those described above, may feel intimidated by testing terminology and concepts and perceive classroom-based assessment as highly technical and beyond their understanding.

The current status of assessment in many collegiate Spanish programs at the course and program levels is riddled with ironies: (1) Many instructors are interested in student learning and are sure it is taking place but are unclear how to validly demonstrate it; (2) the primary mechanism accepted by key stakeholders (e.g., administrators, donors, and parents) to demonstrate effectiveness is through valid assessment, yet many instructors resist attempts to improve it or incorporate it; and (3) persistent complaints from faculty about top-down mandates imposed by external parties such as accrediting agencies precede stiff resistance to take ownership of the process. Instructional staff in Spanish language programs would do well to view assessment literacy not as futile or threatening, or as a distraction from research and teaching in their specialty area, but rather as another arrow in their quiver to showcase their teaching and their students' learning, and to improve both. Higher levels of assessment literacy will only be achieved with increased and persistent efforts to demonstrate to instructors the benefits of valid, reliable assessment of classroom learning at all levels.

## PROGRAM EVALUATION

Our token Spanish student from earlier in the chapter who began with the placement exam before entering a well-conceived and articulated program grounded in a defensible curricular framework and an achievable set of SLOs has now completed all the requirements and is ready to graduate. As she exits the program, she may ask herself "What did I gain from my experience in this Spanish program?" and "What can I now do that I couldn't before?" Unfortunately, in many cases logistical constraints and limited resources preclude a longitudinal analysis of student growth and may lead program evaluators to only look at the achievement of learning outcomes in the aggregate from a cross section of students, essentially nullifying potentially large or small learning gains at the individual level. The heterogeneous nature of Spanish majors who exit a program could possibly mask unique and idiosyncratic growth, or a lack thereof, by individual students. The true beginner may grow tremendously from entrance to exit, but not reach the levels of classmates who entered with much more background, whereas the heritage speaker who entered with superb conversational ability may perform well in oral assessments but may have grown little in acquiring formal reading and writing skills. The diverse nature of incoming cohorts of Spanish students presents unique challenges when programmatic assessments are undertaken.

Spanish language programs at the collegiate level are complex and have many moving parts, such as the students and their backgrounds and goals, the instructional staff and their unique teaching and research proclivities, the integration of newly approved courses, and the shifting content of established courses. Additional complexity is introduced by pressures emanating from a range of sources—accrediting agencies, upper-level administrators, and legislatures, among others. As such, meaningful program evaluation can be an overwhelming task to undertake and one that requires not only faculty buy-in on an intellectual level but also significant contributions from faculty members on a practical level. In many cases, program evaluation has been done incrementally, befitting the needs of a program with only one component being targeted, or a limited number of components, to ensure that meaningful change results (Norris et al. 2009). Norris and Mills (2014) point out that effective, useful program evaluation can (1) shed light on the achievement of goals and on strengths and weaknesses, (2) demonstrate effectiveness to stakeholders, and (3) facilitate the identification of actions plans for improvement.

The realization of these benefits, which have the potential to effect real and lasting change in Spanish tertiary programs, hinges primarily on willful participation by core stakeholders, who then develop a sense of ownership of the process, which increases the use and usefulness of the evaluation (Davis et al. 2016). Michael Patton's (2008) *utilization-focused* framework argues that all attempts at program evaluation should begin by identifying the intended users of the results and by cautiously and honestly anticipating the specific uses. Until these preliminary steps are completed, the process of formulating evaluation questions, selecting methods for data collection, collecting and analyzing the data, and reporting the findings would be futile, because the findings would most likely collect dust on an administrator's shelf.

Once the users have been identified and the uses have been delineated, however, the formulation of effective evaluation questions helps focus the process and the identification of pertinent data and valid methods for collecting them. Davis and others (2016, 6) provide examples of evaluation questions separated into the following categories: needs, expectations, methods, training, instruction, student learning, programs, and resources/support. For example, in the category of program, the authors ask "To what extent is the program implemented as intended?" Spanish language programs in the academy are as diverse as the students who pass through them, and each program must determine which questions are most likely to lead to useful program evaluation. For some programs, heritage language learners' needs remain unaddressed, while for other programs, the needs of students returning from study abroad go unnoticed. As Patton (2008) has so eloquently argued, the effectiveness of program evaluation is best measured by the nature and endurance of the changes that result from it.

## SPANISH POSTSECONDARY PROGRAM AND CURRICULUM SURVEY RESULTS

The assessment section of our national survey included seven of the fifty-five items, with an "other" option for respondents to write in any additional concerns. The items are listed below in descending order of concern, such that the first item with the lowest mean would be the item of most concern on a scale of 1 (very much a concern) to 5 (not a concern at all), with 3 representing neutral. The mean score and overall rank across all items with regard to level of concern appear at the end of each item, as does the percentage who felt the item did not apply to their program:

- Accurate placement of traditional, nonheritage students: 2.297 / 3rd / 2.5 percent;
- Inclusion of coherent course-level student learning objectives: 2.30 / 4th / 1.3 percent;
- Effective system for ongoing program evaluation: 2.31 / 5th / 1.3 percent;
- Inclusion of coherent programmatic student learning objectives: 2.36 / 7th / 2.2 percent;
- Faculty support for evaluation efforts: 2.41 / 9th / 1.3 percent;
- Sufficient instructor training on assessment issues (e.g., writing/use of scoring rubrics, valid test construction): 2.45 / 13th / 1.3 percent; and
- Alignment of assessment instruments with instructors' teaching methods: 2.48 / 14th /1 percent.

Two significant findings rise to the fore: (1) Five of the seven items were ranked among the top ten items of concern across all fifty-five items, with none falling below fourteenth overall; and (2) all seven items scored a mean below 3, indicating that on average all these assessment issues are of concern to the participants. Further analysis demonstrated that the assessment section was of second-most concern among the nine sections. The only other section with a lower average score was the section titled "Other" that appeared at the end of the survey. A somewhat counterintuitive finding was that those who self-identified as having received their highest degree in a field of literary or cultural studies indicated a bit more concern with the assessment items, as indicated by a lower overall mean (2.28) than those trained in linguistics and applied linguistics (2.51). On average, tenured and tenure-track instructors (2.39) responded nearly identically to the nontenured instructor cohort (2.41), with a mean difference of only 0.02.

The two assessment issues of most concern related to the placement of traditional students and the use of coherent student learning objectives at the course level, while the issue of least concern was the alignment of assessment instruments with instructional techniques, though this item was still within the top fifteen items of concern. Participants expressed concern not only about course-level but also program-level issues. Spanish language departments are increasingly called upon to conduct programmatic evaluations by internal or external bodies. As such, it comes as no surprise that "effective system for ongoing program evaluation" was ranked fifth across all fifty-five items. These results indicate that assessment and evaluation are indeed on the minds of postsecondary Spanish language educators.

## A CASE STUDY OF CURRICULAR ADAPTATION AND ASSESSMENT

The incorporation of assessment into the language programs at the two institutions represented by the authors of this book, Brigham Young University (BYU) and the University of Kentucky (UK), have followed very distinct trajectories. As mentioned above, the WebCAPE was designed at BYU and quickly became the most widely used placement exam in several languages. Since the creation of the initial adaptive placement exams, BYU has maintained a strong and ongoing tradition of language assessment development and research, including contributions to the design of ACTFL's reading and listening tests and innovative work with elicited imitation tests. Probably most noteworthy are the programmatic requirements that BYU's unique student and institutional profile allow for, namely, a 0-credit course (SPA 491: Senior Proficiency Evaluation), in which students from all four Spanish major tracks—Spanish, Spanish teaching, Spanish translation, Spanish studies (secondary major)—must complete a certified ACTFL Oral Proficiency Interview, Writing Proficiency Test, Reading Comprehension Test, and Listening Comprehension Test before graduation, with the expectation of achieving at least Advanced Low on the ACTFL proficiency scale. Students who exit BYU's Spanish major do so with a concrete idea of their communicative abilities in the language vis-à-vis a nationally accepted, though far from perfect, proficiency scale. Such a comprehensive assessment system at the postsecondary level is surely the exception and not the norm, but does seems to set a gold standard.

The experience of UK's Hispanic Studies Department may approximate more closely the reality many Spanish programs face, and thus provides an illustrative case study of a program that has dealt with a host of curricular, programmatic, and assessment issues over the last decade. Many readers will find certain aspects of this institution's experience somewhat similar to theirs, whether they are at a large state school or a small private institution, with regard to the need to adapt the curriculum to the demands of students and administrators while not abandoning the principles of a humanistic liberal arts education. By the early 2000s, the UK Department of Hispanic Studies had developed an international reputation, with high-profile scholars in literary studies, and the UK undergraduate curriculum reflected this identity with a multitude of courses in literature and culture but only one linguistics course, in phonetics and phonology; a catchall advanced Spanish language course; and one course in business Spanish—a course avoided by most faculty and lecturers who had been trained in literary and cultural studies. The demographics of the state and city in which UK is located were rapidly changing, adding more Spanish speakers to the region's population and the student body. Students began requesting a greater variety of courses beyond literature, culture, and civilization. At the dean's behest, a specialist in second-language acquisition was hired in 2006 as the second "linguist," joining the director of elementary language instruction. Only a year later, an additional hire was made in the field of historical-comparative linguistics, and the sole linguist of just a few years earlier was suddenly surrounded by two more—per the dean's request, rather than the department's.

Many incoming UK students were entering the program with previous high school experience and placed into the four-semester elementary sequence taught by graduate students in literature after taking the WebCAPE exam. For many years, the curriculum was divided into the elementary language sequence; two fifth-semester pre-major/minor courses; and upper-level literature, civilization, and culture courses. As large numbers of incoming students arrived with previous coursework in Spanish, and with the relatively small numbers of students with no previous experience, two extra courses were added at the first- and second-year levels—High Beginner Spanish (SPA 103) and High Intermediate Spanish (SPA 203)—which were the one-semester curricular equivalent of 101/102 and 201/202, respectively. With a critical mass of professors able to teach courses in linguistics and applied linguistics, additional courses at the upper level were added to enrich the undergraduate offerings. The newly approved courses opened up the curriculum to new areas of study and included courses such as Introduction to Linguistics, Introduction to Translation, Spanish in the World, and Spanish and Globalization. The increased numbers of heritage speakers led to the creation of two courses—Spanish for Bilingual Students (SPA 205) and Written Spanish for Bilingual Students (SPA 215)—that were designed to parallel the third- and fourth-semester courses (SPA 201, 202) and the fifth-semester grammar (SPA 210) and conversation (SPA 211) courses, respectively. Unfortunately, for a variety of reasons, neither of those courses has been taught, although both have been in the course catalogue for over five years.

Basic analyses of students' scores on the WebCAPE and Spanish Language and Culture Advanced Placement scores indicated that the profile of the UK's Spanish students was changing. Between June 2002 and June 2015, 12,826 WebCAPE tests were taken in Spanish, placing students into one of four categories: 0–205 (101: beginning Spanish), 206–344 (103: high beginner), 345–484 (203: high intermediate), or 485 and above (departmental placement but usually 210/211, fifth-semester).[2] In 2002, 21.4 percent of scores placed students into the second two categories; but by 2015, this number had risen to 35.6 percent. Even more impressive was the increase from 1.3 percent of students scoring 485 or higher in 2002 to 14.3 percent in 2015. A growing number of students were scoring at levels beyond the placement exam's ability to discriminate effectively for the purposes of placement into the program. Scores on the AP Spanish language and culture and literature and culture exams demonstrated an equally impressive trend over a shorter period of time. In 2007, 25.3 percent of UK students received at least a score of 3 on the exam, which is the minimum grade needed to receive credit. By 2015, the proportion of students who received at least a 3 increased to 87.2 percent. In 2007, only two students took the Spanish language and literature exam, and only one received at least a 3. Eight years later, nineteen students took it, with seventeen (89.4 percent) receiving a 3, 4, or 5. It was very clear that incoming cohorts of students were arriving on campus with more Spanish ability than previous groups, a discovery that had clear repercussions for placement procedures and programmatic planning.

Students who scored above a certain cut score on the placement exam were referred to the department for an informal assessment by a faculty member via a brief conversation to determine whether they needed either of the fifth-semester courses (grammar and conversation) before taking upper-level courses. Because a greater variety of students were scoring above the highest cut score, it became apparent that a more systematic assessment should be used to accurately determine students' placement and educational needs. Several portions of a practice exam from the Diploma de Español como Lengua Extranjera were given to students, though the grammar and vocabulary section clearly favored peninsular Spanish, with which many of the heritage speakers were totally unfamiliar. For the Hispanic Studies Department, heritage language and advanced student placement is still a work in progress, from the placement instrument that evaluates them to the curriculum that receives them.

For many years, UK's Spanish major required 42 credit-hours, with up to as many as 21 being taken outside the department. The minor required 21 credit-hours, including the fourth-semester course (Spanish 202), both fifth-semester courses, and 12 credit-hours at the 300 level. Neither the major nor the minor had tracks or concentrations, and no exit exam or capstone course was required. Anecdotal reports from instructors of students' subpar communicative abilities in Spanish, coupled with an external review, prompted the revision of the major to allow fewer courses outside Spanish, to require students to declare a concentration, and to categorize all courses as either literature and culture or language and linguistics. The minor was also revised and shifted by one course, such that the fourth-semester course (Spanish 202) no longer formed part of the minor and was replaced by a 300-level course while maintaining intact the 21-credit-hour minimum.

Though the move to a more rigorous major seems reasonable, because it would presumably lead to better learning outcomes for students, it also led to fewer majors. Given the high number of credit-hours that could be used toward an additional major (up to 21) in the humanities or social sciences, Spanish was often combined with other majors at the university. According to data from the UK College of Arts and Sciences, at the end of the spring of 2013—the last semester when students could declare the old major—there were 100 primary majors, 95 secondary majors, and 290 minors. At the end of the spring of 2017, the number of primary majors was 49, secondary/tertiary majors totaled 41, and 418 students were minors. In the course of four years, the number of total majors dropped from 195 to 90, or −54 percent, while the minors increased from 290 to 418, or +44 percent. In an era of revenue-generating and performance-based budget models in higher education, the loss of majors seems unwise; but an academically inferior major unable to produce meaningful outcomes seems unethical, or at the least, unbecoming of professional language educators.

The final piece of this curricular puzzle is the question of assessment, particularly the evaluation of programmatic SLOs. At the request of its regional accrediting agency, the UK Department of Hispanic Studies needed to measure programmatic SLOs, which it did not have. Although the department had a mission statement that appeared in the university bulletin, finite and measurable learning objectives had not been established or assessed previously. Somewhat coincidentally, two years earlier, the department had been asked to prepare a curriculum map in which over two dozen target competencies were mapped onto the existing courses, but not with the intention of being measured. Nevertheless, those that could be measured would serve as the SLOs for the annual undergraduate program evaluation, and the results would, ideally, lead to needed change. As with many assessment initiatives in higher education, achieving widespread faculty participation and follow-up proved difficult because a limited number of faculty members were primarily responsible for the collection, analysis, and reporting of the data to college and university administrators, with minimal impact on concrete practice. This outcome is not altogether surprising, given that many faculty members feel unqualified to engage in empirically driven program evaluation, and may even feel suspicious of or threatened by the results.

UK's Department of Hispanic Studies and its curriculum continue to evolve to meet the intellectual, educational, and professional needs of its students. The hope is that this case study encourages readers to reflect on their own programs and areas that are ripe for change while considering larger issues in Spanish postsecondary education in the United States. Several questions arise as a result of this review of UK's experience: What SLOs should be most valued, and who should determine what those are? How can programmatic outcomes be assessed in meaningful ways, and how can more faculty be engaged in assessment? How can recommendations based on the results of program evaluation make their way into classroom practice? These questions must be answered at the local level, taking into consideration contextual realities and empirical evidence, but need to be based on best practices in curriculum design and a sound understanding of instructed second-language acquisition.

## CONCLUSION

Undoubtedly, the typical postsecondary Spanish language curriculum in the United States and its intended learning outcomes are in transition amid ongoing upheaval in the academy regarding the place of the humanities and the role of foreign language learning more specifically. Central to this discussion is the crucial contribution that assessment can make at all levels to demonstrate the usefulness of language learning in higher education and to validate instructors' diligent efforts. To facilitate the transition to a twenty-first-century educational system that values evidence-based learning outcomes reflective of deep translingual and transcultural competence, Norris and Mills (2014, 1) recommend that foreign language programs and educators "begin to think, innovate, and behave programmatically." Sustainable Spanish programs must adopt approaches to curriculum design that lead to more curricular and programmatic synergies and fewer curricular islands, and that cater less to faculty interests and more to students' academic, intellectual, and professional needs. This requires deep introspection that will surely be difficult and most likely challenge the status quo.

## REFLECTION QUESTIONS

1. Identify the most important skills and knowledge that you feel a Spanish major should acquire in the twenty-first century in the United States upon completion with regard to communicative language ability (listening/speaking, reading/writing), cultural competence, and critical thinking. Justify your list to a partner, and then describe how your list might compare with the list prepared by the average undergraduate Spanish student in the US, from the 101 student to the graduating major.

2. Placement procedures for any Spanish program, whether large or small, are heavily influenced by practical constraints, such as budget allocations, information

technology infrastructure, and personnel availability. Outline appropriate placement procedures for each of the following contexts: (1) unlimited resources, and (2) severely limited resources:

a. A large state school admitting any student in the top 50 percent of her high school class with an average of 2,000 incoming Spanish students each fall (unlimited / severely limited).

b. A small, highly selective liberal arts school with fifty to seventy-five incoming Spanish students each fall (unlimited / severely limited).

3. After reading Bachman and Palmer's (1996) explanation of their formula for test usefulness, identify those components of the formula that are most and least addressed in classroom test construction at your institution, and explain why.

4. Why is valid and useful postsecondary Spanish program language evaluation so difficult? What complexities must be dealt with to ensure that program evaluation is done properly and that the results are used effectively?

5. Why might faculty in the humanities and social sciences resist initiatives to improve assessment in their courses or of their programs? What practical steps can be taken to get more buy-in from faculty with regard to assessment literacy?

## PEDAGOGICAL ACTIVITIES

1. Research the placement procedures currently used at your institution and, if possible, complete any written or computer-based exams. Interview the instructors of courses into which students can place directly via exam, as well as the language program director, or chair, concerning the effectiveness of the current procedures. Gather data pertaining to the utility of cut scores for placement tests, the use of empirical evidence to set cut scores, and the articulation of systematic procedures for advanced and heritage students placing into upper-level courses. Report your findings regarding placement procedures, pointing out any deficiencies as well as how to address them.

2. Identify areas of your program that have recently been scrutinized, either due to internal or external pressures, especially those concerning curriculum and assessment. Potential issues include the following: placement procedures, valid classroom assessment, identification of course-level and programmatic learning outcomes, articulation across courses of the same level and different levels, selection of materials and textbooks, execution of valid and useful program evaluation, and improvement of assessment literacy among instructors and faculty.

3. Identify the department/program mission statement, if available, and any programmatic student learning objectives associated with it. Locate any other related documents (e.g., curriculum map, used to plan and revise the curriculum). Finally, procure course syllabi from one elementary, one intermediate, and one advanced content course. Analyze the relationship between these documents and the extent to which the programmatic planning documents appear to have influenced course-level syllabi.

4. Interview the individual primarily responsible for program evaluation as to (1) the identification of SLOs; (2) the procedures adopted for program evaluation,

including faculty members' roles, evaluation questions, data collection and data analysis procedures, and improvement action plans; and (3) the degree to which the results of program evaluation lead to concrete change.

5. Individually interview two or three graduating seniors—preferably one from each major track, if applicable. In your interview, solicit students' perspectives on global aspects of the program (see question 2 above) rather than opinions on specific instructors or courses, unless they reflect larger tendencies characteristic of the program. Compare their responses with your answer to question 2 above. Read the program SLOs to the students, and ask them to what extent they feel that they achieved them—and if so, how; and if not, why not.

## NOTES

1. For an in-depth discussion of placement testing, see Green 2012.
2. This number includes students' first attempts because some took it more than once.

## REFERENCES

ACTFL (American Council on the Teaching of Foreign Languages). 1986. *ACTFL Proficiency Guidelines*. Hastings-on-Hudson, NY: ACTFL.

———. 2012. *ACTFL Proficiency Guidelines*. Alexandria, VA: ACTFL.

Arens, Katherine. 2009. "Teaching Culture: The Standards as an Optic on Curriculum Development." In *Principles and Practices of the Standards in College Foreign Language Education*, edited by Virginia M. Scott. Boston: Heinle, Cengage Learning.

Bachman, Lyle F., and Adrian S. Palmer. 1996. *Language Testing in Practice*. Oxford: Oxford University Press.

Bernhardt, Elizabeth B. 2006. "Student Learning Outcomes as Professional Development and Public Relations." *Modern Language Journal* 90, no. 4: 588–90.

Bordón, Teresa, and Judith E. Liskin-Gasparro. 2015. "The Assessment and Evaluation of Spanish." In *The Routledge Handbook of Hispanic Applied Linguistics*, edited by Manel Lacorte. New York: Routledge.

Brown, Alan V. 2014. "Foreign Language Course Grades as Prerequisites and Programmatic Gatekeepers." In *AAUSC 2014 Volume: Innovation and Accountability in Language Program Evaluation*, edited by John Norris and Nicole Mills. Boston: Cengage.

Brown, Alan, Troy Cox, and Gregory Thompson. 2017. "A Comparative Discourse Analysis of Spanish Past Narrations from the ACTFL OPI and OPIc." *Foreign Language Annals* 50, no. 4.

Brown, H. Douglas, and Priyanvada Abeywickrama. 2010. *Language Assessment*, 2nd ed. White Plains, NY: Pearson Education.

Byrnes, Heidi, ed. 2006. "Perspectives: Interrogating Communicative Competence as a Framework for Collegiate Foreign Language Study. *Modern Language Journal* 90: 244–66.

Brown, James D. 2011. "Foreign and Second Language Needs Analysis." In *The Handbook of Language Teaching*, edited by Michael H. Long and Catherine J. Doughty. Malden, MA: Wiley-Blackwell.

Byrnes, Heidi, Hiram H. Maxim, and John M. Norris. 2010. "Realizing Advanced FL Writing Development in Collegiate Education: Curricular Design, Pedagogy, Assessment." *Modern Language Journal* 94: 1–221.

Canale, Michael, and Merrill Swain. 1980. "Theoretical Bases of Communicative Approaches to Second Language Teaching and Testing." *Applied Linguistics* 1: 1–47.

Carroll, John B. 1967. "Foreign Language Proficiency Levels Attained by Language Majors Near Graduation from College." *Foreign Language Annals* 1: 131–51.

Chase, Geoffrey. 2006. "Focusing on Learning: Reframing Our Roles." *Modern Language Journal* 90, no. 4: 583–85.

Clark, Martyn K., and Saori Ishida. 2005. "Vocabulary Knowledge Differences between Placed and Promoted EAP Students." *Journal of English for Academic Purposes* 4: 225–38.

Coleman, Algernon. 1929. *The Teaching of Modern Foreign Languages in the United States: A Report Prepared for the Modern Foreign Language Study*. New York: Macmillan.

Cox, Troy, and Randall Davies. 2012. "Using Automatic Speech Recognition Technology with Elicited Oral Response Testing." *CALICO Journal* 29, no. 4: 601–18.

Davis, John McE. 2012. "The Usefulness of Accreditation-Mandated Outcomes Assessment in College Foreign Language Education." Doctoral diss., University of Hawaii at Manoa, Honolulu.

———. 2015. "The Usefulness of Accreditation-Mandated Outcomes Assessment: Trends in University Foreign Language Programs." In *Student Learning Outcomes Assessment in College Foreign Language Programs*, edited by John M. Norris and John McE. Davis. Honolulu: University of Hawaii, National Foreign Language Resource Center.

———. 2016. "Toward a Capacity Framework for Useful Student Learning Outcomes in College Foreign Language Programs." *Modern Language Journal* 100, no. 1: 377–99.

Davis, John McE., Young A. Son, Todd McKay, Francesca Venezia, Amy Kim, and Mina Niu. 2016. Useful Evaluation in Language Programs, GURT 2016 Preconference Workshop, unpublished workshop program.

Hughes, Arthur. 2003. *Testing for Language Teachers*, 2nd ed. Cambridge: Cambridge University Press.

Green, Anthony. 2012. "Placement Testing." In *The Cambridge Guide to Second Language Assessment*, edited by Christine Coombe, Peter Davidson, Barry O'Sullivan, and Stephen Stoynoff. New York: Cambridge University Press.

Green, Anthony, and Cyril Weir. 2004. "Can Placement Testing Inform Instructional Decisions?" *Language Testing* 21, no. 4: 467–94.

Irwin, Robert, and Mónica Szurmuk. 2009. "Cultural Studies and the Field of 'Spanish' in the US Academy." *A Contracorriente: A Journal of Social History and Literature in Latin America* 6, no. 3: 36–60.

Kiely, Richard. 2006. "Evaluation, Innovation, and Ownership in Language Programs." *Modern Language Journal* 90, no. 4: 597–601.

Klee, Carol, Charlotte Melin, and Dan Soneson. 2014. "From Frameworks to Oversight: Components to Improving Foreign Language Program Efficacy." In *AAUSC 2014 Volume: Innovation and Accountability in Language Program Evaluation*, edited by John Norris and Nicole Mills. Boston: Cengage.

Kramsch, Claire. 2000. *Context and Culture in Language Teaching*. Oxford: Oxford University Press.

———. 2006. "From Communicative Competence to Symbolic Competence." *Modern Language Journal* 90: 249–52.

Lafford, Barbara A., Abbott, Ann, and Darcy Lear. 2014. "Spanish in the Professions and in the Community in the US." *Journal of Spanish Language Teaching* 1, no. 2: 171–86.

Lee, James F., and Bill VanPatten. 2003. *Making Communicative Language Teaching Happen*. New York: McGraw-Hill.

Lord, Gillian, and Christina Isabelli-García. 2015. "Program Articulation and Management." In *The Routledge Handbook of Hispanic Applied Linguistics*, edited by Manel Lacorte. New York: Routledge.

Magnan, Sally S. 1986. "Assessing Speaking Proficiency in the Undergraduate Curriculum: Data from French." *Foreign Language Annals* 19, no. 5: 429–38.

Malone, Margaret. 2011. "Assessment Literacy for Educators." www.cal.org/content/download/1516/15923/file/AssessmentLiteracyforLanguageEducators.pdf.

McNamara, Tim. 2000. *Language Testing*. Oxford: Oxford University Press.

Morris, Michael. 2006. "Addressing the Challenges of Program Evaluation: One Department's Experience after Two Years." *Modern Language Journal* 90, no. 4: 585–88.

Nation, I. S. P., and John Macalister. 2010. *Language Curriculum Design*. New York: Routledge.

National Standards in Foreign Language Education Project. 1996. *Standards for Foreign Language Learning: Preparing for the 21st Century*. Lawrence, KS: Allen Press.

Norris, John M. 2004. "Validity Evaluation in Foreign Language Assessment." PhD diss., University of Hawaii at Manoa.

———. 2006. "The Why and (How) of Student Learning Outcomes Assessment in College FL Education." *Modern Language Journal* 90, no. 4: 576–83.

Norris, John M., and Nicole Mills. 2014. "Introduction: Innovation and Accountability in Foreign Language Program Evaluation." In *AAUSC 2014 Volume: Innovation and Accountability in Language Program Evaluation*, edited by John Norris and Nicole Mills. Boston: Cengage.

Norris, John M., John McE. Davis, Castle Sinicrope, and Yukiko Watanabe, eds. 2009. *Toward Useful Program Evaluation in College Foreign Language Education*. Honolulu: National Foreign Language Resource Center.

Omaggio Hadley, Alice. 1986. *Teaching Language in Context*. Boston: Heinle & Heinle.

Paesani, Kate, and Catherine M. Barrette. 2005. "The Role of the Language Program Director within a Three-Dimensional Model of Articulation." In *Language Program Articulation: Developing a Theoretical Foundation*, edited by Catherine M. Barrette and Kate Paesani. Boston: Heinle & Heinle.

Patton, Michael Q. 2008. *Utilization-Focused Evaluation*, 4th ed. Thousand Oaks, CA: Sage.

Rifkin, Benjamin. 2005. "A Ceiling Effect in Traditional Classroom Foreign Language Instruction: Data from Russian." *Modern Language Journal* 89: 3–18.

Rossomondo, Amy. 2012. "The Acceso Project and Foreign Language Graduate Student Professional Development." In *Educating the Future Foreign Language Professoriate for the 21st Century*, edited by Heather W. Allen and Hiram Maxim. Boston: Heinle & Heinle.

Schmitt, Elena. 2014. "Seat Time Versus Proficiency: Assessment of Language Development in Undergraduate Students." In *AAUSC 2014 Volume: Innovation and Accountability in Language Program Evaluation*, edited by John Norris and Nicole Mills. Boston: Cengage.

Schulz, Renate. 2006. "Reevaluating Communicative Competence as a Major Goal in Postsecondary Language Requirement Courses." *Modern Language Journal* 90: 252–55.

Sullivan, Joann H. 2006. "The Importance of Program Evaluation in Collegiate Foreign Language Programs." *Modern Language Journal* 90, no. 4: 590–93.

Swaffar, Janet. 2006. "Terminology and Its Discontents: Some Caveats about Communicative Competence." *Modern Language Journal* 90: 246–49.

Swaffar, Janet, and Katherine Arens. 2005. *Remapping the Foreign Language Curriculum: An Approach Through Multiple Literacies*. New York: MLA.

Swender, E. 2003. "Oral Proficiency Testing in the Real World: Answers to Frequently Asked Questions." *Foreign Language Annals* 36, no. 4: 520–26.

Thompson, L. G., L. T. Cox, and N. Knapp. 2016. "Comparing the OPI and the OPIc: The Effect of Test Method on Oral Proficiency Scores and Student Preference." *Foreign Language Annals* 49, no. 1: 75–92.

Tschirner, Erwin. 2016. "Listening and Reading Proficiency Levels of College Students." *Foreign Language Annals* 49, no. 2: 201–23.

Tyler, Ralph W. 1949. *Basic Principles of Curriculum and Instruction.* Chicago: University of Chicago Press.

University of Kentucky. 2015. *Undergraduate Bulletin.* www.uky.edu/registrar/sites/www .uky.edu.registrar/files/a&s.pdf.

VanPatten, Bill. 2015. "Where Are the Experts?" *Hispania* 98, no. 1: 2–13.

Wall, Diane, Caroline Clapham, and J. Charles Alderson. 1994. "Evaluating a Placement Test." *Language Testing* 11, no. 3: 321–44.

Wesche, Marjorie, T. Sima Paribakht, and Doreen Ready. 1996. "A Comparative Study of Four Placement Instruments." In *Performance Testing, Cognition and Assessment,* edited by Michael Milanovic and Nick Saville. Cambridge: Cambridge University Press.

Wright, Barbara D. 2006. "Learning Languages and the Language of Learning." *Modern Language Journal* 90, no. 4: 593–97.

# 7

# CONNECTING SPANISH LANGUAGE EDUCATION WITH SOCIAL, ECONOMIC, AND POLITICAL REALITIES

> It is not enough simply to add diverse representations . . . of local varieties; educators must engage students in critical examinations of . . . social and political structures, institutions, and processes, including how language is used to reproduce inequality, as well as its liberating possibilities.
>
> —Jennifer Leeman, "Critical Approaches to Teaching Spanish," 2015

Though rather tautological, it is crucial to point out that natural languages facilitate communication between humans whose identity is intricately intertwined with the languages they speak and who form part of various groups, which in turn are embedded in complex social and political structures. Notwithstanding commonly used mechanistic metaphors in second-language acquisition—such as *input, output,* and *information processing* (Pennycook 2001)—to ignore the sociocultural and sociopolitical realities surrounding second-language education is to reduce it to the sterile transmission of information akin to computer code. As such, classroom language learning does not, and has never, occurred in a social, political, historical, and cultural vacuum. What goes on outside the classroom regarding the identity of and relationships between those who use it, and their relationship with those who do not, exerts influence on the teaching and learning of that language in the classroom. As outlined in chapter 2, Spanish language education has a particularly complex history in the United States, in which questions of race, ethnicity, socioeconomic class, and individual and national identity have all been implicated in some form or another.

Each postsecondary Spanish student embodies the confluence of diverse motivations and attitudes—sometimes contradictory, sometimes harmonious—toward the Spanish language and its users, as well as an accumulation of individual life experiences. Though surely many students have not formulated concrete opinions at a conscious level on every sociocultural and sociopolitical issue that might affect their classroom learning, a litany of questions arises about students' motivations, attitudes, and life experiences:

- Did the student enroll in Spanish to fulfill a curricular requirement as quickly as possible, to improve his or her communicative ability, to become more competitive as a future professional, to connect with his or her heritage, to expand his or her worldview and gain greater insights into the cultures and perspectives of those who use the language, or some combination of all these?
- What is the nature of her own sociolinguistic identity and those of close family members and friends? How does she and those closest to her view language learning? Does it depend on the language?
- Does he perceive himself to have a high or low aptitude for language learning? What is his understanding of language variation and *correct* English and Spanish?
- What are her perceptions of the culture of native users of the language in her community, the United States more generally, and those from predominantly Spanish-speaking countries?
- Where does he weigh in on bilingualism, English-only legislation, and linguistic rights? What is his perspective on the role of majority and minority language learning in nation building and solidarity? What underlying ideologies, linguistic and political, influence these perspectives?
- Does she harbor any racial or socioeconomic class prejudices, and what role does language play in perpetuating or eliminating those biases?

Similar questions might be asked of collegiate Spanish instructors, adding additional layers of complexity to the sociocultural dynamic of the Spanish language classroom and the larger milieu of which it is a part.

At the curricular and programmatic level, additional questions surface related to *what* to teach, *how much* of it, at *what levels*, and *what outcomes* to expect. More specifically, how much time should Spanish language educators spend in their classrooms raising students' critical awareness of how language can perpetuate or eliminate inequitable social and political structures, empower or disenfranchise certain groups, and facilitate or undermine social justice? For the collegiate Spanish instructor faced with twenty-five to thirty students in a beginning-level class who struggle to communicate even the most basic messages, it is quite understandable why they might prefer that such content be left to courses in anthropology or (socio-)linguistics rather than second-language courses. Although it is valid to ask how Spanish instructors and curriculum designers can afford to incorporate such content into their teaching with all that they are asked to cover, the realities of twenty-first-century Anglo-American culture and society oblige us to also ask, How can they afford *not* to?

In this chapter, we begin by briefly defining critical approaches to Spanish language teaching as they provide the overarching framework for understanding how social, economic, and political realities external to the classroom might influence postsecondary Spanish language programs. Following this discussion, the chapter reviews historical and contemporary trends in American society concerning the use of Spanish in the United States and how that has shaped current debates regarding American nationalism, English-only legislation, attitudes toward Spanish-English bilingualism, and language ideology.[1] We then present several perspectives on how best to incorporate critical approaches in Spanish language programs, focusing on curricular and programmatic concerns rather than day-to-day classroom pedagogy per se. Finally, we conclude, summarizing the results of our national survey and highlight the importance of situating Spanish language education into the larger sociocultural context of the United States.

## CRITICAL APPROACHES TO PEDAGOGY, APPLIED LINGUISTICS, AND LANGUAGE AWARENESS

Though the relationship between education, oppression, and the emancipation of marginalized populations in society has been studied for centuries, Paolo Freire (1970) provided one of the most lucid explanations of this relationship in the modern era in his seminal book, *Pedagogy of the Oppressed*, which argued that in many cases institutionalized, formal education dehumanizes and oppresses students by restricting their freedom, stifling inquiry, and forcing them to passively receive immutable knowledge imparted by unquestioned authority figures. Other scholars (Giroux 1983; Mclaren 1989) have expanded on Freire's original work and contributed to the intellectually robust field of critical pedagogy that examines how macropolitical structures in society influence power relations in the classroom and students' agency. Scholars in the language sciences have applied the principles of critical pedagogy to second-language learning and teaching contexts more specifically. Our objective in the ensuing discussion is to lay the fundamental conceptual groundwork for critical pedagogy before discussing how the field might inform tertiary Spanish language education in the United States in the twenty-first century.

Pennycook (2004) deconstructs the semantics of the word *critical* in critical applied linguistics, contrasting it with the use of critical in "critical thinking," a phrase used to refer to the application of a set of cognitive skills aimed at achieving increased analytical rigor or as a means to arrive at deeper understanding of a particular issue. He argues that Widdowson's (2001) application of the word *critical* to applied linguistics is insufficient because it only alludes to the recognition of multiple realities and the need to reconcile diverse perspectives in linguistics and language education. For scholars of critical applied linguistics, it is not enough to identify and accept the value of diverse language forms, uses, cultures, and perspectives; they must also delve deeper by questioning how language and culture concretely affect an individual's agency and autonomy. In Pennycook's (2004, 797) view, critical applied linguistics transcends mere description and correlation "between language and society, and instead raises more critical questions to do with access, power, disparity, desire, difference, and resistance. It also insists on a historical understanding of how social relations came to be the way they are."

Similarly, Leeman (2015, 275) observes that a crucial component of critical approaches to language pedagogy is "the dialogic examination of how ideologies, politics, and social hierarchies are embodied, reproduced, and naturalized in language learning and teaching." However, as Leeman notes in the epigraph to this chapter, Spanish language educators must go beyond a simple survey of multiple varieties of Spanish or an overview of the cultural products and perspectives of those who speak it. Leeman stresses that engaging in the intellectual exercise of critiquing oppression "must be accompanied by actions that seek to disrupt and improve on the status quo . . . [and] that result in positive social change." Critical approaches to language pedagogy could not be labeled as such without addressing the sociocultural and sociopolitical realities and forces external to the classroom that implicate the language being taught. Rather than simply equipping language students with linguistic competence to transmit messages within a social and political vacuum, critical pedagogy seeks to empower students as informed agents of change as they strive to rectify power imbalances and to emancipate those whose voices have been silenced and who have been denied access to key discourses.

At the heart of critical approaches to second-language education is the importance of questioning *why* with regard to the relationship between language use and notions of appropriateness. Fairclough (1992, 52) contrasts *critical language awareness* with *language awareness* by highlighting the tendency of the latter to address socioeducational problems by facilitating the acquisition of standard forms and dialects, while the former encourages students to question the standard. Teaching students how to speak a certain way or pointing out which forms to use in certain contexts does not give them insight into why those forms are the standard and who benefits from them remaining the standard: "It is common to find linguists writing about what 'is appropriate' in a speech community rather than what is 'judged to be appropriate' (by particular groups)." Fairclough concedes that critical language awareness should not force students to flout socially constructed conventions of appropriateness to the point of disadvantage and marginalization but should empower them with understanding to facilitate informed choice and engaged linguistic citizenship.

Broad definitions of critical approaches to language learning are helpful to construct an abstract conceptual framework, but it is vital to drill down to the concrete applications of theory and how they might play out in Spanish language programs throughout the United States. A host of relevant topics that fall within the purview of critical pedagogy that could be discussed include the social and political impact of the English-only movement and legislation on bilingual Spanish-English communities; the influence of standard language ideologies on the prestige afforded Peninsular and Latin American varieties of Spanish in university Spanish departments at the expense of US varieties; the propagation of the deficit model for understanding and educating bilingual, migrant students; the loss of Spanish ability and the erosion of ties to the heritage culture among second- and third-generation Latinos as a result of linguistic imperialism.

One unifying thread that has been woven throughout this book is the tremendous diversity present among university Spanish language students. Critical Spanish language pedagogy will most likely be received quite differently by various groups of students, depending on their identity and their social status within society. Although it is beyond the scope of this chapter to describe all possible student reactions, we offer three student profiles that would most likely respond quite differently to critical approaches. For example, the lived experiences of upper-middle-class Anglo-American members of the social, cultural, racial, and linguistic majority acquiring Spanish as elite bilinguals would probably differ from working-class first- and second-generation Latino students with strong ties to Spanish dominant speech communities and relatively little social capital who use highly stigmatized varieties of Spanish and English. The ways in which students of different sociodemographic profiles interpret the larger social and political implications of learning Spanish in the United States in a university classroom will be varied and could be the source of tension, understanding, or both.

## SOCIAL, ECONOMIC, AND POLITICAL CONTEXTS FOR THE TEACHING OF SPANISH

Unlike chapter 2, which provided a brief history of the teaching of Spanish within the current borders of the United States, this section provides richer context for Spanish postsecondary education by delving deeper into the specific social, economic, and political issues related to the place of Spanish in contemporary US society. This discussion incorporates controversial issues in American society—such as racism, discrimination, language policy, and language ideology, among others—that can be seen from different viewpoints and that elicit strong opinions. Although the scope and intent of this chapter do not allow for a detailed analysis of all sides of the various issues covered, we have selected those we feel directly influence contemporary postsecondary Spanish language education.

## "Standard" Language Ideology

Surely there are many points of departure in considering how various sociocultural and sociopolitical forces influence collegiate Spanish language education. We have decided to ground our analysis in the concept of "standard" language ideology and to use it as the lens through which the evolution and impact of contextual realities on Spanish language education in the United States can be understood. Language ideologies are complex constructs that shed light on how speakers view themselves and others and how they make sense of the social, economic, and political issues related to language. Pomerantz (2002, 279) offers a general definition of language ideologies: "[They] shape how people understand themselves and others. By privileging certain ways of understanding people and events in the world, ideologies devalue alternate forms of interpretation and thus reaffirm their own prestige and endurance."

Lippi-Green (2012, 67) provides a definition of *standard* language ideology, influenced by the work of Milroy (2001), Silverstein (1992), and Fairclough (1989): "A bias toward an abstracted, idealized, homogeneous spoken language which is imposed and maintained by dominant bloc institutions and which names as its model the written language, but which is drawn primarily from the spoken language of the upper middle class."

With these definitions in mind, it is not hard to envisage how standard language ideology is implicated in a long list of politically charged issues at the national level:

- the immigration of foreign-born and, particularly, non-English speaking individuals;
- the maintenance of a culturally and linguistically homogeneous nation-state;
- the impact of immigration on the unemployment rate and state of the economy;
- the perpetuation of racism toward ethnically and linguistically diverse groups;

- the marginalization and ghettoization of minority groups;
- the establishment of immersion programs for language majority and minority speakers; and
- the ratification of English-only legislation.

Lippi-Green (2012, 68) argues that standard language ideology lies at the heart of language domination and discrimination and is complicit in a multi-stage language subordination process that can result in overt threats to users of the marginalized language or variety—for example, *If you speak that way you'll never get a good job*. Lippi-Green places much of the blame on the institutions that are supposed to be liberating individuals and expanding their horizons, namely, schools. Put succinctly, she claims that "to suggest that children who do not speak *SAE [standard American English] will find acceptance and validation in the schools is, in a word, ludicrous." Standard language ideol-ogy  surfaces in interpersonal encounters quite commonly when a language majority speaker—feeling empowered by his or her status as a speaker of the standard variety—refuses to share the communicative burden with an interlocutor whose speech is accented or contains other nonstandard features. In cases like these, in which most of the communicative burden has been transferred to the nonnative or nonstandard speaker, an expression such as "I can't understand you" is better understood as "You can't make me understand you." Lippi-Green points out that many speakers of standard varieties, on the contrary, will exert much more effort to repair communicative breakdown when another speaker of the standard variety has been unclear or incoherent, finding reasons to share the communicative burden and prolong the encoun-ter. It is not that efficient and effective communication is not preferred by all, but it is disturbing that a standard variety could be used to devalue variation, to enthrone uniformity, to justify linguistic discrimination, and to limit basic linguistic rights.

## Perspectives on Bilingualism

Field (2011) argues that the first step in understanding how Spanish and Spanish speakers are perceived by many in contemporary Anglo-American society is to consider attitudes toward bilingualism more generally, which have been rather ambivalent and contradictory.[2] On one hand, a university graduate's proficiency in languages other than English is to be applauded and indexes intelligence and achievement, while the analytical and critical think-ing skills of an elementary student whose mastery of a heritage language sur-passes his or her English are questioned. Similarly, foreign language learning for Anglo-Americans at the postsecondary level is more likely to be lauded as beneficial for the economy than strong forms of bilingual education designed to maintain heritage languages in the elementary schools. Though native bilingual ability seems to be beneficial for those initially hired into positions with a high oral service component, it is not as valued for upper-level management positions (Alarcón et al. 2014; Villa and Villa 2005). These ambivalent attitudes are clearly not arbitrary and seem to be driven by social, cultural, political, and economic factors.

According to Field (2011), the three most powerful factors in shaping American attitudes toward bilingualism relate to (1) immigration, (2) education, and (3) language. For many, immigration is intricately intertwined with the status of the economy, the availability of jobs, and the changing profile of residential neighborhoods. Immigration also triggers heated discussions concerning legislation governing residency and citizenship requirements for new arrivals. Education is another key factor, given the role schools play in the inculcation of society's moral values and the connection between an effective educational system and individual and collective economic success. Additionally, notions of what language is and the nature of the language–culture nexus can exert an influence on Americans' perspectives of the need for cultural *and* linguistic homogeneity to achieve national unity and solidarity.

These factors influence each other in dynamic ways, such as when a large influx of immigrants causes the ethnic majority to fear for their jobs as a result of the increased competition from workers willing to accept lower pay. This, in turn, may lead to increased demand for housing, which drives up the rental and real estate markets; or, on the contrary, it may lead to decreased prices as the demographics of a residential area shift and become standardized, and the area becomes less desirable for the ethnic and linguistic majority. Unfortunately, there is a high likelihood that the education of newly arrived immigrants' children will be upstaged by the majority's concern over an overburdened school system. Field (2011, 162) expresses his consternation over the ongoing, highly politicized debate that pits bilingual education against immersive approaches to English as a second language: "If public perceptions are that a certain immigrant or minority group is lazy or does not want to participate in Americanization, . . . then that offending group should expect to be isolated and unwelcome."

Yet the rhetoric involving Mexican immigrants is even more complex. According to Flores (2003, 367), these immigrants are often the protagonists of two concurrent narratives—"the narrative of need and the narrative of the Mexican problem." On one hand, Spanish-speaking immigrants are spoken of by some as lazy, unwilling to learn English, and resistant to culturally assimilate, while on the other hand they can be portrayed as hard working, willing to do jobs others would not, and crucial to the success of the economy. Part of this ambivalent discourse includes internal contradictions as demands are made of Spanish monolingual and Spanish-dominant immigrants to learn English but access to affordable English classes is placed out of reach (DuBord 2014), due to cost, to state-mandated eligibility requirements, or to an extremely taxing work schedule.

During the early days of the United States, when many other concerns were more pressing and cultural enclaves in rural areas were more autonomous, the prevailing sentiment toward bilingualism, Field (2011) argues, was one of acceptance and tolerance. Schools operated primarily under local control, with the community's and children's needs reflected in the curriculum. As such, many schools offered instruction in the heritage languages of communities, with large immigrant populations that were culturally and linguistically homogeneous, particularly German-speaking communities in the eastern United States. However, the nineteenth century was also a time when the doctrine of Manifest Destiny led to the expulsion of Native Americans from their tribal homelands and contributed to the philosophy of one nation, one culture, and one language. The process of Anglicization and assimilation of indigenous and migrant populations culturally, socially, and linguistically reflected the conventional wisdom that language not only influenced thought but also could determine it. The arrival of scores of immigrants at the end of the nineteenth and beginning of the twentieth centuries intensified foreign-born migrants' efforts to Americanize, primarily via acquisition of the English language. The incorporation of Spanish-dominant citizens in the Southwest from lands acquired from Mexico appeared to reflect a maintenance approach; but by the beginning of the twentieth century, it was clear that this approach was unabashedly assimilationist.

The first half of the twentieth century was marred by devastating wars that had a deep impact on Americans' perspectives on foreign languages and, unfortunately, bilingualism and multilingualism. World War I resulted in a steep decline in foreign language enrollments, especially in German, at all levels. The political and social upheaval caused by World War II and the totalitarian regimes that took root immediately after it led to massive migrations within Europe and deep-seeded suspicion of communism, foreigners, and foreignness in the United States, as embodied by McCarthyism. At the same time, the nation was experiencing a period of economic expansion and increased wealth due to advances in technology and the addition of thousands of military personnel to the workforce, who started their own families. The white baby boomer generation benefited socially and economically from the prosperous postwar period, and though it may have led to increased socioeconomic inequality across racial and ethnic groups, Field argues that the increase in personal wealth and prosperity among the white majority resulted in greater acceptance of language minorities, contributing to the emergence of the civil rights movement and the cultural revolution of the 1960s. Several pieces of legislation were passed that contributed to a sympathetic environment conducive to the proliferation of bilingualism and multilingualism: The Civil Rights Act of 1964 prohibited discrimination based on national origin, race, color, and sex, with implications for discrimination based on native language; the Immigration and Nationality Act of 1965 lifted the quota system for immigration; and the Bilingual Education Act of 1967 ensured equal educational opportunity for minority language speakers.

The latter part of the twentieth century and early part of the twenty-first century have reflected the ambivalence mentioned above, as the 1970s, 1980s, and 1990s saw the establishment of immersion and bilingual programs in public schools that were then considered ineffective and were nearly dismantled during the early 2000s in the West and Southwest. Fears among the cultural and linguistic majority surfaced regarding the arrival of increasing numbers of poor, undocumented immigrants from Mexico and Central America, who had limited formal education and struggled to learn English. These fears, coupled with simplistic notions of how languages are learned, were politicized in the form of the English-only movement and accompanying legislation. Those who argue in favor of the English-only movement see it as a necessary and practical step to facilitate commerce and civic engagement, and to avoid social and cultural fragmentation. Those who oppose such legislation see it as an affront to bilingual communities, particularly Spanish-dominant bilinguals, and as a poor cover-up for outright racism, ethnocentrism, and even xenophobia.

The racism and linguistic prejudice that many would argue undergird the English-only movement are juxtaposed with the increased social and commercial intercourse between people of all languages, cultures, and countries facilitated by the internet. *Globalization* has become a buzzword in the mass media, on university campuses, and within university curricula as markets, economies, languages, and cultures interface more easily and more frequently. It would seem logical that any talk of the need to give the rising generation a globalized education would be accompanied by efforts to strengthen language learning. Nevertheless, the worldwide economic recession and, primarily, the increasing international ubiquity and hegemony of English have served to curb many Americans' enthusiasm for foreign language learning and the increased opportunities to interact easily and frequently with speakers of all languages. Moreover, racial, ethnic, and linguistic prejudice and stereotypes continue to overshadow the United States' perspective on multilingualism, despite the desperate need for Americans to achieve greater linguistic proficiency and cultural sensitivity in an increasingly diverse, pluralistic, and globalized world.

## Spanish in the United States

The story of Spanish in the United States is a human, not a linguistic, story, in which social, political, and economic realities have all influenced how those who use Spanish natively have been perceived by the majority of American society, particularly Anglo-Americans. The opinions people form of languages they do not speak are closely associated with the way they view the individuals who speak them and the stereotypes that arise from their cultural customs, worldviews, and social behaviors, particularly those that differ from accepted norms (Field 2011). How American society views French, Spanish, or Chinese people is more likely to reflect their perceptions, and often stereotypes, of French, Spanish, and Chinese speakers and their culture than it is to reflect anything having to do with the structure of the language per se. Lippi-Green (2012) notes the common use of this strategy in theater and film and stridently bemoans its use in movies tailored to children. Indeed, for many among the monolingual Anglo-American majority in the United States, use of the Spanish language evokes strong, negative stereotypes, particularly when spoken by those of a certain ethnic group or socioeconomic class.

Scholars like Field (2011, 174) conclude that such negative perceptions are "rooted in ethnicity" and also "racial and cultural elements." But to speak of ethnic and racial stereotypes and linguistic prejudice without seeking plausible explanations for them is far too reductive and puts the proverbial cart before the horse. In del Valle's (2013) edited volume, *A Political History of Spanish*, del Valle and García (2013, 249–50) claim that the status of Spanish in the United States, historically and presently, is closely tied to the linguistic operationalization of the first words of the US Constitution, "We the people of the United States." They clarify that to pursue the goals stated in the preamble to the Constitution, American nationalists have created policies and discourses that "have aimed at establishing and naturalizing English as the essential instrument for the political articulation of the community and as a symbol of the nation . . . by associating citizenship with knowledge of English and by displacing Spanish and other languages to marginal positions through institutional arrangements and discourses on language."

The desire to construct and consolidate a national identity vis-à-vis the preeminence of English has had clear repercussions for the pervasiveness of "standard" language ideology and the use of other languages at all levels of discourse and in nearly all domains. Moreover, the representation of English and

Spanish in the national imaginary can be explained by the evolution of American capitalism, whereby different social classes strive to defend their socioeconomic interests. Del Valle and García (2013, 251) argue that to understand language ideologies in the US, it is imperative to examine the massive waves of migration from Spanish-speaking countries and the discursive construction of migration, "either as part of the nation's condition or as a threat to its very identity." Notwithstanding the civil rights movement of the 1960s and 1970s and the progress made toward racial and linguistic equality, the racialization of Spanish as a suspicious and foreign element within the country became more conspicuous during the 1980s and 1990s, as large numbers of Spanish speakers migrated to the United States. The English-only movement and the accompanying legislation it championed converted Spanish into a symbolic threat to the country's identity and a stumbling block to its progress. But even more injurious was the deep wound it opened with the large and growing Hispanic and Spanish-speaking populations in the United States.

Unfortunately, the racialization of Spanish and the delegitimization of Spanish and Spanish speakers began much before contemporary efforts at making English a national language gained momentum. Several scholars have traced the marginalization of Spanish and Spanish speakers in the United States, particularly Mexican Americans, from the nineteenth and early twentieth centuries to the present. DuBord (2013) describes the contested status of Spanish on the southwestern frontier in Tucson, in the middle to late nineteenth century, soon after annexation as Mexicans and Anglos struggled to appropriate the discourse surrounding Spanish for diverse purposes. Fernández-Gibert (2013) provides an in-depth, and quite disturbing, analysis of New Mexico's embattled entry into the Union by arguing that the most decisive factor in achieving statehood was the demographic transformation of the territory's population from primarily Spanish-speaking and mestizo to English-speaking and Caucasian. Martinez (2013, 296) provides evidence of the delegitimization and racialization of Spanish by exploring the biosocial categorization of Mexicans in early-twentieth-century Texas as "diseased, dirty and disorderly." Figure 7.1 seems to embody this sentiment. Leeman's (2013, 323) deconstruction of the race and language questions on the United States census demonstrates how it institutionalizes particular ideologies that highlight racial, ethnic, and linguistic difference, specifically those related to the Spanish language: "Whereas early-twentieth-century censuses cast Spanish mother tongue as a hereditary indicator of intra-white difference, the current race, ethnicity, and language questions construct Spanish as the language of Latinos, regardless of whether or not they actually speak it while also imagining a rejection of English."

**Figure 7.1   A Sign Outside a Restaurant in Dimmitt, Texas, 1949**

*Note:* This photograph, "Discrimination, Dimmitt, Texas," by Lee (Russell Werner), 1949, is reprinted by permission of the Dolph Briscoe Center for American History at the University of Texas, Austin.

Although references to overt racism and discrimination during the nineteenth and early twentieth centuries may *not* be surprising to some, Lippi-Green (2012) documents recent manifestations of linguistic intolerance and discrimination toward Spanish-dominant users that are rather unsettling. From the Texas police officers who wrote extralegal citations to drivers without English proficiency to the judge who equated the use of Spanish by parents with their young children to abuse, it is clear that discrimination against Spanish-dominant, ethnic minorities is alive and well in twenty-first-century America. Barrett (2006) found similar evidence of discrimination in his revealing ethnographic research, which documented how racial and linguistic segregation between English-speaking Anglos and Spanish-speaking Latino employees reflected deeply entrenched social hierarchies in the workplace. One linguistic behavior engaged in by many of the Anglo-American workers in Barrett's study has been called *Mock Spanish*, or hyperanglicized Spanish inserted into predominantly English discourse by English-dominant speakers to establish a jocular or pejorative key. Hill (1998, 684) bemoans the use of Mock Spanish in American culture, as in "*Hasta la vista*, baby" (*Terminator* films), arguing that the whites' use of Mock Spanish, or "linguistic disorder," "is rendered invisible and normative, while the linguistic behavior of . . . Spanish-speaking populations is highly visible and the object of constant monitoring." Essentially, what Hill argues is that given their status as the social, cultural, and linguistic majority, Anglo-Americans feel empowered to serve as language brokers, determining which distortions of language, and which languages, are acceptable, comical, or detrimental, and which are not.

Zentella (1996) recounts how disorienting it was for her as a young Latina in the United States to compare the dancing Chiquita banana singing in a heavy Spanish accent with the Latinas in her life. She laments such heavily stereotyped representations of Latinas, calling it the *chiquitification* of Latino cultures, and she identifies three crucial misconceptions it generates: (1) The Hispanic community is culturally homogeneous and refuses to learn English, (2) the varieties of Spanish used in Latin America are inferior to the Castilian varieties used in Spain, (3) speakers from the second generation are really semilinguals or alinguals who lack native-like proficiency in any language. The subordination of Spanish and the deep prejudice toward Spanish-speaking ethnic minorities is not lost on Spanish speakers themselves. as Zentella's reflections demonstrate. When Spanish speakers were asked to identify what they considered to be the primary source of discrimination against them, Hakimzadeh and Cohn (2007) found that nearly half (48 percent) of their survey participants chose *language* rather than other potential sources of discrimination, such as skin color, income, education, and immigration status.

In spite of such compelling evidence for the ongoing linguistic subordination of Spanish and discrimination against Spanish-dominant speakers in the broader Anglo-American society, it continues to be the most commonly taught non-English language at all levels of instruction. Del Valle and García (2013) attribute this apparent paradox to competing ideologies: one that would promote national solidarity and unity vis-à-vis one language and culture and one that would equip citizens of that nation with the necessary skills to compete in an increasingly globalized, capitalistic economy. As Leeman (2006, 38) has observed, increases in Spanish course enrollments do not necessarily indicate concomitant increases in prestige, but rather "the commodification of language and the contemporary fixation on the marketability of particular types of knowledge and education." At this point, two conclusions are in order: (1) Standard language ideology does appear to have influenced perceptions of Spanish in the United States among many of the linguistic and ethnic majority, and (2) language subordination and discrimination are a reality that many native Spanish speakers face in the United States in the twenty-first century, particularly those of mestizo and indigenous heritage, regardless of their legal status.

## CURRICULAR IMPLICATIONS

Although much more could be written concerning language discrimination and subordination, we now turn to how these realities might influence post-secondary Spanish curricula in the United States. As we broach the issue of curricular reform, we return to our hypothetical students from the beginning of the chapter and contemplate how their identity and predispositions toward social justice, language subordination, and linguistic discrimination might influence their reactions to learning Spanish and the inclusion of critical content in Spanish courses of all disciplines and at all levels. For example, how do we respond to Anglo-American students who are not convinced that Mock Spanish has racist or demeaning undertones and that it is harmless and just "for fun," or how do we encourage all students to share the communicative burden with interlocutors regardless of the contextual circumstances, or what do we say to students who insist that Spanish class should only be for acquisition of the linguistic code and that politics and activism have no place in the language classroom? And what if this student is a heritage speaker? For some language students, discussions of "standard" language ideology, discrimination, critical language awareness, and racism may seem peripheral at best and completely irrelevant at worst. Contrarily, instructors who dramatically and abruptly increase the amount of sociopolitical content in their collegiate Spanish classes run the risk of implicitly communicating to students that many Anglo-American monolinguals in society, if not most, are inherently racist, prejudiced, and prone to uncritically accept stereotypes, which, of course, is a stereotype in itself. Therefore, the question of what to teach, how to interweave it with classroom language instruction, and how to evaluate it are difficult issues when it comes to critical pedagogy in the Spanish language classroom and curriculum. Pennycook (2001, 130) notes that one valid critique of critical pedagogy is "its tendency to remain at the level of grand theorizing rather than pedagogical practice."

Ironically, in some ways, widely published textbooks and their ancillary materials are complicit in perpetuating stereotypes and misrepresentations that critical pedagogy aims to combat. Hortiguera (2012) found that many textbook videos were quite reductive in their presentation of each country's culture by presenting the country's geography in dramatic extremes, from arid deserts and exotic jungles to towering volcanoes and frigid glaciers; by describing the inhabitants of each country as festive and jovial, using phrases such as "simple and courageous" (*sencilla y valiente*) and "warm and friendly" (*cálida y amable*); and by limiting much of the cultural history to medieval and renaissance architecture, in the case of Spain, and to indigenous or colonial architecture, in the case of Latin America. Hortiguera also discovered key omissions and an ironic and critical tone when governments were discussed, especially those with political ideologies that could affect American interests. Hortiguera (2012, 18–19) fears that these educational videos strengthen stereotypes because they "do not problematize those representations but rather corroborate them, ironically, in their Spanish classes. By way of a complex apparatus of generalizations, abstractions, omissions, contrasts, or inferences, the *other* is relegated to a marginalized space, folkloric in nature, that identifies it with frivolity, recreation, and hedonism."[3]

Though Herman (2007, 131) concedes that the cultural content of Spanish secondary language textbooks has evolved from the use of rather blatant racial stereotypes (Arizpe and Aguirre 1987; Elissondo 2001), she argues that the primary objective of many textbooks is to help students travel and shop in exotic places. She finds a conspicuous lack of language that would enable students to "describe societal structures, intergroup relations or conflicts, and ethnic or indigenous issues. . . . Indeed, there is no portrayal of a society beyond the atomized level of the individual." Equally disturbing is the tendency to depict school life and educational systems as similar to what most white middle-class students experience in the United States. Throughout their classroom textbooks, students are led to believe that a large majority of teenagers in other cultures have equal access to high-quality low- or no-cost secondary education, that they do not need to work, and that they have plenty of free time to shop and socialize in cafés and restaurants. They see themselves reflected in the pages of Spanish, confirming Kramsch's (1988) concern that the foreign culture is presented as nearly the same as the native culture. Herman points out that this skewed perspective is largely the fault of publishing houses and their self-censorship as they protect their bottom line, but she also blames language teachers for not demanding more substantive sociopolitical content and for not being willing take on difficult issues in their classes.

Not surprisingly, critical approaches to Spanish language education resonate quite strongly with many heritage Spanish speakers who have experienced linguistic discrimination and social marginalization first hand or who have witnessed close family and friends who have. (Correa 2011; Leeman, Rabin, and Román-Mendoz 2011; Pomerantz 2002, 2008; Wright 2007). Heritage speakers may be the target of language-based discrimination on two fronts in the university context: (1) perceived ineptitude with academic English as semilinguals, rather than bilinguals, and (2) use of stigmatized, contact varieties of Spanish considered inferior to normative, monolingual varieties. For many Spanish programs in which standard language ideology has become deeply ingrained in the curriculum and programmatic culture, strict hierarchies arise that marginalize some heritage speakers, ironically, because of their Spanish rather than their English (Villa 2002). Instead of feeling at home in an academic department that validates their linguistic abilities, some feel pushed to the periphery. Valdés and others (2003, 24) document this tendency in one prominent postsecondary Spanish department and conclude that Spanish departments may perpetuate American monolingualism and enthrone English as the national language by transmitting "ideologies of nationalism (one language, one nation), standardness (a commitment to linguistic purity and correctness), and monolingualism and bilingualism (assumptions about the superiority of monolingual native speakers)."

Alvarez (2013, 139) argues that these strong tendencies toward standard language ideology are the result of resistance among Spanish programs and departments to recognize Spanish as another national language and to "de-foreignize their own curricula." For generations, Spanish programs across the United States have focused on monolingual, native varieties of Spanish spoken by foreigners from distant lands—that is, Spain or Latin America, who spoke a pure Spanish untainted by contact with English—a reality reflected by the expertise of most tenured and tenure-line faculty. Subsequently, the message implicitly communicated to students of all ethnicities and backgrounds was that "US Latinos are not desirable representations of the language or culture" (Alvarez 2013, 135). US Spanish speakers have generally occupied the lowest level of the social and linguistic hierarchy within Spanish programs, with native speakers of Spanish at the top, followed by foreign or nonnative speakers (Valdés et al. 2003). To de-foreignize the Spanish curriculum, Alvarez offers several recommendations, such as the use of textbooks that avoid a country-by-country approach, the elimination of explicit demonstrations of derision targeting US Spanish dialects, the integration of more courses focused on US Latino literature and culture, and the academic validation of US Spanish speakers' linguistic assets by providing credit for what they can do instead of solely focusing on how they are deficient.

In spite of the proliferation of research on the pedagogical, linguistic, and cultural needs of heritage language learners of Spanish in the classroom, the largest population of Spanish students in the United States are those without any familial or heritage connection to Spanish and who are part of the ethnic, racial, and linguistic majority, that is, Anglo-Americans. Many of these students may struggle to fully comprehend how language is implicated in issues of power, prestige, discrimination, and racism in society, not having experienced it themselves. Wallace (1999, 102) considers it crucial that white middle-class students receive instruction in critical language study to "challenge social injustices," even if their "immediate interests are not at stake." Moreover, their desire to acquire the language strictly for communicative purposes or for professional advancement may come in direct conflict, in their minds, with a course or curriculum that includes a significant sociopolitical component. Leeman and Rabin (2007) point out that critical approaches to language pedagogy have remained marginal in the undergraduate curriculum and that traditional second-language students, simply due to their identity, should not be deprived of the opportunity to "develop critical agency regarding language" (Leeman and Rabin 2007, 308), in a society where language ideologies abound and can be rather subtle and insidious. Rather than simply focusing on how the acquisition of standard Spanish can improve their own social or professional prospects, Spanish second-language students must also understand how certain language ideologies affect subordinated groups. As ethnic and linguistic dominant groups acquiring socially marginalized languages, Anglo-American students are in a position to become powerful agents of change or idle, yet informed, observers of the status quo.

Glynn, Wesely, and Wassell (2014) address the problem of grand theorizing by providing concrete recommendations on how to incorporate critical pedagogy in the classroom. The authors ground their approach in the five standards from the National Standards for Foreign Language Education (National Standards in Foreign Language Education Project 1996)—communication, cultures, connections, comparisons, and communities—and the three categories of cultural products included in the standards—tangible and intangible *products*, behavioral *practices*, and philosophical *perspectives*. Pedagogically speaking, Glynn, Wesely, and Wassell's volume is theoretically sound and quite comprehensive because it provides guidance on unit and lesson planning, activity types, and assessment procedures accompanied by concrete examples at different levels. Interestingly, in the final chapter, the authors anticipate the questions and concerns that language educators may confront as they integrate social justice instruction into their courses, such as the potential resistance from students and parents—and for the university setting, faculty, and administrators—or the claim that by teaching language students about social justice, instructors are imposing a specific value system. The replacement of commonly accepted topics found in the traditional curriculum of collegiate Spanish programs with those that tackle social justice, critical language awareness, and standard language ideology may prove the most intransigent and difficult to change.

In this section, we offer our own perspectives on what steps can be taken to embed the social, economic, and political realities associated with Spanish and Spanish speakers in the United States more accurately and sensitively into Spanish tertiary education.

First, we use "realities" in the title of this chapter to emphasize that the social and linguistic phenomena we have discussed are, in fact, real and not imagined. Though elementary, intermediate, and advanced language courses are primarily designed to improve students' proficiency, and linguistics and literature courses have their unique disciplinary foci, we can no longer pretend that our students will not confront deeply divisive language ideologies as second-language speakers of Spanish in the United States. Their language proficiency will give them access to communities for which these phenomena are part of everyday life, and we do them a disservice if we leave them unequipped to thoroughly understand them. As several researchers have made clear, with a bit of creativity and sufficient will to do so, social justice and other sociopolitical content can be seamlessly woven into language courses (Glynn, Wesely, and Wassell 2014) and content courses (Leeman and Rabin 2007).

Second, instructors must first possess an understanding and appreciation of language variation, language contact, standard language ideology, linguistic discrimination, language subordination, and critical language awareness before they can help students identify and deconstruct their many social, cultural, and political manifestations. Furthermore, part of our task as Spanish language educators is to sensitively and respectfully inform students concerning the injustices perpetuated against Spanish speakers because of certain language ideologies. Clearly, the degree to which these issues can be broached will depend on the course level and focus. Language program directors and instructors of teaching methods courses should consider the inclusion of these concepts in preservice and in-service training for graduate student instructors and workshops geared toward faculty who may not be familiar with them.

Third, collegiate Spanish programs in the US must de-foreignize their curricula by allowing for a more substantive and concentrated focus on US varieties of Spanish and on sociolinguistic and sociopolitical phenomena that are manifested among domestic Spanish-speaking populations. Although courses in Peninsular and Latin American cultures, civilizations, and literatures need not be replaced, they must be considered just one of several curricular options, both in the number of courses available and in the training and background of faculty hires. In the end, an overwhelming majority of undergraduates will not pursue graduate studies in the culture, literature, or linguistics of any Spanish-speaking population or country, but they will be exposed to US Spanish and the social, economic, and political realities that have an impact on those who use it domestically.

Fourth, while embedding basic principles of language variation and linguistic discrimination—for example, into traditional language, literature, and linguistics courses—is important, it is only the first step. For many students, the principles and concepts discussed will remain at an intellectual level unless students are forced to interface with them outside the classroom in their local communities. Experiential learning is an excellent tool for teaching university students a variety of subjects and skills, but particularly if the objective is to convert intellectual understanding into a more sensitive and political—not partisan—disposition. Departmental administrators must provide incentives for faculty to take on courses with a significant service-learning component that focus on sociopolitical content, given the added demands when working with community partners.

For many years, the Hispanic Studies Department at the University of Kentucky had been rather disconnected from the local Spanish-speaking population in Lexington, in spite of a long-standing course titled "SPA [Science Practical Assessment] 399: Field-Based/Community-Based Education." However, in recent years efforts have been made to better connect undergraduate students with organizations and agencies that serve Spanish-speaking Hispanic populations and to receive credit for doing so. In 2007, the department had a course approved titled "SPA 480: Hispanic Kentucky," which includes a service-learning component. The course was designed to help students study "US Latino history, with primary emphasis on the evolution of the politics of immigration and Spanish in the US" (*University of Kentucky Bulletin* 2007–8). Anecdotally, the students seem to enjoy engaging directly with the local Spanish-speaking community, because the course is in high demand, with the single section offered each semester filling up. Despite progress connecting students with the local community, the majority of the department's faculty members remain rather disconnected from US Spanish and the local Latino population, as it has never hired a tenure-line faculty member whose primary teaching and research areas include US Latino studies or US Spanish and bilingualism.

## SPANISH POSTSECONDARY PROGRAM AND CURRICULUM SURVEY RESULTS

Our national survey included six questions under the section titled "Sociocultural Realities." These six items are listed below with the item of most concern appearing first—the lower the mean value on a scale of one to five the more a concern—and the item of least concern appearing last. The item's mean value and overall rank among all fifty-five items appear following the language of the item, as does the percentage who felt the item did not apply to their program:

- Balanced presentation of international Spanish-speaking cultures in teaching (e.g., textbooks, lectures, presentations, realia, video, music): 2.45 / 12th / 0.7 percent;

- Retention of culturally diverse students at all levels of instruction: 2.53 / 15th / 2.7 percent;
- Recruitment of culturally diverse students at all levels of instruction: 2.59 / 18th / 2.5 percent;
- Integration of US Spanish-speaking sociopolitical component into current course offerings: 2.63 / 23rd / 2.7 percent;
- Accurate depiction of local Spanish-speaking populations in teaching materials: 2.70 / 27th / 1.8 percent; and
- Creation of courses that address issues unique to US Spanish-speaking populations: 2.78 / 30th / 4 percent.

Although all the items represented a concern for the survey respondents, because none of the item's mean values reached 3, or neutral, not one item was within the top ten as far as rank. The most concerning issue was the presentation of international Spanish-speaking cultures, while the least pressing was the creation of courses to address issues unique to US Spanish-speaking populations. However, the difference between the two items was less than half a point (0.33) on a 5-point scale. In comparison with other sections of the survey, this section ranked third, behind "other issues" and "assessment," with a mean item value of 2.61. The rank order of the items' mean values among participants who self-identified as specialists in literature and culture and those who specialized in linguistics and applied linguistics was the same, and was also identical to the overall rank order. However, the mean value of the six items for the literature and culture contingent was 2.43, while the linguists' and applied linguists' responses generated a mean value of 2.83, indicating that the instructors trained in literature and culture found this section a bit more of a concern than their counterparts in linguistics and applied linguistics. Similar to the overall results, untenured instructors were most concerned about striking a balance with the representation of international Spanish-speaking cultures. The mean scores from their tenured and tenure-track instructors, however, placed the retention of culturally diverse students as the item of greatest concern.

One of the most salient findings from this section of our survey research was the fact that none of the participant groups that we analyzed (overall, literature/culture, linguistics/applied linguistics, tenured, nontenured) rated, on average, the "accurate depiction of local Spanish-speaking populations in teaching materials" as more of a concern than a "balanced presentation of international Spanish-speaking cultures in teaching (e.g., textbooks, lectures, presentations, realia, video, music, etc.)." Furthermore, the "creation of courses that address issues unique to US Spanish-speaking populations" was considered of least concern of the six items by all groups analyzed. The trend among all groups to rank issues related to US Spanish-speaking populations as less of a concern than international Spanish-speaking populations seems to lend credence to arguments made by Valdés and others (2003) and Alvarez (2013) that even within university Spanish departments and programs, domestic varieties of Spanish—usually reflective of bilingual communities with frequent contact with English—seem to be less valued than international varieties—usually considered native and monolingual.

## CONCLUSION

One of the most gratifying experiences a Spanish language educator can have is to receive a call from a potential employer wanting to know whether to hire a former high-performing and diligent student. Such was the case with one University of Kentucky student, who only a year or two earlier had been struggling to know how to use her Spanish major professionally as she approached graduation. After Julie (name changed) realized that she did not want to teach, she approached one of her professors, requesting that he supervise an internship at a local pro bono law firm that targets victims of domestic violence, many of whom are undocumented Spanish-speaking immigrants. Her final paper was to outline in detail the steps required of undocumented immigrants to achieve either permanent residency or citizenship in the United States. A second internship at a free and reduced-rate health clinic serving primarily Hispanics further opened the student's eyes to the many realities that this sector of the population confronts. Thus, the call from a social services agency to determine whether to hire her to work with underprivileged, Spanish-speaking groups in the Chicago area was not all that surprising.

Though Julie's case may be a success, her exposure to sociopolitical and socioeconomic realities was more of her doing than it was the doing of a deliberately designed and socially committed curriculum. What this student learned about social justice, prejudice, and power involving Spanish speakers in the United States should have come from a curriculum with explicit goals to that end, rather than as a serendipitous by-product of one student's concern over her professional outlook as a Spanish major. How many more students might be affected in a program that maximizes opportunities for meaningful community-based learning and does not shy away from integrating discussions of linguistic discrimination, subordination, and standard language ideology in its beginning language courses as well as its advanced content courses. In the end, postsecondary Spanish language educators, administrators, and curriculum designers must ask themselves this question: How responsible is it to *not* include substantive sociopolitical content in a curriculum that instructs students in a language that is the site of such frequent discrimination and marginalization within and beyond the walls of the university?

## REFLECTION QUESTIONS

1. Besides those listed at the beginning of the chapter, what other affective and attitudinal questions might you pose about your students? What are your predictions as to their response to our questions and to yours?

2. In your own words, explain the difference between Widdowson's use of *critical* in applied linguistics and Pennycook's.

3. How would you characterize Americans' current perspectives on bilingualism in general, and on Spanish-English bilingualism more specifically? What about the residents of your hometown, the students in your Spanish classes, your family members, or members of different socioeconomic classes? Explain any discrepancies you identify, and whether their perspectives depend on the language pair—for example, Spanish–English, Chinese–English, and French–English.

4. Briefly define standard language ideology in your own words and then identify one manifestation of it within American society that relates to English, Spanish, or both. What are the benefits and drawbacks of standard language ideology for a pluralistic society like the one found in the United States? Why is language, and monolingualism more specifically, so closely tied to nationalism in the United States? Why have so many Latinos taken offense at efforts to pass federal English-only laws?

5. In the United States, discrimination based on race has been well documented. Its linguistic counterpart is discussed much less in the mass media, yet it is quite prevalent among certain groups. Describe cases of linguistic discrimination, prejudice, or marginalization toward Spanish speakers that you have personally witnessed or heard about, and explain why it could be classified as discriminatory or prejudicial. What does it mean when a language is racialized?

6. Describe a situation in which the communicative burden was not shared equally during a conversation between a native speaker of a language and a nonnative speaker. How did you determine that the communicative burden was not shared equally?

7. Identify at least three examples of Mock Spanish in contemporary American society and explain their function. Why did the person choose to use a hyperanglicized Spanish word in their discourse, and what effect did they wish to elicit from their interlocutors? Was the tone pejorative, jocular, both, or neither?

8. Why do Peninsular and Latin American literary and cultural studies, as opposed to US Latino and US Spanish studies, dominate collegiate Spanish programs throughout the country with regard to course offerings, faculty members' specialties, guest speakers, and the like? What arguments can be made for and against a complete overhaul of postsecondary curricula to include a much more substantial representation of US Spanish and US Latino culture? Who might object to such a proposal, and who would champion it? Why?

## PEDAGOGICAL ACTIVITIES

1. Brainstorm ways in which you might incorporate each of the following topics in lower-level Spanish language classes and in upper-level linguistics and literature courses: linguistic prejudice, language variation, standard language ideology, Mock Spanish, communicative burden, critical language awareness.

2. Prepare a survey for beginning or intermediate Spanish language students to assess their opinion on whether the issues mentioned in question 1 above should be included in their particular course and serve as the topics around which the course is structured. Include closed-response items—for example, multiple choice or Likert scale, and constructed-response items (e.g., fill-in-the-blank or short answer).

3. Revisit the assertions made in the chapter regarding many Spanish language textbooks before conducting an analysis of the cultural content of your textbook. Find evidence for and against the arguments made in the chapter.

4. Design a group project for a Spanish language course to be completed in the community with Spanish-dominant speakers that would teach one or more of the concepts mentioned in question 1 above. Prepare instructions with detailed procedures that the students should follow and a rubric on how it will be graded.

5. Prepare a speech of five to seven minutes that could be given to a language program director, department chair, or dean that would argue for more sociopolitical content in the Spanish curriculum from beginning language courses to advanced linguistics, literature, and culture courses.

6. Prepare a one-class lesson plan that would cover at least one of the concepts discussed in question 1.

7. Count the number of courses in your Spanish program whose topical focus is clearly (1) Peninsular literature and culture, (2) Latin American literature and culture, (3) US Spanish literature and culture, and (4) linguistics. Do the same for each faculty member, by determining which of the three areas appears to be their primary specialization. How do the number of courses in each category compare? What about the specializations of the faculty? What explanations can you give for the results?

## NOTES

1. Although we are aware that Spanish-speaking societies in other countries struggle with many of the same issues touched on in this chapter—such as language subordination, and linguistic discrimination and prejudice—our focus in this chapter is squarely on Spanish in the US context and the impact of these phenomena on those residing in the United States.

2. In this section, we draw heavily from Field (2011, chap. 5), given his excellent and in-depth overview of the evolution of American attitudes toward bilingualism and multilingualism from the colonial period to the twenty-first century.

3. Original Spanish: "No cuestionan esas representaciones sino que, por el contrario, las ratifican y corroboran en las propias clases de español. Mediante un complejo dispositivo de generalizaciones, abstracciones, omisiones, contrastes o inferencias se termina otorgándole al otro el espacio folclórico e identificándolo con valores de liviandad, diversión y hedonismo."

# REFERENCES

Alarcón, Amado, Antonio Di Paolo, Josiah Heyman, and María Cristina Morales. 2014. "The Occupational Location of Spanish-English Bilinguals in the New Information Economy: The Health and Criminal Justice Sectors in the US Borderlands with Mexico." In *The Bilingual Advantage*, edited by Rebecca M. Callahan and Patricia C. Gándara. Buffalo: Multilingual Matters.

Alvarez, Stephanie. 2013. "Evaluating the Role of the Spanish Department in the Education of US Latino Students: Un Testimonio." *Journal of Latinos and Education* 12: 131–51.

Alvarez, Steven. 2012. "Brokering Literacies: An Ethnographic Study of Languages and Literacies in Mexican Immigrant Families." PhD diss., City University of New York.

Arizpe, Víctor, and Benigno E. Aguirre. 1987. "Mexican, Puerto Rican, and Cuban Ethnic Groups in First-Year College-Level Spanish Textbooks." *Modern Language Journal* 71: 125–37.

Barrett, Rusty. 2006. "Language Ideology and Racial Inequality: Competing Functions of Spanish in an Anglo-Owned Mexican Restaurant." *Language in Society* 35: 163–204.

Correa, Maite. 2011. "Advocating for Critical Pedagogical Approaches to Teaching Spanish as a Heritage Language: Some Considerations." *Foreign Language Annals* 44, no. 2: 308–20.

Del Valle, José, ed. 2013. *A Political History of Spanish*. New York: Cambridge University Press.

Del Valle, José, and Ofelia García. 2013. "Introduction to the Making of Spanish: US Perspectives." In *A Political History of Spanish*, edited by José del Valle. New York: Cambridge University Press.

DuBord, Elise. 2013. "Language, Church, and State in Territorial Arizona." In *A Political History of Spanish*, edited by José del Valle. New York: Cambridge University Press.

———. 2014. *Language, Immigration, and Labor: Negotiating Work in the US-Mexico Borderlands*. New York: Palgrave Macmillan.

Elissondo, Guillermina. 2001. "Representing Latino/a Culture in Introductory Spanish Textbooks." Document ED478020. ERIC Document Reproduction Service, US Department of Education, Washington, DC.

Fernández-Gibert, Arturo. 2013. "The Politics of Spanish and English in Territorial New Mexico." In *A Political History of Spanish*, edited by José del Valle. New York: Cambridge University Press.

Fairclough, Norman. 1989. *Language and Power*. New York: Pearson Education.

———. 1992. "The Appropriacy of Appropriateness." In *Critical Language Awareness*, edited by Norman Fairclough. New York: Longman.

Field, Frederic. 2011. *Bilingualism in the USA: The Case of the Chicano-Latino Community*. Philadelphia: John Benjamins.

Flores, Lisa A. 2003. "Constructing Rhetorical Borders: Peons, Illegal Aliens, and Competing Narratives of Immigration." *Critical Studies in Media Communication* 20, no. 4: 362–87.

Freire, Paolo. 1970. *A Pedagogia do Oprimido*. São Paolo: Paz e Terra.

Giroux, Henry A. 1983. *Theory and Resistance in Education: A Pedagogy for the Opposition*. New York: Bergin & Garvey.

Glynn, Cassandra, Pamela Wesely, and Beth Wassell. 2014. *Words and Actions: Teaching Languages through the Lens of Social Justice*. Alexandria, VA: American Council on the Teaching of Foreign Languages.

Hakimzadeh, Shirin, and D'Vera Cohn. 2007. "English Usage Among Hispanics in the United States." Pew Hispanic Center. www.pewhispanic.org/2007/11/29/english-usage -among-hispanics-in-the-united-states/.

Herman, Deborah. 2007. "It's a Small World After All: From Stereotypes to Invented Worlds in Secondary School Spanish Textbooks." *Critical Inquiry in Language Studies* 4, nos. 2–3: 117–50.

Hill, Jane. 1998. "Language, Race and White Public Space." *American Anthropologist* 100: 680–89.

Hortiguera, Hugo. 2012. "'They Are a Very Festive People!' El Baile Perpetuo: Comida, Arte Popular y Baile en los Videos de Enseñanza de Español como Lengua Extranjera." *Razón y Palabra* 78. Retrieved from www.razonypalabra.org.mx.

Kramsch, Claire J. 1988. "The Cultural Discourse of Foreign Language Textbooks." In *Northeast Conference on the Teaching of Foreign Languages: Towards a New Integration of Language and Culture*, edited by Alan J. Singerman. Middlebury, VT: Northeast Conference.

Leeman, Jennifer. 2007. "The Value of Spanish: Shifting Ideologies in United States Language Teaching." *ADFL Bulletin* 38, nos. 1–2: 32–39.

———. 2013. Categorizing Latinos in the History of the US Census: The Official Racialization of Spanish. In *A Political History of Spanish.*, edited by José del Valle. New York: Cambridge University Press.

———. 2015. "Critical Approaches to Teaching Spanish as a Local/Foreign Language." In *The Routledge Handbook of Hispanic Applied Linguistics*, edited by Manel Lacorte. New York: Routledge.

Leeman, Jennifer, and Lisa Rabin. 2007. "Critical Perspectives for the Literature Classroom." *Hispania* 90, no. 2: 304–15.

Leeman, Jennifer, Lisa Rabin, and Esperanza Román-Mendoza. 2011. "Identity and Activism in Heritage Language Education." *Modern Language Journal* 95, no. 4: 481–95.

Lippi-Green, Rosina. 2012. *English with an Accent: Language, Ideology, and Discrimination in the United States*, 2nd ed. New York: Routledge.

Martinez, Glenn. 2013. "Public Health and the Politics of Spanish in Early-Twentieth-Century Texas." In *A Political History of Spanish*, edited by José del Valle. New York: Cambridge University Press.

Mclaren, Peter. 1989. *Life in Schools: An Introduction to Critical Pedagogy in the Foundations of Education*. New York: Longman.

Milroy, James. 2001. "Language Ideologies and the Consequences of Standardization." *Journal of Sociolinguistics* 5: 530–55.

National Standards in Foreign Language Education Project. 1996. *Standards for Foreign Language Learning: Preparing for the 21st Century*. Lawrence, KS: Allen Press.

Pennycook, Alastair. 2001. *Critical Applied Linguistics: A Critical Introduction*. Mahwah, NJ: Lawrence Erlbaum.

———. 2004. "Critical Applied Linguistics." In *The Handbook of Applied Linguistics*, edited by Alan Davies and Catherine Elder. Malden, MA: Blackwell.

Pomerantz, Anne. 2002. "Language Ideologies and the Production of Identities: Spanish as a Resource for Participation in a Multilingual Marketplace." *Multilingua* 21: 275–302.

———. 2008. "'Tú Necesitas Preguntar en Español': Negotiating Good Language Learner Identity in a Spanish Classroom." *Journal of Language, Identity, and Education* 7: 253–71.

Silverstein, Michael. 1992. "The Uses and Utility of Ideology: Some Reflections." *Pragmatics: Quarterly Publication of the International Pragmatics Association* 2, no. 3: 311–24.

Villa, Daniel J. 2002. "The Sanitizing of US Spanish in Academia." *Foreign Language Annals* 35, no. 2: 222–30.

Villa, Daniel J., and Jennifer R. Villa. 2005. "Language Instrumentality in a Border Region: Implications for the Loss of Spanish in the Southwest." *Southwest Journal of Linguistics* 24: 169–84.

Wallace, Catherine. 1999. "Critical Language Awareness: Key Principles for a Course in Critical Reading." *Language Awareness* 8, no. 2: 98–110.

Widdowson, Henry G. 2001. "Coming to Terms with Reality: Applied Linguistics in Perspective." *AILA Review* 14: 2–17.

Wright, Wayne E. 2007. "Heritage Language Programs in the Era of English-Only and No Child Left Behind." *Heritage Language Journal* 5, no. 1: 1–26.

*University of Kentucky Bulletin*. 2007–8. www.uky.edu/registrar/content/2007-08-course-descriptions.

Valdés, Guadalupe, Sonia V. González, Dania López García, and Patricio Márquez. 2003. "The Case of Spanish in Departments of Foreign Languages." *Anthropology & Education Quarterly* 34, no. 1: 3–26.

Zentella, Ana Celia. 1996. "The Chiquitification of US Latinos and Their Languages, or Why We Need an Anthropolitical Linguistics." *SALSA III: Proceedings of the Third Annual Symposium about Language and Society—Austin, Texas, Linguistic Forum* 36: 1–18.

# 8

## TRAINING FUTURE SPANISH TEACHERS

The best thing about being a teacher is that it matters. The hardest thing about being a teacher is that it matters every day.
—Todd Whitaker and Beth Whitaker, *Teaching Matters*, 2013

One of the most frequently cited professional outlets used to recruit Spanish language majors, secondary majors, and minors is education, that is, employment as a second/foreign language instructor at the elementary or secondary level. For many students, this seems like a natural fit as they desire to parlay their enthusiasm for language learning and previous successes in the classroom into their livelihood. Moreover, as the number of Spanish enrollments and teacher turnover remain high nationally, large numbers of high school Spanish positions become available each year and augur well for the placement of these students.

Unfortunately, many preservice Spanish instructors are not fully prepared to enter the Spanish classroom on many fronts: (1) subpar levels of oral proficiency in Spanish when compared with state education requirements; (2) insufficient skills to engage large numbers of high school students motivated more by college preparation requirements rather than a desire to achieve translingual and transcultural competence; and (3) inadequate linguistic and pedagogic preparation to teach discipline-specific content in Spanish, such as science and mathematics, as part of an immersion or heritage program. Also of concern for the profession is the level of attrition of practicing language educators.

In a chapter of this scope, it is impossible to address all the variables that have an impact on the training of future Spanish teachers in the twenty-first century. Nonetheless, we address the most pressing concerns for preservice Spanish language education programs as they strive to ensure high-quality instruction at the elementary, secondary, and postsecondary levels. We begin by examining the issue of Spanish teacher candidates' proficiency levels in Spanish before presenting Praxis data that include candidates' scores on the Praxis language and pedagogy examinations. With the increasing number of native Spanish-speaking instructors, we then turn to a discussion of native and non-native instructors in the Spanish classroom. We then explore the demands of teaching in the increasingly common Spanish immersion setting before analyzing the impact of attrition on the field. Finally, we present the results of our national survey regarding the most pressing curricular and programmatic concerns for twenty-first-century Spanish language programs.

## PRESERVICE LANGUAGE PROFICIENCY STANDARDS

In 2002 the American Council on the Teaching of Foreign Languages (ACTFL) recommended that minimum proficiency standards be put in place for preservice language teachers. At that time, the National Council for Accreditation of Teacher Education reviewed and adopted the recommendations by ACTFL regarding the necessary proficiency needed for licensure. Following suit, most states have set minimum proficiency requirements for teacher licensure to empirically measure language competence and to ensure high-quality teaching in the foreign language classroom. For the Spanish language, most states require at least Advanced Low on the ACTFL scale, with some states only requiring a proficiency level of Intermediate High. ACTFL (2002, 4) states that the rationale for the standard is that teachers can only help others learn to communicate in the language if they "themselves exemplify effective communicative skills." Donato (2009) states that the establishment of these minimum proficiency standards has led to many changes in the field of Spanish teaching and in teacher preparation programs, both in their design and redesign, as programs focus more on proficiency.

The value of establishing language standards appears to be supported through research by Hamlyn, Surface, and Swender (2007), who found that 59.5 percent of teaching candidates achieved the Advanced Low level of proficiency on their first attempt. Sullivan (2011) studied over 734 preservice or in-service teachers who had taken the Oral Proficiency Interview (OPI) and found that 72 percent of them self-reported a score of Advanced Low or better on the test. However, 200 students identified as native rather than nonnative speakers of the language they were teaching. Swender and others (2011) investigated the proficiency levels of more than 2,000 teacher candidates from 2006 to 2010 to determine how many had achieved the Advanced Low or Intermediate High level of proficiency. The results showed that across all languages, approximately 55 percent had achieved the required level for their specific language. Nevertheless, the most telling aspect of the research were the large discrepancies between each school's passing rate, with some programs graduating 100 percent of their candidates at the required proficiency level and others reaching 88 percent, 33 percent, 13 percent, and even 0 percent. Indeed, some university programs are failing to prepare teachers to achieve requisite levels of proficiency in the languages that they plan on teaching, even after a five-year program. Finally, Glisan, Swender, and Surface (2013) analyzed the OPI results of 2,890 foreign language teacher candidates of eleven different languages (though 2,094 were from Spanish) and found that 54.8 percent of the test takers met the ACTFL proficiency standard in their language. These studies, for the most part, demonstrate that just over 50 percent of teacher candidates achieve the score necessary to become licensed in their states the first time they take the OPI—a finding that is far from encouraging.

With the minimum oral proficiency requirements in place for preservice teachers, many would consider the OPI to be a high-stakes exam. On the contrary, Aoki (2013, 539) challenges the classification of the OPI and Writing Proficiency Test (WPT) as "high stakes" exams. She argues that they should confirm "what students already are keenly aware of, namely, their own proficiency levels in Interpersonal Communication, Interpretive Listening and Reading, and Presentational Speaking and Writing." The real question may not be which exact level of proficiency should be set as the minimum for preservice candidates, but rather why, and how, it is that students can complete with flying colors preservice programs with such dramatic deficiencies in language ability. Norris (2013, 556) expresses his disappointment this way: "What this discussion reveals more than anything else, sadly, is the disappointing achievement of world/foreign languages education in the United States to date. It is remarkable that we cannot expect these levels of language competency from all of our students (not just the ones who want to be language teachers) before tertiary education, never mind as a result of college study."

This is especially the case for Spanish, because in most parts of the country students have access to native speakers of Spanish close to where they live. Each passing year, Spanish is becoming more available on national television networks, on local radio stations, and at religious services. It is fairly easy in the twenty-first century to access fluent, and even native, speakers of Spanish, which may help students move their proficiency in Spanish beyond Intermediate High and Advanced Low. Norris (2013, 557) declares that "it is high time that we take seriously what four years (!) of college language education should accomplish."

The problem with minimum proficiency requirements is that many students who performed well in their classes, spent time in an immersion setting, and completed the required courses with straight As are still unable to reach the minimum level of proficiency mandated by the state. This can lead to a great deal of resentment among students, and raises serious questions regarding not only the training taking place in the classroom but also the quality of their language training and coursework as well as their immersion experiences. Disgruntled students might respond as Molly did, as reported by Burke (2013, 532):

> Although I have maintained an A average in all of my Education classes and Spanish classes, and I had a very successful trip to Spain, ACTFL tells me that I am not good enough to teach. . . . No matter how many hours I have spent studying to better my Spanish, no matter how many hundreds of dollars I have spent for the testing, I am not good enough in their eyes. ACTFL has single-handedly made me feel like a failure when I am surrounded by nothing but academic success. This, I cannot explain. I have practiced until I've become exhausted. I have written until I can't think. I have paid until I have to borrow money all for one purpose—ACTFL. And even though I have gone through all of this, I am still not good enough in their eyes. Never mind the people who are native speakers that have no background knowledge of second-language acquisition and no creativity— they can pass the test but I can't. Never mind people who have passed the test on a whim but can't connect to a single student. Never mind all of the creativity and ability that I possess to transform Spanish class into the class that opens doors and lights paths for my students' futures. I know how to teach, and more importantly, I know how to teach Spanish. I don't need a piece of paper from ACTFL that tells me that. I see it every day on my students' faces.

This student blames ACTFL for keeping her from achieving her dream of becoming a Spanish teacher. What this student fails to understand is that state education agencies, not ACTFL, set the proficiency levels required for certification and choose the assessments to elicit proficiency (Norris 2013). Although the blame should not be placed on ACTFL, she does highlight a major concern: What can be done with university Spanish students who complete all that they are asked to do and yet fail to meet the proficiency requirement? Or perhaps the better question is, Where did the system fail her before she got to the OPI and WPT? Though Burke (2013) argues that proficiency does not necessarily lead to excellence in language teaching and classroom pedagogy, Tedick (2013) affirms the need for professional standards so that institutions have a way to evaluate the skill level of their students. Just as native speakers who easily pass the OPI and WPT are not naturally endowed with great teaching skills and creativity, neither are nonnatives who do not pass the OPI and WPT. Norris (2013, 555) notes that the benefit of standardized assessments is that all individuals are evaluated using the same instrument, "to ensure minimum competency of language teachers regardless of where they receive their training."

What can be done for those Spanish language teachers who have taken the courses and participated in an immersion experience but still do not demonstrate the necessary proficiency? Burke (2013) recommends that they, first, reflect on their proficiency as well as their preparation and consider why they did not do as well as they needed to. Then she discusses with them a series of interventions meant to improve their exam performance, such as additional writing and extra speaking practice so that they can represent their skills to the best of their ability. For those who scored more than one sublevel below the state-mandated level, she recommends that they participate in an immersion experience or a second one if they have already done so. The concern that Burke raises is that just because foreign language (FL) teachers demonstrate an advanced level of proficiency does not guarantee that they will be more effective K–12 FL teachers. Norris (2013, 557–58) proposes that the profession needs to reconsider whether current assessments are meeting the goals of future language teachers. He states that the profession needs to make sure that any test in place must be one worth teaching to, suggesting that perhaps a different type of assessment would better reflect the needs of the language teaching profession. He proposes the use of integrated performance assessments that would do the following:

(a) simulate actual language use tasks by teachers in language classrooms;
(b) encourage extended, rich performances in the target language as it is used for everything from lesson planning to pedagogic delivery to assessing students;
(c) offer accessible rubrics that spell out what effective teacher language use looks like in the classroom; and
(d) provide numerous opportunities for mentored and scaffolded practice and feedback (e.g., by supervising teachers, by FL faculty) prior to achievement or certification testing.

Regardless of the steps taken, Spanish language teacher candidates need to be aware of the requirements as they enter their language training and take the necessary steps to be proactive in improving their proficiency to meet these requirements. Furthermore, teaching training programs need to reevaluate not only their curriculum but also the assessments and requirements for their language teachers. They need to ensure that there is articulation between candidates' coursework and professional experiences and that a mechanism is in place to help teacher candidates monitor their progress toward meeting minimum language requirements. Finally, scholars of Spanish language education need to provide an empirical basis for the minimum level of proficiency needed for instructors fulfilling diverse roles in Spanish language programs.

## PRAXIS EXAMINATIONS

The Praxis exams are a series of tests that preservice teachers take in many states to receive their licensure. The Praxis for World Languages exams generally consist of at least two exams, one based on knowledge of the second language and culture and the other focused on pedagogical content related to the subject area and level in which the candidates plan to teach. The world languages exam, given in a variety of languages, is required in more states than the content exam. According to the Educational Testing Service's study companion for the Spanish World Language exam, "This test is designed to measure the knowledge, skills, and abilities of examinees who have had preparation in a program for teaching Spanish in grades K–12. Because programs in teaching Spanish are offered at both the undergraduate and graduate levels, this test is appropriate for examinees at either level. All sections of this test are at the Advanced-Low level, as described in the proficiency guidelines of the American Council on the Teaching of Foreign Languages (ACTFL)."

The Spanish World Language exam includes all language modalities as well as cultural knowledge across all modes of communication: interpersonal, interpretive, and presentational. All the questions and response options are given in Spanish and include written and aural texts from different parts of the Spanish-speaking world. The Spanish test is a timed, computer-based exam with a score range from 100 to 200. Currently, thirty-three states require the Spanish World Language exam for candidates seeking licensure or certification as Spanish teachers. To pass the Spanish World Language exam, states determine the cut score, which currently varies from 154 to 168, with twenty-two of the states requiring a score of 168 or better. The most common cut scores among states using the Chinese (164), German (163), and French (162) world language exams are slightly lower.

Using a data set exclusively prepared for and licensed to the authors by the Educational Testing Service, we obtained the results of candidates' Spanish World Language exam for all foreign language teaching candidates from 2010 to 2015. These data allowed us to analyze preservice Spanish teachers' levels of Spanish language proficiency, as measured via their first completion of the "Spanish: World Language (5195)" exam. These aggregated results include examinees' scores grouped by year, state, and demographic variables. In order to compare the results on the Spanish exam with other world languages, we also obtained the results for this time period for "French: World Language (5174)," "German: World Language (5183)," and "Chinese: World Language (5665)." Additionally, the data set also included students' scores on "Principles of Learning and Teaching (5621–5624)" and "World Languages Pedagogy (5841)." With this information, we analyzed the relationship between candidates' mastery of language skills and language pedagogy to make reasonable programmatic and curricular recommendations for the institutions who train them. Because students may take the Praxis exam multiple times, we specifically requested the examinees' initial performance on the world language Praxis exams and then compared it to their initial performance on the pedagogy exams.

The analysis of the Praxis world languages exams revealed several interesting relationships between exam, ethnicity, gender, and score. First, the average score across all languages was 168.72, nearly identical to the mean score on the Spanish Praxis exam, which was 168.26. Despite the lower cut scores set by most states for the other world language exams, the Chinese (183.25) and German (171.65) candidates outperformed the Spanish examinees, whose scores only slightly surpassed those of the French candidates (167.88). Second, ethnic trends emerged from the Chinese and Spanish exam candidates, as 75 percent of those who took the Chinese exam identified as Asian or Asian American, while only 32 percent of the Spanish exam candidates self-identified as Hispanic. The Asian / Asian American candidates scored an average of 188.56, while the Hispanic candidates scored 179.16 on average. In both cases, whites scored lower, but the difference between the ethnic groups was much less pronounced on the Spanish exam, on which whites scored 15.93 points lower than Hispanics yet 54.53 points lower than Asian / Asian American candidates on the Chinese exam. Third, we found that overall only 58 percent of the preservice teachers passed the Spanish exam on their first try—that is, 168 or higher—with Hispanics passing at a much higher rate, 81 percent, than whites, 47 percent. This percentage was consistent with previous research (Glisan, Swender, and Surface 2013; Hamlyn, Surface, and Swender 2007; Swender et al. 2011). Fourth, the female participants, who represented 78 percent of the total Spanish exam candidates, averaged a score of 167.8, while the male participants averaged 169.8. Though this difference may seem minimal, it could be the difference between a pass and fail if 168 is the cut score.

As mentioned above, many preservice teachers also took specialty exams targeting pedagogy, one titled "Principles of Learning and Teaching (5621–5624)" and the other "World Languages Pedagogy (5841)." The passing score for these exams varied by state but generally ranged from 155 to 166. The goal in analyzing scores on these exams was to explore the relationship between examinees' language abilities and pedagogical knowledge. Using a Pearson Product-Moment correlation, we found that there was a weak correlation between scores ($r = .13$), meaning that a high score on the pedagogy portion did not necessarily equate to a high score on the language portion, and vice versa. The students who identified as white scored significantly higher than did Hispanics ($p < .001$), with an average score of 180.09 to 165.33 for the Hispanic group. Once again, the large majority of examinees who took the content exams were women (78 percent), who slightly outscored men.

From a curricular standpoint, these results lead to various conclusions. Students who identified with ethnicities traditionally associated with the language of the exam performed significantly better on the Spanish and Chinese world language exams, which is most likely due to experience with the language and culture outside of class. Candidates who self-identified as white appeared to struggle to meet the proficiency requirements mandated by different states even after fulfilling all curricular requirements for a teaching degree. Even though the white students struggled to meet the proficiency requirements, they surpassed Hispanic candidates on the content exams. The students who identified as white and female performed significantly better on the content exams and significantly worse on the Spanish World Language exam. Apparently, for white, presumably nonnative students, the pedagogical preparation offered by teacher preparation programs surpasses the linguistic and communicative preparation as measured by the Praxis exams. Among all world language tests, the Spanish World Language exam had the largest standard deviation (21.35), representing the sociolinguistic and sociocultural diversity of the candidates. The reasons behind the differential performance of each ethnic group are clearly multifaceted and complex, but it is incumbent on curriculum designers to account for these data and consider the ways in which their curricula may favor one group over another, or at least lead to such divergent outcomes. In summary, preservice teaching programs need to consider how to better prepare nonnative language teachers for the Spanish World Language exam and how to boost Hispanic students' performance on the pedagogy exams.

## NATIVE AND NONNATIVE INSTRUCTORS

Spanish is the first language of millions of individuals in the United States and the second language of millions more, making the available pool of future Spanish language teachers the largest and most diverse of any of the foreign languages taught across the United States. Although many personal variables among Spanish teachers could be addressed in much greater depth, in this section we focus on the differences between native and nonnative Spanish instructors. And though a large body of research exists on this topic for the teaching of English (Moussu and Llurda 2008), only in recent years have studies appeared regarding the sociolinguistic profile of Spanish instructors and their students' preferences.

The traditional bias has often been that the native speaker of the language is in some way an inherently better teacher. Hertel and Sundermann (2009,

469) describe this perceived native speaker advantage as "a greater facility in demonstrating fluent, idiomatically appropriate language; a greater appreciation of the cultural connotations of the language; and an ability to better assess whether a given linguistic form is acceptable or not." Several researchers have looked at the pronunciation of nonnative instructors and found this to be a disadvantage in their teaching as well as their credibility in the classroom (Benke and Medgyes 2006; Lasagabaster and Sierra 2006). One example of the type of discrimination that can take place due to accented speech arose in Arizona in 2010, when the state legislature proposed the "Teachers' English Fluency Initiative in Arizona," which would have removed from classrooms those teachers with heavily accented English who instruct English language learners. As a formal statement endorsed by the faculty of the Department of Linguistics at the University of Arizona pointed out, the disturbing implication of this initiative is that heavily accented speech and ungrammatical speech are the same thing, or that those with accented speech possess inferior pedagogical skills. Many speakers with heavy accents use the language fluently and with impeccable grammar. The fact that the Arizona Department of Education would assume that these are one and the same reflects a lack of understanding of both language acquisition and language pedagogy. Also, though this initiative focused on instructors of English language learners, these same concerns have arisen for nonnative instructors of Spanish in the Spanish classroom.

Preference for the native speaker is evident across languages, but it is particularly evident in English schools around the globe where native language status is given high priority among applicants, and in some cases is a nonnegotiable prerequisite. Rajagopalan (2006, 283) described nonnative instructors of a language as "second-class citizens in the world of language teaching." Although this classification has persisted, little research had questioned this preference for the native speaking instructor until the pioneering work by Phillipson (1992) and Medgyes (1994). Phillipson focused his research on disproving the widely held idea that the native speaker of a language is inherently better than the nonnative speaker, or the *native speaker fallacy*. Medgyes argued that native and nonnative instructors have, not surprisingly, strengths and weaknesses. He, like Phillipson, noted that native speakers are not always able to explain the rules and structures of their language because they acquired it from birth implicitly, without explicit instruction. On the contrary, most second-language learners have acquired their language primarily by explicit means. Medgyes adds that because nonnative speakers have had to learn the language in a similar way to that of their students, they can help them to connect and relate more to the learning process. He claims that nonnative instructors tend to be better instructors because they understand the learning process and can provide strategies to their students that they used to become successful learners. He also found that nonnative instructors were more empathetic to the struggles of learning a foreign language and were able to show learners the result of successful language study. Medgyes determined that native and nonnative speaking instructors had strengths and weaknesses but both had the ability to become successful language instructors with the proper preparation. He added that the biggest concern is that often the nonnative instructor feels inadequate and suffers from linguistic insecurity, which could lead to apprehension and additional stress in the classroom, and in turn might limit their effectiveness.

Hertel and Sunderman (2009) conducted a study to look specifically at students' perceptions of native and nonnative Spanish instructors. They questioned whether undergraduate Spanish students would carry the same bias toward the native Spanish-speaking instructors as had been found in research with English language learners. They included students who were in different courses, at different proficiency levels, and with native Spanish-speaking and nonnative Spanish-speaking instructors. The results of the study mirrored findings from the context of English as a second language (Cheung and Braine 2007; Mahboob 2004), as students perceived that the native speakers were more knowledgeable in the areas of pronunciation and culture. They also had greater confidence in the native speakers' knowledge of vocabulary but were not as confident in their grammatical knowledge. Regarding the teaching of these skills, the students felt that the nonnative speakers could teach grammar better than the native speakers but that the native speakers were better at teaching pronunciation and culture. They concluded that these perceptions changed across proficiency levels and with the identity of their current instructor. Hertel and Sunderman (2009, 478) determined that the higher-proficiency students found native speaking instructors to be "more knowledgeable, to have more teaching ability, and to provide them with more learning potential as compared to learners in lower level courses." They also found that those students who had a native Spanish-speaking instructor at the time of the study expressed a preference for that type of instructor and the same was found for those who had a nonnative Spanish-speaking instructor. Interestingly enough, the variable of previous instructor did not play a role in current preference. Hertel and Sunderman (2009, 479) concluded that "students appreciate NNS [nonnative speaker] instructors' ability to understand and teach grammar and to empathize with their language learning difficulties."

Regarding nonnative Spanish-speaking instructors' self-perceptions, Thompson and Fioramonte (2013) gathered qualitative data on nonnative

Spanish-speaking instructors who were teaching first- and second-year university Spanish courses. The researchers found that three main themes surfaced from their qualitative analysis. First, the instructors were cognizant of the fact that all instructors make mistakes. Although this might seem simplistic, nonnative instructors often forget that native speakers make many errors, both in speech and in writing, that are sometimes shared with their students. The awareness of this fact made some of the instructors less critical of their own mistakes. Second, all the instructors acknowledged that they had preconceived notions not only about themselves but also about other nonnative Spanish instructors regarding pronunciation. The instructors placed a premium on "correct" pronunciation. The concern is that some of the instructors would recommend to students that they take future courses with native speaking instructors so that they could hear "what Spanish is supposed to sound like," in spite of what Thompson and Fioramonte perceived to be good pronunciation. They counter this recommendation, asserting that to use pronunciation as an index of overall linguistic ability is to perpetuate nonnative teacher stereotypes. The instructors in this study had negative stereotypes about themselves and other nonnative instructors that were then passed on to their students—especially in the area of pronunciation. Third and finally, these instructors did not feel that they would be as competent teaching learners at a more advanced level and felt that this was best reserved for native speakers of the language.

The research into native and nonnative instructors provides valuable knowledge for those who are entering the field of Spanish teaching. Beyond physical characteristics, it appears that many students value their instructors' effectiveness differently, depending on their native language. Although these perceptions may be unfounded, they represent the reality that many teachers will face as they enter the teaching profession, both at the primary and secondary levels as well as at postsecondary institutions. Teacher education programs need to prepare both native and nonnative Spanish-speaking instructors for these potential misconceptions. One of the areas of concern, mentioned by Thompson and Fioramonte (2013), was the practice that is common in many universities whereby native Spanish speaking graduate students are automatically assigned to higher-level courses simply because they are native speakers. What message does this send to nonnative instructors, and how does it affect their own linguistic insecurities? Does this practice lead to better instruction for the students? The authors point out that more research needs to be carried out looking at how administrators and supervisors of foreign language departments let these often-unfounded stereotypes influence both their hiring practices and the assignment of courses to nonnative instructors. A better understanding of how these positions are assigned would further inform teacher trainers and future job candidates as to what they need to prepare for and expect in the job market.

## IMMERSION PROGRAMS

Today's Spanish teachers are entering the job market with a larger diversity of program types and student sociodemographics than those in previous generations. Not only have theories and methodologies changed over the years, but the contexts in which they will be called on to teach have changed as well. Teachers are increasingly asked to teach in a variety of settings that present challenges to them and their students. As the prevalence of these unique teaching contexts increases, there is a concomitant upswing in demand for teachers with specialized training to match these instructional contexts. One of these unique contexts that affects Spanish teaching and that is growing throughout the United States is one-way and dual immersion Spanish programs. Although extensive research has been carried out on immersion programs and teacher training independent of each other, the goal of this section is to highlight some of the issues confronting preservice teachers who want to become immersion teachers. One of the biggest challenges is that until recently, few programs existed that prepared teachers with the skills needed to teach in an immersion setting (Met and Lorenz 1997; Tedick and Fortune 2013; Walker and Tedick 2000). Though new preservice training programs have begun to appear in recent years, there are not enough to meet the growing demand for individuals who are able to teach content courses in Spanish. This has resulted in stopgap measures—such as the agreement with the Spanish Ministry of Education, Culture, and Sport to bring in qualified teachers to fill positions that are left empty due to the lack of applicants. For the 2016–17 school year, Spain's Ministry of Education posted on its website that there were more than 850 positions for visiting instructors from Spain in schools across the United States and Canada, with hundreds from other Spanish-speaking countries and hundreds more already teaching in the schools. The problem is so acute in some states that school districts with more resources are luring away dual immersion instructors from others with limited resources. In Oregon, a survey was given in 2014 to school districts to inquire about the need for bilingual teachers. The results indicated that 25 of 37 districts had bilingual teacher openings for the 2014–15 school year. Of the 25 that reported the need for bilingual instructors, 22 reported difficulty filling those vacancies. For that academic year alone, the 25 districts had 172 openings for bilingual teachers, and most of these positions were at the elementary level (Spegman 2015).

The question arises as to what can be done to not only increase the number of trained teachers for dual immersion programs but also help them to be successful in the classroom. Met and Lorenz (1997, 246) consider the ideal immersion teacher as "someone who demonstrates excellent skills in elementary education and who has native or near-native proficiency in the language of instruction." Bernhardt and Schrier (1992) propose that those interested in teaching in a dual language immersion classroom need both sufficient proficiency in the language and pedagogical training at the level they will be teaching if they have any hope of succeeding in the bilingual classroom. Cody (2009, 1) observes that novice immersion instructors are certified to teach elementary school and are proficient in the language but have "little knowledge of immersion pedagogy or what they can expect in their classrooms." Tedick and Fortune (2013, 3) opine that "perhaps the greatest challenge facing teacher educators are change-resistant tertiary-level organizational structures that continue to expect preservice bilingual/immersion teachers to enroll in one program for grade-level appropriate licensure, another to find ongoing support for their second-language proficiency, and yet another for bilingual/immersion specific knowledge and skills." The question then is what can be done to better prepare and train future immersion instructors.

Cody (2009) conducted a study to investigate the curricular challenges faced by new immersion teachers and found four main problems. First, she discovered that teachers were not prepared with the vocabulary and skills needed to relate daily routines to students with no or limited ability in the target language. Second, she found that teachers often were given materials not specifically designed for the immersion classroom and were asked to adapt those materials to their own classroom. The teachers were not prepared to do this and were forced to create many materials of their own of varying degrees of quality. Third, she states that though immersion teachers received professional development, as is required of all teachers, they were also obligated to sift through the training they received and modify it for the immersion classroom. Much of the training maintained only a peripheral relationship to what they wanted to accomplish in the classroom, which resulted in extra work on their part to adapt the materials to their setting. Fourth and finally, though the novice teachers relied on more experienced teachers for advice, they often availed themselves of multiple sources to deal with their concerns in the classroom. Cody (2009, 4) notes the wide variety of colleagues to whom novice immersion teachers would turn for help: "The teachers preferred to get language help from native speakers, curriculum development ideas and teaching techniques from curriculum directors and/or other teachers at their schools, and behavior management strategies from other non-immersion teachers."

In their teacher preparation programs, preservice immersion teachers need to be informed about what immersion education is and encouraged to observe immersion classrooms to determine what they need to do to prepare to teach in this setting. Teacher trainers should be active in making preservice teachers aware of the materials and resources that are available to them and in explaining how to access them, and how to incorporate them effectively. Several universities have started programs offering dual language immersion certificates and minors, such as Brigham Young University (BYU), the University of Minnesota, and San Diego State University. These programs are designed to offer students specialized courses that prepare them for the unique demands of the immersion classroom. As more programs of this type are developed and offered to Spanish language majors, they will appreciate the variety of professional options available to them as future Spanish language educators. Likewise, additional resources in print and online need to be developed for the dual language immersion classroom and made widely available to allow both experienced and new teachers to share materials and ideas. Finally, in addition to these materials, more professional development opportunities and pedagogical training for current and preservice immersion teachers will have a positive impact on current and future teaching practices.

## INSTRUCTOR ATTRITION

Pastor Cesteros and Lacorte (2015, 117) accurately observe that effective language teaching and learning "are only made possible by the use of qualified teachers." The question then remains as to how can programs successfully train qualified instructors and place them in the schools that need them. Although this seems to be a rather straightforward process, the demand for high-quality instructors in Spanish language classrooms of all types and levels is increasing at a higher rate than these individuals are graduating. Newspaper headlines such as "Maine School, Struggling to Find Foreign Language Teacher, Turns to Computer Program" reflect the problems that many schools are encountering in their search for qualified foreign language teachers. The school district in Maine where this newspaper article appeared in 2016 tried to fill a teaching shortage, and when it received zero applicants for the positions, it chose to buy the Rosetta Stone language program and install it on several computers as a substitute for a language program. This raises a major concern as to why so many schools are having problems filling positions across all languages, including Spanish. Researchers and education-related organizations have found that a teacher shortage has existed for many decades (AAEE 2016; Boe and Gilford 1992; Darling-Hammond 1984; Haggstrom, Darling-Hammond, and Grissmer 1988; National Commission on Excellence in Education 1983). Swanson (2010, 306) outlines seven major causes for the shortage of foreign language teachers: "retirement, attrition, increased enrollments, legislation, perceptions of teaching, teacher efficacy, and one's personality and vocational interests."

The teacher shortage is one of the issues facing public schools in Utah and across the United States at both the elementary and secondary levels. The lack of qualified teachers is largely the result of more than 42 percent of teachers leaving the profession in the first five years. In the case of Utah, enough teachers are graduating to fill the demand, but schools are not retaining them, thus creating a chronic shortage. As a result, the Utah State Board of Education decided on an initiative, the Academic Pathway to Teaching (APT), that would potentially alleviate the situation for the affected schools. According to the Utah State Board of Education's website, the APT allows individuals to become teachers without formal licensure if they meet certain requirements: (1) hold a bachelor's degree in any subject related to content area; (2) pass the Praxis test in the content area in which they plan to teach; (3) pay a small application fee; and (4) work with a master teacher as a mentor. The exact role of the mentor vis-à-vis the applicant who is hired with no training is not entirely clear, and no provisions in the law provide any additional compensation for the master teachers who spend additional time with the untrained applicants.

The problem with a policy such as this is that it leads people to wonder why America's children are being taught by untrained novices, as the title of an August 2016 *Washington Post* article claims: "In Utah, Schools Can Now Hire Teachers with No Training Whatsoever." Naturally, the reaction of many current educators to the implementation of this law in the fall of 2016 was very unfavorable. Lincoln Elementary School science teacher Cara Baldree described the new policy "as 'absolutely demoralizing and insulting' by implying that knowledge in a subject area makes a person an automatic teacher." She continues, "Just because you comprehend third-grade math doesn't mean you can teach third-grade math" (Wood 2016). Other educators, such as Doug Corey of BYU's McKay School of Education, have worried that the APT will put inexperienced teachers in the classroom, which "sounds like guaranteed poor outcomes and hurt students" (Wood 2016).

Ironically, this law comes at a time when the Utah State Board of Education has made entering teacher education programs and graduating from them more difficult by raising the requirements for students. Students now must achieve minimum ACT scores (composite, 21; English, 20; math, 19) or SAT scores (critical reading / math, 1,000; with math and reading scores of 450). If a student has a bachelor degree or higher, he or she does not need to meet this testing requirement. In addition, students may not have any grade in a content area lower than a C and must maintain a grade point average of 3.0 or higher. Although the Utah State Board of Education should be applauded for its decision to raise the bar for future teachers, its subsequent decision to create the APT seems problematic. Additionally, the higher standards have an adverse impact on international and other second-language students, who are held to the same standard and required to perform well on the ACT or SAT, or to take a series of exams before they can be admitted to a teacher education program.

Research has found that teachers who enter the teaching field through an alternative route such as the new APT tend to leave the field at a higher rate than teachers who graduate from teacher education programs. The attrition rate of these nontraditional teachers can be as high as 60 percent within the first two years of the profession (Darling-Hammond, Berry, and Thoreson 2001; Lauer 2001). The high turnover in the teaching profession adversely affects not only the students and school districts that must deal with it but also the experienced teachers in a school who are constantly pulled away from their teaching to mentor and train new faculty members. This can lead to burnout on the part of the teachers and contribute to even greater rates of attrition. The focus on teacher training needs to consider how such policies will affect the experiences of trained teachers and especially beginning teachers in schools with high numbers of colleagues without any pedagogical training.

## GRADUATE STUDENT TRAINING

Although there has been growing attention to the training of preservice K–12 teachers by postsecondary Spanish programs, the training of the instructional staff imparting courses within these postsecondary programs has received much less attention. More specifically, the preservice and in-service training of graduate student instructors is an area that has become especially pressing of late, given the increasing numbers of graduate students teaching courses— and this is particularly true in Spanish programs and because the research on and training of these students has been in a period of "stasis" over the past twenty-five years (Allen and Maxim 2013).[1] Schulz (2000) found that before the 1950s, only a few studies had looked into the training of graduate student instructors (Keniston 1922; Waldman 1940). Hagiwara (1969, 90) argues that despite changes in the field during the 1950s and 1960s, the "opportunities for young college teachers to evaluate and increase their language proficiency and teaching skills or increase their knowledge of methodology and linguistics have seldom been available." Early graduate student training consisted of a preorientation, where students would talk about specific university regulations and procedures as well as receive a detailed overview of the syllabus for a specific course that the students would be teaching. The students would also spend time going over ideas for the first week of teaching and would then be given general guidelines on best pedagogical practices. After this, the supervisor would meet with the students with some frequency during the first week of classes and then less frequently throughout the semester. Students were also asked to observe fellow instructors twice during the semester, and their supervisor would observe them just once. This may describe the current practices at many universities across the United States, but it also reflects the routine described by Remak (1957) sixty years ago. Remak was one of the first researchers to address this issue in the *Modern Language Journal*, and it seems that little has changed since then.

Pastor Cesteros and Lacorte (2015, 123) describe four main challenges with graduate student instructor training. First, second-language graduate programs "usually enjoy a greater degree of autonomy than K–12 institutions for the intellectual, scholarly, and pedagogical development of their graduate students." Program supervisors are not required to report to any large institutional body, other than the occasional external departmental review that looks at the entire program and would likely only be reviewed if students were to complain to administrators or if the department were audited by an accrediting agency. Second, typically, the training of graduate student instructors has been carried out by professors whose focus and training are not in the area of applied linguistics or language pedagogy. As many language departments are primarily made up of faculty whose focus is on literature and culture, graduate students receive instruction on language pedagogy from faculty with little to no formal training in the field. Third, language departments generally separate the training of students to teach lower-level language courses from those who teach more advanced literature and culture courses. Not only are there distinct goals between levels but the chasm between the amount and type of training that is needed and what is actually given is also quite broad. Sadly, though the training and preparation for teaching lower-level courses is minimal, the training for the teaching of advanced courses is nearly, if not completely, nonexistent. Finally, there is a lack of research on how the training of graduate student instructors affects their teaching and its impact on their students' learning. Allen and Negueruela-Azarola (2010, 338) offer three suggestions for how to provide "more extensive graduate coursework related to teaching or linking teaching and scholarship, team teaching opportunities, and opportunities to independently teach advanced undergraduate courses." Such recommendations will not resolve all the concerns related to graduate student training, but should help to better prepare these graduate student instructors and in turn provide their students with higher-quality instruction. However well-intentioned these suggestions may be, the scarcity of resources made available for graduate student training remains the proverbial elephant in the room. Although a handful of scholars are developing resources for the training of graduate students (Allen and Maxim 2012; Lieberg 2008), the lack of attention to this important group that has an ever-larger role in the education of university students is quite surprising. Many departments lack the necessary human capital and, unfortunately, interest, to make significant investments in ongoing and meaningful instructor training for all members of the instructional corps, from the first-semester graduate student to the full professor near retirement.

## SPANISH POSTSECONDARY PROGRAM AND CURRICULUM SURVEY RESULTS

The survey we conducted included eight specific questions regarding how much of a concern teacher/instructor training was for the participants in this study. The participants were also given a ninth category, where they could include information from another area that they perceived as a concern. The postsecondary educators were asked to rank each item according to the level of concern that they had for each issue related to teacher/instructor training. Items were ranked on a scale of 1 (very much a concern) to 5 (not a concern at all). We include the overall rank of the item's mean across all fifty-five survey items with regard to the level of perceived concern. These means and ranks were calculated from responses given by approximately seven hundred instructors of all academic backgrounds, ranks, and ages, and from all institution types. The results of the survey show the areas about which the instructors surveyed are most concerned and how these questions ranked in the overall survey. The percentage of respondents who chose the sixth response option, "not applicable to my program," appears last in the information given at the end of each item:

- Sufficient mentoring of university instructors in language teaching (e.g., graduate students, adjunct instructors, lecturers, etc.): 2.82 / 32nd / 8 percent;
- Adequate professional development in language teaching for tenured/ tenure-track professors: 2.85 / 33rd / 7 percent;
- Appropriate balance between theory and praxis in teacher/instructor training at all levels: 2.85 / 35th / 8 percent;
- Deficient language proficiency (oral, writing, etc.) of postsecondary Spanish instructors (e.g., graduate students, part-time/adjunct instructors): 3.28 / 51st / 13 percent;
- Deficient language proficiency (oral, writing, etc.) of K–12 preservice Spanish teachers: 3.28 / 52nd / 25 percent;
- Creation of courses that prepare preservice K–12 teachers for diverse

contexts (e.g., immersion, heritage, traditional FL, Advanced Placement courses): 3.53 / 53rd / 28 percent;
- Availability of qualified cooperating teachers for pre-service K–12 teachers: 3.55 / 54th / 30 percent; and
- Sufficient mentoring of undergraduate student teachers during K–12 school placements by university personnel: 3.56 / 55th / 30 percent.

The greatest concern expressed by the participants on this section of the survey concerned the pedagogical mentoring for university instructors, as this ranked thirty-second out of fifty-five. Closely following this concern was the need for adequate professional development in language teaching for tenured/tenure-track professors as the thirty-third ranked response, followed next by the necessity to find the appropriate balance between theory and praxis in teacher/instructor training at all levels, which was ranked thirty-fifth out of fifty-five. These results demonstrate that the instructors in our study placed some importance on the need for continual training and mentoring to improve their teaching. This is heartening because many of these professors had likely received minimal training in language pedagogy but still perceived it as having value to them. Though ranked in the middle overall, the instructors were concerned with being able to improve their language teaching and apply correct pedagogical principles in the classroom. Language departments and college deans should work with faculty centers and other organizations at their institutions to provide faculty members, both new and experienced, with continued support and workshops specifically related to pedagogy. Recently, for instance, at BYU the Spanish and Portuguese Department started a mentoring program where new and experienced faculty were assigned to observe each other and then meet over lunch to discuss what they had learned as well as offer any suggestions. This benefited both parties because the instructors being observed received feedback from their colleagues and those observing gleaned insights from their colleagues' teaching. This also helped facilitate faculty promotion and tenure and other faculty evaluations because the peer observations enabled multiple colleagues to write letters with informed comments regarding teaching. The letters were included as evidence of the individual's pedagogical development over the course of several semesters. Programs such as these can be very beneficial for instructors at all levels, and were important for the instructors at BYU. On the contrary, peer observations of tenured faculty remain a tough sell at the University of Kentucky because many faculty feel that requiring and documenting class observations by colleagues is intrusive and undermines academic freedom and pedagogical autonomy and creativity.

The other five comments that the participants in the survey were asked to rank according to their level of concern were not technically considered a concern because their mean scores surpassed 3, or neutral, and were of least concern out of all fifty-five items. These items are ranked fifty-first to fifty-fifth, including the lowest-ranked items in the survey. The item that was of least concern to the faculty in this study was the question regarding sufficient mentoring of undergraduate student teachers during K–12 school placements by university personnel. Three of the other four items also dealt with K–12 student teachers or their faculty mentors. This is not surprising, given that many language departments are not involved with the placement and training of student teachers. Often this task is assigned to faculty in education or to a specific faculty member in the department who is solely responsible for all preservice secondary teacher training duties. Four of the five lowest-ranked items were likely not a concern to the population sampled because it was outside their area. This can also be seen, given that from 25 to 30 percent of the participants who responded to these questions marked them as not relevant to their situation. The fifty-first-ranked item also related to teacher training, but specifically to the subpar levels of language proficiency of postsecondary Spanish instructors (e.g., graduate students, part-time/adjunct instructors). Again, the participants in this study were most likely not concerned with this area due to their lack of involvement with the training of graduate students and adjuncts. If such training takes place, it is usually limited to one individual or a small group of faculty whose members serve as the language program director(s).

Compared with all the areas of concern included in the survey, teacher/instructor training ranked the lowest across all levels and specialties and had the highest percentage of responses of "not applicable." Of the nine categories in the survey, concern over teacher/instructor training was ranked ninth overall as being the area of least concern, regardless of academic training or rank. As mentioned above, this is not overly surprising, given that if the responsibilities for some of these areas are in a department, they are generally the responsibility of very few people. The situation at BYU is different from many schools because the Department of Spanish and Portuguese is fortunate to have a pedagogy section, which currently consists of six tenured or tenure track professors and one adjunct professor responsible for observing student teachers in the schools. Given the large number of Spanish pedagogy faculty, many of the duties related to training both undergraduate students and graduate students rest in the department rather than with the School of Education. Additionally, faculty members are often given committee assignments related to their training and are responsible for the observation of adjuncts as well as their training. Although this is not the usual case for language departments, the areas ranked the lowest on the survey are major topics of meetings within the pedagogy section, as faculty members attempt to help the instructors in the department stay up-to-date on current research regarding language teaching and classroom pedagogy.

## CURRICULAR CONSIDERATIONS FOR TEACHER/ INSTRUCTOR TRAINING

The training of teachers is a complex endeavor that requires the preservice or in-service teacher trainer to have knowledge of myriad learning and teaching theories and to be adept at the practical implementation of those theories for future teachers to emulate. Teachers face constant challenges as preservice instructors and as full-time, in-service teachers. Pastor Cesteros and Lacorte (2015) list three main challenges faced by in-service teachers that need to be addressed in curriculum design. First, teachers need better preparation in their undergraduate degree programs, and they should have better contact and communication with other second-language colleagues. Second, many programs still favor a grammar-focused curriculum, relying on methods that worked in the past instead of teaching preservice teachers to be innovators. Third and finally, there is still a gap between language courses and the education courses that students are required to take to graduate. This gap between language skills and content is likely part of a larger disconnect between a liberal arts curriculum and that of education departments. Language and education departments need to collaborate to develop programs that do not operate independently of one another but rather in a more integrated fashion, so that students' overall experience results in more effective classroom teachers in practice and not just on paper.

With respect to developing the necessary skills and abilities for the next generation of Spanish teachers, several organizations have recommended what these skills are and how to teach them. The Instituto Cervantes is a public institution created by the Government of Spain in 1991 to promote the teaching, study, and use of Spanish throughout the world, and to contribute to the spread of Hispanic cultures abroad. In 2012, the Instituto Cervantes produced a manual (Moreno 2012), in which it shares eight key competencies, with additional subcompetencies that all foreign language and second-language teachers should possess (table 8.1). These eight categories reflect the overall characteristics that Spanish programs need to consider as they prepare future teachers with these skills.

Pastor Cesteros and Lacorte (2015) propose several areas within teacher training where improvements need to be made. Second-language and foreign

**Table 8.1    Key Competencies of Foreign Language and Second-Language Educators**

**Organize learning situations**
- Diagnose and meet the needs of students.
- To promote the use and reflection on the language.
- Plan teaching sequences.
- Manage the classroom.

**Evaluate the students' learning and performance**
- Use tools and evaluation procedures.
- Ensure good practices in evaluation.
- Promote constructive feedback.
- Involve the student in the evaluation.

**Involve students in controlling their own learning**
- Encourage and ensure that the student manages the resources and means available to learn.
- Integrate teaching tools to reflect on the learning process.
- Encourage the student to define his or her own learning project.
- Motivate students to take responsibility for their own learning.

**Develop professionally as an instructor in the institution**
- Analyze and reflect on the teaching practice.
- Define a personal plan for ongoing training.
- Be involved in the professional development of the teaching team.
- Participate actively in the development of the profession.

**Facilitate intercultural communication**
- Be involved in the development of one's intercultural competence.
- Adapt to the cultures of the environment.
- Encourage intercultural dialogue.
- Encourage the student to develop his or her intercultural competence.

**Actively participate in the institution**
- Work as a team in one's institution.
- Get involved in the improvement projects of one's institution.
- Promote and disseminate good practices in one's institution.
- Know the institution and integrate into it.

**Use information and communication technology (ICT) in the performance of work**
- Engage in the development of one's own digital competence.
- Develop digital environments and learn to use available computer applications.
- Take advantage of the didactic potential of ICT.
- Encourage students to use ICT for learning.

**Manage feelings and emotions in the performance of work**
- Manage your own emotions.
- Motivate yourself at work.
- Develop interpersonal relationships.
- Engage in the development of the student's emotional intelligence.

language methodology textbooks need to be informed by current research and ongoing studies in second-language acquisition. For example, too many textbooks fail to account for the sociocultural aspects of language teaching. They also suggest that a larger proportion of preservice and in-service training could be done using electronic teaching portfolios (Atienza 2009; González Argüello and Pujolà Font 2008; Pastor Cesteros 2012), which would allow teachers to customize their training to their own needs and future positions. These electronic portfolios would allow teachers to better capture the full array of their teacher preparation. Similarly, teachers need to receive specialized training for the variety of courses that they may be asked to teach. This chapter has mentioned some of the challenges of teaching immersion courses, but other challenges may come in the form of courses for heritage students; mixed classes with native, heritage, and nonnative students; and content courses in areas traditionally not included in the Spanish curriculum. Teachers need training not only to be more marketable but also to become more prepared for the diversity that exists in today's Spanish language classroom. Finally, Pastor Cesteros and Lacorte mention the need for active participation in professional organizations that can help create professional training opportunities and connect teachers from different areas to facilitate collaboration. Several organizations exist worldwide that can serve Spanish teachers, such as the Asociación para la Enseñanza del Español como Lengua Extranjera and the American Association of Teachers of Spanish and Portuguese, as well as national organizations for all foreign language teachers, such as the American Council on the Teaching of Foreign Languages. Involvement of teachers at all levels, for both preservice and in-service, in these organizations can make a difference across language departments and in teacher training programs.

## CONCLUSION

The preparation of Spanish language instructors is not without its challenges, and much work needs to be done to improve not only teacher education programs but also the conditions that teachers face as professionals. Spanish teachers today have a much different set of students than in previous years. Many Spanish teachers instruct mixed groups of students in the same class that consist of nonnative, native, and heritage learners. Thus, teachers need to be equipped with the tools necessary to address a variety of student needs in the same classroom. The demand for Spanish immersion teachers continues to grow, yet the number of programs preparing teachers for this context is still lacking. There needs to be more and better coordination and collaboration between schools of education and language departments to ensure high quality preservice training.

Nonnative, preservice teachers need to maximize opportunities for increasing their proficiency and cultural knowledge, which does not travel abroad. With Spanish speakers throughout the United States, preservice teachers need only look as far as the neighborhoods where they live, or online, to find opportunities to engage with the language and culture. The large number of Spanish speakers throughout the United States makes training future teachers different from teaching other languages. Teacher training programs need to incorporate more experiential learning into their programs to provide students with the opportunity to serve and learn at the same time, and to stay in touch with the cultures and peoples who use Spanish on a daily basis. By so doing, students can gain valuable experience and knowledge while helping the community and working with others, and at the same time developing their proficiency and a better understanding of the Hispanic community around them.

Finally, all efforts at improving Spanish teachers will be for naught if within a few years the majority of trained teachers have left the teaching profession. Programs need to better prepare teachers to confront the complex sociocultural, sociopolitical, programmatic, and curricular realities that they will encounter in the classroom and in the community. In addition, state and local governments and community organizations must take a harder look at how they can better support teachers, especially those who are beginning their academic careers.

## REFLECTION QUESTIONS

1. How does a teacher's proficiency level affect student achievement and learning in the classroom? What level of proficiency do you feel instructors should demonstrate? How does the level of the course they are teaching affect the required proficiency level? What about cultural competence?

2. What options should be available to preservice teachers to measure their proficiency, other than the OPI? What about the other language skills?

3. What role should native language play in the assignment of teaching responsibilities for faculty members, adjuncts, and graduate students? Should upper-level language and culture courses be limited to native speakers? Explain.

4. Many practicing teachers cite a lack of respect and professionalism as the main reasons for leaving the profession—not salary. What can be done to address this?

5. Why do you think that schools are accepting teachers who have no formal training in the classroom? What other solutions could work to solve teacher shortages?

6. A large portion of survey participants found the category regarding teacher training not to be relevant to them. What should the role of faculty members be in training both preservice teachers and graduate instructors? Should the responsibility for this training reside in colleges of education or with faculty who have specific pedagogical training? How could other faculty members contribute to this training?

7. How are graduate student instructors trained at your institution? What additional support and training would improve the quality of their teaching? How is the ongoing pedagogical training of tenured and tenure-line faculty addressed? How is their teaching evaluated?

8. Students often enter the classroom with preconceived notions about the effectiveness of native and nonnative instructors. What can be done to prepare students for the variety of instructors that they will have in language courses?

9. Does your institution offer specific training for immersion instructors? If so, describe how this training differs from the nonimmersion program.

## PEDAGOGICAL ACTIVITIES

1. Many language teachers base much of their teaching on what they have observed from others, either as a student or as a colleague. Observe the class of an instructor whom you respect as someone who demonstrates excellence in the classroom. Take detailed notes on what he or she does that is effective. Write a reflection on what you can do to be more effective as a language instructor.

2. Visit your institution's faculty professional development or teaching center, or its equivalent. Find out what resources are offered for faculty members to improve their teaching. Also, find out about the resources available to graduate student instructors and who is responsible for their training. Go to one of the workshops or other events sponsored by either the faculty center or graduate college.

3. Interview one of the faculty members responsible for training Spanish teachers. Find out what some of the main challenges are for teachers in your region. Ask about job placement and retention in your area. Finally, ask about what recommendations they would offer future Spanish language teachers.

4. Find an article published in the last two years related to an area of your teaching that you would like to improve (reading, writing, grammar, culture, etc.). The article can be a research article or a synthesis, "best practices" article focused on classroom practices and strategies. Read the article and develop a new activity for your own language classroom based on the reading. Use the activity in your classroom, and evaluate how the activity helped your students in their learning.

## NOTE

1. Although this section focuses primarily on graduate student instructors and their training, even less research has looked at the ongoing pedagogical training of other instructors, such as contractual staff, tenure-line staff, and tenured professors.

## REFERENCES

AAEE (American Association for Employment in Education). 2016. *Educator Supply and Demand Report 2015–16: Executive Summary.* Evanston, IL: AAEE. www.aaee.org/re sources/Documents/2015-16_AAEE_Supply_Demand_Summary.pdf.

ACTFL (American Council on the Teaching of Foreign Languages). 2002. *ACTFL/ NCATE Program Standards for the Preparation of Foreign Language Teachers (Initial level– Undergraduate and Graduate) (For K–12 and Secondary Certification)*. Alexandria, VA: ACTFL. http://www.ncate.org/LinkClick.aspx?fileticket= percent2FudOr9ZQCW0 per cent3D&tabid=676.

Allen, Heather, and Hiram Maxim. 2012. "Foreign Language Graduate Student Professional Development—Past, Present, and Future." In *AAUSC 2011 Volume: Educating the Future Foreign Language Professoriate for the 21st Century*, edited by Heather Allen and Hiram H. Maxim. Boston: Heinle & Heinle.

Allen, Heather Willis, and Eduardo Negueruela–Azarola. 2010. "The Professional Development of Future Professors of Foreign Languages: Looking Back, Looking Forward." *Modern Language Journal* 94, no. 3: 377–95.

Aoki, Michelle. 2013. "The Role of Testing Language Proficiency as Part of Teacher Certification." *Modern Language Journal* 97, no. 2: 539–40.

Atienza, Encarna. 2009. "El Portafolio del Profesor como Instrumento de Autoformación." *marcoELE* 9: 1–19.

Benke, Eszter, and Peter Medgyes. 2006. "Differences in Teaching Behaviour between Native and Non-Native Speaker Teachers: As Seen by the Learners." In *Non-Native Language Teachers: Perceptions, Challenges, and Contributions to the Profession*, edited by Enric Llurda. New York: Springer Science & Business Media.

Bernhardt, Elizabeth, and Lesley Schrier. 1992. "The Development of Immersion Teachers." In *Life in Language Immersion Classrooms, Volume 86*, edited by Elizabeth Bernhardt. Clevedon, UK: Multilingual Matters.

Boe, Erling, and Dorothy Gilford. 1992. "Teacher Supply, Demand, and Quality: Policy Issues, Models, and Data Bases." Washington, DC: National Academies Press.

Burke, Brigid M. 2013. "Looking into a Crystal Ball: Is Requiring High-Stakes Language Proficiency Tests Really Going to Improve World Language Education?" *Modern Language Journal* 97, no. 2: 531–34.

Cheung, Yin Ling, and George Braine. 2007. "The Attitudes of University Students towards Non-Native Speakers: English Teachers in Hong Kong." *RELC Journal* 38, no. 3: 257–77.

Cody, Jae. 2009. "Challenges Facing Beginning Immersion Teachers." *ACIE Newsletter–The Bridge*. http://carla.umn.edu/immersion/acie/vol13/no1/Bridge_nov_2009.pdf.

Darling-Hammond, Linda. 1984. *Beyond the Commission Reports: The Coming Crisis in Teaching*. Santa Monica, CA: RAND Corporation.

Darling-Hammond, Linda, Barnett Berry, and Amy Thoreson. 2001. "Does Teacher Certification Matter? Evaluating the Evidence." *Educational Evaluation and Policy Analysis* 23, no. 1: 57–77.

Donato, Richard. 2009. "Teacher Education in the Age of Standards of Professional Practice." *Modern Language Journal* 93, no. 2: 267–70.

Feinberg, Robbie. 2016. "Maine Grapples with 'Crisis-Level' Foreign Language Teacher Shortage." *Maine Public*, October 26. http://mainepublic.org/post/maine-grapples-crisis-level -foreign-language-teacher-shortage#stream/0.

Glisan, Eileen W., Elvira Swender, and Eric A. Surface. 2013. "Oral Proficiency Standards and Foreign Language Teacher Candidates: Current Findings and Future Research Directions." *Foreign Language Annals* 46, no. 2: 264–89.

González Argüello, Vicenta, and Pujolà Font, Joan-Tomás. 2008. "El Uso del Portafolio para la Autoevaluación Continua del Profesor." *Monográficos MarcoELE* 7: 92–110.

Haggstrom, Gus W., Linda Darling-Hammond, and David Grissmar. 1988. *Assessing Teacher Supply and Demand.* Santa Monica, CA: Rand Corporation.

Hagiwara, Michio P. 1969. "Training and Supervision of College Foreign Language Teachers." *Foreign Language Annals* 3, no. 1: 90–107.

Hamlyn, Helen, Eric Surface, and Elvira Swender. 2007. "What Proficiency Testing Is Telling Us about Teacher Certification Candidates." Presentation at the Annual Conference of the American Council on the Teaching of Foreign Languages, San Antonio, November.

Hertel, Tammy Jandrey, and Gretchen Sunderman. 2009. "Student Attitudes toward Native and Non-Native Language Instructors." *Foreign Language Annals* 42, no. 3: 468–82.

Jordan, Miriam. 2010. "Arizona Grades Teachers on Fluency." *Wall Street Journal,* April 30. www.wsj.com/articles/SB10001424052748703572504575213883276427528.

Keniston, Hayward. 1922. "The Role of the Graduate School in the Training of the Modern Language Teacher." *Modern Language Journal* 7, no. 1: 1–4.

Lauer, Patricia. 2001. *A Secondary Analysis of a Review of Teacher Preparation Research.* Denver: Education Commission of the States.

Lasagabaster, David, and Juan Manuel Sierra. 2006. "What Do Students Think about the Pros and Cons of Having a Native Speaker Teacher?" In *Non-Native Language Teachers: Perceptions, Challenges, and Contributions to the Profession,* edited by Enric Llurda. New York: Springer Science & Business Media.

Lieberg, Carolyn. 2008. *Teaching Your First College Class: A Practical Guide for New Faculty and Graduate Student Instructors.* Sterling, VA: Stylus.

Mahboob, Ahmar. 2004. "Native or Nonnative: What Do Students Enrolled in an Intensive English Program Think?" In *Learning and Teaching from Experience: Perspectives on Non-Native English Speaking Professionals,* edited by Lia Kamshi-Stein. Ann Arbor: University of Michigan Press.

Medgyes, Peter. 1994. *The Non-Native Teacher.* London: Macmillan.

Met, Myriam, and Eileen B. Lorenz. 1997. "Lessons from US Immersion Programs: Two Decades of Experience." In *Immersion Education: International Perspectives,* edited by Robert Johnson and Merrill Swain. Cambridge: Cambridge University Press.

Ministry of Education, Culture, and Sport. "Profesores Visitantes en EEUU y Canadá." www.mecd.gob.es/eeuu/convocatorias-programas/convocatorias-eeuu/ppvv.html.

Moreno Fernández, Francisco. 2012. "Las competencias claves del profesorado de lenguas segundas y extranjeras." http://cvc.cervantes.es/ensenanza/biblioteca_ele/competencias/competencias_profesorado.pdf.

Moussu, Lucie, and Enric Llurda. 2008. "Non-Native English-Speaking English Language Teachers: History and Research." *Language Teaching* 41, no. 3: 315–48.

National Commission on Excellence in Education. 1983. *A Nation at Risk: The Imperative for Educational Reform.* Washington, DC: National Academies Press.

National Standards Collaborative Board. 2015. *World-Readiness Standards for Learning Languages,* 4th ed. Alexandria, VA: National Standards Collaborative Board. www.actfl.org/publications/all/world-readiness-standards-learning-languages.

Norris, John M. 2013. "Some Challenges in Assessment for Teacher Licensure, Program Accreditation, and Educational Reform." *Modern Language Journal* 97, no. 2: 554–60.

Pastor Cesteros, Susana. 2012. "Portafolio Docente y Evaluación del Profesorado de ELE." *Tinkuy: Boletín de Investigación y Debate* 19: 5–27.

Pastor Cesteros, Susana, and Manel Lacorte. 2015. "Teacher Education." In *Routledge Handbook of Hispanic Applied Linguistics,* edited by Manel Lacorte. New York: Routledge.

Phillipson, Robert. 1992. *Linguistic Imperialism.* Oxford: Oxford University Press.

Rajagopalan, Kanavillil. 2006. "Non-Native Speaker Teachers of English and Their Anxieties: Ingredients for an Experiment in Action Research." In *Non-Native Language Teachers: Perceptions, Challenges, and Contributions to the Profession*, edited by Enric Llurda. New York: Springer Science & Business Media.

Remak, Henry H. H. 1957. "The Training and Supervision of Teaching Assistants in German." *Modern Language Journal* 41, no. 5: 212–14.

Schulz, Renate A. 2000. "Foreign Language Teacher Development: MLJ Perspectives, 1916–1999." *Modern Language Journal* 84, no. 4: 495–522.

Spegman, Abby. 2015. "Wanted: Bilingual Teachers for English-Spanish Classrooms." *Bulletin*, October 19. www.bendbulletin.com/localstate/education/3603182-151/wanted -bilingual-teachers-for-english-spanish-classrooms.

Sullivan, JoAnn Hammadou. 2011. "Taking Charge: Teacher Candidates' Preparation for the Oral Proficiency Interview." *Foreign Language Annals* 44, no. 2: 241–57.

Swanson, Peter B. 2010. "Teacher Efficacy and Attrition: Helping Students at Introductory Levels of Language Instruction Appears Critical." *Hispania* 93, no. 2: 305–21.

Swender, Elaine, Eric Surface, Ruth M. Cahoon, and Eileen Glisan. 2011. "Advancing Professional Standards: Are Teachers and Programs Making the Grade?" Paper presented at the annual convention of the American Council on the Teaching of Foreign Languages, Denver, November 18–20.

Tedick, Diane J. 2013. "Embracing Proficiency and Program Standards and Rising to the Challenge: A Response to Burke." *Modern Language Journal* 97, no. 2: 535–38.

Tedick, Diane J., and Tara W. Fortune. 2013. "Bilingual/Immersion Teacher Education." In *The Encyclopedia of Applied Linguistics*, edited by Carol Chapelle. Hoboken, NJ: Blackwell.

Thompson, Amy S., and Amy Fioramonte. 2013. "Nonnative Speaker Teachers of Spanish: Insights from Novice Teachers." *Foreign Language Annals* 4, no. 45: 564–79.

Utah State Board of Education. "Academic Pathway to Teaching (APT)." www.schools.utah .gov/cert/APT.aspx.

Waldman, Mark. 1940. "The Selection of Heads of Modern Language Departments, Appointments of Modern Language Teachers, and Their Supervision." *Modern Language Journal* 24, no. 7: 510–25.

Walker, Constance L., and Diane J. Tedick. 2000. "The Complexity of Immersion Education: Teachers Address the Issues." *Modern Language Journal* 84, no. 1: 5–27.

Whitaker, Todd, and Beth Whitaker. 2013. *Teaching Matters: How to Keep Your Passion and Thrive in Today's Classroom*, 2nd ed. New York: Routledge.

Wood, Benjamin. 2016. "Utah Teachers Decry 'Demoralizing,' 'Insulting' Licensing Rule at School Board Hearing." *Salt Lake Tribune*, July 26. www.sltrib.com/news/4161600-155 /utah-teachers-decry-demoralizing-insulting-licensing?fullpage=1.

# 9

# TECHNOLOGICAL ADVANCES IN SPANISH LANGUAGE EDUCATION

> Computers will not replace teachers; teachers who use computers will
> eventually replace teachers who don't.
> —Ray Clifford, "The Status of Computer-Assisted
> Language Instruction," 1987

Many technological developments have taken place in language education since the mid–twentieth century, when the only technology available to supplement second-language classroom teaching and learning was quite rudimentary, consisting of chalk and a chalkboard, a Xerox machine to make individual copies, and in some cases a reel-to-reel projection system, and later on a slide projector. However, more recent developments in technology have twenty-first-century educators excited as well as slightly apprehensive—excited for the potential of increased learning gains and student motivation, and apprehensive regarding their ability to effectively implement these innovations. The vast majority of postsecondary classrooms are equipped with computers connected to the internet that allow users to connect asynchronously and synchronously with individuals and classrooms that were previously unreachable, or were unreachable without leaving the classroom. In addition, the traditional classroom has changed, in that students are now able to access other classrooms from any digital device and connect with fellow students and their teachers from anywhere in the world. This chapter discusses how the careful design of online and blended, or hybrid, courses in accord with the principles of second-language acquisition can increase the effectiveness of these courses.

In this chapter, we discuss how technology can be integrated into the Spanish curriculum, and how this implementation can help educators meet institutional objectives and national standards in the acquisition of Spanish as a second language. We also comment on the potential impact of increased use of technology on macro issues at the programmatic and curricular levels. Although educational technologies are constantly changing, this chapter focuses on how they can be implemented into the Spanish language curriculum to facilitate students' language learning and to assist educators as they navigate the ever-changing curricular and programmatic landscape. And though most technologies are not unique to Spanish, how they are integrated into the twenty-first-century curriculum present unique challenges as well as opportunities for postsecondary Spanish educators.

## ONLINE AND BLENDED LEARNING ENVIRONMENTS

As computer technology has become more fully integrated into the language classroom, specifically via mobile access to the internet on individual devices, so have the attempts to implement it in innovative ways to maximize benefits for the learner and to improve the quality of instruction. Universities are increasingly offering online and blended Spanish courses at all levels for a variety of reasons, including limitations in physical classroom space, the demands of an increasingly mobile student body whose members want classes that fit into their schedule, and the scheduling difficulties that arise as more and more students enroll in university courses. Somewhat ironically, the advances in computer technology have essentially distanced students and teachers spatially by taking them out of the classroom to instruct and learn from wherever they choose. The addition of online and blended course options to the Spanish curriculum is an area that has received widespread attention and that has seen intense research in recent years, given the ubiquity of electronic devices with internet access and the tremendous convenience it affords students and instructors. However, convenience does not automatically translate into effectiveness, particularly with such a complex and interpersonal undertaking as second-language teaching and learning. Too often, advances in technology have been passed on to instructors without an understanding of the underlying theoretical framework or without training necessary to make effective use of them. Researchers and instructors in a variety of fields have been exploring how to deliver content, enhance the overall learning experience, and, more important, facilitate students' skill acquisition via online and blended course delivery. In truth, the field of foreign languages was one of the last to undertake research in this area, which commenced in earnest with Adair-Hauck, Willingham-Mclain, and Young (2000), whose study examined French programs at Carnegie Mellon University. Since that time, many studies have looked at best practices in the online and blended classroom and from a curricular perspective. Chapelle (2009, 750) warns that technology in and of itself offers no panacea to the learning of languages: "Based on their work with technology in other domains, most people would probably readily agree that technology alone is not the answer, but that a real solution will draw on technology in a manner that is informed by professional and scientific knowledge about SLA [second-language acquisition]."

The development of online and blended Spanish courses must be designed in light of second-language acquisition theory, as well as the curricular and instructional objectives of individual programs. Moreover, as we discuss below, the impact of students' motivation for enrolling in online and blended courses, as well as the effect on vertical program articulation, must also be carefully considered.

**Transactional Distance**

One of the foundational theories in the field of online and blended instruction is the concept of transactional distance (Moore 1997, 22). Transactional distance describes "the universe of teacher–learner relationships that exist when learners and instructors are separated by space and/or by time." Although the concept of transactional distance is not limited to online and blended courses, it is an important concept in understanding how to develop effective curricula for virtual modes of delivery. According to Moore (1991, 5), "Physical separation leads to psychological and communication gap, a space of potential misunderstanding between the inputs of instructor and those of the learner. It is a continuous rather than a discrete variable, a relative rather than an absolute term. In any educational program, there is some transactional distance, even where learners and teachers meet face to face. Special organizations and teaching procedures are essential."

As Moore notes, the major challenge of the online and blended environment can be broken down into two main areas, which in turn have an impact on the transactional distance between learners and instructors. The first area referred to by Moore (1997, 24) is that of interactional dialogue, which occurs between the instructor and students, either in a face-to-face setting or mediated through technology. Although the terms interaction and dialogue can often be used synonymously, Moore makes a key distinction between these terms: "The term 'dialogue' is used to describe an interaction or series of interactions having positive qualities that other interactions might not have. A dialogue is purposeful, constructive, and valued by each party. Each party in a dialogue is a respectful and active listener; each is a contributor, and builds on the contributions of the other party or parties."

This is different from interactions, which from Moore's point of view can be both positive and negative. He reserves the use of dialogue for only the constructive and "synergistic nature" of the interactions between instructors and students. An increase in these positive dialogues between instructors and students in online and blended courses helps to mitigate the transactional distance, creating a more positive experience and increasing the likelihood of students not only remaining in the course but also increasing their involvement and commitment to learning. The role of the instructor is to facilitate the dialogue between students and provide them with ample opportunities to have positive interactions and to create opportunities where this positive dialogue can take place between the instructor and the students within the flexible framework that the online/digital classroom affords.

The second area relates to the degree of structure of online and blended programs. Highly structured programs, whether they are face-to-face courses or online and blended courses, tend to increase the transactional distance between participants, given that such programs do not permit for modifications based on the dialogue between instructors and students. Highly structured courses are quite common in many university Spanish programs, given that lower-level courses are often taught by adjuncts or graduate students. Program directors create a more highly structured curriculum to maintain uniformity across courses. If a program is so highly structured that it dictates a prescribed use of every minute of time involved in an online and blended classroom, then this rigidity increases the transactional distance as well. Moore (1997, 23) describes these highly structured programs, declaring that "there is no dialogue and therefore no possibility of reorganizing the programme to take into account inputs from learners." It is understood that transactional distance is part of every classroom, and the fact that a class is described as face-to-face does not preclude it from being part of this reality. This is particularly the case in many large auditorium-style lecture classes, where there is minimal interaction between students and instructors and the instructor is simply there to present content and possibly answer a few questions. An attempt is made to mitigate this effect after the large group meeting, by having the students meet with teaching assistants in smaller groups, where the learners are then expected to interact with their fellow students and the teaching assistant. This type of setting is sometimes found in upper-level Spanish courses and graduate-level courses.

Face-to-face Spanish classes have the potential for less transactional distance, given their smaller size and relatively greater amount of dialogue between all parties involved; but this can create this distance if the instructor simply stands in front of the class and addresses the students, without the students expecting or needing to interact with the instructor. Understanding the role of transactional distance is important in the design of online and blended Spanish courses. The challenge in these courses is to recreate the dialogic learning environment typical of a face-to-face class and thus limit the transactional distance. Both students and instructors need to feel part of a community and feel that they can and do interact with other members of that community. Creating this sense of community in the online and blended Spanish course through technology is one of the principal goals of these courses.

### Interaction in the Online and Blended Course

In the online and blended classroom, instructors need to be aware of the diverse types of interactions that form part of this learning environment. The three possible types of interaction in most teaching settings, including on-line and blended courses, are (1) interactions between the learners and the content; (2) interactions between learners; and (3) interactions between the learners and the instructors (Moore 1989, 2). The first type of interaction occurs between the learners and the content, and refers to the expectations of students concerning their role in interacting with the content that is presented to them through the electronic medium and in the face-to-face portion of a blended course. Moore defines interaction with the content as "the process of intellectually interacting with the content that results in changes in the learner's understanding, the learner's perspective, or the cognitive structures of the learner's mind." How is the content presented? What does the learner need to do to respond to the content? Is there any type of interaction with the content, or is the online platform merely a delivery method for the content? As mentioned above, if the electronic medium is simply a delivery method for the content, then the transactional distance is greatest and very little interaction will take place with the content. Students will not access the learning materials and interact with them unless they see the importance of these as they relate to grades and knowledge, or need to do so in support of student–teacher or student–student interactions.

The second type of interaction in the online and blended classroom is between the learners themselves. These are interactions facilitated by the instructor to create a greater sense of community and lessen the transactional distance. How do learners engage with one another? How are these interactions evaluated? What degree of collaboration should be expected by learners in online and blended classes? What is the most effective way to bring learners together? How can learners become part of an online and blended classroom? In research carried out looking at studies into collaborative writing assignments through the use of wikis, blogs, and the like, scholars have found that learners who participated in these assignments felt a greater sense of pride in their accomplishments, were motivated by the fact that they were addressing a real audience, and were able to look at their writing in a way that working alone did not provide (Lee 2009; Oskoz 2010; Oskoz and Elola 2014). Wichadee (2014) studied students in a blended course and found that they claimed that group projects and assignments were much more difficult to schedule and complete when students were not consistently meeting on campus, and this was due in large part to the design of the courses. The teachers needed to develop assignments that encouraged and facilitated student interaction. In the face-to-face Spanish classroom, many students are used to completing group or pair projects, and this can benefit them as they interact together and use their language skills to produce a final product. Often, in the online and blended course, students assume that the course will be a completely autonomous and independent learning experience; but as previous studies have shown (Rovai and Jordan 2004), interaction between students fosters language learning and a sense that they are part of a community of learning.

Finally, the third type of interaction is between learners and the instructor. If learners are expected to participate and are to feel connected to a class, they need to interact with the instructor rather than simply perceive him or her as an electronic wizard behind a digital curtain. Interaction between the instructor and the students does not always need to be synchronous in nature, but it does need to occur regularly. This interaction will also help the instructors to communicate via chats, messages, and video conferences, or in face-to-face conversations with the students in Spanish and to assess how they might need to adjust the course to improve the students' skills in the classroom.

These three types of interactions not only characterize the online and blended classroom but also make up the structure of any classroom setting. When designing online and blended courses, language instructors need to determine the types of interactions that will take place and how these interactions will help them to meet the course objectives and the program's goals. Because the development of online and blended courses begins with the establishment of course objectives and alignment with program goals, the initial stages in course design should facilitate the format of the interactions expected from both learners and instructors. Although the overarching principles are the same in considering the types of interaction in a classroom, the delivery and structure of online and blended courses compared with face-to-face courses may, in fact, result in differential learning outcomes. Using the online and blended classroom to teach Spanish to students can function as a form of differentiated instruction, in which certain students may thrive more than in the face-to-face setting. If different types of interaction are created, students in the online and blended course can use their language abilities, and thus they may become more confident as they acquire the language or discuss advanced language and culture.

## Community of Inquiry

In addition to the concept of transactional distance and the various types of learner interactions, Garrison and Archer (2003) developed a model for online course design titled Community of Inquiry, which is based on some of the same principles mentioned above. In their model, Garrison and Archer divide the online environment according to the type of engagement and processes. Although these concepts are similar to the types of interactions mentioned above, they present unique features as well. They divide their model into social presence, cognitive presence, and teaching presence, using a Venn diagram that can be seen in figure 9.1.

Social presence can be defined as "the ability to project one's self and establish personal and purposeful relationships" (Garrison 2007, 63). Garrison asserts that three main aspects make up the concept of social presence: "effective communication, open communication, and group cohesion." Early research into online and blended courses focused on this notion of social presence, which is essential to the implementation of effective programs and classes. Social presence is important in establishing a sense of community and purpose, but Garrison argues that the social and cognitive aspects must interface so that collaboration takes place. This is further supported by sociocultural theory, which declares that learning takes place through interaction and mediation (Lantolf 2000; Lantolf and Thorne 2006). One of the concerns of the online and blended Spanish class is that the students will not engage in the requisite social interaction that has been shown as necessary for successful language acquisition. As learners purposively collaborate to complete meaningful assignments, they will be able to learn more than if carrying out the tasks by themselves. The notion of social presence is reflected in activities that not only necessitate collaboration but also benefit the students through their collaboration. If information is only being gathered through electronic means and the collaboration is artificially created in hopes of forcing interaction, then students will quickly perceive this as an unproductive use of their time and resources and will find more efficient means to complete the task.

The second area is that of cognitive presence, defined as "the exploration, construction, resolution and confirmation of understanding through collaboration and reflection in a community of inquiry" (Garrison 2007, 65). Garrison states that cognitive presence is directly related to the progressive development of inquiry within an electronic environment. He refers to this as practical inquiry and defines it as a situation where "participants move deliberately from understanding the problem or issue through to exploration, integration and application." This would be beneficial for Spanish language learners, given that collaboration and interaction are key components of the acquisition process. If learners can work together to negotiate meaning in the online and blended course, then this collaboration will reflect the type of interaction that is hoped for in authentic communicative settings. Meyer (2003) observed that the greatest challenge for students is moving them from the stage of inquiry to problem solving or resolution. Students can be quite

**Figure 9.1    Community of Inquiry Model**

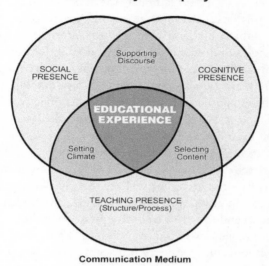

Community of Inquiry

*Source:* Reprinted with the permission of Elsevier from "Critical Inquiry in a Text-Based Environment: Computer Conferencing in Higher Education," by D. Randy Garrison, Terry Anderson, and Walter Archer, *The Internet and Higher Education* 2, nos. 2–3 (2000): 87–105.

successful in the inquiry state in online and blended courses, but Meyer states that to move students past this, the instructor needs to develop tasks suitable to this domain as well as provide guiding questions that lead online learners to practical applications of the material being covered. Additionally, as with social presence, meaningful collaboration needs to be present when completing tasks; otherwise, students will not work together to draw conclusions and promote learning. This can be accomplished by creating a digital information gap, where each individual possesses necessary information to facilitate the completion of the task. To complete an assignment, learners may be required to collaborate electronically through peer reviews, comments and reactions to posts by other peers, and interviews between peers.

Another concern for the online and blended classroom is the variation in the type of instructor comments given to students (Vaughan 2004). Teachers were found to give fewer design and facilitation comments in online and blended courses, but the number of direct instruction comments increased. Whereas direct instruction comments are designed to change students' behaviors and lead them toward a specific goal, design and facilitation comments are mainly supportive dialogue meant to encourage student interaction with minimal shaping of a discussion. Garrison (2007, 66) states, "It is very important to facilitate and yet not dominate the discourse and, at the same time, be prepared to provide crucial input to ensure that the community moves to resolution. As a subject matter expert, relevant information should be interjected and diagnoses of misconceptions are crucial to productive discourse."

This problem can be avoided by providing groups with clear goals as to what they need to do. Garrison also notes that cognitive development and group dynamics can be enhanced by increasing students' metacognitive awareness of the stages of inquiry as well as of how each individual contributes to group goals. Too often in online and blended courses, the resultant group work is simply a series of monologues submitted independently with no cognitive collaboration present. Pawan and others (2003) recommend that students self-code their collaborative comments to raise their metacognitive awareness regarding their role in group work, which will help the students see how they fit into their group and to have a cognitive presence in the classroom.

Finally, no language classroom, regardless of the method of delivery, can function well without considering the impact of the instructor's teaching presence. The physical presence in the face-to-face classroom cannot be replicated in the online and blended classroom, but this does not mean that teaching presence is not an important aspect. Research has shown that the teaching presence of the instructor can influence not only student learning but also student satisfaction with the course and the overall sense of community that students feel (Shea, Pickett, and Pelz 2004; Wu and Hiltz 2004). Garrison (2007) divides teaching presence in the online and blended course into three main areas: design, facilitation, and direct instruction. Regarding these three areas, students need to have explicit guidance in their interactions to avoid merely the exchange of "serial monologues" (Pawan et al. 2003). Meyer (2003, 63–64) declares that "faculty may need to be more directive in their assignments for threaded discussions, charging the participants to resolve a particular problem, and pressing the group to integrate their ideas."

The design of online and blended courses requires the teaching of strategies and techniques that will facilitate a higher level of thinking and interaction among participants in a class. Gilbert and Dabbagh (2005, 14) found that "the number and type of facilitator postings also increased the level of interaction between students." This shows that as students perceive more engagement from the instructor, they will also respond in kind. This relates to the concept of transactional distance, where students feel less of a distance because of the participation of their instructor, thus creating a community of inquiry with which students not only engage but of which they also feel part. Instructors are then able to facilitate the learning process and help students to such an extent that the line between direct instruction and facilitation may even be blurred and students and instructors may engage in meaningful interactions at all times in the online and blended classroom.

## TELECOLLABORATION

One of the ways to connect Spanish language learners in the online and blended classroom as well as the face-to-face classroom is through online conversation partners. Research into telecollaboration has experienced an increase in growth in recent years and is related to the pedagogical tool of connecting language learners from different countries so that they are able to use their language skills to teach each other (Youngs, Ducate, and Arnold 2011). This is called by many different names—such as telecollaboration, tandem learning, and online intercultural exchanges. Helm (2015, 197) describes this type of exchange as "the practice of engaging classes of geographically dispersed learners in online intercultural exchanges using internet communication tools for the development of language and/or intercultural competence." The rationale behind telecollaboration is based on fundamental principles of second-language acquisition. Sauro (2011, 380) argues that "interactional adjustments are seen as tools for facilitating comprehension and for triggering cognitive processes (e.g., noticing the gap and uptake) deemed essential for L2 development." Researchers in second-language acquisition have long proposed that languages are learned through social interaction, requiring both input and output, which form part of the process of negotiating meaning between learners (Long 1991; Firth and Wagner 2007; Pica, Kanagy, and Falodun 1993; Swain and Lapkin 1995).

Instructors have been using technology to connect students for years, and research on connecting language learners remotely is vast and diverse. Early projects that connected language learners before the internet and mobile devices involved sending letters to pen pals. This type of asynchronous exchange evolved with the appearance of the internet and email into what became known as key pals. With key pals, language learners communicated with one another through email exchanges that arrived instantly but were asynchronous because the receiver of the message had an extended period of time in which to compose a response. With the increased availability of the high-speed internet, the necessity to communicate via asynchronous means has grown into a vast series of programs and services that connect language learners from different countries through synchronous audio and video connections. In these conversations, learners are not only able to talk with members of the target language and culture but are also able to connect visual clues from their interlocutor that are germane to face-to-face exchanges.

Telecollaboration brings students who are motivated to learn a second language together with other learners with similar desires. The benefit of these online conversations goes beyond mere language practice and embodies all the major requirements needed to acquire a language. The benefit for learners of Spanish is threefold. First, there are a large number of Spanish speakers all over the world in a variety of countries with varied cultural backgrounds. Second, many Spanish speakers are interested in learning English as a foreign language and thus are very willing to exchange time speaking Spanish for help with their English. Finally, there are corresponding times zones across Latin America that directly align with those in the continental United States. These facts make connecting Spanish language learners to native speakers relatively easy. Chun (2015) claims that telecollaboration not only improves language proficiency but also cultural knowledge and intercultural awareness. Helm (2015, 198) attributes a host of learning benefits to telecollaboration: "increased motivation and linguistic output, gains in language development, accuracy and fluency, intercultural communicative competence, pragmatic competence, learner autonomy, online literacies, and multimodal communicative competence."

The acquisition of cultural knowledge stands out as a particularly valuable product of these exchanges especially because it is one of the areas where language teachers often struggle in their teaching (Lange 2003). In these conversational exchanges, learners engage in meaningful interactions, in which they must make their output understood by a sympathetic nonnative speaker of the target language as well as receive input that requires extensive interaction. Although the interlocutors tend not to be monolingual speakers of just one language, they are generally considered native speakers of one of the languages being used to communicate and learners of one of the languages of which their partner is a native speaker.

The benefits of telecollaboration require successful curricular development and implementation in order to succeed. Blake (2013, 17) states that "teletandem" learning can have "an enormous contribution to make to the L2 curriculum if teachers will become familiar enough with the technology to be able to incorporate it into the students' out-of-class assignments." In a study carried out by Ceo-DiFrancesco, Mora, and Serna Collazos (2016) with learners of Spanish, the authors found that by connecting the online conversations to the curriculum of the language program, learners not only increased in their overall oral and aural proficiency but also in their intercultural competence. They found this because the telecollaboration was such a vital part of their curriculum that it not only connected students outside the classroom with the native speakers but also brought many insights into the face-to-face meetings that were relevant and informed classroom activities. Helm (2015, 197) further found that "telecollaboration offers opportunities for universities to support their internationalization strategies by 'globalizing their curriculum' and engaging learners in dialogue with peers in distant parts of the world." She goes on to explain that even though this offers the potential for many universities to improve their language curriculum, telecollaboration has failed to become mainstream even though more expensive programs such as study abroad are firmly embedded in almost every university campus. Because one of the concerns of the online and blended classroom is a lack of group and pair work, telecollaboration can serve to help mitigate this gap along with other pair and group assignments that instructors develop in their curriculum. The benefit of telecollaboration is that it allows instructors in the online and blended Spanish classroom to assign students topics and conversations that they can carry out with native speakers to develop their communicative and cultural competence.

## SPANISH POSTSECONDARY PROGRAM AND CURRICULUM SURVEY RESULTS

The survey included seven specific questions regarding how much of a concern online and blended teaching was for the participants in this study. The participants were also given an eighth category, where they could add information from another area that they perceived as a concern. Participants ranked each item on a scale of 1 (very much a concern) to 5 (not a concern at all). We also include the overall rank of the item's mean across all fifty-five survey items with regard to the level of perceived concern. These means and ranks were calculated from responses given by approximately seven hundred instructors of all academic backgrounds, ranks, ages, and from all institution types. The results of the survey show the areas where the instructors surveyed are most concerned and how these questions ranked in the overall survey. The percentage listed last under each question represents the number of participants who felt the item did not apply to their program:

- Impact of online and blended instruction on face-to-face, interpersonal language skills: 2.85 / 34th / 15 percent;
- Development of online and blended courses: 2.90 / 38th / 12 percent;
- Use of online and blended courses to fulfill foreign language requirements: 2.93 / 39th / 15 percent;
- Availability of technology to support online and blended instruction: 2.98 / 40th / 13 percent;
- Availability of training for instructors of online and blended courses: 2.99 / 41st / 12 percent;

- Vertical articulation of online and blended courses with traditional face-to-face courses: 3.08 / 46th / 17 percent; and
- Attrition of students before completion of online and blended courses: 3.21 / 49th / 18 percent.

The greatest concern for the instructors surveyed concerned the impact that online and blended courses would have on the skill development of students, especially with regard to their interpersonal skills in face-to-face interactions. The other areas received similar rankings by the participants in this study. Given that a 3 is a neutral score, the participants in this study did not find the area of online teaching to be of too much concern. It is interesting to note that the questions received similar ranks, ranging from thirty-fourth to forty-ninth out of fifty-five questions. Four of the areas were ranked in sequence from thirty-eighth to forty-first and pertained to the development of online courses, the use of online courses to fill requirements, the availability of adequate technology, and the incorporation of training for instructors. The area of least concern among the instructors who participated in this survey was the retention of students involved in these courses; but this is also the question with the highest share of participants who said it was not relevant to them (18 percent). Given that many of these courses have not mitigated the transactional distance between learners and instructors in the online and blended domain, the implementation of these types of courses, especially when poorly carried out, has led to high rates of attrition. Heyman (2010) states that one of the biggest concerns in online education stems from the high attrition rates in fully online programs compared with traditional classes. A study by Herbert (2006) found that the attrition rate for online courses was 10 to 20 percent higher than traditional face-to-face classrooms. Smith (2010) found that 40 to 80 percent of online students dropped out of these courses.

Although this survey provides valuable information on the concerns that instructors face, it is not known how relevant online courses are at the institutions surveyed, especially given that 12 to 18 percent of the respondents stated that questions were not applicable. Although there has been a dramatic increase in online and blended courses in some academic disciplines, others have been more reticent in developing such courses for their disciplines, including foreign language education. The number of courses offered by the various institutions represented by the participants is not known. Also, similar to other areas of Spanish teaching, it is likely that a limited number of faculty members are involved in the teaching of language courses in an online and blended setting. Of the nine categories in the survey, concern over online and blended issues was ranked eighth overall, just ahead of teacher training, as being the area of least concern. When participants' responses are analyzed by academic background and rank, we found that those instructors whose highest degree was in the area of literature and culture were less concerned about online and blended courses than were their colleagues in linguistics or applied linguistics. This could be the result, as with other areas, of not having personally offered many courses in this format. Tenured and tenure-track instructors were the least concerned group, with an average section score that placed it ninth, or last, of all sections included. However, for all other types of instructors, the online and blended section had a mean rating that placed it slightly higher, at seventh out of nine. This may be because many language programs have moved some of their lower-level courses to an online or blended format and these courses are typically taught by instructors, graduate students, adjuncts, and other nontenured line staff and less by tenured and tenure-track faculty.

## CURRICULAR CONSIDERATIONS FOR THE IMPLEMENTATION OF TECHNOLOGY

Johnson and others (2011, 3) provide reasons for considering the implementation of online and blended courses into the curriculum. Contemporary university students expect the flexibility that online and blended courses offer, as "digital natives" who are part of a mobile generation that wants to access their courses whenever they want and wherever they are. This is especially important for institutions that tend to have a large proportion of the student body who are nonresident commuters. For community colleges and universities as well, being able to send the courses to students allows for greater access and increases the numbers of students that an institution can accept, which in turn benefits the university's bottom line. If 20 percent of courses are offered in an online and blended format, then additional classes may be scheduled on campus, allowing students to take courses according to the format that best suits them. Additionally, the authors observe that "the world of work is increasingly collaborative, giving rise to reflection about the way student projects are structured." The online environment allows synchronous and asynchronous communication between students, which will better prepare them for the future and the varied employment opportunities that they will have. Though it is important to know how to collaborate in face-to-face settings, it is equally important to know how to work with individuals at a distance to design projects, prepare presentations, and plan and organize themselves successfully. The successful development of online and blended language courses allows for students to prepare to use their language skills in a variety of career settings. In the blended course, further research is needed to determine what the best use of class time is. Because many activities and learning take place outside class in the blended environment, face-to-face time should not be squandered in lectures and other activities that can more effectively be done using the online portion of the class. Many instructors try to maximize class time for group and pair activities and for conversations in which learners are then able to apply what they have been studying outside the classroom.

However, Rubio and Thoms (2013) raise concerns regarding the curricular concerns of implementing online and blended courses in language programs. First, time and resources need to be allocated so that the implementation and maintenance of these programs is successful. They claim that language program directors need time, training, and flexibility to be able to manage online and blended programs. Much of the initial investment into online and blended courses comes at the beginning of the program, when it is being established. Each program needs to consider the makeup of its students, the nature of program outcomes, and the availability of technological support, not to mention administrative support for curricular changes. Rubio and Thoms further assert that language program directors should receive a course release to experiment with new technology and also learn how the technologies work, research the types of online and blended programs that exist and how each one works, confirm the selection of a textbook that will work for the type of course they hope to design, and have time allotted to train new instructors on the course innovations being developed.

Second, course redesign and training for instructors is paramount for those considering online and blended learning in their Spanish program. As with the design of all language courses, the notions of input, output, interaction, and feedback are still very relevant and need to be considered. As discussed above, many of these fundamental areas in the field of second-language acquisition are closely related to the notion of transactional distance and the types of interactions that learners have in the second-language classroom with the instructor, fellow students, and the content. Simply providing learners with an online delivery system without having key principles of second-language acquisition solidly in place will provide students, at best, with a substandard education and, at worst, cause them frustration and lead to the abandonment of study.

Garrett (1991, 74) warned early on when technology was still quite limited that "technology that can be taken for granted is already light years ahead of the profession's ability to integrate a principled use of it into the classroom and the curriculum." Though this warning is more than twenty-five years old, it resonates even more now, as technology continues to advance in ways beyond the comprehension of both language educators and the population at large. Those who spearhead the training of instructors need to consider the profiles of the individuals who typically teach many of the lower-level university courses, namely, adjuncts, graduate students, and other full- and part-time instructors. The majority of these instructors, and tenure-line in-structors as well, are of course reluctant to take on additional assignments and responsibilities for little or no compensation. The wide range of backgrounds that these instructors represent must be taken into consideration with regard to their teaching experience, educational background, and familiarity with the technologies that make up online and blended courses.

At Brigham Young University, many part-time employees have been teach-ing for twenty or more years and form part of a generation of faculty who not only did not use modern technology in their early teaching but also were not taught as students with current technologies. These instructors face the same challenges that many others face in dealing with students who have not known a world where the internet did not exist. The current generation of stu-dents is often referred to as "digital natives," while their instructors are "non-natives," or perhaps "second-language learners" with respect to technology. As more online and blended courses are developed and as technologies change, instructors need training to incorporate technology into their teaching and stay abreast of ongoing developments in educational technology. If instruc-tors have only taught in a face-to-face setting, they will surely need help con-verting materials, lessons, and instruction formats to the online and blended model. In addition, they require assistance in setting course objectives and goals that promote student interaction and development in their classes.

The third consideration that needs to be addressed relates to the quality-versus-cost debate. Institutions need to consider the best design to meet the needs of their particular students. Though it has been established that online and blended courses result in monetary savings, this fact alone should not be reason enough to increase the numbers of these courses. The quality of in-struction should be the driving force behind the development of new online and blended courses, not the amount of savings. Can the instruction given in these courses truly enhance students' acquisition of the language? Rubio and Thoms (2013, 4–5) state that online and blended courses "should be consid-ered as an opportunity to facilitate the integration of content and language from the introductory levels of instruction, address the needs and draw on the strengths of a variety of learners, foster the formation of communities of learners, improve linguistic outcomes, and adopt pedagogies that are well grounded in SLA [second-language acquisition] theories."

The final consideration mentioned by Rubio and Thoms (2013, 5) is the importance of developing assessment instruments that reflect the medium of course delivery and course objectives. Too often, online and blended courses use the same exams and learning benchmarks as face-to-face courses. Assess-ments need to reflect not only what is taught but also how it is taught. These assessments need to take into account the technology being employed; the presence of different learning styles among students; and the need to measure student engagement, retention, and satisfaction. These assessments need to "address how new modes of delivery meet the needs of a changing student population, in terms of both facilitating their linguistic gains and addressing their social and cognitive needs."

Aside from many of the learning opportunities provided by online and blended courses, there are many practical reasons to create these courses. As mentioned, it has been found that these courses can save institutions money, which is increasingly important given the nature of state budgets and ongoing economic challenges. These courses also make it possible to offer courses to a more diverse population of students, who for a variety of reasons are unable to attend other university classes during typical times when these courses are offered. An experience that one of the authors had as a professor in Florida helps to illustrate measures that some departments are forced to take as a result of contracting budgets. The Modern Language Department decided to move all 4-credit language classes meeting four times a week to only meeting three times a week via the creation of blended and fully online classes. The main reason provided by the administration for this change was not the documented success of online and blended courses in achieving learning outcomes, but rather as a way to resolve the difficulty of scheduling classes that met four days a week and dealing with growing numbers of students and limited seats. In order to assist the registrar's office, blended and online classes were developed to alleviate this problem. Thus, often practical and logistical considerations necessitate the creation of online and blended courses rather than compelling empirical evidence as to their effectiveness; yet even in these cases, instructors and programs who are well informed can create well-designed courses that maximize the benefits these courses offer students. However, poorly designed courses with objectives that do not take into account different learning domains often end up simply removing a face-to-face class meeting and replacing it with menial online tasks that do not engage the students. Care needs to be taken so that this is not the result of moving all or some of a course's content to the online and blended environment. Online and blended Spanish courses are ones that have been designed using the key principles mentioned above. As Rubio and Thoms (2013, 4–5) declare, "the decision to 'go blended' should be considered as an opportunity to facilitate the integration of content and language from the introductory levels of instruction, address the needs and draw on the strengths of a variety of learners, foster the formation of communities of learners, improve linguistic outcomes, and adopt pedagogies that are well grounded in SLA theories."

One of the other areas of consideration for the implementation of online and blended courses is how these courses will be articulated within the framework of face-to-face courses. Most institutions offer a variety of modes of delivery—from fully online to blended to traditional face-to-face. Institutions need to consider how students will transition between these different modes of delivery. What challenges will they face? What will students bring to each of these types of classrooms? How can instructors and institutions best prepare students for being successful as they progress in the curriculum? Because university courses typically award credit-hours that are based on seat time and contact hours, the online and blended course needs to reenvision what this means and how it will be represented in the digital environment. Students who come from online and blended courses should be equal to their face-to-face counterparts; otherwise, they will struggle as they move between classes and formats and will end up unfairly disadvantaged.

Another important consideration vis-à-vis online and blended courses involves the selection of materials. Because the publishing industry is monetarily driven, many Spanish language textbooks currently contain information and activities that have been designed with the online and blended course in mind but are not specifically designed solely for these courses. The Spanish language textbook publishing industry has yet to figure out a balance between the traditional face-to-face course and the online and blended course, which has led publishers to capture an area right in the middle of these two types of teaching with differing degrees of success. As more online and blended courses are created, it is crucial that sound pedagogical design based on current second-language acquisition theories inform the design of textbooks and materials destined for these courses. In the meantime, many programs are finding ways to provide materials for these courses through a combination of open source and open access materials.

Blyth (2012) argues for the use of open educational resources (OER) for online and blended courses and offers three recommendations for those who intend to use OER. First, he recommends that educators learn how to locate OER using a variety of websites, including creativecommons.org and nflrc .msu.edu/lrcs.php. He asserts that using trusted websites that have peer-reviewed resources will increase the quality of the materials. Second, he encourages instructors to join organizations that peer review materials and create a collection of materials that can be shared with others. Finally, he encourages instructors to become language learners again and study a language using OER to remember how it feels to be a beginner and to identify the types of materials that are best in learning a language. Materials developed for online and blended courses need to specifically address the structure of these courses, either through traditional publishing routes or through open access.

Winke, Goertler, and Amuzie (2010) suggest that instructors who are considering implementing online and blended courses should first take a course themselves on an online and blended platform to see how it works and to reflect on the pros and cons of this type of learning. Taking a course would also allow instructors to see where they need to improve their knowledge of the technologies that are used in the online and blended course. Second, they should use a teach–review–revise approach, both during initial development and after the course is in place to always allow themselves to be improving and modifying their courses to better fit their students' and the course's objectives. The notion that an instructor need not make any further modifications once an online and blended course is created is a myth and greatly disadvantages students. Third, in the blended class, instructors should allow for students to provide feedback on the online component of the course and do the same with the fully online class as well. How do students feel that about the activities? Do they feel that their time outside the classroom is valuable? What do they believe could be done to better integrate the face-to-face and online components of the classroom? Involving students and valuing their input allows them to take a certain degree of ownership of the course and feel more like contributors to their own educational experience. Finally, even though students are "digital natives," they possess a wide range of digital skills and could benefit from basic instruction, including a lesson on the value and benefits of online and blended courses.

## CONCLUSION

High-quality teaching is not limited to one specific mode of delivery, whether it be online, blended, or face-to-face. Many educators criticize the use of technology in online and blended language courses. In most cases, it is not the technology that is problematic, but rather the implementation of the technology, especially when it is not rooted in sound pedagogy and second-language acquisition theory and does not consider the complex and multifaceted nature of language learning and curriculum design. Much like the questionable conclusions of empirical research based on suspect data, the adage "garbage in, garbage out" seems to apply to the online and blended classroom.

Of the studies that have been carried out comparing online, blended, and face-to-face courses, the results have favored the blended course. In a study of three different graduate education courses, Rovai and Jordan (2004) found that the blended course produces a higher "mean connectedness score" than traditional or online courses and a higher "adjusted mean learning score" than the online course. In deciding whether or not to develop these courses, curriculum designers need to consider the objectives and goals of their programs and determine how the implementation of online and blended courses will affect these goals.

Successful implementation of online and blended courses can be achieved and meet institutional goals and objectives with careful design and planning. Difficulties arise when the driving force behind the implementation of online and blended courses is the saving of money or classroom space. Although this motivation to develop online and blended is not in and of itself problematic, it tends to be symptomatic of an institution that is not willing to invest significant resources for their proper development, and for effective learning and teaching more generally. Development of online and blended courses may fall on the overworked shoulders of a language program director or even an adjunct or part-time instructor. Subsequently, these courses may then be assigned to untrained instructors who do what they can with a poorly designed curriculum and insufficient training on how to manage the online and blended classroom. Not surprisingly, this has an adverse impact on students and can cause problems as these students continue their studies in face-to-face classes. However, this problem is not unique to the online and blended classroom, in that students who come from poorly designed and badly taught courses, regardless of the format, have a disadvantage in subsequent courses. Elola and Oskoz (2014, 224) sum this, up declaring that "language professionals therefore need to have a sound and current theoretical background to decide how a particular tool might assist their students' linguistic development." Future research needs to examine audioconferencing and videoconferencing, especially in Spanish (Blake 2013). Although some studies are being carried out, there is still a paucity of research in this area, not only comparing face-to-face classes with online and blended classes but also research looking into how best to increase the fluency of students in all areas of language acquisition, especially with the blended classroom.

## REFLECTION QUESTIONS

1. How do the online and blended language courses offered at your institution mitigate transactional distance? If no language courses are offered, how do other online and blended classes address transactional distance?

2. This chapter mentions the need for instructors to interact with their students in the online and blended classroom. How often do you think these interactions should occur? What is the most effective way to engage learners with their instructors through computer-mediated communication? What is the best way to hold virtual office hours? What do Spanish students in an online and blended class expect the instructor's availability to be?

3. In an era when second-language study and the humanities are under fire, how do we ensure that putting courses online does not diminish their stature and prestige in the academy? Do we undermine the value of language study by offering online and blended courses? How does it affect the perception of Spanish, which already

struggles to stave off racism, stereotypes, and social marginalization among the lay public?

4. Telecollaboration seems to be an excellent way to connect language learners. What challenges to telecollaboration might surface in the Spanish classroom? How might telecollaboration contribute to the foreignizing of the Spanish curriculum, meaning that some students may feel that Spanish speakers are only available from far away places via the internet?

5. Many institutions like the idea of online and blended courses because they feel they are able to increase enrollment, given that the space used is virtual. Do enrollment caps matter as much in an online and blended language course? Should they be the same as face-to-face courses? Explain.

6. Although many language courses are given in an online and blended format, which courses do you feel are the best fit for this model? Explain.

7. Many language programs are now offering online and blended classes, whereas some other subjects are more resistant to offering their classes virtually. Why do you think some programs and areas of study are slow to do so?

8. How could you incorporate telecollaboration into the classroom? How would you grade it? What criteria would you use to determine the success or failure of telecollaboration?

9. If you have taken an online and blended Spanish course or other such course, how much interaction did you have with the instructor and the other students in the class? How could the structure of the course have been changed to increase the interaction between participants? Would you have wanted a greater connection to the instructor and the students? Why or why not?

10. Given that online courses have a higher dropout rate, how could this affect the number of students who might declare a major or minor in Spanish? What can be done to encourage students in online courses to pursue their studies beyond the language requirement or the basic levels of Spanish?

## PEDAGOGICAL ACTIVITIES

1. After the discussion in the chapter about training instructors for delivering online courses, find out what training is offered at your university to prepare teachers for these courses. Are online training courses offered? Are training materials available to help instructors develop new courses? Who provides assistance with the technology needed in online courses? Write a summary of your findings.

2. Collaboration is an important part in learning a language. Pick a lesson that you have used for a face-to-face class, or one that you have seen used, and change it to one that could be used in the online and blended classroom. Describe how the students would collaborate. Discuss how you would ensure collaboration among students, as well as how you would assess the effectiveness of the collaboration and the activity.

3. One of the major concerns of offering Spanish courses in an online and blended format is the lack of speaking practice and interaction among the students. Do an internet search to find four online services that help to connect language learners.

Create a table that provides the following information about each of the four services: name of service, cost per conversation, length of conversation, and types of learners using the service.

4. Interview the basic language director for your Spanish program regarding the online and blended courses that are offered:

a. What are the goals in offering these courses? Why not offer them face-to-face?

b. When were the first online or blended Spanish courses offered?

c. How much growth in online and blended courses has occurred in recent years?

d. How have students responded to the implementation of online and blended courses?

If there are no online courses, then ask about the plans for the future with regard to online Spanish courses.

## REFERENCES

Adair-Hauck, Bonnie, Laurel Willingham-McLain, and Bonnie Earnest Youngs. 2000. "Evaluating the Integration of Technology and Second Language Learning." *CALICO Journal* 17, no. 2: 269–306.

Anderson, Terry, Liam Rourke, D. Randy Garrison, and Walter Archer. 2001. "Assessing Teaching Presence in a Computer Conferencing Context." *Journal of the Asynchronous Learning Network* 5, no. 2: 1–17.

Blake, Robert J. 2013. *Brave New Digital Classroom: Technology and Foreign Language Learning*. Washington, DC: Georgetown University Press.

Blyth, Carl. 2012. "Opening Up Foreign Language Education with Open Educational Resources: The Case of *Français interactif*." In *Hybrid Language Teaching and Learning: Exploring Theoretical, Pedagogical and Curricular Issues*, edited by Fernando Rubio and Joshua J. Thoms. Boston: Cengage.

Ceo-DiFrancesco, Diane, Oscar Mora, and Andrea Serna Collazos. 2016. "Developing Intercultural Communicative Competence across the Americas." In *New Directions in Telecollaborative Research and Practice: Selected Papers from the Second Conference on Telecollaboration in Higher Education*, edited by Sake Jager, Malgorzata Kurek, and Breffni O'Rourke. Dublin: Research-publishing.net.

Chapelle, Carol A. 2009. "The Relationship Between Second Language Acquisition Theory and Computer-Assisted Language Learning." *Modern Language Journal* 93, no. 21: 741–53.

Chun, Dorothy M. 2015. "Language and Culture Learning in Higher Education via Telecollaboration." *Pedagogies: An International Journal* 10, no. 1: 5–21.

Clifford, Ray. 1987. "The Status of Computer-Assisted Language Instruction." *CALICO Journal* 4, no. 4: 9–16.

Elola, Idoia, and Ana Oskoz. 2014. "Toward Online and Hybrid Courses." In *The Routledge Handbook of Hispanic Applied Linguistics*, edited by Manel Lacorte. New York: Routledge.

Firth, Alan, and Johannes Wagner. 2007. "Second/Foreign Language Learning as a Social Accomplishment: Elaborations on a Reconceptualized SLA." *Modern Language Journal* 91, no. s1: 800–819.

Garrett, Nina. 1991. "Technology in the Service of Language Learning: Trends and Issues." *Modern Language Journal* 75, no. 1: 74–101.

Garrison, D. Randy, and Walter Archer. 2003. "A Community of Inquiry Framework for Online Learning." In *Handbook of Distance Education*, edited by Michael Grahame Moore and William G. Anderson. Mahwah, NJ: Lawrence Erlbaum Associates. http://ltc-ead.nutes.ufrj.br/constructore/objetos/Handbook_Of_Distance_Education.pdf.

Garrison, D. Randy, Terry Anderson, and Walter Archer. 2000. "Critical Inquiry in a Text-Based Environment: Computer Conferencing in Higher Education." *The Internet and Higher Education* 2, nos. 2–3: 87–105.

———. 2003. "A Theory of Critical Inquiry in Online Distance Education." In *Handbook of Distance Education*, edited by Michael Grahame Moore and William G. Anderson. Mahwah, NJ: Lawrence Erlbaum Associates. http://ltc-ead.nutes.ufrj.br/constructore/objetos/Handbook_Of_Distance_Education.pdf.

Gilbert, Patricia K., and Nada Dabbagh. 2005. "How to Structure Online Discussions for Meaningful Discourse: A Case Study." *British Journal of Educational Technology* 36, no. 1: 5–18.

Helm, Francesca. 2015. "The Practices and Challenges of Telecollaboration in Higher Education in Europe." *Language Learning & Technology* 19, no. 2: 197–217.

Herbert, Michael. 2006. "Staying the Course: A Study in Online Student Satisfaction and Retention." *Online Journal of Distance Learning Administration* 9, no. 4: 300–17.

Heyman, Errin. 2010. "Overcoming Student Retention Issues in Higher Education Online Programs: A Delphi Study." PhD diss., University of Phoenix.

Johnson, Larry, Rachel Smith, H. Willis, Alan Levine, and Keene Haywood. 2011. *The 2011 Horizon Report*. Austin: New Media Consortium.

Lange, Dale L. 2003. "Implications of Theory and Research for the Development of Principles for Teaching and Learning Culture." In *Culture as the Core: Perspectives on Culture in Second Language Learning*, edited by Dale Lange and R. Michael Paige. Charlotte: Information Age.

Lantolf, James P. 2000. *Sociocultural Theory and Second Language Learning*. New York: Oxford University Press.

Lantolf, James P., and Steven L. Thorne. 2006. *Sociocultural Theory and the Genesis of Second Language Development*. New York: Oxford University Press.

Lee, Lina. 2009. "Promoting Intercultural Exchanges with Blogs and Podcasting: A Study of Spanish–American Telecollaboration." *Computer Assisted Language Learning* 22, no. 5: 425–43.

Long, Michael H. 1991. "Focus on Form: A Design Feature in Language Teaching Methodology." *Foreign Language Research in Cross-Cultural Perspective* 2, no. 1: 39–52.

Meyer, Katrina A. 2003. "Face-to-Face versus Threaded Discussions: The Role of Time and Higher-Order Thinking." *Journal of Asynchronous Learning Networks* 7, no. 3: 55–65.

Moore, Michael G. 1989. "Editorial: Three Types of Interaction." *American Journal of Distance Education* 3, no. 2: 1–6.

———. 1991. "Editorial: Distance Education Theory." *American Journal of Distance Education* 5, no. 3: 1–6.

———. 1997. "Theory of Transactional Distance." In *Theoretical Principles of Distance Education*, edited by Desmond Keegan. New York: Routledge.

Oskoz, Ana, ed. 2010. "Mediating Discourse Online." *Modern Language Journal* 94, no. 2: 349–50.

Oskoz, Ana, and Idoia Elola. 2014. "Promoting Foreign Language Collaborative Writing through the Use of Web 2.0 Tools and Tasks." In *Technology-Mediated TBLT: Researching Technology and Tasks*, edited by Marta González-Lloret and Lourdes Ortega. Amsterdam: John Benjamins.

Pawan, Faridah, Trena M. Paulus, Senom Yalcin, and Ching-Fen Chang. 2003. "Online Learning: Patterns of Engagement and Interaction among In-Service Teachers." *Language Learning & Technology* 7, no. 3: 119–40.

Pica, Teresa, Ruth Kanagy, and Joseph Falodun. 1993. "Choosing and Using Communication Tasks for Second Language Instruction." In *Tasks and Language Learning: Integrating Theory and Practice*, edited by Graham Crookes and Susan Gass. Clevedon, UK: Multilingual Matters.

Rovai, Alfred P., and Hope Jordan. 2004. "Blended Learning and Sense of Community: A Comparative Analysis with Traditional and Fully Online Graduate Courses." *International Review of Research in Open and Distributed Learning* 5, no. 2: 1–13.

Rubio, Fernando, and J. Thoms. 2013. "Hybrid Language Teaching and Learning: Looking Forward." In *AAUSC 2012 Volume: Issues in Language Program Direction—Hybrid Language Teaching and Learning—Exploring Theoretical, Pedagogical, and Curricular Issues*, edited by Fernando Rubio and Joshua J. Thoms. Boston: Heinle & Heinle.

Sauro, Shannon. 2011. "SCMC for SLA: A Research Synthesis." *CALICO Journal* 28, no. 2: 369–91.

Shea, Peter J., A. M. Pickett, and William E. Pelz. 2004. "Enhancing Student Satisfaction through Faculty Development: The Importance of Teaching Presence." *Elements of Quality Online Education: Into the Mainstream* 5: 39–59.

Smith, Belinda G. 2010. "E-Learning Technologies: A Comparative Study of Adult Learners Enrolled on Blended and Online Campuses Engaging in a Virtual Classroom." PhD diss., Capella University.

Swain, Merrill, and Sharon Lapkin. 1995. "Problems in Output and the Cognitive Processes They Generate: A Step towards Second Language Learning." *Applied Linguistics* 16, no. 3: 371–91.

Vaughan, Norman D. 2004. "Investigating How a Blended Learning Approach Can Support an Inquiry Process within a Faculty Learning Community." PhD diss., University of Calgary.

Wichadee, Saovapa. 2014. "Factors Related to Students' Performance of Hybrid Learning in an English Language Course." *International Journal of Distance Education Technologies* 12, no. 1: 74–90.

Winke, Paula, Senta Goertler, and Grace L. Amuzie. 2010. "Commonly Taught and Less Commonly Taught Language Learners: Are They Equally Prepared for CALL and Online Language Learning?" *Computer Assisted Language Learning* 23, no. 3: 199–219.

Wu, Dezhi, and Starr Roxanne Hiltz. 2004. "Predicting Learning from Asynchronous Online Discussions." *Journal of Asynchronous Learning Networks* 8, no. 2: 139–52.

Youngs, Bonnie, Lara Ducate, and Nike Arnold. 2011. "Linking Second-Language Acquisition, CALL, and Language Pedagogy." In *Present and Future Promises of CALL: From Theory and Research to New Directions in Language Teaching*, edited by Nike Arnold and Lara Ducate. San Marcos, TX: Computer Assisted Language Instruction Consortium.

# 10

# CHARTING A COURSE FORWARD

> There are two important, related aspects to any major curriculum change—the change that occurs in the curriculum, and the change that needs to occur in the minds of the various people affected by the curriculum.
>
> —I. S. P. Nation and John Macalister,
> *Language Curriculum Design*, 2010

The fundamental premise of this book is that Spanish is no longer a foreign language in much of the United States, but rather a second language, and that this rather straightforward assertion carries with it extensive and complicated sociocultural, educational, curricular, and sociopolitical implications for postsecondary Spanish curricula. The argument that Nation and Macalister make in the epigraph above is that concrete changes made to the curriculum—such as adjustments to the pedagogical and assessment instruments incorporated in the classroom, the content covered by course syllabi, or the nature of placement and promotion procedures—may all be for naught if there is no change in the mind-set of those who are tasked with deploying the curriculum. If this is indeed the case, several questions arise, such as the following: Who is affected, or threatened, or appeased, by the changing nature of Spanish in the United States and the curricular adaptations that such changes necessitate in postsecondary programs, and why? Who benefits from maintaining the status quo in collegiate Spanish teaching, and who might feel repressed by it? The answers to these questions will, in part, be rooted in each stakeholder's understanding of such fundamental concepts as the nature of language, instructed second-language acquisition, "standard" language ideology, nation-state building, and language variation. The consequences of decisions based on these answers will also greatly affect the viability of Spanish as a staple in the future postsecondary academic landscape.

As we close our macro needs analysis of Spanish postsecondary curricula in the United States, we return to our national survey of Spanish language educators from various disciplinary backgrounds and academic ranks. The survey was not designed to delve into the particulars of individual program struggles, but rather to cast a broad net in identifying overarching areas of concern for participants, for whatever reason. In this chapter we first present the results from the two sections of the survey that still have not been analyzed, namely, the *other* section and the *national standards* section. Following this analysis, we synthesize the issues presented in the chapters, pointing out the relationships between them, the tensions they create, and how they can be dealt with constructively. We do this through the lens of Nation and Maclister's (2010) model of second-language curriculum design and Dubin and Olshtain's (1986) model for language program policy. Finally, we outline additional issues that can and should be addressed to set the course for the future of postsecondary Spanish language education and that would be the most beneficial for students, instructors, and the academy overall.

## SPANISH POSTSECONDARY PROGRAM AND CURRICULUM SURVEY RESULTS

A crucial step before recommending changes to Spanish tertiary curricula is to determine what changes practicing Spanish educators see as most pressing. In designing the survey, we had to selectively choose from a long list of topics that might have relevance for contemporary Spanish language educators regardless of context. The items we included were grouped by category, with an *other* category intended to capture those issues that did not fit into any particular category and that were unrelated to each other. In this section, we first present the results from the *other* section before exploring the respondents' uses of the options "not applicable to my program" and "unfamiliar with concept(s)." The results from the *standards* section are then treated in a subsequent section. Somewhat unexpectedly, the section that presented the greatest concern across all respondents, on average, was the one titled "other." Its six items had the lowest average mean across all sections of the survey and also included the two items of the fifty-five survey items that were of most concern for respondents.

In keeping with the pattern established in previous chapters, we present the six items from the *other* section in order, from those items of most to least concern, where a score of 1 indicates "very much a concern," and 5 is an item considered "not a concern at all." The item's mean value and rank among the fifty-five items appear after the item, as well as the percentage of respondents who indicated that the item was "not applicable to my program":

- Helping students value learning Spanish for reasons other than employment: 2.09 / 1st / <1 percent;
- Providing access to study abroad programs for all interested students: 2.19 / 2nd / 1.7 percent;

- Addressing the curricular needs of true beginners with no previous Spanish language instruction: 2.33 / 6th / 1.7 percent;
- Addressing the needs of students with different reasons for pursuing Spanish: 2.40 / 8th / 1.5 percent;
- Differentiating instruction for students at various proficiency levels in the same classroom: 2.43 /11th / 1.5 percent; and
- Addressing differential student learning outcomes from participation in study abroad programs: 2.59 / 21st / 4.1 percent.

We begin by looking closely at the item that was considered of most concern among all fifty-five when participants' responses were averaged, regardless of discipline or rank. When the responses were grouped by discipline—that is, literature and culture and linguistics and applied linguistics, and rank (i.e., tenured / tenure track and nontenure track)—this item maintained its spot as the item of most concern on the survey. Among the four cohorts mentioned above, those who identified literature and culture as their primary area of specialty expressed the most concern that contemporary students conceive of Spanish as simply a tool for improved employment prospects, which is not altogether surprising. Though the item is fairly short, its content and participants' responses are rather illuminating, and are illustrative of a recurrent theme throughout the book: that to some extent, Spanish has been disconnected from the literature, cultures, and realities of those who speak it and has become, for many students, primarily another arrow in their professional quiver. Another interesting finding is that participants' level of concern with items in this section seemed to maintain an inverse relationship with the percentage who found the items "not applicable" to their particular program. The item of most concern was marked as being not applicable by fewer than 1 percent of respondents, and none of the section's items were considered irrelevant by more than 4.1 percent of respondents. In other words, the issues in this section were of concern to many respondents, and relatively few found them not applicable to their programs.

The great irony, of course, with the concern that students consider Spanish primarily as a bridge to greater marketability is that one of the principal recruitment strategies used by many Spanish language educators to attract students to their courses and programs of study is to make this same argument: that improved Spanish language competence—presumably facilitated by completion of formal Spanish programs—will allow greater access to professional opportunities and economic markets. Foreign language administrators, professors, and college-level recruiters are encouraging students to declare a minor or second major in Spanish to help boost their employability, which may have repercussions for how students perceive of their Spanish studies and the sorts of courses they might prefer. For instance, at Brigham Young University (BYU), educators and administrators in the College of Humanities have mounted a well-orchestrated campaign to market an academic initiative titled "Humanities+" to students majoring in fields outside the humanities, such as business, education, and preprofessional programs. As expected, the goal is to convince nonhumanities students to enroll in humanities courses, with the focal point of the effort being continued and advanced language study. The Humanities+ website (http://humanities.byu.edu/about-the-col lege/humanitiesplus/) includes promotional videos and a blog with a long list of articles from popular news media outlets—such as the *Wall Street Journal, Forbes,* and the *New York Times*—that extol the virtues and marketability of a liberal arts education.

Another BYU initiative that was developed at the same time as BYU's Humanities+ was a language certificate that students can earn by taking three advanced (third-year) courses: the first, focused on Spanish grammar, reading, and writing; the second, a survey of Spanish language literature; and the third, a culture course with a focus on either Latin American or Iberian culture. Students' successful completion of these three courses results in a notation on their transcript stating that they completed the BYU language certificate program. The creation of this program has led to dramatic increases in enrollment in those courses that fulfill the requirements. Since the program's inception in 2010, more than 1,860 certificates have been awarded across fifteen languages, and the Spanish language has been awarded the most certificates. As of April 2017, 1,008 Spanish BYU language certificates have been awarded, which equals 54 percent of all BYU language certificates earned. The other 46 percent of BYU language certificates earned are shared across the other fourteen languages. Interestingly, it took four years for the first 1,000 language certificates to be earned, but since the 1,000th certificate was awarded, almost an additional 1,000 have been earned in just two years. This has been equal to an average expected growth of 10 percent a year in the number of language certificates earned. The advantage to this certificate program in part addresses the concerns raised in this survey. The goal of the certificate is to engage students in language study beyond first- and second-year courses. In addition, the certificate exposes them to language, literature, and culture in a way that they would not have been if they had stopped after beginning or intermediate Spanish. Finally, what has resulted from this program is that many students who start with the plan to only complete the certificate often decide they enjoy the classes they are in and continue on to minor or major in Spanish and thus are exposed to the language, literature, and culture in a much more profound way. A somewhat similar initiative in progress at the University of Kentucky attempts to make a similar case for language study, along with majors in science, technology, engineering, and mathematics. Efforts such as these are becoming increasingly common, and though Spanish has been somewhat immune to decreasing enrollments as compared with French and German, the apparent demotion of serious and singular study of second languages—and their cultures, literatures, and civilizations—has mobilized even the Spanish contingent of the humanities corps.

Though it would be hard to find a Spanish language educator who would not applaud a student's professional success as a result of his or her achieving Spanish proficiency and cultural sensitivity, as humanists and social scientists, most Spanish instructors bristle to think that enrollments in their courses and programs of study are mainly driven by vocational considerations or neatly packaged and deftly marketed language certificate programs. Yet the current sociocultural and sociopolitical climate in higher education has turned apathetic and even hostile toward language education, resulting in budgetary cuts for many foreign language programs at state-funded public institutions. Moreover, at the federal level, many politicians have threatened to defund agencies that have long provided crucial funding for academics conducting research or engaging in creative projects in the arts and humanities, such as the National Endowment for the Arts and the National Endowment for the Humanities. Such rhetoric has put many Spanish language educators on the defensive. Several qualitative responses from survey participants reflected this sentiment:[1]

- "Trying to keep our department alive despite major cuts to funding"—*and from the same participant:* "Attracting majors to the program, as incoming freshmen"; "Loss of tenured faculty, replaced (if replaced) by contract faculty."
- "Severe budget cuts"—*and from the same participant:* "Lack of support for humanities and languages."
- "Convincing evil dean of business and justice studies not to eliminate foreign language major"—*and from the same participant:* "Convincing colleagues to not eliminate foreign language requirement."
- "Ensuring sufficient enrollment in department courses"—*and from the same participant:* "Preventing tenure-stream literature faculty from having upper-level courses cancelled due to low enrollment."
- "Value of languages other than English among colleagues in other disciplines."
- "Advocating for foreign language study across the campus."

Of the comments cited above, at least two might shed light on the defensive stance that many Spanish language educators are taking in the current climate and the mechanism whereby many programs are being undercut. One respondent noted the use of contract faculty to replace lost tenure-track positions, if they are replaced at all: "Loss of tenured faculty, replaced (if replaced) by contract faculty." The second quotation that has explanatory power pertains to low enrollments in upper-level courses: "Preventing tenure-stream literature faculty from having upper-level courses cancelled due to low enrollment." What both quotations indicate is that the demand for tenured faculty is decreasing as the number of upper-level course enrollments decreases, and vice versa. The cumulative effect of this trend toward fewer tenure-line positions is the diminished intellectual and programmatic presence and prestige of Spanish in the curriculum of institutions of higher education. This results in the offering of fewer courses at advanced levels, making it more difficult for students to find ones that fit their schedules, which in turn further decreases enrollment. Thus, as fewer upper-level courses are offered and as tenured faculty retire, they are replaced by adjuncts or are not replaced at all. This deterioration may feed the mentality among administrators and powerful faculty in disparate disciplines that foreign language departments serve primarily a "service" function by focusing on lower-level courses and by facilitating completion of university- or college-imposed requirements for majors from other disciplines.

In some departments with graduate programs, a particularly insidious tendency may surface: to assume that the existence of a graduate program makes the entire program untouchable. One rather smug comment from a participant, offered only partially tongue in cheek, declared that "since we have a PhD, we don't need anyone else to tell us how to teach." Nonetheless, in most cases, the deterioration of the undergraduate program and the decrease in upper-level enrollments translates into more courses being taught by lecturers and tenure/tenure-track faculty and fewer courses available for graduate student instructors. This shift in staffing, in turn, negatively affects graduate student recruitment, because fewer teaching lines are available for incoming students. In the worst case scenario, fewer and fewer students apply to a graduate program with limited funding opportunities, and graduate course enrollments plummet, as does the number of defended dissertations. This often translates into a top-heavy department with tenured faculty teaching courses with a low number of students, resulting in astronomical instructional costs per student and claims by deans that the language departments are the most expensive to run. Such was the accusation made on several occasions to the Department of Hispanic Studies at the University of Kentucky, as upper-level undergraduate and graduate course enrollments fell to historic levels, all while the department argued tirelessly for the maintenance of enrollment caps of no more than twenty in fifth-semester courses and twenty-seven in the first four-semester sequence. In some cases, associate professors were finishing the semester in their 300- and 400-level courses with ten students, and their graduate courses with four or five students. Though the status and economics of undergraduate and graduate education are not the focus of this book, the success and survival of the two have become increasingly more interdependent and deserve much greater attention in the literature.

The second item of most concern in the survey was also found in the *other* group and related to the need to provide access to study abroad to all interested students. Among the four subgroups of instructors analyzed—that is, tenure-line versus non–tenure line, literature/culture versus linguistics / applied linguistics—only the linguists' ratings did not rank this item as the one of second-highest concern, though the item was ranked fifth-highest among the fifty-five items for the linguists. At first glance, these items appear to pertain to two different domains in language teaching; but in reality, they are quite closely connected. Apparently, the instructors participating in this survey are concerned that their students only see Spanish as a springboard, or tool, used to improve their employment prospects and not as a means to broaden their social, cultural, and intellectual horizons. Strictly instrumental or utilitarian motives for language learning may lead to significant learning gains by students, but are not ones that most language educators strive to cultivate in their students.

As students of language, literature, and culture, many instructors yearn for their students to connect with other cultures and peoples, and to do so in ways that help students properly situate their own culture among the many possibilities. The experience of living as a linguistic and cultural minority and realizing that one's own culture may actually be considered foreign and "weird" to large numbers of people can be transformative. Thus, it would seem that by adequately addressing the issue of second-highest concern in the survey, the first may also be addressed. The issue of study abroad is a particularly vexing one—because, on one hand, it offers dramatic potential for transformative educational experiences; but on the other hand, it is often undermined by intractable financial limitations at both the institutional and personal levels. Primarily for this reason, the topic has not been broached in this volume, but it is worthy of careful and serious consideration at the curricular and programmatic level by scholars in the field.

Though many additional analyses could be conducted on the survey results, the final analysis we include here are the percentage of respondents who indicated that a particular item was not "applicable" to their program or was an item with which they were "unfamiliar" in the case of the *standards* section. Not surprisingly, the section whose items had the largest mean percentage considered "not applicable" or "unfamiliar" was the *teacher training* section (18.6 percent). Understandably, for many programs without a preservice teacher preparation program, these items seemed irrelevant. Somewhat less expected was the finding that the *online / hybrid instruction* section had the next-highest mean percentage, with no item falling below 11 percent. The average share of "not applicable" responses to items in this section was 14.6 percent. Apparently, for many survey participants the integration of online and hybrid instruction still has not become a reality in their particular programs, rather than not a concern. The qualitative comments left by several respondents reflect the conflicted state of online and hybrid approaches to Spanish education. One respondent was very positive about online education and its future, noting that "we have wonderful support for online courses at the institutional level, both expertise and funding," while another expressed frustration that the Spanish Department and the Online Education Department were "two separate entities (i.e., the Spanish Department has essentially little say about online course offerings)." A third respondent bemoaned the imposition of online teaching, stating "administration imposed online venue for FL [foreign language] course." What seems to undergird all three comments is an apparent desire among central administration staff members that online courses gain traction in language curricula. Finally, one participant offered a simplistic, potentially sarcastic, perspective regarding online and hybrid education: "Assign students online gr[aduate] exercises and *no one* needs to attend class—free time for teachers too."

Several competing narratives appear to be at play concerning online and hybrid Spanish language courses in the academy, with each appropriating scholarship on the effectiveness of such models to further their arguments. For many faculty members with an extremely negative view, online language education is anathema to the enterprise of a humanistic approach to language learning and represents the eventual elimination of the professoriate and the place of language learning in higher education. Others are not nearly as fatalistic, and view online language learning via large courses without nearly as much resentment, but consider it simply a thinly masked attempt at increasing revenues by administrators. For other well-informed instructors steeped in second-language acquisition and pedagogy, online learning is the wave of the future and an inevitability that is crucial to the engagement of technology-savvy students and to the mere survival of language learning in the academy. Regardless of the narrative one adopts, it appears that online and hybrid models have yet to gain real traction among the programs represented by our survey participants.

## THE WORLD-READINESS STANDARDS

The World-Readiness Standards for Learning Languages—formerly the Standards for Foreign Language Learning: Preparing for the 21st Century—were the result of a collaborative project undertaken by an eleven-member task force representing a variety of languages and instructional levels to "define content standards—what students should know and be able to do—in language learning" (www.actfl.org). These standards, which were first published in 1996 and were revised in 2015, resulted from a three-year grant awarded by the US Department of Education, and, according to the American Council on the Teaching of Foreign Languages (ACTFL), they represent "an unprecedented consensus among educators, business leaders, government, and the community on the definition and role of language instruction in American education" (www.actfl.org). Indeed, the standards, their curricular recommendations, and the language associated with them have penetrated nearly every level of foreign language education and have gained great momentum; but they seem to stall at the postsecondary level—particularly after the initial four-semester sequence.

The four items included in the survey related to these standards appear below, with the item with the lowest mean, or item of most concern, appearing first; and the item with the greatest mean, or of least concern, appearing last. Once again, the mean value appears alongside the rank of the item given at the end of each item. The percentage that appears below indicates the proportion of respondents who indicated that they were "unfamiliar" with the concept. This language differed slightly from the other sections, whose sixth option was used to indicate that the issue addressed by the item was not applicable to the participant's program:

- Integration of multiple modes of communication into course design (i.e., interpretative, presentational, interpersonal): 2.6 / 20th / 2.9 percent;
- Inclusion of the 5 Cs (communication, connections, communities, cultures, and comparisons) in course design: 2.64 / 25th / 4.1 percent;
- Implementation of ACTFL's 90/10 recommendation on the use of the target language / native language in the classroom: 2.7 / 28th / 5.1 percent; and
- Incorporation of "can-do" statements into the Spanish curriculum: 3.0 / 43rd / 8.7 percent.

The *standards* section did not elicit many qualitative responses from participants, but those that were included seemed illustrative of the sentiments shared by many colleagues from our anecdotal observations. The first perspective that merits mention is the simple lack of familiarity with the standards, as we mentioned above. One respondent noted that "I personally am concerned but most of my department is unfamiliar with these concepts. I utilize them." In our experience, those who have little contact with the first four-semester sequence of their programs may be less familiar with the standards or be totally unaware of their existence. The second perspective follows from the first and was one of resistance, dismissal, and a feeling of imposition: "Academic freedom means we do our own thing. Who needs standards?" For some colleagues, the codification of content to be taught or the ways in which it should be conceived, even at the somewhat abstract level of the standards, is overstepping bounds and is intellectually repressive.

## The 5 Cs: Communication, Cultures, Connections, Comparisons, and Communities

One of the goals of asking our survey participants about the World-Readiness Standards for Learning Languages (National Standards Collaborative Board 2015) was not only to better understand their concerns but also to see how these standards fit into the broader scope of this book. The purpose of this section is to discuss how the 5 Cs—communication, connections, communities, cultures, and comparisons—relate to curricular development across the topics covered in the book's chapters.

### COMMUNICATION

One of the foremost goals in the Spanish classroom is to allow students to practice their Spanish and to create an authentic need to use the language. Many teachers attempt to artificially create this need in the classroom by developing information gap activities with elaborate prompts and contrived situations in an attempt to replicate realistic settings. As discussed in chapter 4, the integration of service-learning projects provides an authentic, communicative way for speakers not only to use the language but also to address the larger social, economic, and political realities found in the Spanish-speaking world (see chapter 7). In pedagogical terms, service learning may be the most realistic and motivating information gap activity there is! The communication standard stresses the use of language for communication in real-life situations, emphasizing "what students can do with language" rather than "what they know about language." Students are required to use the target language and to accomplish certain tasks based on the needs of the individuals and/or organization being served, and these tasks can vary depending on the level and needs of the student and community. Students need to not only communicate about one specific topic or theme but also use the language to converse with community members about areas of interest to them. These tasks can also be related to courses on Spanish for specific purposes, wherein students are able to focus their interactions with native speakers on their specific area of study. When appropriately designed, service-learning tasks will require students to communicate in both oral and written form, interpret oral and written messages, show cultural understanding when they communicate, and present oral and written information to various audiences for a variety of purposes. In addition to service learning, the discussion in chapter 9 of online and blended courses addresses the ability of students in these courses to communicate via different digital platforms with native speakers. These electronic exchanges, which are not limited to the classroom, allow learners to develop this communication standard as well as learn about people around the world.

## CULTURES

The vast number of cultures and peoples that constitute the Spanish-speaking world present a unique challenge to the language educator who wants to provide students with an understanding of this richness. Experiencing other cultures firsthand helps to develop a better understanding and appreciation of the relationship between other languages and their corresponding cultures. Additionally, individuals are often unaware of the nuances of their own culture because, for many, there are limited opportunities to truly reflect on one's cultural identity until this identity is juxtaposed with another. Culture learning is a fundamental and important component of the Spanish postsecondary classroom, and it thus facilitates students' understanding of other people's points of view, ways of life, and contributions to the world. The *culture* standard refers to the need for students to learn about the products, practices, and perspectives of the target culture.

Products that arise from a particular culture are defined as "tangible (e.g., a painting, a piece of literature, a pair of chopsticks) or intangible (e.g., an oral tale, a dance, a sacred ritual, a system of education)" (National Standards Collaborative Board 2015, 6). These products are the manifestation of the culture's perspectives. For instance, when students are taught about the great architecture of the Mayan Empire or the great cathedrals of the Catholic Church, they may go away with minimal understanding of the importance of these monuments if the cultural perspectives they represent are not discussed. Too often, the culture taught in the classroom focuses solely on a given culture's cultural artifacts or products without delving into the perspectives they embody.

The second component of "cultures" has reference to culturally charged practices. Cultural practices are defined by ACTFL as "patterns of behavior accepted by a society and deal with aspects of culture such as rites of passage, the use of forms of discourse, the social 'pecking order,'" and the use of space. In short, they represent the knowledge of "what to do when and where" (National Standards Collaborative Board 2015, 6). It is difficult to expect students to understand the cultures of those who speak the second language and to interact successfully with members of that culture if they do not have a knowledge of what is acceptable behavior within that culture. Occasionally, teachers engage students in defining and discussing the practices and behaviors of the target culture(s), but students are seldom able to understand the perspectives that members of the target culture embrace.

Cultural perspectives are defined as "the philosophical perspectives, meanings, attitudes, values, beliefs, ideas that underlie the cultural practices and products of a society. They represent a culture's view of the world" (National Standards Collaborative Board 2015, 1). These perspectives are essential, in that they enable learners to better understand the subtleties in the behaviors of members of the target culture and hopefully debunk the notion that other cultures do things "incorrectly." Too often in the Spanish language classroom, culture lessons emphasize the curious and unique traditions, architecture, and customs of people who are different from the learner. In the discussion of heritage learners in chapter 3, it was mentioned how these learners are a valuable resource for the classroom because they are cultural insiders to differing degrees. They are parts of families who have lived the many experiences discussed in Spanish classes. The Spanish curriculum needs to develop ways to include the resources in a community to connect with the cultures that surround it. Whether it is through service learning, where they achieve a firsthand perspective on the culture and may even directly ask the cultural insider about what they are learning in the school setting, or in their training to become future language teachers and are exposed to students from a diverse background, programs need to implement specific and measurable goals for the acquisition of culture to truly develop as culturally informed speakers of Spanish.

## CONNECTIONS

Instruction in world languages must be connected to other subject areas and disciplines within and beyond the academy to remain relevant in higher education. Because the demand for linguistically competent and culturally informed speakers has increased in all sectors of contemporary Anglo-American society, it is imperative that university curricula also reflect these changes across all disciplines. Content from other subject areas is integrated with world language instruction through lessons that are developed around common themes, as is commonly found in the courses on Spanish for specific purposes. Students are able to see how their use of the language can relate to the business community, the medical field, translation and interpretation services, and many other areas. As students are exposed to the wide range of fields in which Spanish is used, they are not only confronted with language-related issues but are also forced to delve into other subject areas and to make connections to other disciplines. Thompson (2012, 56) placed students in several different organizations as part of a service-learning curriculum in both conversation and content courses, in which the students had to connect their language skills with a wide range of topics. He describes the activities and organizations, stating that

> with Junior Achievement, the day care center, and the youth program, students were teaching young bilingual community members in small classroom settings. With the community center and the Alzheimer's awareness program, students worked with Spanish-speaking community members teaching them about resources and services available to them. In addition, in the Alzheimer's awareness program and Junior Achievement, the students had to translate the materials used by the organizations from English to Spanish in order to be able to use them to teach the community members. Finally, the students who worked with the health care center and the Hispanic Chamber of Commerce acted as translators and the first point of contact for the people who entered into those facilities and needed assistance.

As can be seen from this study, the students were signed up for Spanish conversation and other Spanish content courses, but their interaction with the community allowed them to develop linguistic skills in the target language, with which they could then return to the classroom and employ in other interactions in Spanish.

The benefits of these interactions were not limited to the Spanish language classroom. The students were also able to take this information and apply it to their other courses and areas of study. Increasingly, language students have a distinct academic minor or secondary major, with which they can gain experience through connecting disciplines outside the language classroom to their study of Spanish. The MLA report (2007) makes a strong case for the expansion of foreign language study to disciplines and majors beyond the humanities and social sciences. The future medical student can serve in a hospital with limited-proficiency community members and assist them as they communicate with doctors, thereby helping the community members but also benefiting the language student by allowing him or her to practice the target language. In addition, these students gain valuable knowledge about the workings of a particular hospital or clinic and how they deal with linguistic and cultural minority groups, experiences that surely can assist them in their future career goals. Students studying elementary or secondary teaching can get practical experience by working in schools or with other youth programs. This not only helps them prepare for their future profession but also makes them more keenly aware of the needs of a population of students that they are likely to find in their classes. Often, beginning teachers have little experience with the classroom before doing their student teaching; developing a more diverse curriculum can better prepare them for these challenges. Making connections between the curriculum and needs of the community can be challenging at times, but the value of this experience will benefit the learning and growth of all involved. To not make these connections in the twenty-first century would truly mean to miss out on a valuable opportunity.

## COMPARISONS

Students are encouraged to compare and contrast languages and cultures by discovering patterns, making predictions, and analyzing similarities and differences. This formulation and testing of hypotheses is valuable for their overall linguistic development and may help to increase their cultural sensitivity. The typical default when one encounters a new situation is to rely on the cultural norms of his or her upbringing or those that are familiar. The Spanish curriculum needs to find ways to facilitate students making the comparisons between their own culture, beliefs, and practices with those around them, and especially with the Spanish-speaking world. Service learning is one way that provides students with the opportunity to not only recognize their own culture and beliefs but also to appreciate differences, as they observe and interact with the Spanish language and the many cultures that speak it within their own community. It also may allow them to consider the behaviors and reasons behind others' decisions and the actions of another culture, or their own. Dubinsky (2006) states that reflection is one of the key elements of being able to successfully compare one's own culture, beliefs, and practices with those of other people who may see the world differently. If students are not asked to directly compare the cultures and languages with which they are working, they miss out on one of the key elements of successful language development and may fail to see any comparisons. Students can reflect on their learning with fellow classmates. This collaboration is valuable as they negotiate the meaning of their experiences and collectively develop an understanding of the customs and cultures with which they have had contact. This would be especially valuable in the heritage classroom, where learners may have diverse cultural and linguistic backgrounds but also unique experiences with the Spanish language and culture. As heritage learners work with one another or with second-language learners of Spanish in mixed classrooms, these opportunities will prove invaluable to their educational experience.

## COMMUNITIES

For students, extending their learning experiences from the Spanish language classroom to their home and to multilingual and multicultural communities

**Figure 10.1   Logo of the World-Readiness Standards for Learning Languages**

*Source:* National Standards Collaborative Board, *World-Readiness Standards for Learning Languages, 4th Edition.* Alexandria, VA: National Standards Collaborative Board, 2015.

emphasizes that they are living in a global society. Activities used to accomplish this may include field trips, use of email and the internet, clubs, exchange programs and cultural activities, service learning, school-to-work opportunities, and opportunities to hear speakers of other languages in the school and classroom. Putting students in contact with the community can change the student who participates and thus help him or her to become more civically and socially minded, leading to a lifetime of involvement. This practice gets the students away from the school and from sitting behind a desk into the community to employ the language that they are learning.

Taken as a whole, these 5 Cs can be easily woven together and interconnected through all of the aspects covered in this book (figure 10.1). Whether in the heritage language classroom, in the training of future teachers, in online and blended courses, or in the courses on Spanish for specific purposes, the successful integration of the 5 Cs needs to form part of the twenty-first-century curriculum and guide program development and assessments.

## SYNTHESIS AND SUMMARY

At the outset of this book, we mentioned that one of our goals was to conduct a sort of macro needs analysis of postsecondary Spanish language education in the United States as we move further into the twenty-first century and as the number of Hispanics and Spanish speakers in the country grows. As part of this needs analysis, we have reviewed relevant research, both others' and our own, while arguing that certain aspects of the collegiate Spanish language curriculum are necessarily affected by the increased use of Spanish in American society and in the academy. Although we have not addressed every curricular consideration relevant to all postsecondary contexts, we have targeted those components we feel are most pressing, both in the main body of the chapter as well as in the reflection questions and pedagogical activities.

Our goal has been to examine issues that have resonance on a national level and that Spanish postsecondary programs may confront in the twenty-first century. Of the many models proposed for curriculum design and language program policy, those developed by Nation and Macalister (2010) and Dubin and Olshtain (1986) provide a coherent conceptual frame for understanding Spanish postsecondary programs in the twenty-first century. The argument we have made throughout the book, in essence, is that Dubin and Olshtain's and Nation and Macalister's models have clear and unmistakable implications for Spanish language teaching and learning in the university setting. Although no foreign language taught in the American academy should be considered outside the reach of these models, the situation of Spanish in the United States presents a rather unique case study. Admittedly, our treatment of postsecondary Spanish curriculum has more directly addressed certain facets of these models more than others, with a clear emphasis on programmatic (e.g., "needs"), rather than on theoretical (e.g., "principles") or pedagogical ("format and presentation") issues—in the case of Nation and Macalister's model, for example. However, our treatment of macro issues in curriculum design and program development should not be interpreted as meaning to slight the principles of sound second-language acquisition theory or classroom pedagogy because they are clearly key components of curriculum design and evaluation. Surely, the relationship between second-language acquisition and curriculum design and program development—as well as the idiosyncrasies of individual classrooms and the students and instructors who inhabit them—merit full attention and study elsewhere. In this section, we use these models to synthesize and reflect on what we have proposed throughout this book (figure 10.2).

Though Dubin and Olshtain's (1986) model clearly overlaps with Nation and Macalister's with regard to the centrality of a contextual analysis, it focuses more explicitly on the sociocultural and sociopolitical realities that exert influence on second-language programs. This model invites us to consider larger trends in society that might influence Spanish programs and the vitality of Spanish teaching and learning in the United States. More specifically, the outer circle contains four sources of information, each comprising an equal fourth of the circle with arrows pointing inward, symbolizing the

**Figure 10.2    Dubin and Olshtain's Model of Language Program Policy Design**

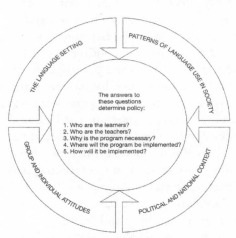

*Source:* Fraida Dubin and Elite Olshtain, *Course Design: Developing Programs and Materials for Language Learning.* Cambridge: Cambridge University Press, 1986.

direct influence they exert on the determination of language program policy: "The language setting"—the presence or absence of native speakers in society; "Patterns of language use in society"—opportunities to use the language outside the classroom; "Political and national context"—legitimacy or official recognition given the language by governing bodies; and "Group and individual attitudes"—opinions of language majority speakers toward the language. Throughout the book, we have argued that significant numbers of native Spanish speakers ("The language setting") can be found in nearly all US states, including those that only twenty years ago had relatively few native speakers, and that the use of Spanish is rather ubiquitous in American society, available in print, electronic, and face-to-face encounters. However, in spite of the broadening scope and reach of the Spanish language in American society, it struggles to be granted official status politically ("Political and national context"), institutionally, academically, and to be imbued with prestige and legitimacy ("Group and individual attitudes") by the language majority speakers.

In chapters 2 and 7, we traced the history of the Spanish language and the teaching of Spanish from colonial times to the present within territories currently circumscribed within borders of the United States. In these chapters, we explained the powerful impact that "standard" language ideology has had on the perceived need by some to maintain a linguistically and culturally homogenous nation-state and how this directly affects the status of Spanish in the United States and the racialization and marginalization of ethnically diverse Spanish speakers. These sociopolitical realities most assuredly influence students' perspectives and motivations on the learning of Spanish in the classroom.

One particularly poignant case in which sociocultural and sociopolitical realities intersect with pedagogical and acquisition-related considerations is the situation of heritage language learners and heritage language pedagogy, an issue addressed in chapter 3. Heritage language education serves as a lightning rod or, better yet, litmus test for the degree to which Spanish teaching will thrive in the twenty-first century, for three main reasons. First, the allocation of precious educational resources and monies to the teaching of Spanish, the language of a predominantly marginalized minority, to members of those same marginalized minorities would index a true commitment to equal access to bilingualism for all students, regardless of sociolinguistic and socioethnic background. Second, the linguistic and, more important, sociocultural validation that strong forms of bilingualism and heritage language learning at all levels would communicate to Latino and Anglo students could be educationally and personally transformative. Secondary and postsecondary Anglo-American students enrolled in traditional foreign language Spanish courses at institutions with a strong commitment to heritage language education may begin to realize that Spanish is much more than simply a commodity to be traded on the labor market but rather a significant cultural semiotic. Third, the recognition of the need for unique pedagogies and thematic content in harmony with students' diverse proficiency levels, routes to acquisition, and cultural background opens the door to greater understanding of the complexities of classroom language pedagogy more generally in the twenty-first century, even in the traditional Spanish as a foreign language classroom.

We turn now to Nation and Macalister's (2010) rather comprehensive conceptualization of curriculum design. What Nation and Macilister denominate as "needs" and "environment" appears to cover Dubin and Olshtain's (1986) entire outer circle, if interpreted liberally at a general level. The unique contribution of Nation and Macalister's model is to connect principles, needs, and environment to the inner circle of goals, which is enveloped by content and sequencing, format and presentation, and monitoring and assessment. It is the inner circle of Nation and Macalister's model where well-designed curricula make the most difference, that is, in practical classroom-level application. Given the scope of this book, we have chosen to maintain our discussion at a rather general level with regard to "goals," "content and sequencing," "format and presentation," and "monitoring and assessment." However, each of these crucial elements of curriculum design finds expression throughout the book. Chapter 3 addresses the best format and presentation for instructing learners who bring implicit linguistic and cultural knowledge to the Spanish classroom. Likewise, chapters 4 and 9 discuss instructional strategies and pedagogical approaches vis-à-vis service learning and technology that have a direct impact on format and presentation. Chapters 5 and 8 focus on content by analyzing Spanish for specific purposes and the training of Spanish teachers. Finally, chapter 6 provides an overview of issues bearing on what can be expected of a postsecondary Spanish language program with respect to the achievement of learning outcomes and students' progression toward those objectives, that is, "monitoring and assessment."

In the case of both models, what is conspicuously absent from the two-dimensional, static, schematic representation is the dynamic interrelationships between each component of the models. The prominence of one node of Nation and Maclister's model might better be represented by an enlargement of that particular node as compared with others. Likewise, the strength of connection between nodes may require a much thicker line to represent a sort of hierarchy within the model between its constituent parts. In Dubin and Olshtain's model, the quarter turn given each of the four sources of information influencing program policy may expand to cover nearly half the circle rather than a quarter or less than an eighth. The task for the local Spanish curriculum designer is to determine the particular features of these models and their hierarchies and weights, given the realities of their local context.

## ADDITIONAL CONSIDERATIONS

There are other key curricular issues in collegiate Spanish language education that we mentioned at the outset in chapter 1 that are not addressed in the book due to space and scope. In our view, these issues merit further attention elsewhere if Spanish language education in the twenty-first century is to realize its potential. In this section, we limit the discussion of these issues but highlight areas ripe for further inquiry.

The first issue we highlight here, study abroad, was of particular concern for the educators who completed our national survey. The incorporation of study abroad into collegiate Spanish language education is a particularly thorny one for most programs. Several issues arise with regard to study abroad, such as (1) controlling costs to increase student access, (2) discerning the place and role of the study abroad experience in graduation requirements, (3) improving current study abroad configurations to maximize gains in language learning and cultural awareness, (4) increasing access to reasonably priced study abroad experiences for in-service teachers, and (5) incorporation of meaningful and rigorous service learning abroad. Even more fundamental is whether too much focus on study abroad perpetuates the tendency to "foreignize" the Spanish curriculum. Unlike most other non-English languages taught in the United States, Spanish is spoken by such large communities in certain regions of the country, where immersive experiences similar to a study abroad trip might conceivably be had within the borders of the United States. Of course, this would presuppose a willingness among Spanish program administrators, faculty members, and curriculum designers to value domestic varieties of Spanish and corresponding cultures enough to allow their students to be exposed to and, presumably, acquire these contact varieties of Spanish.

Another interesting trend in Spanish higher education that has only recently begun to surface pertains to the use of immersive models of postsecondary education. For instance, Georgetown College, a small liberal arts college near the University of Kentucky, has established an immersion program in which incoming students can take many of their general education courses in Spanish (www.georgetowncollege.edu/land/ie/). Similar to immersion programs at the elementary and secondary levels—in which, for example, students learn science and math in Spanish—students take courses in history, philosophy, and other subjects in Spanish rather than English. Programs such as these generate myriad questions and logistical concerns, but are the perfect embodiment of what postsecondary curricula might look like if Spanish were truly considered a second national language, or at least a second institutional language.

In our chapter on assessment, we only briefly mentioned the idea of a required proficiency exam for all graduating seniors. Although many programs already make use of an exit exam focused on proficiency such as BYU, there are various ways to implement such a requirement. Some prefer that it serve a gatekeeping function and risk having it be construed as punitive or even adversarial if a student's graduation depends on achieving a certain level. Others use such exams or assessment protocols for informational purposes only, both for the student and the program. In light of the ubiquity of Spanish in modern American society, the inclusion of such exams seems logical; but the impact of such assessments on the student, his or her self-efficacy, and his or her linguistic ego must also be considered, as should the impact on the program and the instructors.

## CONCLUSION

In their introduction to the 2014 issue of the annual volume published by the American Association of University Supervisors, Coordinators, and Directors of Language Programs, Norris and Mills (2014, 1) note that "FL programs . . . are facing the heightened need . . . to begin to think, innovate, and behave programmatically." In many cases, what seems to undercut progress in Spanish language programs is the simple fact that for many programs, the notion of "program" has been quite loosely construed, and looser still is stakeholders' (e.g., instructors, students, and administrators) understanding of their role in the program. Before the admonition by Norris and Mills can be heeded, Spanish postsecondary educators must engage in the simple task of defining the word "program." Is it a mission statement and departmental student learning outcomes listed on a printed page or on a website? Do the students make up the program, or is it those who write the curriculum, or those who teach it? Is it the compilation of syllabuses stored on the department's website or in a filing cabinet? Are the tenured/tenure-line faculty and their research publications part of the program? Is it the major program of study, the minor, or the student's entire education seen as one integrated whole? Can any of these pieces be missing from the puzzle and there still be something we could call a "language program"? To behave programmatically would seem to imply a collaborative, joint endeavor taken on by multiple individuals with some commonality of purpose or objective that can only be achieved as a group.

The landscape in which postsecondary Spanish language education takes place in the twenty-first century has changed considerably over the last twenty years and will continue to change. Although the sociocultural, socioeducational, and sociopolitical landscape evolves, it is imperative that the postsecondary curriculum do the same, as well as those who consider themselves part of an undergraduate program. Indeed, to teach and learn Spanish in the United States represents a dramatically different experience for instructors and students when compared with other languages and thus requires close examination of heretofore-undefined terms, roles, and responsibilities. We have identified a subset of issues that must be addressed if Spanish language education is to remain a robust and vital element that is highlighted in the foreground of the American educational landscape rather than being relegated to a remote corner of the background.

## REFLECTION QUESTIONS

1. In general, which aspects of a Spanish collegiate-level curriculum are most intractable and difficult to change? Why? Which are the most difficult in your given context?

2. In the introduction, we noted that some may be resistant to change and others may welcome it. Are there particular stakeholder profiles that could be pointed to as more or less willing to welcome change? How could those who are resistant to change be persuaded?

3. The survey did not request participants to explain why the item about viewing Spanish as a tool for better employment caused such concern. What conclusions can

you draw about why this item was rated as of most concern across all fifty-five? What might this mean with respect to students' and instructors' expectations for the goals of Spanish language education?

4. How are we to interpret the items with a high percentage of respondents who considered them "not applicable" to their program? As you review the survey items (see the online appendix, available on the publisher's website, press.georgetown.edu), identify any items that you feel would not be applicable to your program.

5. What are the advantages and disadvantages of national standards written by task forces convened by large professional teaching organizations such as ACTFL? In your mind, are standards mostly helpful, overly prescriptive, or even restrictive?

6. Have the World-Readiness Standards influenced the design of upper-level culture, civilization, literature, and linguistics courses at your institution? Why, or why not? Is the language of these standards familiar to professors in your program who do not teach lower-level language courses? Why, or why not?

7. Closely review the two models analyzed in the chapter. Are any elements of curriculum design or sources of information for language program policy missing? In the case of Spanish postsecondary education, which components of each model seem to be the most important currently? Why?

8. Peruse the Humanities+ website (http://humanities.byu.edu/about-the-college /humanitiesplus/). Why is such an elaborate and concerted effort made by Brigham Young University, and others, to connect the humanities and employment? Are this sort of website and this approach apt to result in more advanced language study by non–language majors? Why, or why not?

## PEDAGOGICAL ACTIVITIES

1. Design a lesson plan to be delivered in English for a Spanish course of any level or topical focus that uses the Humanities+ website. Ensure that your lesson engages students with the underlying issues that elicited the creation of the website. Encourage students to voice their opinions regarding their language study that is related to their professional aspirations, and also their language study and personal development that are unrelated to their career.

2. For the next three lesson plans you design, identify which of the 5 Cs each activity addresses, realizing that an activity may address more than one. After the third lesson plan, tally the number of times each of the 5 Cs was incorporated and explain any notable patterns. In subsequent lessons, make an effort to include those Cs that were less frequently used.

3. Prepare a short, multiple-choice quiz of five questions covering information on the 5 Cs. Select five instructors in your Spanish program with various disciplinary backgrounds, academic ranks, professional profiles, and teaching persuasions to complete the quiz. Engage each in a short debriefing interview to follow up on their answers to the questions and to ask about their familiarity with and use of the 5 Cs in their teaching.

4. Review Dubin and Olshtain's (1986) and Nation and Macalister's (2010) models with two colleagues and ask them which components are the most crucial for the success of your particular program. Request that they explain their answer.

## NOTE

1. All responses are reproduced verbatim without alteration to spelling or grammar.

## REFERENCES

Brigham Young University. 2017. "Humanities+." http://humanities.byu.edu/about-the -college/humanitiesplus/.

Dubin, Fraida, and Elite Olshtain. 1986. *Course Design: Developing Programs and Materials for Language Learning.* Cambridge: Cambridge University Press.

Dubinsky, James. 2006. "The Role of Reflection in Service Learning." *Business Communication Quarterly* 69, no. 3: 306–11.

Georgetown College. 2017. "Inmersión en Español at Georgetown College." www.george towncollege.edu/land/ie.

MLA (Modern Language Association). 2007. "Foreign Languages and Higher Education: New Structures for a Changed World." www.mla.org/Resources/Research/Surveys -Reports-and-Other-Documents/Teaching-Enrollments-and-Programs/Foreign-Lan guages-and-Higher-Education-New-Structures-for-a-Changed-World.

Nation, I. S. P., and John Macalister. 2010. *Language Curriculum Design.* New York: Routledge.

National Standards Collaborative Board. 2015. *World-Readiness Standards for Learning Languages,* 4th ed. Alexandria, VA: National Standards Collaborative Board. www.actfl.org /publications/all/world-readiness-standards-learning-languages.

Norris, John M., and Nicole Mills. 2014. "Introduction: Innovation and Accountability in Foreign Language Program Evaluation." In *AAUSC 2014 Volume: Innovation and Accountability in Language Program Evaluation,* edited by John Norris and Nicole Mills. Boston: Cengage.

Thompson, Gregory L. 2012. *Intersection of Service and Learning: Research and Practice in the Second Language Classroom.* Charlotte: Information Age.

# APPENDIX: DESCRIPTION OF DATA SETS

To chart the growth of Spanish language education in the United States, primarily in the second half of the twentieth century and the first two decades of the twenty-first century, we analyzed several relevant data sets. These data come from various sources and helped inform our analyses of the current status of postsecondary Spanish language education and curricular and programmatic implications for the future.

## MLA DATA AND REPORTS

The Modern Language Association (MLA) was founded in 1883 and is the largest professional organization of postsecondary modern language educators at the national and international levels. As part of its mission, the MLA collects and publishes on its website (www.mla.org) information pertaining to foreign language education at the tertiary level, from enrollment totals to curricular and programmatic trends in language departments, among many other reports. One of the most cited reports is the Language Enrollment Database, which includes the results of a nationwide survey that has been sent to institutions of higher education every few years since 1958. In addition to the data that constitute the enrollment database, more recently the MLA has collected data on the number of enrollments that correspond to upper- and lower-level courses, as well as the number of American university students who have declared language or literature as primary and secondary majors.

## WORLD LANGUAGE (FOREIGN LANGUAGE) ADVANCED PLACEMENT EXAMINATIONS

The Advanced Placement (AP) data that are referred to throughout this book come from two distinct data sets licensed to the authors by the College Board covering the period from 1979 to 2014. The first data set details the number of modern foreign language exams given from 1994 to 2014 in each state, and allows for the totals to be filtered by state, year, foreign language exam, score, gender, dominant ("best") language, and ethnic and racial background. Two extra variables were derived by the College Board at the request of the authors and were added to the data set: heritage speaker status; and an additional Hispanic category that conflated Mexican American, Puerto Rican, and other Hispanic students. For a student to be identified as a heritage speaker in the database, he or she had to have lived or studied for a month or more in a country where the language is spoken *and* have used the language regularly at home. The second data set made available to the authors provided summary statistics for all AP exams taken between 1979 and 1993. The summary tables included tallies for all AP exams nationwide from each racial and ethnic group and reported their scores on a scale from 1 to 5.

## UNDERGRADUATE SPANISH COURSE CATALOGS

Undergraduate Spanish courses and program configurations from seven prominent private and public American universities that had digitally archived university course catalogs and university bulletins were studied longitudinally from the late nineteenth to the early twenty-first centuries (private: Brigham Young University and Stanford University; public: University of Arizona; University of Kentucky; University of California, Los Angeles; University of Minnesota; and University of Wisconsin–Madison). Two additional public universities were included in the initial analysis, though it was discovered after the coding had begun that records were not available back to the early twentieth century. The course descriptions but not degree requirements for The Ohio State University were available from 1963 to the present, while the University of Iowa had course descriptions *and* degree requirements accessible from 1970 to the present. This survey of course catalogs was not meant to be exhaustive or to sample from all institution types or regions, but was used to provide a rough gauge of how Spanish language education evolved during the twentieth century. We are cognizant of the fact that course naming conventions, curricular structures, and programmatic configurations change over time and that the course titles and descriptions printed in the course catalogs may not exactly reflect the content that was taught or whether the course was actually taught in that particular year. Moreover, the courses were placed in only one category (e.g., elementary language, literature, culture, and linguistics), though their content may have overlapped with other categories. Notwithstanding these limitations, we feel that our analysis of these course catalogs and the classification system adopted provide a useful tool for determining what university Spanish language curricula might have looked like at each time interval.

Once the nine universities were selected and contemporary curricula were preliminarily reviewed, the researchers created categories in which to place each course from an institution's Spanish curriculum. Those categories included Spanish for the professions, translation/interpretation, elementary language, advanced language, culture, linguistics, literature, teaching, service learning, heritage/native language, and independent/directed studies. In addition to the coding of courses at each time interval, the presence of a major, minor, and tracks within the major or minor were noted, as were the number of credit-hours or courses needed for completion of each program of study. The programmatic configurations and academic terminology from the early twentieth century were difficult to compare with the late twentieth and early twenty-first century, but were included nonetheless. The coding of the number and type of Spanish courses and major/minor options available began with the earliest bulletin year accessible for each university, in some cases as early as the mid-1800s, and then was continued every ten years, from 1900 until 2000. From 2000 to 2015, the courses and programs were coded every five years to achieve greater granularity in the analysis. Our focus is primarily on the second half of the twentieth century and the first two decades of the twenty-first century, given the greater similarity in overall curricular structures and publishing conventions of university bulletins.

# SPANISH POSTSECONDARY PROGRAM AND CURRICULUM SURVEY

The authors created an online survey with Likert-scale items to elicit in a very broad manner current Spanish language educators' "perceptions of the most pressing programmatic and curricular issues in Spanish education at your institution overall." The survey was distributed electronically via electronic listservs, professional discussion boards and email distribution lists, and personal contacts to reach Spanish educators of all ranks, from full professors at research institutions to adjunct, contract faculty at two-year community colleges to inexperienced first-year graduate students teaching beginning courses. When the survey was closed and the results were analyzed, approximately seven hundred educators had completed some or all of the survey. The survey aimed at capturing Spanish language educators' concerns at a general level regarding specific curricular and programmatic issues at their institutions, and it did not provide any information on why the respondents chose the responses they did. For example, the individual instructor may not have any problem in his or her own class with a particular issue but may feel that others in the program do and thus consider the issue a concern.

The survey included several demographic and institutional questions before requesting respondents' reactions to fifty-five statements associated with the following areas of concern in contemporary Spanish language education: service learning, heritage/native language learners, Spanish for specific purposes, assessment, sociocultural realities, teacher/instructor training, online/hybrid instruction, national standards, and other issues. Each section contained between four and eight Likert-scale questions, with an "other" option for respondents to include other areas of concern. The 5-point Likert scale ranged from "very much a concern" to "not a concern at all," with an additional sixth option, "not applicable to my program." Given our concern that some foreign language educators may not recognize the terminology and concepts that appeared in the national standards section, the sixth response option available was "unfamiliar with concept(s)."

# ETS PRAXIS DATA

The preservice training of foreign language instructors as part of their university studies to fill positions at public and private institutions, primarily at the secondary level, has received particular attention among scholars in applied linguistics. One of the most pressing concerns for many teacher trainers is the level of candidates' foreign language proficiency. In 2010 the Educational Testing Service (ETS) began offering world language exams in the most commonly taught languages, and many states have begun requiring it of preservice teachers seeking state certification. As such, the authors were licensed ETS Praxis data from 2010 to 2015 that included candidates' de-identified scores on their first attempt at the Spanish, French, and German world language exams, as well as their scores from their first attempt at any other of the

Praxis series exams, including Principles of Learning and Teaching: Early Childhood / Grades 7–12, and World Languages Pedagogy. These data will allow for direct comparisons between candidates' language and pedagogical knowledge and abilities.

## WEBCAPE DATA FROM THE UNIVERSITY OF KENTUCKY

Nearly without exception, postsecondary world language programs have placement procedures that attempt to match incoming students' levels of linguistic competency with the program's course levels. In many cases, these procedures consist of an exam whose score determines the placement of the student in the program. For many years, one of the most widely used exams has been the WebCAPE (Web-Based Computer Adaptive Placement Exam), designed at Brigham Young University and currently licensed to and distributed by Perpetual Works, Inc. This exam tests students' grammar, vocabulary, and reading abilities via multiple-choice items delivered online. After extensive field testing, students' responses to each of the test's items were submitted to complex mathematical procedures using Item Response Theory, which allow for precise calibrations of each item's difficulty level. In this way, the exam is able to quickly, interactively adapt to students' respective ability levels, producing a score in as short as 20 to 25 minutes. This efficient approach to program placement appealed to many schools and, as of the summer of 2016, was used by approximately 660 colleges and universities across the country (Dustin Thacker, Perpetual Technology Group, personal communication). De-identified WebCAPE scores from 12,826 Spanish, 2,988 French, and 1,009 German tests taken by University of Kentucky students from June 2002 to June 2015 were analyzed to allow for comparisons of the raw number of placement exams taken in each language and the average score levels. At the University of Kentucky, students took the exam in a proctored environment in the department office; but they were able to take the exam more than once, given the variable nature of the test items presented to them. Before the scores were de-identified and analyzed, students with identical first and last names or identification numbers were located, and only their first attempt at the exam was included.

## INSTITUTIONAL DATA

On several occasions, we cite compelling institutional data collected at our respective universities, the University of Kentucky and Brigham Young University. These two universities and their Spanish programs clearly do not and cannot represent the wide variety of programs across the United States and their respective curricula and stakeholders. However, Brigham Young University and the University of Kentucky represent two rather distinct profiles—one, a large, rather selective, private religious university in the Intermountain West; and the other, a large, public land-grant research university in the Southeast. In including these schools, we had two goals: (1) to demonstrate in a concrete way how the trends and curricular phenomena we reference are manifest in real programs, even those of very distinct profiles, like ours; and

(2) to encourage readers to investigate and corroborate the trends we have identified in our institutions by engaging in similar research at their institutions. We cite a variety of statistics from the number of majors and minors to the number of AP exam candidates and their scores, all of which serve to illustrate the changing nature of Spanish postsecondary education.

# INDEX

Figures, tables, and notes are indicated by *f*, *t*, and *n* following the page number.

AAPPL (Assessment of Performance toward Proficiency in Languages), 126–27, 137

Abbott, Annie: *Comunidades*, 72; on employment opportunities, 104, 113; on LSP, 98, 113; on service learning, 76, 84; on the silo walls metaphor, 135

academic advisers, 126–27

Academic Pathway to Teaching (APT), 192–93

accented speech, 55–56, 157, 164, 186

accountability, 15, 40, 124, 137

achievement, 5, 8, 89–90, 128–32, 138–39

ACTFL. *See* American Council on the Teaching of Foreign Languages

ACT scores, 192, 193

Adair-Hauck, Bonnie, 207

Adler-Kassner, Linda, 74

administrative support, 6, 37, 59, 86, 220

advanced-level courses: for heritage language learners, 51; instructor training for, 194; low enrollment in, 235–36; placement testing and, 125; service learning for, 78–79, 91, 92–93; for Spanish LSP, 108; standards for, 130; transactional distance and, 209; two-tiered model and, 37–38, 134–35; at the University of Kentucky, 143

Advanced Placement examinations: data sets from, 19n1, 253; heritage language learners and, 56–57, 253; increase in, 13, 29; statistics on, 4, 29, *30f*, 142; at the University of Kentucky, 143

African Americans, 2

Alarcón, Irma, 62

Allen, Heather, 194

Alonso, Carlos, 6, 7, 22

Alvarez, Stephanie, 167

American Association of Teachers of Spanish and Portuguese, 19n3, 25, 32, 102–3, 200

American Association of University Supervisors, Coordinators, and Directors of Language Programs, 249–50

American Community Survey, 2

American Council on the Teaching of Foreign Languages (ACTFL): AAPPL and, 126–27, 137; Brigham Young University and, 141; instructor training and, 200; Integrated Performance Assessment model, 132; learner standards and, 54–55; Praxis for World Languages exams and, 183; on proficiency levels, 15, 129, 137, 141, 179–80, 181. *See also* 5 Cs; World-Readiness Standards for Learning Languages

American Sign Language, 3

Amuzie, Grace L., 223–24

Anglicization, 159

Anglo-American society: bilingualism and, 13, 157–61; critical language studies and, 167–68; perspectives on Spanish in, 11, 161–64, 247; territorial expansion and, 25–27

anthropology, linguistic, 16

Aoki, Michelle, 180

AP exams. *See* Advanced Placement examinations

applied linguistics: bilingualism and, 33; critical, 153–54; curriculum design and, 7; heritage language learners and, 59; instructor specialties in, 40–41, 59; motivation and, 65; performance-based approach and, 31; Praxis data and, 255; research on, 24

appropriateness, language use and, 154, 155
APT (Academic Pathway to Teaching),
192–93
Archer, Walter, 211–15
Arens, Katherine, 8, 130, 131
Arizona, 5–6, 186, 254
Army Specialized Training Program, 35
Arnó-Macià, Elisabet, 101
arts and humanities programs, funding for,
234
Asian/Asian Americans, Praxis exam scores
for, 184
Asociación para la Enseñanza del Español
como Lengua Extranjera, 200
aspectual distinction, 61
assessed curriculum, definition of, 128–29
assessment, 124–50; case study of, 141–45;
current status of, 137–38; exit exams
for, 249; importance of, 145; instructor
training for, 136, 137–38; integrated
performance, 182; language tests for,
136; of LSP, 100; of online and blended
courses, 221–22; pedagogical activities
for, 146–47; reflection questions on, 145–
46; of service learning, 77, 77f, 89–90; of
Spanish LSP courses, 109–10; of student
learning outcomes, 132–36; survey
results on, 139–41. See also placement
procedures and testing; proficiency levels;
program evaluation
assessment literacy, 137–38
Assessment of Performance toward Proficiency
in Languages (AAPPL), 126–27, 137
assimilation, 64, 159
audioconferencing, 225
Audio-Lingual Method, 35
audio recording assessments, 90
aural skills, 17, 52
Axsom, Trish, 84

Bachman, Lyle F., 109, 136
Baldree, Cara, 192
barbarism, 49, 68n1
Barreneche, Gabriel Ignacio, 79–80, 81, 93

Barrette, Catherine M., 134, 163–64
Basturkmen, Helen, 101, 115
Beaudrie, Sara M., 49–50, 53, 62, 63, 64, 66
beginning-level classes. See lower-level
courses
behavior, cultural practices and, 140–42
behaviorism, 35
Bellini, Carlo, 23
Beltrán, Blanca, 98, 102, 120n3
Bernhardt, Elizabeth B., 38, 190
bilingual education, 31–33, 158, 160. See
also dual immersion programs
Bilingual Education Act of 1967, 31, 160
bilingualism: diversity of, 55–56; English-
only movement and, 155; equal access to,
247; grammar courses and, 142; heritage
language learners and, 33, 48, 64–65; of
Hispanic children, 107; immigrants and,
31–33, 158–59; informal style of, 48,
49; legislation and, 160; perspectives on,
13, 64, 157–61; Spanish-dominant, 16;
standard language ideology and, 167; US
Spanish dialects and, 172
Blake, Robert J., 216
blended courses. See online and blended
courses
Bloom, Melanie, 80–81
Blyth, Carl, 223
Bok, Derek, 99–100
Bordón, Teresa, 136
Bowles, Melissa, 53–54, 65, 66, 110
Brecht, Richard, 49–50
Brigham Young University (BYU): course
catalogs from, 254; dual immersion
program at, 191; heritage language
learners and, 51; Humanities+ initiative,
233; institutional data from, 256–57;
language certificate program of, 233;
mentoring program at, 196; online and
blended courses at, 221; pedagogy section
at, 197–98; service learning program
of, 88–89; WebCAPE exam and, 125,
136–37, 141, 142–43, 147n2, 256
Bringle, Robert G., 84

Brown, Alan V., 5–6, 135–36
Brown, James D., 9
Burke, Brigid, 181, 182
business meetings, in English, 107
business Spanish courses: availability of, 41; connections standard and, 241; heritage language learners and, 106; prerequisites for, 110; sociocultural realities and, 111–12; Spanish LSP and, 116; student profile for, 104; textbooks for, 105; at the University of Kentucky, 107; upper-level management and, 106–7
Byrnes, Heidi, 8, 39, 124, 129–30
BYU. *See* Brigham Young University

Cabrillo, Juan Rodríguez, 22
California, 254
Campus Compact, 75, 89
Canale, Michael, 129
capitalism, 162. *See also* employment opportunities; markets
Carnegie Mellon University, 207
Carney, Terri M., 93–94
Carr, Peter, 1
Carreira, María, 2, 52
Carroll, John B., 129
Catholic Church, 23
Cengage, 102
Census statistics (US), 2, *3t*, 48, 162
Ceo-DiFrancesco, Diane, 216
Chapelle, Carol A., 207
Chávez, César, 33
children: bilingual, 107, 159; as heritage language learners, 33, 64; immigrant, 31–32, 158; movies for, 161; service learning with, 78, 79, 82, 91; standard language ideology and, 157. *See also* elementary schools; secondary schools
Chinese: World Language exam, 183–84
Chomsky, Noam, 35, 99
Choy, Susan P., 65
Christianization, 23
Chun, Dorothy M., 216
civic engagement, 74–75, 76–77, 82, 89, 160

Civil Rights Act of 1964, 160
civil rights movement, 31, 33, 160, 162
Clapham, Caroline, 110, 113
Clark, Martyn K., 127
Clarke, John, 23
Clifford, Ray, 206
code-switching, 48–49
Cody, Jae, 190
cognitive presence, 212–13
Cohn, D'Vera, 164
Cold War, 27, 28
Coleman, Algernon, 130
Coleman Report, 35
collaboration: cognitive, 214; comparisons standard and, 243; face-to-face interactions and, 215–17, 219; MLA report on, 40; online and blended courses and, 212–13, 219; service learning and, 81, 89; telecollaboration for, 215–17
College Board, 4, 13, 19n1, 29, *30f*, 56–57, 253
commodification of languages, 6, 29, 164
commonly taught languages (CTL), 5–6
communication, definition of, 76
communication standard (5 Cs), 54, 76–77, *77f*, 239–40
communication technology, 99
communicative competence: breakdown of, 157; Canale and Swain on, 129; content courses and, 131–32; Hymes on, 15, 35; LSP and, 99; natural languages and, 151; oral skills and, 78–79, 130; performance-based approach and, 31; translingual and transcultural, 7, 13, 40, 42, 128, 145, 178. *See also* proficiency levels
communism, 27
communities standard (5 Cs), 54, 76–77, *77f*, 243–44, *244f*
community-engaged learning. *See* service learning
Community of Inquiry model, 211–15, *213f*
community service learning. *See* service learning

commuter-oriented institutions, 74, 219

comparisons standard (5 Cs), 54, 76–77, *77f*, 243, *244f*

computer-based instruction, 191, *199t*, 200. *See also* online and blended courses

*Comunidades* (Abbott), 72

connections standard (5 Cs), 54, 76–77, *77f*, 241–43, *244f*

content courses: communicative competence and, 131–32; connections standard and, 241–43; language certificate program and, 233–34; learning outcomes for, 135; service learning and, 7, 242–43; sociopolitical realities and, 169; Spanish LSP and, 109–10, 112, 117

contract faculty, 116, 234–35

conversation courses, 78–80, 90, 91, 92–93, 242–43

Cook, William, 25

Corder, Stephen P., 35

Corey, Doug, 192

Correa, Maite, 32

course catalogs, undergraduate, 36–37, *37t*, 42, 135–36, 254

course-level objectives, 128

course-level outcomes, 134

critical applied linguistics, 153–54

"Critical Approaches to Teaching Spanish" (Leeman), 151

critical language awareness, 154–55, 168

critically needed languages, 28

critical thinking, 81, 153–54

Crooks, Robert, 74

cross-cultural competence. *See* cultural sensitivity; transcultural competence

CSL (community service learning). *See* service learning

CTL (commonly taught languages), 5–6

Cubillos, Jorge H., 102

cultural context. *See* sociocultural realities

cultural knowledge, 39, 55, 81–83, 109, 183, 216

cultural perspectives, 241

cultural practices, 140–42

cultural products, 168, 240

cultural sensitivity: comparisons standard and, 243; employment opportunities and, 107, 110–11, 112; service learning and, 80–83, 88, 243

cultural studies: Advanced Placement exams and, 143; course catalogs on, 36–37; curriculum design for, 130–32; definition of, 76; heritage language learners and, 63–64; humanities education and, 130, 131; instructors for, 59, 187, 194; language certificate program and, 233–34; vs. the literary approach, 38; NAEP assessment framework and, 77, *77f*; need for, 152–53; service learning and, 73, 75; specialists in, 40–41, 59, 115; standards for, 130; survey results on, 236. *See also* sociocultural realities

cultures standard (5 Cs), 54, 76–77, *77f*, 240–41, *244f*

curriculum, intended, enacted, assessed, and learned, 128–29

curriculum design: case study of, 141–45; contemporary, 11–12; de-foreignization of, 169; environment analysis for, 10–11, 12, 19n2; 5 Cs and, 239–44; for heritage language learners, 14, 49, 62–66; for instructor training, 198–200, *199t*; internalization of, 100; key issues in, 11–12, 37–41, 248–49; Nation and Macalister's model of, 247–48; needs analysis for, 9–10, 12, 244–45; for online and blended courses, 219–24; pedagogical activities for, 251–52; progressive expansion of, 34–37; reflection questions on, 250–51; for service learning, 86–93; situation analysis for, 10–11; for Spanish LSP, 109–13; for sustainable programs, 145; tradition of, 40, 42; for the twenty-first century, 244–48

curriculum mapping, of learning outcomes, 134–35

Dabbagh, Nada, 214

Daniel, Shirley J., 107

d'Arlach, Lucia, 81

Dasenbrock, Reed W., 6

"Data on Second Majors in Language and Literature, 2001-2013" (MLA), 39

data sets and surveys, 12, 253–57; Campus Compact, 75, 89; course catalogs for, 36–37, *37t*, 42, 135–36, 254; on heritage language learners, 47–60; institutional data and, 256–57; from the MLA, 253; from the Praxis exams, 178, 183–85, 255–56; on service learning, 84–85; WebCAPE exam and, 125, 136–37, 141, 142–43, 147n2, 256. *See also* Advanced Placement examinations; Spanish Postsecondary Program and Curriculum Survey

Davis, John McE., 139

deficit model, 66, 155

del Valle, José, 161, 162

de Miranda, Francisco, 24

dental terminology, 111–12

Dewey, John, 72

Dialang diagnostic exam, 137

dialects, 49, 55–56, 66, 154, 167, 172

digital natives, 221, 224

Dings, Abby, 41, 42

Diploma de Espanol como Lengua Extranjera, 143

Direct Method, 34–35

discipline-specific language, 11, 17, 107–9, 114, 118, 178

discrimination: accented speech and, 186; legislation on, 160; linguistic, 157, 160, 161–64, *163f*, 166–67, 169–70. *See also* racism

"Discrimination, Dimmitt, Texas" (Lee), *163f*

domestic violence, 172

Donato, Richard, 179

Douglas, Dan, 101, 109

Doyle, Michael S., 116

drop outs, 65. *See also* retention of students

dual immersion programs, 91, 189–91

Dubin, Fraida, 18, 244–47, *246f*, 248

Dubinsky, James, 243

DuBord, Elise, 162

Ducar, Cynthia, 63, 66

Eastern Michigan University, 102

Eastern Seaboard, 23, 26

economic downturns, 73, 160

economic factors. *See* socioeconomic factors

Ecuador, 111–12

Educational Testing Service (ETS), 255–56

electronic teaching portfolios, 200

Elementary and Secondary Education Act of 1965, 31

elementary schools: employment opportunities in, 178, 189; heritage language learners in, 63; immigrant children in, 31; instructor proficiency for, 183–85; LSP courses in, 108; service learning and, 79–81, 242–43; student teachers in, 197

Elola, Idoia, 225

employment opportunities: cultural sensitivity and, 107, 110–11, 112; discipline-specific language for, 11, 17, 107–9, 114, 118, 178; humanities education and, 100; for instructors, 178, 189; LSP and, 11, 99–100; multilingualism and, 108; proficiency levels and, 11, 28, 39; service learning and, 73; Spanish LSP and, 104–8, 110–12, 113, 118; survey results on, 232–35; with transnational businesses, 99, 107, 112; in upper-level management, 106–7, 108, 158; value of college education for, 36. *See also* job market

enacted curriculum, definition of, 128–29

Ene, Estela, 114

English as a second language: immersion programs for, 158; immigrant access to, 159; instructors for, 186, 187; needs analysis for, 134; telecollaboration and, 216

English composition courses, 84

English for specific purposes (ESP): definition of, 100; emphasis on, 15, 102; research agenda for, 113; sociopolitical realities and, 111; vs. Spanish LSP, 120n1; student profile for, 104

English language: business meetings in, 107; as the international lingua franca, 27–28, 98–99, 102, 107, 160, 161–62; loanwords in, 2; as the national language, 161–62, 167; territorial expansion and, 26
English language learners. *See* English as a second language
English-only movement, 32, 155, 160, 162
environment analysis, 10–11, 12, 19n2
ESP. *See* English for specific purposes
*Español para el bilingüe* (Marrone), 48–49, 68n1
ethnic groups, 81, 159–60, 161, 184–85. *See also* minority groups; Spanish-speaking communities
ethnocentrism, 83, 160
ETS (Educational Testing Service), 255–56
evidence-based learning outcomes, 145
exit exams, 143, 249
expansion activities, 18
experiential learning, 11, 14–15, 72, 74, 170. *See also* service learning
Eyler, Janet, 83

face-to-face interactions: collaboration and, 219; heritage language learners and, 55; online and blended courses and, 17, 218, 219–20, 222, 223, 224, 225; service learning and, 76, 77; with Spanish-speaking communities, 16; transactional distance and, 209
faculty: for advanced-level courses, 135; on assessment, 140; contract, 116, 234–35; for LSP, 115–16, 117; oral ability of, 34; promotion of, 116; as subject specialists, 40–41, 115; two-tiered structure and, 38. *See also* instructors; tenured/tenure-line faculty
Fairclough, Marta, 52, 60–61, 65–66, 154–55, 156
false beginners, 33–34
Felix, Angela, 52–53
Fernandez-Gibert, Arturo, 162
Feuer, Rachel, 81

Feuerverger, Grace, 47
Field, Frederic: on bilingualism, 31, 157, 158, 159–60; on the Hispanic population, 2; on national security, 28; on stereotypes, 161; on territorial expansion, 26
Fioramonte, Amy, 187–88
first-generation students, 65
Fischer, Gerhard, 8
Fishman, Joshua, 48
5 Cs, 54, 76–77, *77f,* 98, 130, 168, 239–44, *244f*
Flagship Proficiency Initiative, 129
Flores, Lisa, 158–59
Florida, 55–56, 88, 222
Fooks, Paul, 23
foreign-born speakers. *See* native speakers
foreign language programs, 249–50; curriculum design for, 8, 9–11; learning objectives of, 39–40; two-tiered model for, 7, 37–38, 39, 40, 132, 134–35
foreign languages: Cold War and, 27; for enrichment, 26–27; vs. host languages, 32; vs. a second language, 7, 9, 11, 13
"Foreign Languages and Higher Education: New Structures for a Changed World" (MLA), 7–8, 13
Fortune, Tara W., 190
Foster, William, 49
free trade agreements, 28
Freire, Paolo, 153
French language, 3, 27, 129
French language programs, 25, 207
French: World Language exam, 183–84, 255
Fryer, T. Bruce, 102, 115–16
funding, 66, 127, 234, 235, 237

Galloway, Vicki, 111
García, Jesús Suárez, 2, 10, 19n2
García, Ofelia, 161, 162
Garrett, Nina, 220
Garrison, D. Randy, 211–15
gender differences, in Praxis exam scores, 184, 185

general Spanish majors, 104, 108
Georgetown College, 249
Georgetown University, 8, 104, 127–28, 130
German language, 27, 159
German language programs, 25, 26, 127–28, 130
German: World Language exam, 183–84, 255
Gilbert, Patricia K., 214–15
Giles, Dwight E., 83
Glisan, Eileen W., 180
globalization, 28, 160–61, 217
Gloria, Alberta M., 65
Glynn, Cassandra, 168
Goertler, Senta, 223–24
graduate programs, 25, 194, 235–36
graduate student instructors, 91, 135, 137, 193–95, 202n1, 235
graduation requirements, 6, 25, 134, 141, 248, 249
grammar: accented speech and, 186; assessment of, 256; heritage language learners and, 52, 61; placement testing for, 125, 128, 143; service learning and, 90, 92
grammar courses: advanced, 41, 126; bilingualism and, 142; instructors for, 187, 198; language certificate program and, 233; as prerequisites, 110
Green, Anthony, 126, 127–28
Grosse, Christine U., 100, 103, 114
group projects, in online and blended courses, 210–11, 214
Guatemala, 112

*haber* (to have), 60–61
Hadley, Omaggio, 129
Hakimzadeh, Shirin, 164
Halliday, Michael A. K., 15, 99
Hamlyn, Helen, 179
*Harvard Business Review*, 105
Harvard Council on Hispano-American, 24
Harvard University, Smith Professorship, 24, 25, 34, 41–42
Hatcher, Julie A., 84

health clinic internship, 172
Heining-Boynton, Audrey L., 36
Helm, Francesca, 215, 216–17
heritage language learners (HLLs), 11, 14, 47–71; Advanced Placement exams and, 56–57, 253; bilingualism and, 33, 48, 64–65; code-switching and, 48–49; comparisons standard and, 243; course catalog offerings for, 36; current programs for, 49–51; curriculum design for, 14, 49, 62–66; definition of, 48; grammar and, 52, 61; increase in, 14, 47; informal style of, 48, 49, 52; instructor training for, 58, 65–66; lack of courses for, 14; low proficiency, 61–62; marginalization of, 166–67; in mixed classrooms, 52–53, 55, 56, 59, 63; in the nineteenth century, 159; outcomes for, 53–54; Pedagogical Activities for, 66–67; placement testing of, 58–59, 60–62, 65, 125, 127; proficiency levels of, 5, 17, 48, 61–62, 64, 106; program evaluation for, 138, 139; reflection questions on, 66; research agenda for, 62, 66; second language learners and, 51–57, 64; sequence of courses for, 63; service learning and, 63–64, 66, 79, 106; sociocultural and sociopolitical realities for, 62, 65, 241, 247; Spanish LSP for, 106; standards and, 54–56; survey results on, 47–60; textbooks for, 48–49, 50
Herman, Deborah, 166
Hertel, Tammy J., 41, 42, 185–86, 187
Heyman, Errin, 218
higher education: accreditation of, 133; budget models in, 144; principal objectives of, 99–100; trends in, 98–99, 234
high intermediate-level courses, 50, 125, 131, 142
high schools. *See* secondary schools
Hill, Jane, 164
*Hispania*, 19n3, 25
Hispanic community. *See* Spanish-speaking communities

Hispanics/Latinos: Advanced Placement data on, 253; heritage language learners identifying as, 56; market for, 28–29, 105, 106; Praxis exam scores for, 184; statistics on, 2, 29, 48

HL (host language), 32

HLLs. *See* heritage language learners

Holsapple, Matthew, 82–83

home Spanish speakers, 2, *3t*, 29. *See also* heritage language learners

horizontal program articulation, 134, 136

Hortiguera, Hugo, 165–66, 174n3

host language (HL), 32

human capital, service learning and, 75

Humanities+ initiative, 233

Humanities Departmental Survey of 2012.13, 39

humanities education: communicative competence and, 130; cultural studies and, 130, 131; employment opportunities and, 100; funding for, 234; interdisciplinary programs and, 114; second majors in, 39, 144; trends in, 73, 145; value of, 38, 130; vs. vocationally focused curriculum, 98

Humphries, Jeffrey, 105

Hyland, Ken, 99, 109–10, 111

Hymes, Dell H., 15, 35, 99

Iberian Peninsula, 24, 25. *See also* Peninsular Spanish

identity: individual, 151; Mexican-American, 33; national, 151, 161–62; positive, 82

immersion programs: dual, 91, 189–91; for English as a second language, 158; growth of, 17; history of, 160; for instructors, 182; instructors for, 179, 189–91, 200; one-way, 189; proficiency levels and, 5, 180–81; vs. study abroad, 249

immigrants and immigration: bilingualism and, 31–33, 158–59; Mexican, 29, 38, 158–59; Spanish-speaking, 162; territorial expansion and, 26; twentieth century,

27–31; undocumented immigrants, 29, 82, 160, 172

Immigration and Nationality Act of 1965, 160

imperialism, 27, 155

independent and directed study, 36

indigenous languages, 23, 159.166

indirect tests, 127–28

information gap activities, 213, 239–40

information technology, 99. *See also* online and blended courses

Ingold, Catherine, 49–50

inquiry, development of, 212–13

in-service training, 193–95, 198, 200

institutional culture, 104, 113–16

institutional data, 256–57

Instituto Cervantes, 198

instructors: for advanced-level courses, 135; background of, 16–17; employment opportunities for, 178, 189; graduate student, 91, 135, 137, 193–95, 202n1, 235; for grammar courses, 187, 198; immersion programs and, 179, 182, 189–91, 200; key competencies for, *199t*; learning objectives and, 132; native and non-native, 178, 185–89, 201; for online and blended courses, 213–15, 219, 223–24, 237; peer observations of, 196; Praxis for World Languages exams for, 183–85; preservice, 12, 17, 91, 169, 178, 179–82, 183–85, 189–91, 193–95, 200–201; professional development for, 190, 191, 196, 198; proficiency levels of, 178, 179–82, 197; research on, 186–88; self-perception of, 187–88; on the service learning workload, 87, 93; shortage of, 191–92; for Spanish LSP, 113–16, 117; specialties of, 59, 200; teaching presence of, 214–15; turnover of, 178, 191–93, 201; understanding of sociocultural/political realities by, 169

instructor training, 16–17, 178–205; for assessment, 136, 137–38; curriculum design for, 198–200, *199t*; for graduate student instructors, 193–95, 202n1; for heritage language learners, 58, 65–66; for immersion programs, 200; for online and blended courses, 220–21, 225; pedagogical activities for, 202; for preservice instructors, 178; reflection questions on, 201–2; for service learning, 84, 91; for Spanish LSP, 114; survey results on, 195–98

Integrated Performance Assessment model, 132, 182

intellectualism, vs. pragmatism, 39

intended curriculum, definition of, 128–29

interactional dialogue, 208

interactions, 208, 210–11, 220. *See also* face-to-face interactions

Interagency Language Roundtable, 129

intercultural exchanges, 215–17

interdisciplinary programs, 104, 113, 114, 131

intermediate-level courses: for heritage language learners, 50, 51, 63; high, 50, 125, 131, 142; low, 51, 125; placement testing and, 125; service learning for, 91

international cultures, 165–66, 171, 172. *See also* cultural studies; sociocultural realities

international students, content courses for, 109–10

internships, 11, 74, 172

interpretation. *See* translation and interpretation

Iowa, 254

Irwin, Robert, 5, 36–37, 38, 131–32

Isabelli-García, Christina, 135

Ishida, Saori, 127

Item Response Theory, 136–37, 256

Jefferson, Thomas, 1

Jimenez de Cisneros, Francisco Cardinal, 23

job market, 11, 28, 36, 39, 158, 232–35. *See also* employment opportunities

Johnson, Larry, 219

Jordan, Hope, 224

José, Alán, 100, 102, 103, 107, 108, 113

*Journal of Spanish Language Teaching*, 11

Kedia, Ben L., 107

Kelly, Nataly, 105

Kelm, Orlando, 106, 108

Kentucky. *See* University of Kentucky

Keup, Jennifer R., 84

key pals, 215

Klee, Carol, 133

Kramsch, Claire, 100, 166

Lacorte, Manel: on census statistics, 2; on commodification of languages, 6; on the emic perspective, 10, 19n2; on heritage language learners, 65–66; on instructors, 191, 194, 198, 200; on the status of Spanish, 10–11

Lafford, Barbara A.: on employment opportunities, 104, 113; on LSP, 98, 100, 108, 113, 115; on service learning, 84; on the silo walls metaphor, 135

Lancaster University, 137

language acquisition: bilingual education and, 31; online and blended courses and, 208; research on, 12; of second languages, 35; service learning and, 72–73, 93; social presence and, 212; specialists in, 40–41; telecollaboration and, 215

language awareness, critical, 154–55, 168

language certificate programs, 233–34

language-culture nexus, 158

Language Enrollment Database, 253

language for specific purposes. *See* LSP; Spanish LSP

language ideologies, 156–57, 169. *See also* standard language ideology

"Language Learners as Teachers" (Barreneche), 93

language loss, 48–49, 66

language majors, 39, 40, 41, 137, 178, 191

languages: commodification of, 6, 29, 164; commonly taught, 5–6; critically needed, 28; indigenous, 23, 159.166; natural, 151

languages other than Spanish (LOTS), 5
language subordination, 15, 157, 164, 165, 169
Latin America, 6, 28, 155, 166, 216
Latin Americanists, 38
Latin American studies, 38, 169
Latinas, stereotypes of, 164
Latinos. *See* Hispanics/Latinos
Latino studies, 38, 170
Lave, Jean, 111
law firm internships, 172
LCTL (less commonly taught languages), 5–6
LDT (lexical decision task), 61
Lear, Darcy: on employment opportunities, 104, 113; on LSP, 98, 113; on service learning, 76, 84; on the silo walls metaphor, 135; on Spanish LSP, 108
learned curriculum, definition of, 128–29
learner-content interactions, 210
learner-instructor interactions, 210, 211
learner-learner interactions, 210–11
learning goals & objectives, 39–40, 128, 132–38, 140, 144
learning outcomes, 15, 53–54, 132–36, 138–39, 145
Leavitt, Sturgis E., 23, 24, 25
lecture classes, 209
lecturers, 235
Lee, James F., 78, 131
Leeman, Jennifer, 25, 29, 51–52, 151, 154, 168
legal Spanish, 106
less commonly taught languages (LCTL), 5–6
lexical decision task (LDT), 61
liberal arts education, 129, 198, 233. *See also* humanities education
life experiences, diversity of, 151–52
linguistic anthropology, 16
linguistic competency, 60, 62, 75, 131
linguistic discrimination, 157, 160, 161–64, *163f*, 166–67, 169–70
linguistics, 15, 24, 41, 59, 99. *See also* applied linguistics

linguistics courses, 36, 92, 130, 134–35, 169
Lippi-Green, Rosina, 156, 161, 163
Lipski, John, 4–5
Liskin-Gasparro, Judith E., 136
literacy, 130, 137–38
literary studies: Advanced Placement examinations, 143; cultural studies and, 38; early education in, 24; instructor specialty in, 59; instructor training for, 194; language certificate program and, 233–34; vs. language programs, 6; role of, 169; service learning and, 90, 92; specialists in, 40–41, 115; standards for, 130; statistics on, 41; survey results on, 236; upper-level courses and, 38. *See also* Spanish literature
loanwords, 2
Long, Mary K., 102, 103, 108, 114
Longfellow, Henry, 24
Lord, Gillian, 135
Lorenz, Eileen B., 190
LOTS (languages other than Spanish), 5
lower-level courses: emphasis on, 235; for heritage language learners, 50; instructor training for, 194; MLA report on, 7; online and blended, 220–21; placement testing and, 125; service learning for, 80–81, 91; sociocultural realities and, 152; for Spanish LSP, 108; standards for, 130; students in, 33–34; two-tiered model and, 37–38, 134–35
low intermediate-level courses, 51, 125
LSP (language for specific purposes), 15, 98–100; background for, 98–100; challenges for, 103–4; definition of, 100–101; needs analysis for, 105; research agenda for, 113; subject areas of, 100. *See also* Spanish LSP
Lynch, Andrew, 53, 61

Macalister, John, 9, 10, 18, 230, 245, 247–48
Macías, Reynoldo, 1, 10–11
Magnan, Sally S., 129
Maine, 191

majors: connections standard and, 242; double, 84; general Spanish, 104, 108; humanities, 100; language, 39, 40, 41, 137, 178, 191; marketability of, 232–35; socioeconomic factors and, 100; at the University of Kentucky, 143–44

Malone, Margaret, 137

management, upper-level, 106–7, 108, 158

Manifest Destiny, 159

marginalization: Freire on, 153; of heritage language learners, 166–67; of minority groups, 111–12; of the other, 166, 174n3; of Spanish-speaking communities, 25, 246–47; standard language ideology and, 157

markets, 28–29, 105, 106, 164. *See also* employment opportunities; job market; socioeconomic factors

Marrone, Nila, 48–49, 68n1

Martinez, Glenn, 51–52, 55, 104, 162

mass media, Spanish language, 131–32

Master, Peter, 113, 114

Maxim, Hiram H., 8, 39, 124, 129–30

McCarthyism, 159

Medgyes, Peter, 186–87

medical Spanish, 101, 106, 108, 114, 117, 241

Melin, Charlotte, 133

mentoring, 182, 192, 193, 196, 197

merit-oriented systems, 112

Met, Myrian, 190

metacognitive awareness, 214

Mexican-Americans, 33, 38, 162, 253

Mexican immigrants, 29, 38, 158–59

Mexican studies, 38

Meyer, Katrina A., 212–13

*Michigan Journal of Community Service-Learning*, 89

Mills, Nichole, 139, 249–50

Milroy, James, 156

Minnesota, 191, 254

minority groups: Census statistics on, 2; marginalization of, 111–12; retention of students and, 84; statistics on, 29, 48; stereotypes of, 81, 82, 83

minors (academic), 39, 84, 143–44, 232–35, 242

missionary service, 51

mission statements, 132–33, 144

mixed classrooms, heritage language learners in, 52–53, 55, 56, 59, 63, 243

MLA. *See* Modern Language Association

Mock Spanish, 163–64

Model of Language Program Policy Design (Dubin and Olshtain), 244–47, *246f,* 248

Modern Language Association (MLA): Ad Hoc Committee report, 7–8, 40, 41, 100, 113, 242; "Data on Second Majors in Language and Literature, 2001-2013," 39; data sets from, 253; establishment of, 25; "Foreign Languages and Higher Education: New Structures for a Changed World," 7–8, 13; *Profession,* 6; on student enrollments, 2–3, 29, *30f,* 73; on translingual and transcultural competence, 128

*Modern Language Journal,* 8, 25, 103, 194

monolingualism, 27–28, 32, 64, 167

Montrul, Silvina, 48, 53–54, 63, 65, 66

Moore, Michael G., 208, 209, 210

Mora, Oscar, 216

motivation: diversity of, 151–52; for heritage language learners, 65; service learning and, 80; socioeconomic factors and, 28–29; telecollaboration and, 216; types of, 5, 6; utilitarian, 6, 24, 28, 42, 118, 236

multilingualism, 108, 160, 243–44. *See also* bilingualism

Muthiah, Richard N., 84

NAEP (National Assessment of Educational Progress), 77, *77f*

Nation, I. S. P., 9, 10, 18, 230, 245, 247–48

National Assessment of Educational Progress (NAEP), 77, *77f*

National Center for Educational Statistics, 83–84

National Council for Accreditation of Teacher Education, 179

National Defense Education Act of 1958, 27
national identity, 151, 161–62
nationalists, 161
national language: English as, 161–62, 167; second, 1–2, 6, 22, 167, 230
national security, 27, 28
National Standards Collaborative Board, 54, 76, 239, 240, 241, *244f*
National Standards for Foreign Language Learning. *See* World-Readiness Standards for Learning Languages
national survey. *See* Spanish Postsecondary Program and Curriculum Survey
Native Americans, 159
native speaker fallacy, 186–87
native speakers: accented speech of, 55–56, 157, 164, 186; increase in, 246; as instructors, 178, 180, 185–89, 201; interactions with, 1; Praxis exam scores for, 184; service learning and, 79; telecollaboration and, 216. *See also* Spanish-speaking communities
naturalistic approaches, 35
natural languages, 151
needs analysis, 9–10, 12, 244–45; for LSP, 105, 108; macro, 13, 244–45; for student learning outcomes, 134
Negueruela-Azarola, Eduardo, 194
New Mexico, 162
Noel, Garret, 23
non-native speakers, as instructors, 178, 185–89, 201
Norris, John N.: on foreign language programs, 249–50; on German language programs, 8; on language and culture learning, 130; on learning goals, 39; on oral proficiency, 129–30; on placement testing, 127–28; on proficiency standards, 180, 181, 182; on program evaluation, 139; "Realizing Advanced FL Writing Development," 124
North American Free Trade Agreement of 1994, 28
Northeast states, 23, 26, 50

OER (open educational resources), 223
Office of Postsecondary Education, 108
Ohio State University, 254
Olshtain, Elite, 18, 244–47, *246f,* 248
online and blended courses, 12, 17, 206–29; assessment of, 221–22; attrition rates for, 218; communication standard and, 240; Community of Inquiry model and, 211–15, *213f;* curriculum design for, 219–24; face-to-face interactions and, 17, 218, 219–20, 222, 223, 224, 225; implementation of, 224, 225; instructors for, 213–15, 219, 223–24, 237; instructor training for, 220–21, 225; language acquisition theory and, 208; management of, 220; pedagogical activities for, 226–27; quality versus-cost debate on, 221, 222, 225; reflection questions on, 225–26; research on, 207, 224, 225; survey results on, 217–19, 237; telecollaboration and, 215–17; textbooks for, 220, 223; transactional distance and, 208–9, 214–15, 218, 220; types of interactions in, 210–11, 220
online marketing, 105
open educational resources (OER), 223
Oral Proficiency Interview (OPI), 78, 129, 137, 179–80, 181
Oral Proficiency Interview by computer (OPIc), 137
oral skills: bilingualism and, 158; characteristics of, 78; communicative competence in, 130; the Direct Method for, 34–35; need for, 29, 31, 131; online courses and, 17; proficiency levels for, 17, 34, 38, 78, 129–30, 131, 179–80; service learning and, 78–81
Oregon, 189
Oskoz, Ana, 225
the other, marginalization of, 166, 174n3
outcomes. *See* learning outcomes

Paesani, Kate, 134
Palmer, Adrian S., 109, 136

Pastor Cesteros, Susana, 191, 194, 198, 200
Patton, Michael, 139
Pawan, Faridah, 214
pedagogy. *See* teaching methodology
*Pedagogy of the Oppressed* (Freire), 153
peer observations/reviews, 90, 196, 213, 223
Peninsular Spanish, 24, 25, 38, 143, 155, 169
Pennycook, Alastair, 153–54, 165
performance-based approach, 31, 126, 141
Peris, Ernesto, 102
Perpetual Works, Inc., 256
"Perspectives" discussion (*Modern Language Journal*), 8
Petrov, Lisa Amor, 82
Phillipson, Robert, 186
phonetics courses, 55–56, 142
Pilland, William, 84
placement procedures and testing, 11, 15–16, 125–28; AAPPL for, 126–27, 137; computer-based alternatives for, 137; cultural and social factors in, 62; for heritage language learners, 58–59, 60–62, 65, 125, 127; indirect tests for, 127–28; language tests for, 136; pedagogical activities for, 146; performance-based, 126; for reading ability, 126, 127, 129; reflection questions on, 145–46; survey results on, 140; WebCAPE exam for, 125, 136–37, 141, 142–43, 147n2, 256; for writing ability, 125, 127. *See also* Advanced Placement examinations
political context. *See* sociopolitical realities
*A Political History of Spanish* (del Valle and García), 161
Pomerantz, Anne, 156
Ponce de Leon, Juan, 22
postwar World War II period, 159–60
Potowski, Kim, 52, 66
pragmatism, 39, 90
Praxis for World Languages exams, 178, 183–85, 255–56
precollege language requirements, 17
prerequisites, 14, 27, 72–73, 109–10, 135–36, 186

preservice instructors, 17, 169; for immersion programs, 189–91; Praxis data on, 183–85, 255–56; proficiency levels for, 179–82; service learning and, 91; training for, 12, 178, 193–95, 200–201
Principles of Learning and Teaching exam, 183–85, 256
private language schools, 35
*Profession* (MLA), 6
professional development, 190, 191, 196, 198
professional opportunities. *See* employment opportunities
professional organizations, 200
proficiency levels: ACTFL tests of, 15, 137, 141, 179–80, 181; employment opportunities and, 11, 28, 39; exit exam for, 249; of heritage language learners, 5, 17, 48, 61–62, 64, 106; for immersion programs, 5, 180–81; of instructors, 178, 179–82, 197; for oral skills, 17, 34, 38, 78, 129–30, 131, 179–80; Praxis for World Languages exams for, 183–85; research on, 129–30; standards for, 179–82; for teacher certification, 8, 181. *See also* placement procedures and testing
program, definition of, 250
program evaluation, 113, 136, 138–39, 140–41, 146
pronunciation, 35, 186, 187, 188. *See also* accented speech
Public Academy of the City of Philadelphia, 23
public schools, 35, 191–92. *See also* elementary schools; secondary schools
Puch, José María de Tomás, 99, 120n2

racism, 25, 33, 156, 160–61, 162–64, 246–47
Rajagopalan, Kanavillil, 186
reading ability: ACTFL's exams on, 129, 141; advanced-level courses and, 27, 38, 51, 223; "barbarisms" and, 49; emphasis on, 34; heritage language learners and, 52, 53, 138; placement testing for, 126, 127, 129; service learning and, 77, 80, 91, 92

"Realizing Advanced FL Writing Development" (Byrnes, Maxim and Norris), 124
receptive language skills, 33, 48, 52, 53, 60, 126
Relaño-Pastor, Anna Maria, 63
Remak, Henry H., 194
retention of students, 65, 83–84
Richards, Jack C., 9–10
Robby, Matthew A., 82
Roberts, Sam, 48
Rosetta Stone language program, 191
Rovai, Fernando, 224
Rubio, Fernando, 129, 220, 221, 222
Ruiz, Richard, 32
Russia, 27, 28

SAE (standard American English), 157
Sánchez, Bernadette, 81
Sánchez López, Lourdes, 8, 118
Sánchez Pérez, Aquilino, 23, 26, 28, 44n3, 44n4, 44n5
San Diego State University, 191
SAT scores, 192, 193
Sauro, Shannon, 215
Schmidt, Adeny, 82
School of Foreign Service Program (Georgetown University), 104
Schrier, Leslie, 190
Schwarzenegger, Arnold, 2
Science Practical Assessment (SPA) 205, 50
secondary schools: employment opportunities in, 178; enrollment demographics for, 4, 31; heritage language learners in, 63; instructor proficiency for, 183–85; LSP courses in, 108; preservice teacher in, 17; service learning and, 242–43; student teachers in, 197
second language programs, 9–11; critical approaches to, 153–55; heritage language learners and, 51–57, 64; sociocultural and sociopolitical realities and, 151–53, 165–66
second languages: commodification of, 6,
29, 164; vs. a foreign language, 7, 9, 11, 13; language acquisition theory on, 12, 35
second national language, 1–2, 6, 22, 167, 230
self-evaluations, 90
September 11, 2001, terrorist attacks, 28
sequence of courses, 63, 108, 113, 133, 142, 238
Serna Collazos, Andrea, 216
service learning, 14, 72–97; for all classroom levels, 91–93; assessment of, 77, 77f, 89–90; benefits of, 93–94; civic engagement and, 74–75, 76–77, 82, 89; community partners for, 63–64, 74–75, 78, 81–82, 84, 87–89, 90, 170, 242–43; content courses and, 7, 242–43; for conversation courses, 78–80, 242–43; cultural sensitivity and, 80–83, 88, 243; curriculum design for, 86–93; heritage language learners and, 63–64, 66, 79, 106; information gap activities and, 239–40; instructor training for, 84, 91; internships for, 172; oral skills and, 78–81; pedagogical activities for, 95; reflection questions on, 94–95; research on, 72, 77–84, 89; retention of students and, 83–84; Spanish LSP and, 118; statistics on, 36; survey results on, 84–85
SHL (Spanish heritage learners), ,241, 247
silo walls metaphor, 115–16, 135
Silva-Corvalán, Carmen, 61
Silverstein, Michael, 156
Simon, Paul, 28
situation analysis, 10–11, 17
Skinner, B. F., 35
SLOs (student learning objectives), 140
SLOs (student learning outcomes), 132–36
Smith, Abiel, 24
Smith, Rachel, 218
Smith Professorship, 24, 25, 34, 41–42
social constructivism, 99
social justice, 168, 169
social presence, 212
sociocultural realities, 5, 6, 12, 16,

151–53, 172; bilingualism and, 157–61; critical approaches to pedagogy and, 154; curriculum design and, 165–70; environment of, 10–11; heritage language learners and, 62, 65; LSP and, 100; Model of Language Program Policy Design (Dubin and Olshtain) on, 244–47, *246f*, 248; pedagogical activities for, 174; reflection questions on, 173; of Spanish in US society, 155–56, 161–64; Spanish LSP and, 110–12; standard language ideology and, 156–57; survey results on, 170–72; textbooks on, 200; of textbook videos, 165–66, 174n3

sociocultural theory, of learning, 212

socioeconomic factors: bilingualism and, 158–59; LSP and, 99, 100, 111–12; as motivation, 28–29; selection of a major and, 100; Spanish-speaking communities and, 12, 16

sociolinguistic profile, 15, 42, 48, 106, 185, 247

sociolinguistics, 4, 6, 16, 169

sociopolitical realities: critical approaches to pedagogy and, 154; curriculum design and, 165–70; Model of Language Program Policy Design (Dubin and Olshtain) on, 244–47, *246f*, 248; pedagogical activities for, 174; reflection questions on, 173; of Spanish in US society, 155–56, 161–64; standard language ideology and, 156–57

Soneson, Dan, 133

Southeast states, 50, 256

Southern states, 2, 23, 25–27, 41

Southwest states, 23, 25–27, 41, 50, 159

SPA (Science Practical Assessment) 205, 50

Spain: colonization by, 23; Iberian Peninsula, 24, 25; Instituto Cervantes, 198; Peninsular Spanish of, 24, 25, 38, 143, 155, 169; textbook videos of, 165–66

*Spanish and Portuguese for Business and the Professions* (American Association of Teachers of Spanish and Portuguese), 103

Spanish heritage learners (SHL). *See* heritage language learners

"Spanish in the Professions" (Lafford, Abbott and Lear), 98

Spanish language: Advanced Placement examinations, 4, 13, 19n1, 29, *30f*, 56–57; American Community Survey on, 2; dialects of, 55–56, 66; Peninsular Spanish, 24, 25, 38, 143, 155, 169; racialization of, 162–64, *163f*; as the second national language, 1–2, 22, 230; as a second vs. foreign language, 7, 9, 11, 13; as spoken in the home, 2, *3t*, 29; statistics on, 42; United States history of, 22; utilitarian uses for, 38–39; value of, 118

Spanish language proficiency. *See* proficiency levels

Spanish language programs: in course catalogs, 36–37, *37t*, 42; early history of, 23–24; foreignization of, 248–49; history and evolution of, 13, 22–46, 254; identity crisis and, 6; in the nineteenth and early twentieth century, 24–25; statistics on, 36, *37t*; in the twentieth century, 27–31, 254; in the twenty-first century, 31–34, 250

Spanish language service provider (LSP), 135

Spanish literature: Advanced Placement examinations, 4, 13, 19n1, 29, *30f*, 56–57, 143; emphasis on, 24, 25, 34; service learning and, 92; subject specialists in, 115. *See also* literary studies

Spanish LSP (language for specific purposes), 15, 98–123; assessment of, 109–10; background for, 98–100; challenges for, 103–4; course levels available for, 108; curriculum design for, 109–13; discipline-specific language in, 107–8; diversity of, 100; employment opportunities and, 104–8, 110–12, 113, 118; vs. ESP, 120n1; for heritage language learners, 106; instructors and, 113–16, 117; needs analysis for, 108; pedagogical activities for, 120; prerequisites for, 110;

Spanish LSP (*continued*)
program evaluation for, 113; reflection questions on, 119; research agenda for, 100–102; service learning and, 118; sociocultural realities and, 110–12; student profile for, 104–9; survey results on, 116–18; teaching methodology for, 100–103; textbooks for, 102–3, 105

Spanish Ministry of Education, Culture, and Sport, 189

Spanish Postsecondary Program and Curriculum Survey, 231–37; on assessment, 139–41; description of, 255; on instructor training, 195–98; intent of, 230–31; largest "not applicable" responses on, 236–37; on online and blended courses, 217–19, 237; "other" section of, 231–36; qualitative responses from, 234–35, 237; on service learning, 84–85; on sociocultural realities, 170–72; on Spanish LSP, 116–18; "standards" section of, 231, 236, 238–39; "teacher training" section of, 236–37; on the World-Readiness Standards, 238–39

Spanish-speaking communities: accurate portrayal of, 171–72; attitudes toward, 153, 161, 174n1; bilingual education for, 31–33; communities standard and, 243–44; English-only movement and, 155, 162; experiential learning and, 14–15; heritage language learners and, 55, 66; marginalization of, 25, 246–47; market for, 28–29, 105, 106; service learning and, 63–64, 74–75, 78, 81–82, 84, 87–89, 90, 170, 242–43; sociopolitical realities of, 12, 16; Spanish LSP and, 118. *See also* heritage language learners

"Spanish: The Foreign National Language" (Alonso), 22

Spanish World Language exam, 183–85, 255

Spell, Jefferson R., 24, 25

standard American English (SAE), 157

standard language ideology, 156–57; divisive nature of, 164, 166–67, 168, 169, 246–47; heritage language learners and, 64–65; national identity and, 161–62

state education agencies, 181

"The Status of Computer-Assisted Language Instruction" (Clifford), 206

stereotypes: acceptance of, 165; of Latinas, 164; of minority groups, 81, 82, 83; multilingualism and, 160–61; of nonnative instructors, 188; of Spanish-speaking communities, 161

stimulus-response psychology, 35

student enrollment: in advanced-level courses, 235–36; attendance statistics and, 36; decrease in, 3, 5, 73, 235–36; foreign language, 2–3, *4f,* 29, *30f,* 73; in service learning programs, 86; in Spanish language courses, 2–3, 4–5, *4f,* 6, 13, 29, *30f,* 73, 164; in Spanish LSP, 104–5, 104–9; "the Spanish problem" and, 4–5; statistics on, 29, *30f,* 164; trends in, 13; twenty-first century demographics and, 31

student learning objectives (SLOs), 140, 144

student learning outcomes (SLOs), 132–36

student populations: Advanced Placement data on, 253; diversity of, 10–11, 14, 155; first-generation, 65; retention rates for, 65, 83–84; statistics on, 10–11, 14, 48

student teachers, mentoring for, 197

study abroad programs, 5, 41, 111–12, 236, 248–49

Sundermann, Gretchen, 185–86, 187

superlanguages, 102

Surface, Eric A., 179, 180

Swaffar, Janet, 8, 130

Swain, Merrill, 129

Swanson, Peter, 191–92

Swender, E., 129, 179, 180

systemic-functional linguistics, 15, 99

Szurmuk, Monica, 5, 36–37, 38, 131–32

Taylor, M., 114–15

teacher certification, proficiency levels for, 8, 181

teachers. *See* faculty; instructors

Teachers' English Fluency Initiative in
Arizona, 186

teacher training. *See* instructor training

*Teaching Language in Context* (Hadley), 129

*Teaching Matters* (Whitaker and Whitaker),
178

teaching methodology: Audio-Lingual
Method of, 35; critical approaches to,
153–55, 167–68; the Direct Method for,
34–35; for heritage language learners,
66; history and evolution of, 34–37;
naturalistic approaches for, 35; Praxis
exams on, 183–85; service learning as,
74; for Spanish LSP, 100–103; textbooks
on, 200

teaching presence, 214–15

*Teaching Spanish to the Hispanic Bilingual:
Issues, Aims and Methods* (Valdés), 48

Teagle Report, 40

technical content, 107, 108, 110, 115, 137

technology, 17, 99, 120n2, 137. *See also*
online and blended courses

Tedick, Diane J., 181, 190

telecollaboration, 215–17

television networks, Spanish language, 2,
131–32

tenured/tenure-line faculty: advanced-level
courses and, 38; on assessment, 140;
lower-level courses and, 7; on online and
blended courses, 219; peer observations
of, 196; professional development for,
196; replacement of, 234–35; service
learning and, 86; specialties of, 115–16

*Terminator* movies, 2

territorial expansion, nineteenth century,
25–27

Texas, 60–61, 162, 163, *163f*

textbooks: for business Spanish, 105;
for heritage language learners, 48–49,
50; vs. needs analysis, 134; for online
and blended courses, 220, 223; for
Spanish LSP, 102–3, 105; on teaching
methodology, 200

textbook videos, 165–66, 174n3

Thompson, Gregory L., 62, 63–64, 78–79,
88, 187–88, 242

Thoms, J., 220, 221, 222

Tickner, George, 24

Tier 1 and Tier 2 languages, 133

Title VII of the Elementary and Secondary
Education Act, 31

*The Tongue-Tied American: Confronting the
Foreign Language Crisis* (Simon), 28

transactional distance, 208–9, 214, 218, 220

transcultural competence, 7, 13, 40, 42,
128, 145, 178

translation and interpretation: connections
standard and, 241; course offerings for,
41; heritage language learners and, 36,
106; service learning and, 87–88, 89, 242

translingual competence, 7, 13, 40, 42, 128,
145, 178

transnational businesses, 32, 99, 107, 112

tripartite integrated curriculum structure,
9, 109

Troike, Rudolph, 114–15

Tschirner, Erwin, 129

two-tiered model, 7, 37–38, 39, 40, 132,
134–35

Tyler, Ralph W., 133

UK. *See* University of Kentucky

undergraduate course catalogs, 36–37, *37t*,
42, 135–36, 254

undocumented immigrants, 29, 82, 160, 172

United Way of Central Florida, 88

University of Arizona, 5–6, 186, 254

University of California, Los Angeles, 254

University of Central Florida, 55–56

University of Houston, 60–61

University of Iowa, 254

University of Kentucky (UK): assessment
and curricular adaptation at, 141–45,
147n2; business Spanish courses and,
107, 110, 112; course catalogs from, 254;
enrollment changes for, 235–36; heritage
language learners in, 50–51; institutional

University of Kentucky (*continued*)
data from, 256–57; internships and,
172; language certificate program and,
233–34; mission statement of, 132,
144; placement testing by, 126–27; SPA
399: Field-Based/Community-Based
Education, 170; SPA 480: Hispanic
Kentucky, 170; Spanish 101 students at,
33–34; WebCAPE exam and, 256
University of Minnesota, 191, 254
University of Wisconsin-Madison, 254
"University Students' Language Learning"
(Feuerverger), 47
Univisíon, 2
upper-level courses. *See* advanced-level courses
upper-level management, 106–7, 108, 158
Uscinski, Izabela, 101, 102, 103, 108, 114
US Constitution, 161
US Department of Education, 39, 238
Utah, 192–93
utilitarian motivation, 6, 24, 28, 42, 118, 236
utilization-focused framework, 139

Valdés, Guadalupe, 48, 55, 62, 167, 172
VanPatten, Bill, 40–41, 42, 105, 115, 131
Vaughn, Augustus, 23
Vaught, Geoffrey M., 114
*Verbal Behavior* (Skinner), 35
verb forms, 60–61
vertical program articulation, 12, 15, 63,
135–36, 137
videoconferencing, 225
videos, textbook, 165–66, 174n3
vocabulary knowledge, 52, 60–61, 64, 108,
127, 187, 190
vocationally focused curriculum, 98, 233–
34. *See also* employment opportunities
Voght, Geoffrey M., 100
volunteerism, vs. service learning, 75

Wallace, Catherine, 167–68
*Washington Post*, 192
Wassell, Beth, 168
Watters, Ann, 74

WebCAPE (Web-Based Computer Adaptive
Placement Exam), 125, 136–37, 141,
142–43, 147n2, 256
Wehling, Susan, 72
Wenger, Etienne, 111
Wesely, Pamela, 168
Whitaker, Beth, 178
Whitaker, Todd, 178
white society. *See* Anglo-American society
Wichadee, Saovapa, 210–11
Widdowson, Henry, 154
William and Mary College, 24
Willingham-Mclain, Laurel, 207
"Will Spanish Help You Reach the US
Hispanic Market? It Depends" (Kelly), 105
Winke, Paula, 223–24
Wisconsin, 254
World Languages Pedagogy exam, 183–85,
256
World-Readiness Standards for Learning
Languages, 237–44, *244f;* 5 Cs and,
76–77, 168, 239–44; heritage language
learners and, 54–55; lower-level courses
and, 130; service learning and, 14;
Spanish LSP and, 98; student learning
outcomes and, 132
World War I, 26, 159
World War II, 26, 27, 159
WPT (Writing Proficiency Test), 180, 181
writing ability: "barbarisms" and, 49; Byrnes,
Maxim, and Norris on, 8; collaborative
assignments for, 210; emphasis on, 34;
genre-focused approached to, 130; heritage
language learners and, 51, 53, 60, 61, 138;
language certificate program and, 233; of
native speakers, 188; placement testing
for, 125, 127; proficiency levels and, 180;
service learning and, 77, 90, 92
Writing Proficiency Test (WPT), 180, 181

Youngs, Bonnie Earnest, 207
Y-Serve program, 88–89

Zentella, Ana Celia, 164

# ABOUT THE AUTHORS

ALAN V. BROWN (PhD, second-language acquisition and teaching, University of Arizona) is an associate professor of Spanish applied linguistics in the Hispanic Studies Department at the University of Kentucky. As an applied linguist, he teaches courses in a wide variety of fields—from second-language acquisition to Spanish phonetics and introductory linguistics to translation to teaching methods and assessment. Likewise, his research explores disparate aspects of second-language learning, classroom teaching, assessment, and curriculum development. He has published in journals such as the *Modern Language Journal*, *Foreign Language Annals*, and *Hispania*.

GREGORY L. THOMPSON (PhD, second-language acquisition and teaching, University of Arizona) is an associate professor of Spanish pedagogy at Brigham Young University. He has taught courses on language pedagogy, bilingualism, Spanish phonetics, and applied linguistics, as well as courses on the development of language skills. He has published articles in *Foreign Language Annals*, *Hispania*, and other journals on his varied research areas, including code-switching in the foreign language classroom; heritage language learners; service learning and language acquisition; bilingualism and languages in contact; and placement examinations and language testing. He also has published two books: *Intersection of Service and Learning: Research and Practice in the Second Language Classroom*; and *Spanish in Bilingual and Multilingual Settings around the World*.

CPSIA information can be obtained
at www.ICGtesting.com
Printed in the USA
BVHW03s0512200318
510862BV00005B/12/P